INTERNATIONAL MACROECONOMICS

ISBN 978-1-4875-0360-4 (cloth)   ISBN 978-1-4875-1833-2 (EPUB)
ISBN 978-1-4875-2277-3 (paper)   ISBN 978-1-4875-1832-5 (PDF)

Library and Archives Canada Cataloguing in Publication

Title: International macroeconomics : dynamic and multi-sectoral models / Kit Pasula.
Names: Pasula, Kit, author.
Description: Includes bibliographical references and index.
Identifiers: Canadiana (print) 20250311305 | Canadiana (ebook) 20250311321 | ISBN 9781487522773 (paper) |
ISBN 9781487503604 (cloth) | ISBN 9781487518325 (PDF) | ISBN 9781487518332 (EPUB)
Subjects: LCSH: Macroeconomics—Textbooks. | LCGFT: Textbooks.
Classification: LCC HB172.5 .P37 2026 | DDC 339—dc23

Cover design: Tamara Hawkins
Cover image[s]: Maxger/Shutterstock.com

We welcome comments and suggestions regarding any aspect of our publications – please feel free to contact us at news@utorontopress.com or visit us at utppublishing.com.

Every effort has been made to contact copyright holders; in the event of an error or omission, please notify the publisher.

The manufacturer's authorised representative in the EU for product safety is Mare Nostrum Group B.V., Mauritskade 21D, 1091 GC Amsterdam, The Netherlands. Email: gpsr@mare-nostrum.co.uk

We wish to acknowledge the land on which the University of Toronto Press operates. This land is the traditional territory of the Wendat, the Anishnaabeg, the Haudenosaunee, the Métis, and the Mississaugas of the Credit First Nation.

University of Toronto Press acknowledges the financial support of the Government of Canada and the Ontario Arts Council, an agency of the Government of Ontario, for its publishing activities.

International Macroeconomics

Dynamic and Multi-Sectoral Models

KIT PASULA

UNIVERSITY OF TORONTO PRESS
Toronto Buffalo London

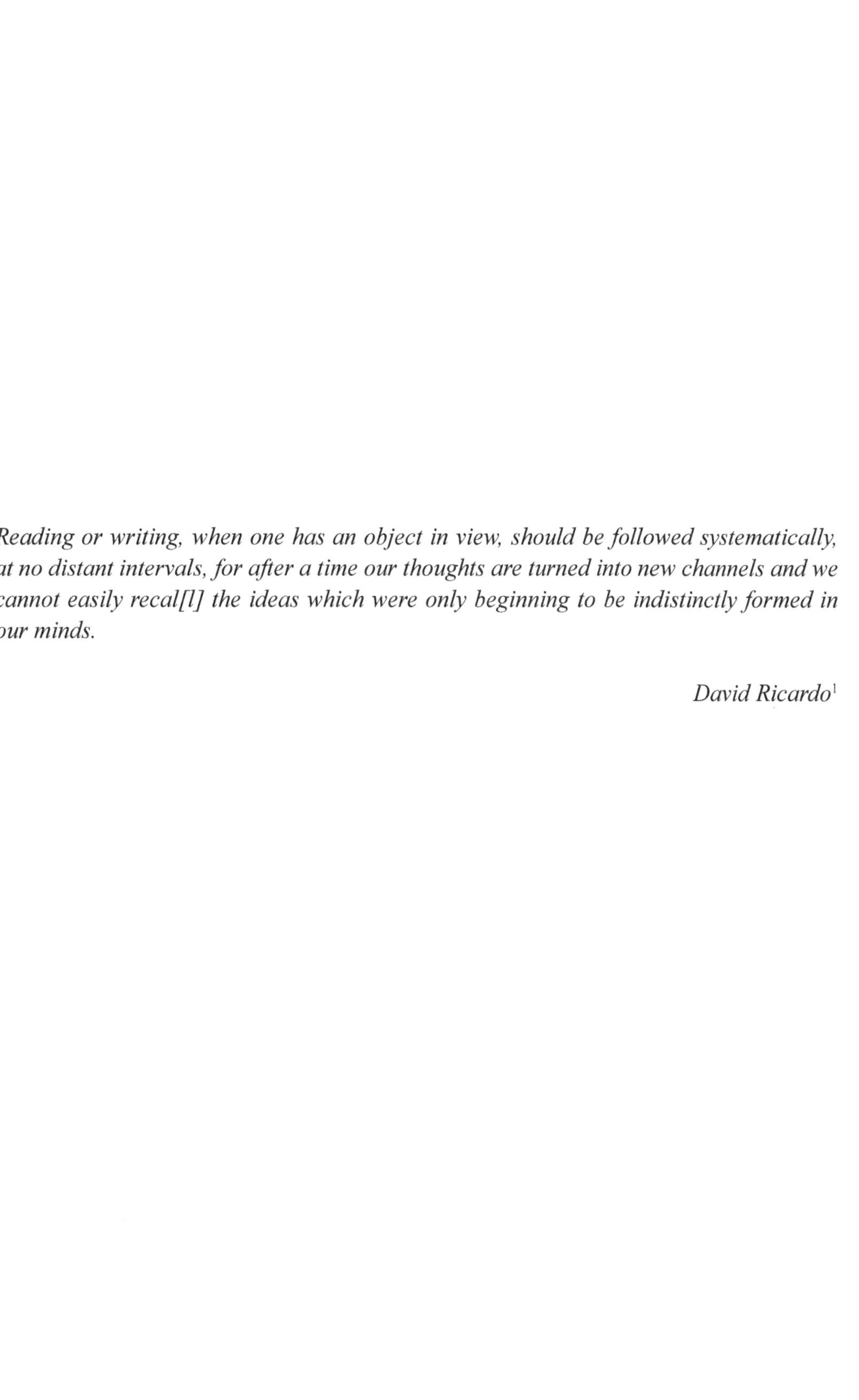

Reading or writing, when one has an object in view, should be followed systematically, at no distant intervals, for after a time our thoughts are turned into new channels and we cannot easily recal[l] the ideas which were only beginning to be indistinctly formed in our minds.

David Ricardo[1]

Contents in Brief

Part V: Topics in International Macroeconomics   253

Table of Contents

Preface

This book provides lectures on the core topics in undergraduate international macroeconomics. The approach in this book differs from that in existing books in that it gives significantly more prominence to dynamic and multi-sectoral models. This is consistent with graduate-level courses and academic research in international macroeconomics. The structure and content should be appealing to students, general readers, and lecturers. The analysis is logical and straightforward, and there are many interesting and enlightening empirical applications.

The analytical approach emphasizes a choice-theoretic framework, dynamic models (both real and monetary), financial and business cycle models that highlight expectations, and multi-sectoral models that incorporate sectors such as the manufacturing, resource, and service sectors. Each chapter focuses on providing an economic analysis, but the empirical elements supplement the reader's understanding. These elements are not summaries of empirical studies by academic economists, but rather a presentation of relevant data and an immediate economic analysis. It is as if the author and the reader are examining the data together, applying the relevant international macroeconomic theory.[2]

The analysis is conducted with diagrams and equations, with each chapter written at a level appropriate for intermediate undergraduates. Some professors may regard parts of the book as more appropriate for fourth-year or honors courses in international macroeconomics. But all the material can be presented in the standard undergraduate course, without any advanced mathematics needed. A core diagram, along with a few key equations, is sufficient to provide the fundamental analysis of each chapter.

This book, like others, contains more content than can be covered in a one-semester course.[3] The lecturer would typically omit three or four chapters and the latter parts of certain chapters, while including certain appendixes and small segments of omitted chapters. Each chapter is relatively self-contained, so the lecturer has flexibility with the order in which topics are presented.

The empirical elements tend to focus on Canada, but many are based on other countries. The theoretical analyses are, without exception, discussed in general terms, always using phrases like the domestic price level rather than the Canadian price level.

I have been lecturing on this material for many years.[4] Students have often commented that they enjoyed the course because of the realism of the models and analysis. This impression comes not only from the applications but also from the fact that dynamic and multi-sectoral models are inherently more realistic than the standard models in undergraduate economics.

The book has the elements of a monograph, written for the general reader with an interest in international macroeconomics based on dynamic and multi-sectoral models. The book provides extensive references to academic literature, citing seminal literature and directing the reader to advanced empirical studies. And while understanding the theory is an essential prerequisite to applying the analyses to events in the global economy, the empirical elements in the book are well-designed to satisfy the interests of the general reader. To provide a few examples, there are discussions related to movements in Canada's net exports over a period that encompasses the Great Recession, the long-term movements in the US real interest rate over the past five decades, the phenomenal sectoral productivity growth in Japan under Bretton Woods, the large increases in China's foreign exchange reserves between 1996 and 2005, and other interesting historical episodes like the depreciations of the French franc in the early 1920s and the Italian lira in the late 1970s.

The book includes a variety of interesting and enlightening empirical elements (along with numerous comments regarding difficulties in conducting and interpreting empirical analyses). Of course, these empirical elements will also be of considerable interest to undergraduates mastering the theory and empirics of international macroeconomics.

NOTES

1   David Ricardo, October 29th, 1815, in a letter to Hutches Trower.
2   An exercise section, labelled "Data Analytics," provides details on applied exercises, with specific instructions on data collection and the completion of well-defined analyses.
3   The coverage of topics is not comprehensive, and the author's inclinations may have resulted in omissions of models or approaches that others would have included.
4   The two most recent topics were added in 2014 and 2020. The dynamic model with a non-traded good has been included since 2014, and the two-country dynamic model of real interest rates and current account balances was added in 2020.

Acknowledgments

I learned an immense amount from my professors at the University of Alberta and the University of Toronto, including the skills that allow me to work out the correct analyses of well-defined economic problems. While these skills allow for beneficial academic research, diligent economics lecturers learn that these same skills allow them (with pen and paper) to expand their own knowledge and significantly improve their lectures. Knowledge acquired through this channel is contained within these pages.

I have also benefited from teaching courses in international macroeconomics at UBC Okanagan and other Canadian universities. Professors learn from their students. The classroom provides an excellent learning environment, with the direction of learning at times from student to professor.

Various friends, including professors and former students with graduate degrees in economics, read specific chapters and provided comments and suggestions that improved the book. This group includes Lee Bailey, Todd Campbell, Jesse Johal, Niki Kupchenko, Thomas Palmer, Bill Woloschuk, Keith Yacucha, Lijun Zhang, and Ziyu Zhang. Kate Pasula and Brett Pasula provided assistance on various editorial matters. I am grateful to all of these individuals. In addition, I received suggestions from a number of anonymous reviewers retained by the publisher. Any errors that remain are my own.

I also want to thank Statistics Canada, the Federal Reserve Bank of St. Louis (FRED), the International Monetary Fund, and the Groningen Growth and Development Centre. The data from these sources are used in the plots in the chapters. These organizations do such an excellent job in providing access to the numbers that economists use in their empirical analyses.

I am proud to have a book published by UTP, the academic press of the university where I completed a Ph.D. in Economics. I am especially grateful to Jennifer DiDomenico, now editorial director at UTP, who worked on my book project over many years. I have also benefited from the editing and marketing expertise of others at UTP, including Megan Hunt, Leah Connor, Tina Eng, and Aditi Parikh, and from editing services provided by Aalap Trivedi. I am grateful to them all.

I thank family and friends for making life enjoyable, as well as listening to and providing guidance on matters related to the book. And I am indebted to John Floyd and Allan Hynes, my professors at the University of Toronto. I benefited not only from their lectures but also from the assistance they provided in my academic work. I am grateful for their wisdom, guidance, and encouragement.

PART I

The Exchange Rate, Interest Rates, and Expectations

CHAPTER 1

The Exchange Rate in the Very Short Run

1. INTRODUCTION

The exchange rate measures the value of one currency in terms of another currency, such as the exchange rate between the Canadian dollar and the US dollar or between the euro and the yen. This chapter examines the determination of the exchange rate in the very short run (a very short period of time, such as one day).

Exchange rates, like stock prices, have considerable short-term volatility, with short-term movements often associated with investors responding to new information in the marketplace. The very short-run theory of the exchange rate, like the theory of stock prices, is based on a core principle in financial economics: the actions of investors result in the equalization of (risk-adjusted) expected returns on alternative investments. With the analysis focusing on investments in domestic bonds and foreign bonds, this principle results in a dynamic relationship that links interest rates, expectations, and the exchange rate. This relationship implies that, in the very short run, the exchange rate is affected by factors such as interest rates and investors' expectations.

The focus of each chapter is on theoretical analysis, but it still provides the related empirical evidence. In addition, each chapter includes applied exercises, with detailed instructions and data sources, in a section called "Data Analytics." The approach of combining theory with empirics enhances one's understanding of both international macroeconomics and the workings of the global economy.[1]

2. THE EXCHANGE RATE

Consider, for example, the Canadian dollar–US dollar exchange rate. If one has $1 Canadian, how many US dollars is this worth? Or if one has $1 US, how many Canadian dollars does one get in exchange?

In the financial press, the exchange rate is typically quoted as US cents per Canadian dollar. But the exchange rate can also be quoted as the inverse of this number: the number of Canadian cents per US dollar. For example, suppose that $1 Canadian is worth 66 2/3 cents US. How much is $1 US worth in terms of Canadian dollars? If 66 2/3 cents US is worth $1 Canadian, another 33 1/3 cents US is worth another $0.50 Canadian. In total, $1.00 US is worth $1.50 Canadian. Either measure can be used:

- $0.6667 US = $1 Canadian is the same as $1.50 Canadian = $1 US

When presenting factual information, this book may use either measure. In the theoretical analysis, the exchange rate is defined as the units of domestic currency per one unit of foreign currency (for example, units of Canadian dollars per US dollar, such as $1.50 Canadian equals $1 US). The exchange rate is denoted by the symbol s, and domestic residents can think of s as the price of the foreign currency. For a Canadian, the variable s indicates how many Canadian dollars are needed to buy one US dollar.

The following terminology is used:

(a) a depreciation of the domestic currency (an appreciation of the foreign currency):
- If the variable s rises, say, from 1.25 to 1.33, the price of the foreign currency has increased; the domestic currency has depreciated, or decreased in value, and the foreign currency has appreciated;

(b) an appreciation of the domestic currency (a depreciation of the foreign currency):
- If the variable s falls, say, from 1.25 to 1.20, the price of the foreign currency has decreased; the domestic currency has appreciated, or increased in value, and the foreign currency has depreciated.

3. LONG-TERM MOVEMENTS IN THE EXCHANGE RATE

Figure 1.1 depicts movements in the Canadian–US dollar exchange rate, using monthly data from 1980 to 2024. The variable on the vertical axis is the number of US cents per Canadian dollar, so a fall in the line represents a depreciation of the Canadian dollar (the data are taken from the Statistics Canada CANSIM database).[2]

The Canadian dollar tended to depreciate in the early 1980s, falling from 87 cents US in 1980 to 70 cents US in 1986. The Canadian dollar tended to appreciate in the next five years, reaching 89 cents US in 1991. The Canadian dollar then began a long-term fall for the rest of the 1990s, with a low point of 64 cents US in 1998. In the early 2000s, the Canadian dollar dropped to a further low of 62.5 cents US in 2002. Between 2002 and 2008, the Canadian dollar appreciated to a level above par. This appreciation was phenomenal, with the value of the Canadian dollar rising more than 60 per cent. The Canadian dollar then depreciated by more than 20 per cent amid the 2008–2009 financial crisis and recession and appreciated back to a level above par by 2011. In the next major change, the Canadian dollar depreciated from par

Figure 1.1: Canadian–US dollar exchange rate

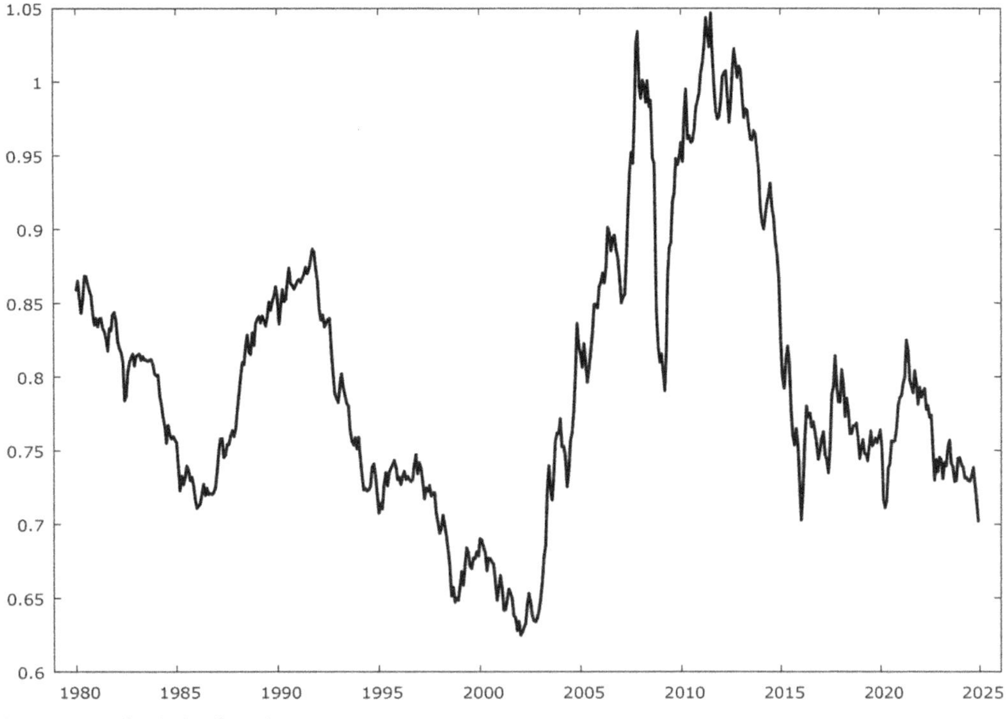

Data source: Statistics Canada

in 2013 to 75 cents US in late 2016. Thereafter the Canadian dollar moved sharply up and down, primarily in the range between 70 and 80 cents. The possible causes of these long-term changes in the exchange rate, as well as their impact on the economy, are examined at various points in the book.

The analysis in this chapter focuses on the very short-term changes in the exchange rate, such as daily changes (financial sites on the internet often show exchange rate movements over the last five business days). These changes are explained by factors that affect the expected returns on domestic and foreign bonds.

4. EXPECTED RETURNS ON DOMESTIC AND FOREIGN BONDS

Consider a domestic investor with a one-year time horizon, and suppose the investor is considering whether to invest in a 1-year domestic bond or a 1-year foreign bond. If, for example, the domestic interest rate equals 3 per cent and the foreign interest rate is 1 per cent, which bond should the investor buy?

The expected and actual return on the domestic bond equals 3 per cent. If the domestic investor buys the domestic bond today and holds it for the full year, the percentage return will be 3 per cent. The interest rate on a 1-year domestic bond, denoted as i_t, equals 3 per cent, where the subscript t denotes "today."

To calculate the expected return on the foreign bond, one needs to consider the different transactions. For a domestic investor, there are three transactions: (1) sell domestic currency in exchange for foreign currency *today*, where today's exchange rate is denoted as s_t; (2) use the foreign currency to purchase a one-year foreign bond *today*, where today's foreign interest rate is denoted as i_t^*; and (3) *one year from today*, cash in the foreign bond and sell the foreign currency for domestic currency, where the exchange rate in one year is denoted as s_{t+1} (the subscript t+1 denotes one year into the future from today). Note that, because the future is uncertain, the expected return will depend on the *expected* future exchange rate, denoted as s_{t+1}^e.

While s_t and i_t^* are known today, the investor needs to generate the expected future exchange rate s_{t+1}^e. Based on information available today, the investor must assess how the exchange rate may move over the next year, and formulate a best estimate of the exchange rate one year into the future. The expected return on the foreign bond for domestic investors has two components:[3]

$$expected\ return\ on\ the\ foreign\ bond = i_t^* + \frac{s_{t+1}^e - s_t}{s_t}.$$

The first component is today's foreign interest rate, and the second component is the expected rate of appreciation of the foreign currency (relative to the domestic currency) over the next year. This second component requires further explanation.

Suppose the exchange rate today, s_t, equals 1.20, but the investor expects the exchange rate to be 1.26 in one year (s_{t+1}^e equals 1.26). Consider a Canadian investor as the domestic investor who buys US dollars today for $1.20 Canadian and expects to sell US dollars in one year for $1.26 Canadian. The investor expects to make an additional return from buying at a lower price today relative to the price expected to sell at in one year. The expected rate of appreciation of the foreign currency (relative to the domestic currency) equals 0.06/1.20, or 5 per cent. For a domestic (Canadian) investor, the expected return on the foreign (US) bond is 6 per cent, calculated as

$$i_t^* + \frac{s_{t+1}^e - s_t}{s_t} = 0.01 + \frac{1.26 - 1.20}{1.20} = 0.01 + 0.05 = 0.06.$$

The Time Diagram

Consider Figure 1.2, where the exchange rate is measured on the vertical axis and time is on the horizontal axis. As noted, time t means today and time t+1 represents one year into the future. This diagram is a useful tool, and it is called the time diagram for the exchange rate. The exchange rate, s_t, at time t equals 1.20, and the expected future exchange rate, s_{t+1}^e, equals 1.26. The investor expects the foreign currency to appreciate by 5 per cent over the next year. If an investor buys foreign currency today for 1.20 and then sells foreign currency in one year for 1.26, the investor would indeed make a 5 per cent return from buying the foreign currency low and selling it high.

Figure 1.2: Time diagram

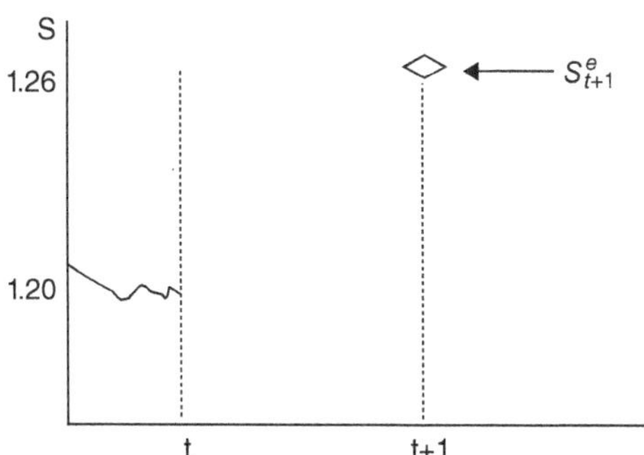

The investor's expectation may not be correct. But investors base their investment decisions on the best possible prediction of the future, given the information available today.

Risk-Neutral Investors

Which bond is the better investment? In general, investors are concerned with both the expected returns and the relative riskiness of alternative investments. But certain investors, called risk-neutral investors, focus exclusively on expected returns. Under risk neutrality, an investor always prefers an investment with a higher expected return (regardless of the risk) and is indifferent between any two assets, only if they have the same expected return. For simplicity, this chapter assumes that investors are risk-neutral. Chapter 2 discusses the risk premium on foreign bonds and how changes in it affect today's exchange rate.

Based on these numbers, the expected return on the domestic bond equals 3 per cent and the expected return on the foreign bond equals 6 per cent. The risk-neutral domestic investor will prefer the foreign bond to the domestic bond. Note that the domestic investor will prefer the foreign bond even though the domestic interest rate is higher than the foreign interest rate.

5. INDIVIDUAL BEHAVIOR AND MARKET BEHAVIOR

In financial markets (such as bond, stock, and foreign exchange markets), prices adjust quickly to eliminate any great investment opportunities that arise. In the analysis of financial markets, it is essential to distinguish between actions taken by an individual and actions taken by many (or all) individuals at once. Consider an example.

Suppose that, all of a sudden, an investor realizes that the expected return on an asset has increased substantially. This investor, acting alone, would experience an increase in demand for the asset and would want to buy more units of this asset at the initial market price. This action is an example of individual behavior.

But if all investors experienced the same increase in expected return, all individuals will not be able to purchase the asset. The quantity of the asset is fixed and held by other investors. The market behavior of investors will lead to investors bidding higher and higher prices, with no investors willing to sell the asset. Indeed, the investors who own the asset are, like everyone else, submitting higher bids in an attempt to acquire more units of the asset. In the very short run, the price will be quickly bid up to a level where the bidding stops, with no trades having been made (assuming all investors have identical expectations). At the new equilibrium point, the expected return on the asset is again no higher than the expected returns on alternative assets. These actions reflect market behavior.[4]

The same type of adjustment occurs in the foreign exchange market, with the exchange rate changing quickly to eliminate any opportunities for superior returns that may arise.

6. INTEREST RATE PARITY AND EQUILIBRIUM IN THE FOREIGN EXCHANGE MARKET

In the very short run, the exchange rate is determined by the variables that affect the expected returns on domestic and foreign bonds. The exchange rate is affected not only by changes in domestic and foreign interest rates but also by changes in the expected future exchange rate. Thus, like stock prices, the exchange rate is affected by changes in expectations.

For simplicity, the following assumptions are adopted: all investors are risk-neutral, all investors have the same expected future exchange rate, and the domestic economy is "small" (meaning that changes in the domestic economy have no effect on variables in the large foreign economy).

In equilibrium, there is no incentive to buy or sell. Investors are content holding the quantity of assets (domestic and foreign bonds) they are currently holding. Equilibrium occurs when domestic and foreign bonds have the same expected return:

$$i_t = i_t^* + \frac{s_{t+1}^e - s_t}{s_t}.$$

This equation is the *interest rate parity*, or *IRP*, condition. Note that the IRP condition implies that expected returns are equal (interest rates need not be equal for IRP to hold).

It is the actions of investors that force the IRP condition to hold. Suppose, for example, that the IRP condition does not hold, with the domestic interest rate equal to 6 per cent, the foreign interest rate equal to 4 per cent, and the expected rate of appreciation of the foreign currency (relative to the domestic currency) equal to 7 per cent (all investors have the same expected future exchange rate and, therefore, the same expected rate of appreciation of the foreign currency). For domestic investors, the expected returns are 6 per cent on domestic bonds and 11 per cent on foreign bonds. What will happen?

To simplify, hold the two interest rates and the expected future exchange rate fixed. In this case, the exchange rate does all the adjusting to restore equilibrium. Based on these numbers, everyone wants to shift into foreign bonds. Domestic investors try to buy foreign currency (try to sell domestic currency). They bid higher and higher prices for foreign currency, because no one will sell foreign currency at the original price: everyone wants to buy foreign currency and sell domestic currency (note that focusing on the actions of domestic residents is for convenience, as foreign residents are not willing to sell their own currency at this level).[5] This action causes the price of foreign currency to rise. In other words, the foreign currency appreciates, and the domestic currency depreciates. This increase in s_t, holding s_{t+1}^e fixed, continues until it causes the expected rate of appreciation of foreign currency to fall from 7 per cent to 2 per cent. At this point, an equilibrium situation exists. The domestic interest rate and the expected return on foreign bonds both equal 6 per cent, with the foreign interest rate equal to 4 per cent and the expected rate of appreciation of foreign currency equal to 2 per cent.

In equilibrium, IRP holds.[6] If a change occurs to create a situation where it does not hold, the exchange rate adjusts to restore the equilibrium condition.

Exogenous and Endogenous Variables

The foreign interest rate and the expected future exchange rate are taken to be exogenous variables, meaning variables held fixed unless it is indicated that they have changed exogenously. The exchange rate and the domestic interest rate are endogenous variables that adjust in response to the exogenous changes that occur.

For the next few sections, the exchange rate is the sole endogenous variable, and the domestic interest rate is held fixed. This approach simplifies the analysis and allows us to focus on exchange rate determination. The joint determination of the exchange rate and the domestic interest rate is examined concisely in Section 11 and comprehensively in Chapter 2.

7. THE FOREIGN INTEREST RATE AND THE EXCHANGE RATE

Suppose the domestic interest rate equals 7 per cent, the foreign interest rate is 4 per cent, and the expected rate of appreciation of foreign currency is 3 per cent. This situation is an equilibrium situation, denoted as point A in Table 1.1, with the expected returns on both assets equal to 7 per cent (for risk-neutral investors, domestic and foreign bonds are equally good investments). Suppose there is an exogenous increase in the foreign interest rate to 6 per cent. Holding the domestic interest rate and the expected future exchange rate fixed, how does this change affect the exchange rate and the expected rate of appreciation of foreign currency in the very short run? That is, how are these variables affected today?

Immediately after the increase in the foreign interest rate, denoted as point B in Table 1.1, foreign bonds are a better investment because their expected return exceeds the domestic interest rate. Domestic investors want to increase their holdings of foreign bonds and *try to* buy foreign currency (try to sell domestic currency). Because all investors have the same expectation, no one is willing to sell foreign currency at the initial exchange rate. But domestic investors are willing to bid higher prices for the foreign currency, because there is a 2 per cent differential in expected returns. So, the foreign currency is bid up in value, and this process continues until the foreign bonds are no longer a superior investment. This situation is denoted as point C, where the expected returns are again both equal to 7 per cent. In the process, the increase in s_t has, for a given s_{t+1}^e, reduced the expected rate of appreciation from 3 per cent to 1 per cent. In the new equilibrium, the expected returns on domestic and foreign bonds are equal.

Table 1.1: Increase in the foreign interest rate

	i_t	i_t^*	$\dfrac{s_{t+1}^e - s_t}{s_t}$	$i_t^* + \dfrac{s_{t+1}^e - s_t}{s_t}$
A	7%	4%	3%	7%
B	7%	6%	3%	9%
C	7%	6%	1%	7%

Figure 1.3: Time diagram

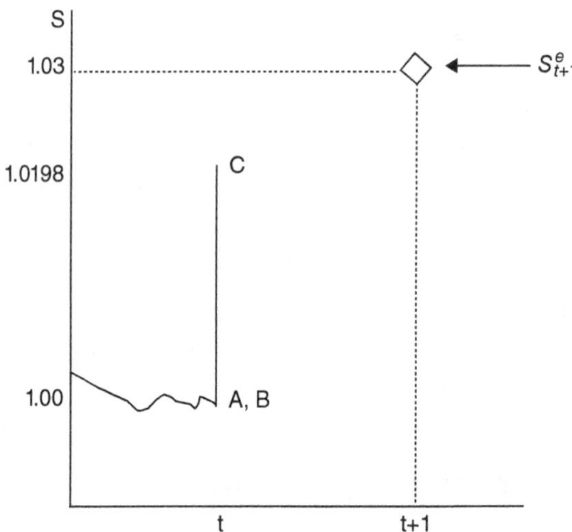

This case is also shown on the time diagram in Figure 1.3, where the initial exchange rate equals 1.0 and the expected future exchange rate equals 1.03. The initial exchange rate, s_t, is at point A. Point B is immediately after the exogenous increase in the foreign interest rate, so that today's exchange rate has not yet had time to change. As investors try to buy foreign currency, s_t increases. Investors bid up today's exchange rate in an attempt to acquire foreign currency (to be able to buy foreign bonds). The new equilibrium is established at point C. The value of s_t at point C is the exchange rate that generates an expected rate of appreciation of the foreign currency of 1 per cent with a given expected future exchange rate equal to 1.03. Therefore, the equilibrium s_t equals 1.0198. At this new equilibrium, foreign and domestic bonds have the same expected return. For a domestic investor, the domestic bond earns 7 per cent for sure and the foreign bond is expected to earn 7 per cent, the latter being a combination of the 6 per cent return on the foreign bond interest earnings and the expected 1 per cent return from the expected appreciation of the foreign currency over the next year.

The adjustment in the exchange rate occurs quickly. When the foreign interest rate increases, the exchange rate rises quickly to point C as investors bid higher and higher prices in an attempt to acquire foreign currency. International bond traders are constantly monitoring these markets such that any superior expected return opportunities are eliminated quickly. While these traders are attempting to earn higher returns, the competitive environment between traders (with the same expected future exchange rate) causes the exchange rate to move quickly to the new equilibrium point.

8. NEWS AND THE EXCHANGE RATE

News is an important factor causing changes in the exchange rate in the very short run. Exchange rates, like stock prices, are asset prices. It is not surprising that stock prices are influenced by news, and it should not be surprising that news is a critical factor in very short-term movements in the exchange rate.[7] Any news that causes investors to revise their expectations of the level of the future exchange rate immediately causes today's exchange rate to change.

Suppose that, in the initial equilibrium, the domestic interest rate equals 5 per cent and the foreign interest rate equals 4 per cent. In equilibrium, the current exchange rate, s_t, will be 1 per cent less than the expected future exchange rate, s_{t+1}^e (if the current exchange rate equals 1.00, the expected future exchange rate equals 1.01). Both domestic and foreign bonds have expected returns equal to 5 per cent (denoted as point A in Table 1.2 and Figure 1.4).

Suppose some news causes an increase in the expected future exchange rate, an increase in s_{t+1}^e from 1.01 to 1.08 (hold domestic and foreign interest rates fixed). Immediately after this change, the expected rate of appreciation of the foreign currency is 8 per cent (point B in the table). With today's exchange rate at 1.00 and the expected future exchange rate at 1.08, an investor that bought foreign currency today at 1.00 and sold this foreign currency next year at 1.08 would make an 8 per cent return. With the foreign interest rate equal to 4 per cent, the expected return on the foreign bond has therefore increased to 12 per cent.

Because foreign bonds have a higher expected return than domestic bonds, investors have an incentive to shift funds into foreign bonds. Investors try to buy foreign currency (try to sell domestic currency). Because all investors have the same expectation, no investor is willing to sell foreign currency for 1.00. Investors therefore bid higher prices in an attempt to acquire foreign currency. Investors would bid, for example, 1.04 in an attempt to acquire foreign currency. At s_t equal to 1.04 (point BB in the table and on the figure), the expected rate of appreciation of foreign currency is 3.85 per cent and the expected return on foreign bonds is 4 per cent plus 3.85 per cent, or 7.85 per cent. This expected return is still greater than the 5 per cent return on domestic bonds. This process of bidding higher prices for foreign currency continues, as investors attempt to acquire foreign currency by selling domestic currency. In the new equilibrium, denoted as point C, the price of foreign currency (in terms of units of domestic currency) equals 1.0693.[8] Expected returns on domestic and foreign bonds both equal 5 per cent, and the two bonds are regarded as equally good investments.

A change in the expected future exchange rate causes a change in today's exchange rate. In this example, news caused a depreciation of domestic currency (relative to foreign currency) on the foreign exchange market today.

News and Changes in the Expected Future Exchange Rate

There are many factors that cause changes in expectations. The most common factors are statistics and announcements that provide information on the current and future state of the domestic or foreign economy and on the current and future policy in the two countries. In terms of the Canadian–US dollar exchange rate, examples of statistics could be Statistics Canada releases on

Table 1.2: Increase in the expected future exchange rate

	i_t	i_t^*	$\dfrac{s_{t+1}^e - s_t}{s_t}$	$i_t^* + \dfrac{s_{t+1}^e - s_t}{s_t}$
A	5%	4%	1%	5%
B	5%	4%	8%	12%
BB	5%	4%	3.85%	7.85%
C	5%	4%	1%	5%

Figure 1.4: Time diagram

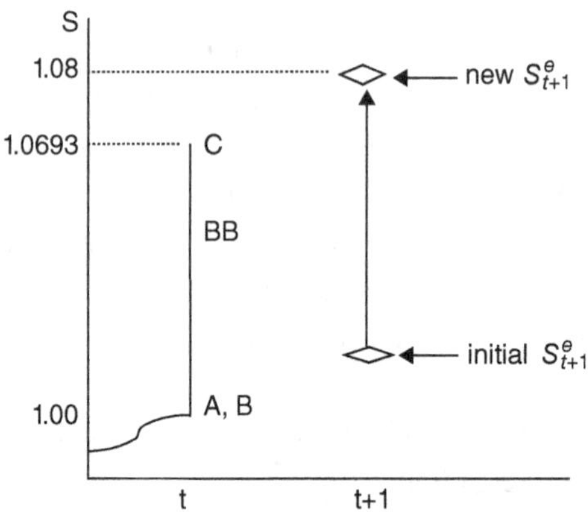

new orders of durable goods, the leading economic indicator, or the consumer price index. Indeed, there are scores of statistics released by the government statistical agencies relevant to the future states of the Canadian and American economies.[9] An example of an announcement could be a Bank of Canada statement on the future state of the economy or on possible monetary policy actions in the near future.

With each statistical release or announcement, bond and currency traders assess the new information and determine how the news affects their view regarding where the exchange rate is expected to be one year into the future. If these traders can consistently predict the future better than other investors, they will be able to earn higher actual returns.[10] With traders working for pension funds, mutual funds, and banks, there is a strong incentive to outperform "the market." But while there are incentives to try to earn superior returns on a consistent basis, the assumption that all investors have the same expected future exchange rate means that this is not possible.

Investors Equalize Expected Returns, But Actual Returns Can Differ

Based on what is known today, the actions of risk-neutral investors equalize expected returns on the two assets. Domestic and foreign bonds are equally good investments, based on information available today. Expected returns are also called ex ante returns, where the Latin phrase ex ante means "before the event." But there is no guarantee that actual returns will be the same. Many things can happen between today and next year, so the actual exchange rate at time t+1 can differ from what was expected a year earlier. Therefore, actual or ex post returns can differ, where ex post means "after the event."

For example, suppose i_t equals 5 per cent, i_t^* equals 4 per cent, and domestic investors purchase foreign currency at s_t equal to 1.0 (expecting s_{t+1} to be 1.01). If the actual time t+1 exchange rate equals 0.89, the actual returns for domestic investors will be 5 per cent on the domestic bond and −7 per cent on the foreign bond (the latter being the sum of 4 per cent on interest and −11 per cent on the change in the exchange rate).[11] The actions of risk-neutral investors equalize expected returns, but this in no way guarantees the equality of ex post returns.

9. A MARKET-BASED MEASURE OF THE EXPECTED FUTURE EXCHANGE RATE

While the expected future exchange rate is a variable in investors' minds, there is a variable that, under certain conditions, is a good proxy for the expected future exchange rate. This variable is the forward exchange rate.[12] The forward exchange rate is an exchange rate set today for the exchange of two currencies on some future date, typically 90 days, 180 days, or 1 year into the future.

Let F_t^{t+1} denote the 1-year forward exchange rate, measured as Canadian dollars per US dollar. The forward exchange rate is set at time t for the exchange of US and Canadian dollars at time t+1 (one year in the future). The forward exchange rate is set today in a contract between someone who has agreed to sell US dollars in one year (in exchange for Canadian dollars) with another person who has agreed to buy US dollars in one year (in exchange for Canadian dollars). When all investors are risk-neutral (with the same expectation), the actions of investors cause the equilibrium forward exchange rate to equal the expected future exchange rate:

$$F_t^{t+1} = s_{t+1}^e.$$

Why does this condition hold? Consider an example, with s_{t+1}^e equal to $1.23 Canadian. A risk-neutral investor would be willing, using a forward contract signed today, to agree to buy US dollars in one year for less than or equal to $1.23 Canadian. If this investor gets a forward exchange rate of, say, $1.21, the investor would agree to buy US dollars for $1.21 Canadian. This investor would expect to be able, at time t+1, to sell these US dollars for $1.23 Canadian (generating an expected profit, based on information available today). Another risk-neutral investor would be willing, using a forward contract signed today, to sell US dollars in one year for more than or equal to $1.23 Canadian. If this investor gets a forward exchange rate of, say, $1.25, the investor would agree to sign the forward contract today. This investor would think that they will be able to buy US dollars on the spot market at time t+1 for $1.23 (the s_{t+1}^e), and then get $1.25 when US dollars are sold, as agreed in the forward contract, thus generating an expected profit. But market forces will move the forward exchange rate to an equilibrium level. In this case, the actions of risk-neutral investors will drive the equilibrium forward exchange rate, set today, to $1.23. This level of the forward exchange rate is the only level with both a willing buyer and a willing seller.

Figure 1.5: Spot and forward exchange rate

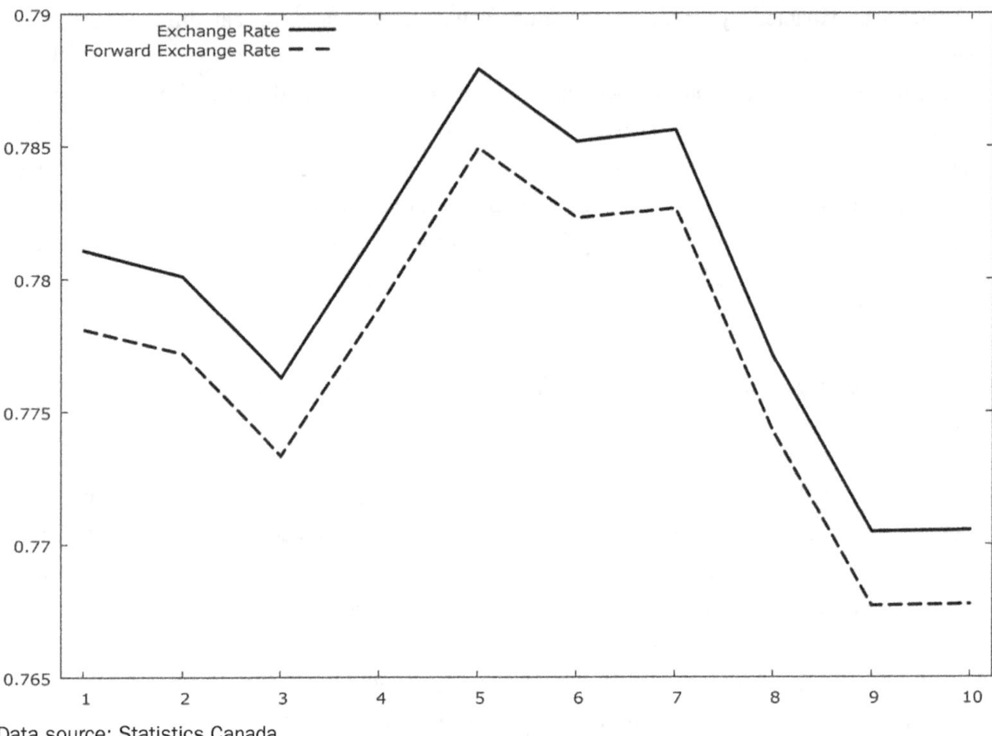

Data source: Statistics Canada

Spot and Forward Exchange Rates

Figure 1.5 shows the exchange rate and the forward exchange rate for ten business days from January 5, 2004, to January 16, 2004 (as a typical example).[13] These two variables move closely together. If movements in the forward exchange rate are interpreted as representing movements in the expected future exchange rate on that day, it is evident that changes in the expected future exchange rate are an important determinant of exchange rate fluctuations in the very short run (an applied exercise in Data Analytics examines the co-movement between spot and forward rates over recent periods).

10. THE EXCHANGE RATE AND WORLD COMMODITY PRICES

For countries with large resource sectors, changes in world commodity prices can have a significant impact on the domestic economy, including on the foreign exchange value of the currency. In resource-rich countries with flexible exchange rates, such as Australia, Canada, and New Zealand, the exchange rate tends to be correlated with world commodity prices.[14] In Canada, for example, significant quantities of exports are from four resource sectors: forestry, agriculture, metals and minerals, and energy.[15] And there is a correlation between movements in the Canadian–US dollar exchange rate and the "commodity price index," a weighted-average of the US dollar prices of goods in these four sectors. The Canadian dollar tends to depreciate when

Figure 1.6: Exchange rate and commodity price index

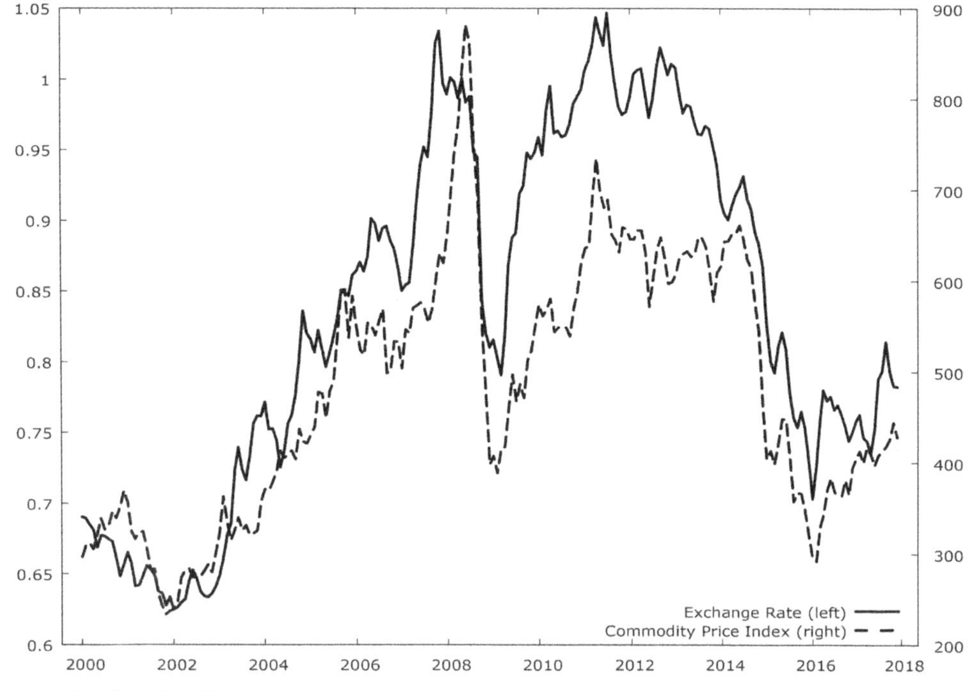

Data source: Statistics Canada

the commodity price index decreases and tends to appreciate when the commodity price index increases.[16]

An Explanation Based on Expectations and Interest Rate Parity

Suppose there is a decrease in the world demand for all resource commodities, causing a decrease in both the expected future and current prices of these commodities on world markets. Traders may infer that the fall in prices will cause a sustained weakness in the Canadian resource sector and the Canadian economy in general, and extrapolate that this weakness will result in a sustained depreciation of the Canadian dollar.[17] If traders interpret the news of a decrease in world resource prices in this way, these traders will decrease their expected future value of the Canadian dollar and then take actions that cause the Canadian dollar to depreciate today. The news of the fall in world resource prices is matched by a depreciation of the Canadian dollar today.[18]

Empirical Evidence

There are many factors that can cause the exchange rate to change, and other factors could offset the possible effect of a change in commodity prices. But the evidence in Figure 1.6, based on monthly data, indicates that the two series have moved relatively closely together in this century.[19] The sharp appreciation of the Canadian dollar between 2002 and 2008 was unprecedented in Canadian economic history, with the Canadian dollar rising in value by

Table 1.3: Increase in the expected future exchange rate

	i_t	i_t^*	$\dfrac{s_{t+1}^e - s_t}{s_t}$	$i_t^* + \dfrac{s_{t+1}^e - s_t}{s_t}$
A	4%	4%	0%	4%
B	4%	4%	5%	9%
C	6.4%	4%	2.4%	6.4%

more than 60 per cent. Over the same period, the index measuring world commodity prices rose from below 300 to almost 900, also a phenomenal increase (although commodity prices, in general, are quite volatile). The commodity price index and the Canadian dollar collapsed together at the onset of the 2008 financial crisis, and both variables trended upward over the subsequent few years. In the period after 2014, both variables moved back down to lower levels.

The link between the exchange rate and commodity prices is also evident in other periods, with further evidence presented in subsequent chapters and in Data Analytics.[20]

11. NEWS, THE EXCHANGE RATE, AND THE INTEREST RATE

In previous sections, the domestic interest rate was held fixed. In a more general framework, changes in the expected future exchange rate may cause changes in both the exchange rate and the domestic interest rate. While an increase in the domestic interest rate (relative to the foreign interest rate) is often regarded as being associated with an increase in the value of the domestic currency, this relationship need not hold. It is possible for the domestic currency to depreciate even though the domestic interest rate has increased on that day.

Suppose that, in the initial equilibrium (denoted as point A in Table 1.3), i_t and i_t^* equal 4 per cent, both s_t and s_{t+1}^e equal 1.20, and then there is an increase in the expected future exchange rate to 1.26. Holding the foreign interest rate fixed, how does this exogenous change affect the exchange rate and the domestic interest rate in the very short run? With an increase in s_{t+1}^e from 1.20 to 1.26, there is an expected appreciation of the foreign currency (relative to the domestic currency) of 5 per cent. As foreign bonds now have a higher expected return than domestic bonds, two different attempted transactions occur immediately. First, domestic investors try to buy foreign currency (sell domestic currency), causing the price of the foreign currency, s_t, to be bid up. Second, investors try to sell domestic bonds, causing today's bond price to fall and the domestic interest rate to rise.

In the new equilibrium, the domestic currency has depreciated, and the domestic interest rate has increased. If the exchange rate increases to 1.23 in the new equilibrium, there is an expected rate of appreciation of the foreign currency of 0.03/1.23, or approximately 2.4 per cent. The domestic interest rate, in this case, will increase to 6.4 per cent. The expected returns on domestic and foreign bonds are equal (point C in the table), and an equilibrium situation exists. Thus, bad news about the future value of the domestic currency (an increase in s^e_{t+1}) causes both a depreciation of the domestic currency today and an increase in the domestic interest rate today.

This relationship is examined further in Chapter 2, both theoretically and empirically. An applied exercise in Data Analytics examines the daily movements in the exchange rate and the interest rate (differential) around the time of an important event in Canadian political history, the 1995 Quebec Referendum.[21]

12. CONCLUSION

This chapter outlined the interest rate parity condition and explained how changes in today's exchange rate act to equalize the expected returns on domestic and foreign bonds. In the very short run, the exchange rate is affected both by interest rates and by news that alters investor expectations regarding the future exchange rate. Indeed, news can play a significant role in the very short-term movements in the exchange rate.[22]

The core of the analysis in this chapter held the domestic interest rate fixed. While this assumption allowed the analysis to focus on exchange rate determination, exogenous shocks impacting financial markets may affect both the exchange rate and the domestic interest rate.[23] The next chapter continues the analysis of exchange rate determination in the very short run but incorporates a richer financial structure that allows for the joint determination of the exchange rate and the interest rate.

PRACTICE QUESTIONS

1. Fill in the blanks
   (a) If $1 Canadian is worth $0.6667 US, then $1 US is worth $_____ Canadian.
   (b) The exchange rate at time t is denoted s_t. An increase in s_t means that the domestic currency has _____ (relative to the foreign currency) today, or that the price of foreign currency (in terms of domestic currency) has _____ today.
   (c) The expected return on a foreign bond for domestic investors equals the foreign interest rate plus the _____ rate of _____ of the foreign currency (relative to the domestic currency).
   (d) Suppose interest rate parity holds, today's interest rate on a 1-year domestic bond equals 4 per cent, and today's interest rate on a 1-year foreign bond equals 1 per cent. Investors expect the foreign currency (relative to the domestic currency) to _____ by _____ per cent over the next year.
   (e) Suppose interest rate parity holds. If, today, the domestic interest rate is 5 per cent and the foreign interest rate is 3 per cent, investors expect the foreign currency to _____ over the next year. Based on today's numbers, the domestic bond _____ better investment.

2. Fill in the blanks
   (a) If the domestic interest rate equals 7 per cent, and the expected rate of appreciation of the foreign currency (relative to the domestic currency) equals 2 per cent, the equilibrium expected return on foreign bonds for a domestic investor equals ______ per cent.
   (b) The ______ is a market-based measure of the expected future exchange rate.
   (c) An exogenous increase in the foreign interest rate (holding the domestic interest rate and the expected future exchange rate fixed) causes the domestic currency to ______ (relative to the foreign currency) in the very short run.
   (d) The commodity price index is a weighted average of the US dollar prices of products from four sectors of the Canadian economy: forestry, ______, ______, and energy.
   (e) Suppose that, at time t, the domestic interest rate is 3 per cent, the foreign interest rate equals 1 per cent, and the equilibrium exchange rate equals 1.0. The market expects the time t+1 exchange rate to equal ______. If the actual time t+1 exchange rate equals 1.09, the actual 1-year return on foreign bonds for domestic investors will equal ______ per cent.
3. Using numbers and a time diagram for the exchange rate, explain how an exogenous increase in the foreign interest rate from 2 per cent to 6 per cent affects the exchange rate in the very short run. Assume that the domestic interest rate is fixed at 4 per cent and the expected future exchange rate does not change.
4. Using numbers and a time diagram, explain how an increase in the expected future exchange rate (an increase in s_{t+1}^e from 1.03 to 1.08) affects the exchange rate and the expected rate of appreciation of the foreign currency in the very short run. Hold the domestic interest rate fixed at 4 per cent and the foreign interest rate fixed at 1 per cent.
5. Suppose that, in the very short run, domestic and foreign bonds are equally good investments (interest rate parity holds), with the domestic interest rate equal to 5 per cent and the foreign interest rate equal to 12 per cent. What do investors expect to happen to the exchange rate over the next year? Explain using interest rate parity and a time diagram.
6. Would it ever make sense for domestic investors to purchase a foreign currency bond today if these investors expected the foreign currency to depreciate (relative to the domestic currency) by 20 per cent over the next year? Explain.

DATA ANALYTICS

1. Collect monthly data on the Canadian–US dollar exchange rate and the forward exchange rate, beginning with data in January 2012 (available in CANSIM Table 176-0064). Plot these series on the same plot over the period since 2012, as

well as over shorter periods of a year or two. Comment using the analysis in the chapter.

2. Download data on the commodity price index from CANSIM Table 176-0076. Convert these weekly data to quarterly data. Convert the monthly spot exchange rate data into quarterly data, and invert the data such that the exchange rate is measured as Canadian dollars per US dollar. Plot the commodity price index and the exchange rate on the same plot, beginning with the first quarter of 2012 (measure each series on a separate axis). Have these series tended to move together? Comment.

3. (a) The Quebec referendum on sovereignty was held on October 30, 1995. Collect daily data on the Canadian–US dollar exchange rate and the 91-day Canadian Treasury bill interest rate for the month of October. The CANSIM series numbers for these daily variables are V121716 and V39065 (note that the exchange rate is measured at noon). Collect daily data on the US 91-day Treasury bill interest rate from FRED, the Federal Reserve Bank of St. Louis database. Create a time-series plot of the exchange rate and the Canadian–US interest rate differential, with each variable measured on a separate axis. Comment.

(b) There were many poll results announced in the pre-Referendum period. Fox, Andersen, and Dubonnet (1999) provide information on poll results, as well as comments on important events during this period. Using the plot from part (a), discuss whether the announced poll results may have affected the financial variables.

APPENDIX A: INTEREST RATE PARITY, THE APPROXIMATION, AND THE EXACT EXPRESSION

Suppose an investor has $100 Canadian to invest, with i_t equal to 7 per cent and i_t^* equal to 10 per cent. Suppose the current exchange rate, s_t, equals 1.25.

By investing $100 Canadian in the Canadian bond, the investor will, after one year, have $107 Canadian. The payoff in one year, in Canadian dollars, equals

$$\$100\left(1+i_t\right) = \$100\left(1.07\right) = \$107 \ Canadian.$$

Consider the US bond. The $100 Canadian is converted to $100 Cdn/$s_t$, or $80 US because s_t equals 1.25. The $80 US is used to purchase a US bond, which in one year becomes $100 Cdn/$s_t$ $(1+i^*_t)$ or $88 US when the US interest rate equals 10 per cent. To convert this US dollar payoff back to Canadian dollars, the investor will sell these $88 US on the foreign exchange market in one year. Suppose that, based on information available today, the investor expects the exchange rate to equal 1.20 in one year: s_{t+1}^e equals 1.20. Then the $88 US is expected to be sold for $105.60 Canadian in one year. The expected payoff in one year, in Canadian dollars, equals

$$\frac{\$100}{S_t}\left(1+i_t^*\right)s_{t+1}^e = \frac{\$100}{1.25}(1.10)1.20 = \$105.60 \ Canadian.$$

For a Canadian investor, the expected return on the US bond equals 5.6 per cent.

Based on these numbers, the Canadian bond has a higher expected payoff in one year. The Canadian bond pays \$107, for sure, in one year, whereas the US bond is expected to have a payoff of \$105.60 Canadian in one year.

Market forces result in the equalization of the equilibrium expected returns on Canadian and US bonds. The actions of investors will cause changes that result in the interest rate parity condition holding as an equality:

$$\left(1+i_t\right) = \frac{\left(1+i_t^*\right)s_{t+1}^e}{S_t}.$$

This condition is the exact specification of the IRP condition, rather than the approximation used in the chapter. This exact specification can be rewritten as

$$i_t = i_t^* + \frac{s_{t+1}^e - S_t}{S_t} + i_t^*\left[\frac{s_{t+1}^e - S_t}{S_t}\right].$$

The approximation ignores the last term, the cross-product term, because it is small relative to the sum of the first two terms. If i_t^* equals 0.04 and $\frac{s_{t+1}^e - S_t}{S_t}$ equals 0.02, the cross-product term is 0.0008, whereas the sum of the first two terms equals 0.06. It is convenient to base the analysis on the approximation. This type of approximation is widely used in financial economics.

APPENDIX B: COVERED INTEREST RATE PARITY

Suppose a Canadian investor buys US dollars today, uses these US dollars to purchase a 1-year US bond today, and signs a forward exchange contract today that commits them to sell US dollars in one year at the forward exchange rate, denoted F_t^{t+1}. With the forward contract, the investor has guaranteed the Canadian dollar payoff in one year:

$$\frac{\left(1+i_t^*\right)F_t^{t+1}}{S_t}.$$

There is no risk in this investment. The payoff in Canadian dollars and the percentage return are guaranteed. Market forces will cause the payoff to equal the payoff from buying a 1-year Canadian bond:

$$\left(1+i_t\right) = \frac{\left(1+i_t^*\right)F_t^{t+1}}{s_t}.$$

This result is called the covered interest rate parity condition.[24] It holds even if risk neutrality does not hold.[25]

NOTES

1 The empirical elements are not summaries of empirical studies by academic economists, but rather a presentation of relevant data and an analysis based on the theory in that chapter. The book also provides extensive references to the academic literature, citing seminal literature and directing the reader to empirical studies.

2 The data are monthly, CANSIM series numbers V37426 and V111666275 (the first series terminated in April 2017, and the second series starts in January 2017).

3 This equation is an approximation, but typically a good approximation (see an appendix). Note that the analysis ignores taxes and transactions costs.

4 On this general point, see the comments in Floyd (1995, 145–46).

5 In the initial situation, the expected return on the domestic bond for a foreign investor equals −1 per cent, that is, the 6 per cent domestic interest rate minus the 7 per cent expected rate of depreciation of the domestic currency.

6 This condition is called the uncovered IRP condition, emphasizing that foreign bonds are a risky asset for domestic residents. The risk can be eliminated using a forward exchange rate contract, yielding a covered IRP condition (see section 9 and an appendix).

7 This point has long been understood by international macroeconomists. See the comments, for example, in Johnson (1976) and Mussa (1979).

8 For most exchange rates, the daily changes are not this large. But the same principles apply regardless of the magnitude of the change.

9 While these statistics are about recent *past* performance, the statistics are news in that there is new information. But the announcement must be news. If the statistical organization announces a 2.3 per cent increase in a variable and everyone was expecting 2.3 per cent, this is not news.

10 If a trader correctly foresees a future appreciation of the foreign currency (and others do not), this trader will be able to acquire foreign currency at the existing exchange rate and will earn higher returns than other investors.

11 While this is a simple point, it is often misunderstood. Of course, the same point is true for other investments. One could purchase shares in a company today and expect a 5 per cent return on the stock, but the actual one-year return could be negative or very high.

12 The price of foreign currency on the futures market (the futures price) is also a good measure.

13 The forward exchange rate is the Canada–US dollar 90-day forward rate (CANSIM series V121727). The series number for the daily exchange rate data is V121716.

14 See, for example, Chen and Rogoff (2003).

15 These commodities are Canada's *claim to fame* in international trade. One could say that, in terms of Canada's exports, the acronym *FAME* refers to forestry, agriculture, metals and minerals, and energy.

16 In the late 1980s, the interest rate policy of the Bank of Canada was regarded as a key factor contributing to the rising Canadian dollar. John Crow, the Bank of Canada Governor, noted that the appreciation of the dollar was related to the rise in commodity prices (see, for example, Crow 1993b).

17 Or traders may infer that the fall in commodity prices will move inflation below the Bank of Canada's target range, so that the Bank will undertake an offsetting policy action that results in a depreciation.

18 Other explanations are provided in future chapters that examine multi-sectoral models (with sectors such as services, manufacturing, and resources), but any explanation of the very short-run co-movement needs to incorporate the expected future exchange rate and the interest rate parity relationship.

19 The commodity price index is CANSIM V52673496. Exchange rate data are the same as in Figure 1.1.

20 Ferraro, Rogoff, and Rossi (2015) examine, among other items, the relationship between oil prices and the Canada–US dollar exchange rate on a daily basis. For an analysis that links the commodity price index, the exchange rate, and the expected future policy interest rate, along with empirics based on monthly data, see Devereux and Smith (2021).

21 In 1995, the Quebec government announced a sovereignty referendum for October 30. During the campaign, polling results were announced and participants made speeches and announcements. Indications of greater support for sovereignty may have resulted in decreases in the expected future value of the Canadian dollar. In the four business days between October 19 and October 24, the Canadian dollar fell from 74.8 to 73 cents US, and the short-term interest rate increased from 6.55 per cent to 7.13 per cent. And the referendum result on October 30 generated the opposite effects. On the next day, the Canadian dollar rose from 73.4 to 74.6 cents US, and the short-term interest rate fell from 6.9 per cent to 5.9 per cent (the CANSIM numbers for the daily exchange rate and interest rate data are V121716 and V39065).

22 There is a vast empirical literature related to testing elements of interest rate parity. This literature is discussed by, among others, Cumby and Obstfeld (1984), Engel (1996, 2014, 2016), Floyd (2010), Lewis (2011), and Lothian (2016).

23 The "overshooting" result, formulated by Dornbusch (1976), is discussed extensively in Chapter 2.

24 Taxes and transactions costs are ignored.

25 Under risk aversion, the equilibrium forward exchange rate is not equal to the expected future exchange rate, but it differs by a risk premium. Chapter 2 discusses the risk premium.

The Exchange Rate and the Interest Rate in the Very Short Run

1. INTRODUCTION

The exchange rate and the domestic interest rate are determined jointly in the sense that both variables respond to exogenous shocks impacting financial markets. Many factors, including exogenous changes in the money supply, cause both the exchange rate and interest rate to change. To get a more complete understanding of exchange rate determination in the very short run, the model needs a richer financial structure. This chapter takes a step in this direction by incorporating the concept of portfolio equilibrium, allowing for an analysis of the interaction between bond markets and foreign exchange markets. The analysis focuses on the domestic economy, taken to be a small economy with foreign variables regarded as exogenous.

With the aim of gaining a better understanding of the very short-term movements in the exchange rate and the domestic interest rate, the following questions are addressed. How do changes in the money supply affect the exchange rate and the interest rate in the very short run? If news is the main factor causing changes in the exchange rate, is it possible for the domestic currency to depreciate on the same day that the domestic interest rate has increased relative to the foreign interest rate? What factors cause the exchange rate to "overshoot" its long-run equilibrium level in the very short run? Under what conditions does undershooting occur? How do changes in the risk premium affect the exchange rate and the domestic interest rate in the very short run?

2. PORTFOLIO EQUILIBRIUM

Portfolio equilibrium requires that domestic residents be content with their existing holdings of assets. The assets are domestic bonds, foreign bonds, and domestic money. In equilibrium, there is no incentive to buy or sell domestic or foreign bonds and no incentive to alter the amount of money currently being held. Portfolio equilibrium requires interest rate parity to hold and the money market to be in equilibrium.[1]

Interest Rate Parity

The actions of investors ensure that the risk-adjusted expected returns on domestic and foreign bonds are equalized (the time horizon of investors is one year). In equilibrium, the interest rate parity (IRP) condition holds:

$$i_t + \varphi_t = i_t^* + \frac{s_{t+1}^e - s_t}{s_t},$$

where the following notation is used: time t represents today and time t+1 represents one year from today; i_t is the interest rate on (1-year) domestic bonds today; φ_t is the risk premium on foreign relative to domestic bonds today; i_t^* is today's interest rate on (1-year) foreign bonds; s_t is today's exchange rate, defined as the number of units of domestic currency per unit of foreign currency (an increase in s is a depreciation of the domestic currency); and s_{t+1}^e is the exchange rate *expected* to hold at time t+1, based on information available today. The following terminology is used: s_{t+1}^e is the expected future exchange rate, $[\frac{s_{t+1}^e - s_t}{s_t}]$ is the expected rate of appreciation of the foreign currency (relative to the domestic currency), and $[i_t^* + \frac{s_{t+1}^e - s_t}{s_t}]$ is the expected return on foreign bonds for domestic investors.

It is convenient to assume that the risk premium is exogenous and to set its initial value equal to zero. This assumption is akin to risk neutrality, where investors focus exclusively on the expected returns of assets. With a zero-risk premium, the interest rate parity condition is

$$i_t = i_t^* + \frac{s_{t+1}^e - s_t}{s_t}.$$

The actions of investors ensure that interest rate parity holds. When it does not hold, investors attempt to make trades in the foreign exchange and bond markets and these actions serve to equalize expected returns. In equilibrium, interest rate parity holds and investors are content with their existing holdings of foreign and domestic bonds.

All investors are assumed to have the same expected future exchange rate. The foreign interest rate, the risk premium, and the expected future exchange rate are exogenous. These variables are held fixed but can change exogenously (for some exogenous changes, it is logical to change the expected future exchange rate at the same time).[2] The exchange rate and the domestic interest rate are endogenous variables.

Money Market Equilibrium

In equilibrium, the nominal money supply, M_t^s, equals nominal money demand, M_t^d :

$$M_t^s = M_t^d.$$

In equilibrium, the amount of money in existence, the supply of money, equals the amount of money the public *wants to hold*, the demand for money.[3]

The nominal money supply is controlled by the central bank. In a flexible exchange rate regime, the central bank has exact control of the nominal money supply[4] (this is not true under a fixed exchange rate, where the money supply is an endogenous variable). Under a flexible exchange rate, all changes in the money supply are exogenous changes that occur at the discretion of the central bank. The central bank can change the nominal money supply through open market operations (the central bank buys or sells domestic bonds on the bond market) and deposit switching operations (the central bank deposits money into or withdraws money from accounts at private banks).

The public holds money primarily for transactions purposes, but the demand for money is determined within the overall portfolio allocation decision. In terms of transactions demand, the nominal demand for money depends on both the price of goods (denoted P) and the real income of domestic residents (denoted y). The variables P and y are fixed in the very short run, so the desired amount of money demand for transactions purposes is constant. But given that money is assumed to earn zero interest,[5] the quantity of money demanded moves inversely with the expected return on alternative assets. With the expected returns on domestic and foreign bonds equalized under IRP, one can represent this effect on money demand using the interest rate on domestic bonds. Portfolio effects on money demand can also arise through various factors (such as changes in expected future interest rates), represented as exogenous changes in a variable labeled X_t. The nominal demand for money is specified as follows (where the notation L represents "is a function of"):

$$M_t^d = P\,L\left(y, i_t, X_t\right).$$

This equation for nominal money demand represents the amount of money the public wants to hold, given the variables P, y, i_t, and X_t.

Portfolio Equilibrium

Portfolio equilibrium is depicted in Figure 2.1, with the domestic interest rate on the vertical axis and nominal money balances on the horizontal axis. This diagram incorporates both equilibrium conditions:

- The domestic interest rate equals the expected return on foreign bonds, so that i_t equals $i_t^* + \dfrac{s_{t+1}^e - s_t}{s_t}$, as represented by the horizontal line; and
- Nominal money demand, represented by the downward sloping curve M_t^d, equals the nominal money supply, represented by the vertical line denoted M_t^s.

There is portfolio equilibrium at point A, where the nominal money supply equals 160 and the domestic interest rate equals 0.04. At this interest rate, the position of the money demand curve indicates that money demand equals 160. Domestic residents are willingly holding the existing quantity of money, so the money market is in equilibrium. When the horizontal line intersects the vertical axis at 0.04, this implies that the expected return on foreign bonds equals 0.04. Because

Figure 2.1: Portfolio equilibrium

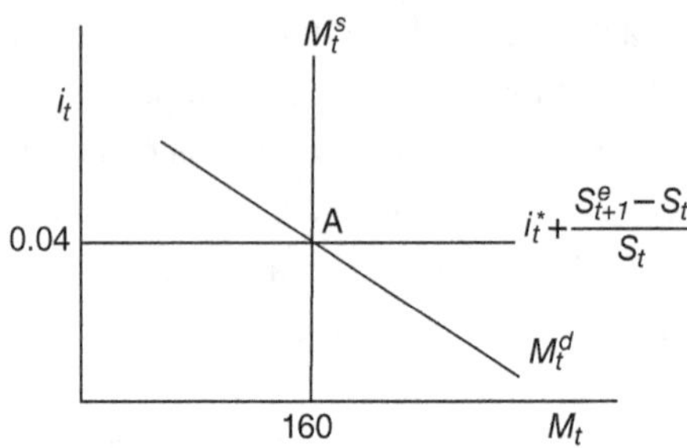

the domestic interest rate also equals 0.04, interest rate parity holds and investors are content with their existing holdings of domestic and foreign bonds. Money market equilibrium holds, and interest rate parity holds. There is portfolio equilibrium.

The exogenous variables are i_t^*, φ_t, s_{t+1}^e, M_t^s, and X_t, and the variables P and y are fixed. The two endogenous variables are the exchange rate s_t and the domestic interest rate i_t (an appendix reviews the relationship between the bond price and the interest rate).

In the initial equilibrium, it is assumed that domestic and foreign interest rates both equal 0.04, or 4 per cent. Interest rate parity then implies that investors expect the exchange rate to stay at its current level over the next year. Investors know that the exchange rate can rise or fall going forward, with various probabilities, but the expected future value of the exchange rate equals today's exchange rate. If s_t equals 1.0, s_{t+1}^e equals 1.0. In the figures, the initial equilibrium is denoted as point A and the new equilibrium is denoted as point C (if a point B is included, it represents a point immediately after an exogenous change, when asset prices have not yet changed).

3. TEMPORARY CHANGES IN THE MONEY SUPPLY

Suppose there is a temporary increase in the nominal money supply, meaning that M_t^s increases but the expected future money supply is unchanged. With no long-term change in the money supply, there is no long-run effect on the exchange rate (or the price level). It is assumed that investors understand that the change is temporary (it is therefore logical to hold the expected future exchange rate fixed).

How does the temporary increase in the money supply affect the exchange rate and the domestic interest rate in the very short run? The increase in today's money supply shifts the money supply line to the right in Figure 2.2, so that the initial effect is an excess money supply at the initial interest rate. As the public attempts to buy domestic bonds, the domestic bond price is bid up and the interest rate falls.[6] At the same time, the public attempts to purchase foreign currency to be able to purchase foreign bonds. This bidding on the foreign exchange market causes the price of foreign currency to be bid up, and the domestic currency depreciates. As s_t increases, for a given s_{t+1}^e, the expected return on foreign bonds falls and the horizontal line shifts down. In the new equilibrium at point C, the domestic interest rate is lower and the domestic currency has depreciated.

With the new equilibrium domestic interest rate equal to 0.032 (as shown on the figure) and the foreign interest rate equal to 0.04, investors no longer expect the exchange rate to remain at

Figure 2.2: Temporary increase in money supply

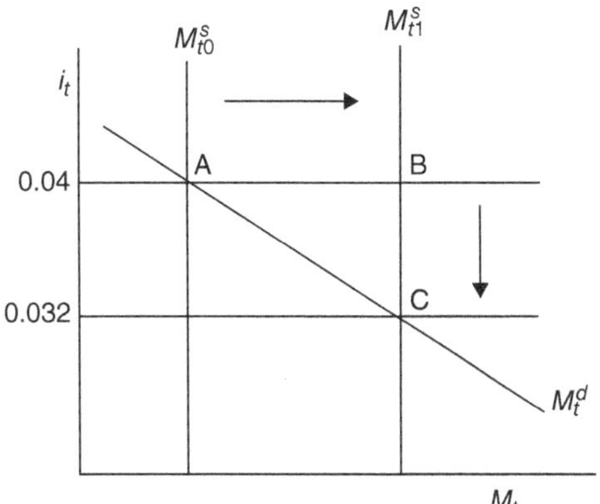

its current level over the next year. Although the expected future exchange rate is still equal to 1.0, the new equilibrium exchange rate equals approximately 1.008. Over the next year, investors expect the foreign currency to depreciate by 0.8 per cent (the expected rate of appreciation of the foreign currency is −0.8 per cent). The expected return on foreign bonds for domestic investors is 3.2 per cent, the 4 per cent on interest earnings less the 0.8 per cent on the expected change in the exchange rate. Domestic and foreign bonds are equally good investments.

4. PERMANENT CHANGES IN THE MONEY SUPPLY

Suppose the nominal money supply increases permanently, with both the time t and time t+1 money supply increasing from 100 to 110. How does this permanent increase in the money supply affect the exchange rate and the domestic interest rate in the very short run? Given that the change is permanent, the expected future exchange rate is affected.

On the Expected Future Exchange Rate

With a permanent increase in the money supply, the public knows that the long-run effect is a depreciation of the domestic currency (and an increase in the domestic price level).[7] Therefore, when an increase in the money supply is regarded by the public as being permanent, the expected future exchange rate increases *today*. A permanent 10 per cent increase in the money supply causes a permanent 10 per cent fall in the value of the domestic currency. The expected future exchange rate increases from 1.0 to 1.10.

Effects on the Interest Rate and the Exchange Rate

With an increase in the money supply *and* an increase in the expected future exchange rate, there are two initial effects in Figure 2.3. The money supply line shifts to the right, and the horizontal line representing the expected return on the foreign bond shifts upward (as s^e_{t+1} increases *today*).

Figure 2.3: Permanent increase in money supply

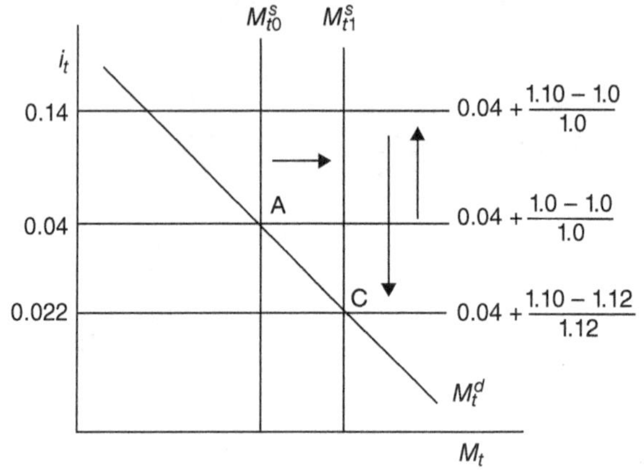

Immediately after these changes, there is an excess supply of money and the expected return on foreign bonds exceeds the domestic interest rate. As the public attempts to buy foreign currency, the domestic currency depreciates on the foreign exchange market. As s_t increases, the horizontal line shifts downward. This adjustment process occurs rapidly, and a new equilibrium is reached at point C in the figure. The domestic interest rate is lower, and the domestic currency has depreciated.

Overshooting

With an increase in the money supply, and no shift in the money demand function, the equilibrium domestic interest rate must fall.[8] The very short-run depreciation of the domestic currency must be larger than the depreciation that occurs in the long run when the domestic price level is flexible (assume, for simplicity, that the economy reaches a new long-run equilibrium by time t+1). This result is called the overshooting result: with a permanent increase in the money supply, the exchange rate moves by a larger amount in the very short run than in the long run.[9]

Does overshooting have to occur? Given the lower domestic interest rate, overshooting must occur. Suppose that when s_{t+1}^e increases from 1.0 to 1.10, the domestic currency only depreciated to a level of 1.10 in the time diagram depicted in Figure 2.4. If today's exchange rate equals the expected future exchange rate, the expected rate of appreciation is 0 per cent. But with the domestic interest rate less than the foreign interest rate, this cannot be an equilibrium situation: foreign bonds are a superior investment at this level of the exchange rate. Investors striving for a higher expected return will therefore cause the domestic currency to keep depreciating until point C is reached. With the foreign interest rate equal to 4 per cent and the domestic rate equal to 2.2 per cent, the expected rate of appreciation of the foreign currency must equal −1.8 per cent in the new equilibrium.

5. NEWS, THE EXCHANGE RATE, AND THE INTEREST RATE

What is the relationship between the domestic interest rate (relative to the foreign interest rate) and the exchange rate in the very short run?

Figure 2.4: Time diagram

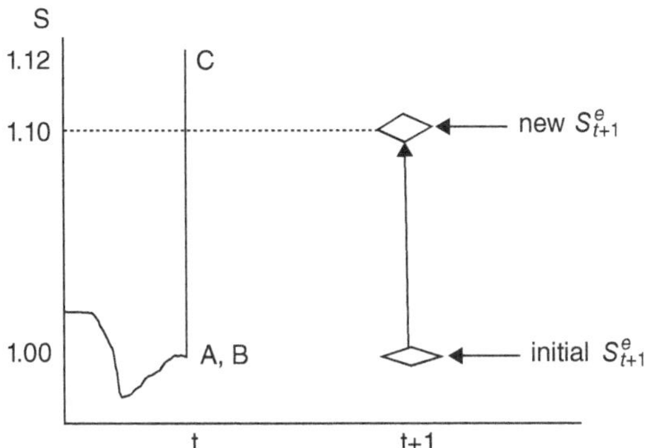

When current-period monetary factors are the main driving force causing the interest rate and the exchange rate to change, the relationship is as follows:[10] when the domestic interest rate *falls* (relative to the foreign interest rate), the domestic currency depreciates (and vice versa). The same result occurs when there is an exogenous change in the foreign interest rate (holding the domestic interest rate and the expected future exchange rate fixed).

But this relationship does not always hold. It is possible that, when the domestic interest rate *rises* (relative to the foreign interest rate), the domestic currency depreciates (and vice versa). The main cause of the change in the exchange rate in this case is news, often with news associated with real, or non-monetary, factors.[11] The change in the domestic interest rate is associated with either a temporary change in the money supply or an exogenous temporary shift in money demand, as explained in the following subsections.

A Change in Expectations and a Temporary Change in the Money Supply

Suppose there are two changes that occur at time t: an exogenous increase in s^e_{t+1} and an exogenous *temporary* decrease in the nominal money supply. In Figure 2.5, the initial equilibrium is at point A where both foreign and domestic bonds have an expected return of 0.04 and the money supply equals money demand. Some news then causes an increase in s^e_{t+1} (from 1.0 to 1.03), and the horizontal expected return line shifts upward. At the initial exchange rate and interest rate, the expected return on foreign bonds exceeds the domestic interest rate. As the public tries to buy foreign currency on the foreign exchange market, bidding higher prices for foreign currency, the domestic currency depreciates. As s_t rises, for the new given level for s^e_{t+1}, the expected return on foreign bonds falls. If the central bank held the money supply fixed, the domestic currency would depreciate by the same amount as the change in the expected future exchange rate (the new equilibrium would be back at point A). But if the central bank decreases the money supply, the equilibrium point is at C. The news, in conjunction with the central bank action, has resulted in a depreciation of the domestic currency and an increase in the domestic interest rate.

When the central bank decreases the money supply, the magnitude of the depreciation of the domestic currency is moderated. The central bank may be operating under a "managed float," where the central bank has decided to moderate the very-short-run movements in the exchange rate. More

Figure 2.5: Increase in s^e_{t+1} and decrease in M^s_t

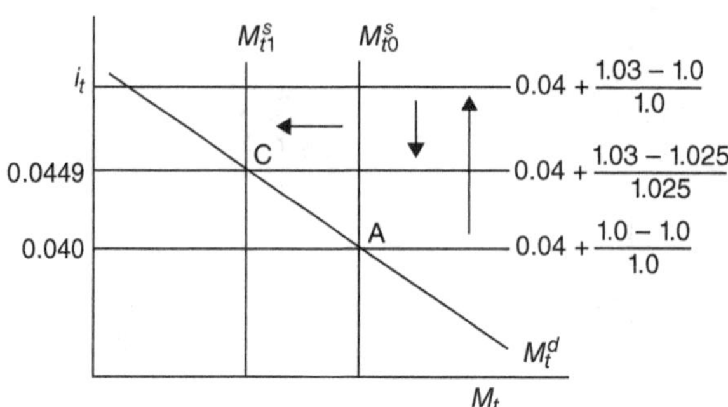

generally, the central bank may be operating in a policy environment where both the interest rate and the exchange rate are incorporated into the central bank's analysis in determining the appropriate policy reaction. With a lower value for the domestic currency, the central bank may regard an upward movement in the domestic interest rate as the appropriate policy.[12]

Note that the change in s^e_{t+1}, in conjunction with the change in the interest rate, results in *undershooting* in the very short run. The expected future exchange rate s^e_{t+1} increases by 3 per cent and the current spot exchange rate increases by 2.5 per cent. The exchange rate may be a volatile asset price, but in this case, the exchange rate does not overshoot its long-run equilibrium level.

A Change in Expectations and a Temporary Shift in Money Demand

Suppose there are two changes that occur at time t: an exogenous increase in s^e_{t+1} and an exogenous *temporary* increase in the demand for money (at each level of the interest rate). The increase in the expected future exchange rate shifts the horizontal expected return line up in Figure 2.6, and the exogenous increase in money demand shifts the money demand function to the right. At the initial exchange rate and interest rate, the expected return on foreign bonds exceeds the domestic interest rate, and the demand for money exceeds the supply of money. Domestic residents will try to buy foreign currency on the foreign exchange market and try to sell domestic bonds on the domestic bond market (to acquire additional money balances). The attempt to purchase foreign currency causes the domestic currency to depreciate today, shifting the horizontal expected return line back toward its original level. The attempt to sell domestic bonds causes the bond price to fall, increasing the domestic interest rate. The new equilibrium position is at point C. In the very short run, there is a depreciation of the domestic currency and an increase in the domestic interest rate.

What causes the exogenous increase in the demand for money in the very short run? With the news that caused the increase in the expected future exchange rate, domestic residents may also change their view regarding the *future* domestic interest rate. That is, investors may now expect a higher interest rate in the near future. This change in the expected future interest rate causes today's money demand function to shift to the right. At today's initial interest rate, the public desires

Figure 2.6: Increase in s^e_{t+1} and increase in M^d_t

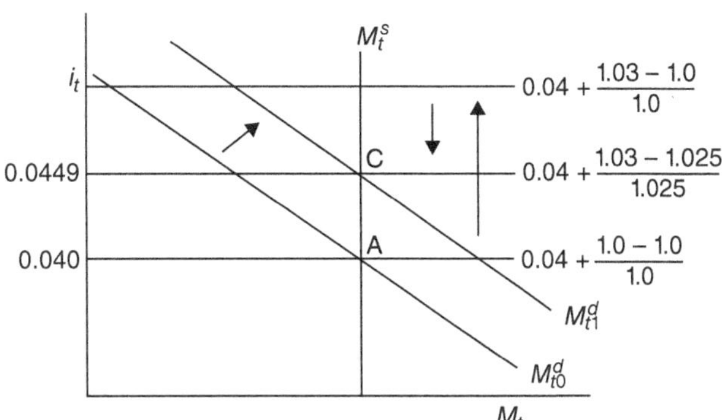

to shift out of bonds and into money holdings. The plan is to hold additional money balances for a while and then repurchase domestic bonds in the near future when the domestic interest rate moves higher. But the attempt by the public, today, to sell domestic bonds causes today's interest rate to rise.[13]

It is important to emphasize that both the depreciation of the domestic currency and the increase in the domestic interest rate can occur without any trades occurring. The public *attempts* to buy foreign currency and *attempts* to sell domestic bonds, but no trades need to occur.[14] The asset prices – the exchange rate and the domestic bond price – adjust quickly to levels that form the basis of the new portfolio equilibrium. Also, note that exchange rate undershooting again occurs in the very short run.

6. EXOGENOUS CHANGES IN THE RISK PREMIUM

With a nonzero risk premium, the IRP condition is

$$i_t + \varphi_t = i_t^* + \frac{s^e_{t+1} - s_t}{s_t}.$$

If investors regard foreign bonds as riskier, the risk premium φ_t is positive and the expected return on foreign bonds is greater than the equilibrium interest rate on domestic bonds (investors are assumed to be risk-averse, so that risk neutrality does not hold).[15] If φ_t equals 1 per cent and the domestic interest rate equals 3 per cent, the equilibrium expected return on foreign bonds, measured as $[i_t^* + \frac{s^e_{t+1} - s_t}{s_t}]$, is 4 per cent. The higher expected return on foreign bonds does not mean that foreign bonds are a better investment. Rather the higher expected return simply compensates investors for holding the riskier asset (if the expected returns were the same, risk-averse investors would not want to hold the riskier bond). In equilibrium, investors are content with their existing holdings of these assets. The two bonds are regarded as equally good investments.

Fluctuations in the risk premium cause fluctuations in the exchange rate and the domestic interest rate. Suppose there is an exogenous increase in the risk premium from 1 per cent to 2 per cent (hold the foreign interest rate and the expected future exchange rate fixed). This exogenous change means that, all of a sudden, investors regard the foreign bond as an even riskier asset.[16] Immediately after the exogenous change, the domestic interest rate exceeds the risk-adjusted expected return on foreign bonds:

$$i_t > i_t^* + \frac{s_{t+1}^e - s_t}{s_t} - \varphi_t.$$

At the initial exchange rate and domestic interest rate, domestic bonds are regarded as better than foreign bonds. As the public tries to sell foreign currency, the domestic currency appreciates (s_t falls) and the term $\left[\frac{s_{t+1}^e - s_t}{s_t}\right]$ increases. Likewise, the public tries to buy domestic bonds, inducing an increase in the bond price and a decrease in the domestic interest rate.[17] In the new equilibrium, the risk-adjusted expected returns on foreign and domestic bonds are equalized.

The increase in the risk premium provides another example where, even though the domestic interest rate falls relative to the foreign rate, the domestic currency appreciates. And the opposite change – an exogenous decrease in the risk premium – results in a depreciation of the domestic currency and an increase in the domestic interest rate.[18]

7. CO-MOVEMENT BETWEEN THE EXCHANGE RATE AND THE INTEREST RATE DIFFERENTIAL

In theory, the co-movement between the exchange rate and the interest rate differential can be positive or negative. In many instances involving news or changes in the risk premium, a depreciation of the domestic currency is associated with a rise in the domestic interest rate relative to the foreign interest rate (and vice versa).

Figure 2.7 shows the results for Canadian–US data over the period 1980:1 to 2013:7, using monthly data.[19] The interest rates are Treasury bill rates, and the exchange rate is measured such that an increase is a depreciation of the Canadian dollar.[20] To present information on the co-movements, the scatter plot depicts the percentage change in the exchange rate on the vertical axis and the change in the interest rate differential on the horizontal axis.

As is evident, neither case predominates. Both cases have occurred often in financial markets over the past three decades. If a simple linear regression analysis is conducted, the relationship is positive (suggesting that a depreciation of the Canadian dollar tends to be associated with a relative increase in the Canadian interest rate). But the main insight is that both cases are common (as suggested by the theoretical analysis).

The exercise in Data Analytics re-examines the issue using data since 2013.

Figure 2.7: Percentage change in exchange rate and change in interest rate differential

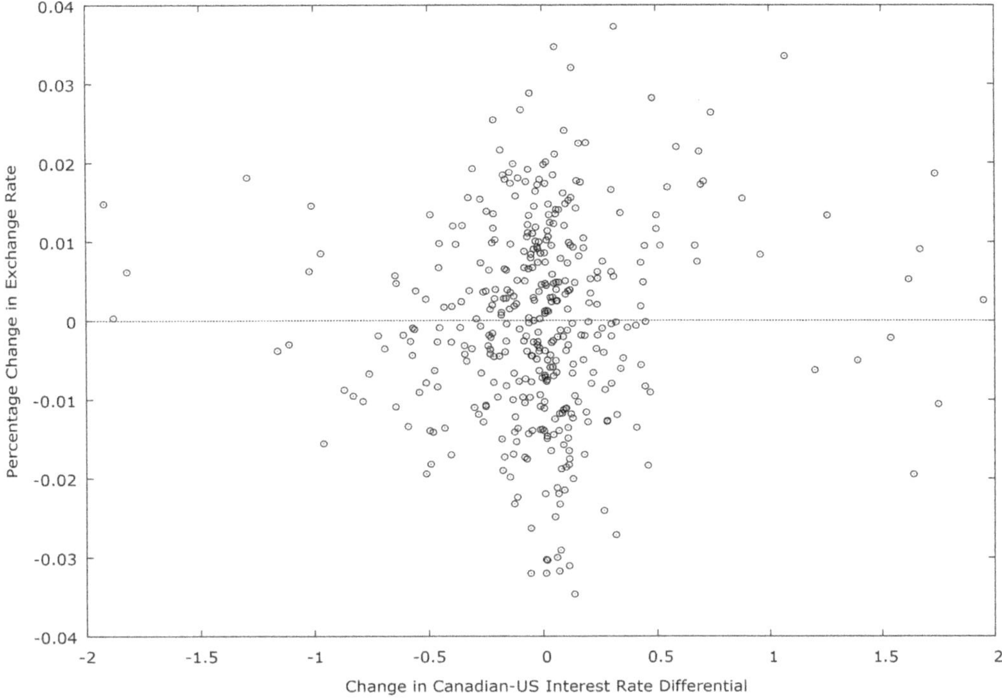

Data sources: Statistics Canada and Board of Governors of the Federal Reserve System via FRED

8. INTEREST RATES AND THE EXCHANGE RATE BEFORE AND AFTER THE 2008 FINANCIAL CRISIS

In September 2008, global financial markets were rocked by the onset of the financial crisis. Stock price indexes around the globe fell sharply, and central bank actions lowered interest rates. Central banks chose expansionary monetary policies in an attempt to moderate the recession that was widely expected to occur. How did interest rates and the exchange rate move in the period before and after the crisis?

Figure 2.8 plots the Canadian and US interest rates over the period 2008:1 to 2009:12. Interest rates moved lower in both countries in the first part of 2008 and were aggressively pushed down by the central banks after the onset of the financial crisis.[21] The interest rate differential at first widened from about 100 basis points to 155 basis points in late 2008 (when the Federal Reserve pushed the US interest rate down close to 0 per cent), but the differential collapsed to less than 20 basis points by the spring of 2009.

Yet with relatively small movements in the Canadian–US interest rate differential, there were large movements in the exchange rate. The Canadian dollar first depreciated by over 20 per cent in late 2008, and then rebounded in 2009 with an appreciation of almost 20 per cent. There was, of course, much news impacting financial markets throughout this period. But movements in world commodity prices played a significant role with respect to news regarding the Canadian economy.

Figure 2.8: Short-term interest rates

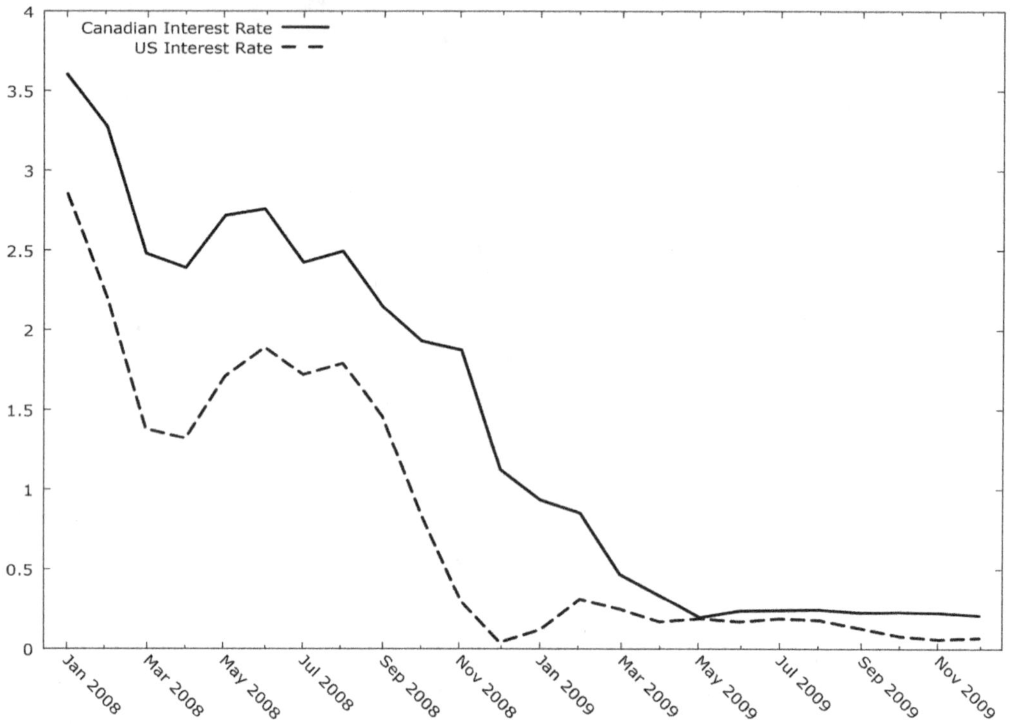

Data sources: Statistics Canada and Board of Governors of the Federal Reserve System via FRED

As shown in Figure 2.9, the timing of the sharp depreciation of the Canadian dollar in late 2008 coincided with the collapse in world commodity prices (as measured by the commodity price index).[22] And the subsequent appreciation of the Canadian dollar was associated with a large increase in world commodity prices (in 2009, the commodity price index increased by about 25 per cent).

9. CONCLUSION

Exogenous factors impacting financial markets can cause changes in both the exchange rate and the domestic interest rate. In the very short run, the exogenous factors affecting foreign exchange and bond markets can be news that alters investor expectations, changes in the nominal money supply, shifts in money demand, changes in the foreign interest rate, and shifts in the risk premium on foreign bonds. Of course, news that changes expectations occurs on an ongoing basis, so this factor is constantly bombarding foreign exchange and bond markets.[23]

The volatility in the foreign exchange market suggested that the exchange rate may be overshooting its long-run equilibrium level. But it is recognized that daily movements in the domestic interest rate can serve to moderate (rather than amplify) the daily movements in the exchange rate (and indeed that the exchange rate can change without any change in interest rates). These insights

Figure 2.9: Exchange rate and commodity price index

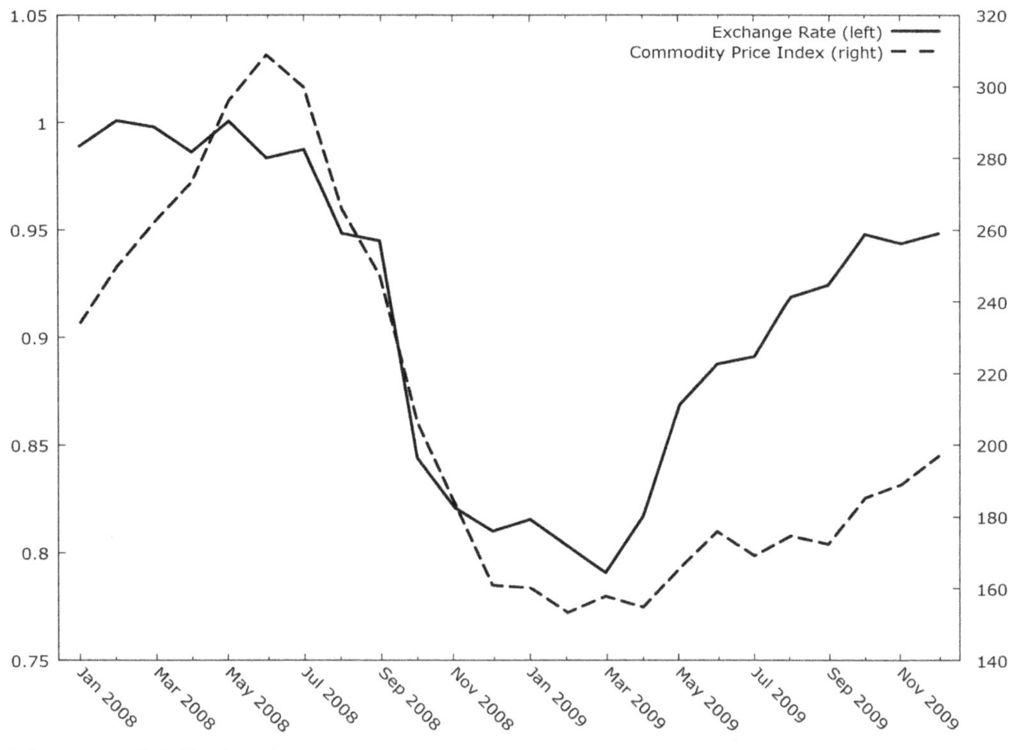

Data source: Statistics Canada

have been garnered by analyzing a model that incorporates portfolio equilibrium and examining the empirical evidence with respect to short-term movements in the exchange rate and interest rates.[24]

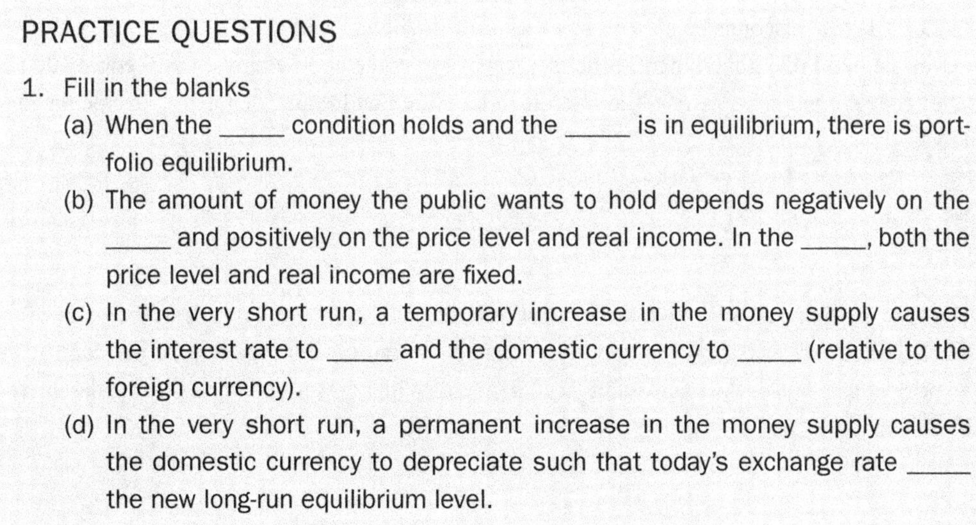

PRACTICE QUESTIONS

1. Fill in the blanks
   (a) When the _____ condition holds and the _____ is in equilibrium, there is port-folio equilibrium.
   (b) The amount of money the public wants to hold depends negatively on the _____ and positively on the price level and real income. In the _____, both the price level and real income are fixed.
   (c) In the very short run, a temporary increase in the money supply causes the interest rate to _____ and the domestic currency to _____ (relative to the foreign currency).
   (d) In the very short run, a permanent increase in the money supply causes the domestic currency to depreciate such that today's exchange rate _____ the new long-run equilibrium level.

(e) Suppose the domestic currency depreciates and the domestic interest rate increases in the very short run. This change could have been caused by _____ in s^e_{t+1} and an exogenous _____ in the demand for money.

2. Explain how a temporary increase in the money supply affects the exchange rate and the domestic interest rate in the very short run. Use the portfolio equilibrium diagram.

3. Using the portfolio equilibrium diagram, along with a time diagram for the exchange rate, explain why overshooting can occur in the very short run in response to a permanent increase in the money supply.

4. Is it possible for the domestic currency to depreciate on the same day that there has been an increase in the domestic interest rate? Explain (hold the foreign interest rate fixed).

DATA ANALYTICS

1. Redo the scatter plot in Figure 2.7, with the sample beginning in 2013 (see section 7 for data sources). Comment on the relationship between the change in the interest rate differential and the percentage change in the exchange rate.

2. Using the same data, create one time-series plot for Canadian and US interest rates and another plot for the exchange rate. Over this period, have movements in interest rates played a large role in influencing the exchange rate? Discuss.

APPENDIX: INTEREST RATES AND BOND PRICES

Consider a 1-year discount bond. The face value of the bond, denoted F, is the amount that the issuer of the bond (the government) promises to pay when the bond expires. Let F equal 100 and denote today's bond price as P^B_t. The interest rate on the bond today, denoted i_t, is calculated as follows:

$$i_t = \frac{F - P^B_t}{P^B_t}.$$

Because the face value is fixed, the interest rate (or yield) on the bond falls as the price of the bond rises (and vice versa). If the bond price equals 95, the interest rate is 5.26 per cent. If the bond price equals 90.91, the interest rate is 10 per cent. With a lower bond price today, the interest rate is higher.

NOTES

1   At a point in time, individuals decide on the portfolio allocation of assets (the portfolio allocation decision). The saving decision determines, over a period of time, how much after-tax income is saved.

2   In some chapters, the expected future exchange rate is endogenous and depends on exogenous variables.

3   For a discussion of the academic literature on money demand, see McCallum and Goodfriend (1989).

4   The central bank controls the monetary base, and the money supply is determined by the base and the money multiplier. While the actions of banks and the public can affect the multiplier, the central bank can always offset changes in the multiplier and set the money supply at the level it desires.

5   Currency earns zero interest; interest rates on transactions-type bank accounts are assumed to equal zero.

6   If the central bank deposits some new money into the private banks, these banks initially have excess bank reserves and will eliminate these excess funds by purchasing interest-earning assets.

7   This issue is examined in Chapter 8.

8   The expected future interest rate (the interest rate expected to hold at time t+1) is not affected by a permanent (one-time) increase in the money supply, so the money demand function does not shift.

9   This celebrated result, first set forth by Dornbusch (1976), was regarded as providing a possible explanation of the volatility in foreign exchange markets.

10 For both temporary and permanent changes, exogenous decreases in the demand for money have the same effects as exogenous increases in the supply of money.

11 The news could be related to future real variables such as productivity, the terms of trade, and export demand. This case may also arise with news associated with expected future monetary factors.

12 This policy could be consistent with a central bank policy framework that, over the medium term (such as a year or two), focuses on the inflation rate and the growth rate of real GDP.

13 All investors have the same view, so no one is willing to purchase bonds at the initial interest rate. As the public tries to sell bonds, the bond price falls until today's interest rate rises to a level where the public is willing to buy. In the new equilibrium, the public is indifferent between buying, selling, and holding.

14 That interest rates can change without any trades in the market has long been recognized by economists. See, for example, the discussion in Keynes (1936, 198). Paul Volcker (former Chair of the Federal Reserve, 1979 to 1987) has highlighted the role of changing expectations in driving daily movements in interest rates (see Volcker 2007, 171).

15 The consumption capital asset pricing model (CCAPM) of the risk premium is based on the intertemporal theory of consumption with uncertainty. See, for example, the discussion in Cochrane (2001), Lustig and Verdelhan (2007, 2011), and Lewis (2011). The CCAPM explains the magnitude and sign of the risk premium, as well as the factors that may cause it to change (there is a risk premium for any two assets).

16 It could also be caused by a change in tastes, with investors becoming more risk averse.

17 The extent of any decrease in the interest rate depends on changes in money supply and demand.

18 Some economists have placed emphasis on the risk premium as a determinant of exchange rates and interest rates. See, for example, Duarte and Stockman (2005), Alvarez et al. (2009), and Cochrane (2011). Pasula (2016) discusses the risk premium under a fixed, but adjustable, exchange rate.

19 The figure excludes seven outliers to allow a better visual representation of the other almost 400 points. The points excluded are a month in 1980 when the differential rose by more than 200 basis points and months in 2003, 2004, 2007, 2008, and 2009 when the percentage change in the exchange rate exceeded 4 per cent.

20 The exchange rate and the Canadian 91-day Treasury bill interest rate are CANSIM series V37426 and V122484. The US interest rate is a Treasury bill rate, taken from the FRED database at the Federal

Reserve Bank of St. Louis. The data are monthly (with daily data, care needs to be taken as the exchange rate and interest rates may be measured at different times of the day).

21 Both US and Canadian money supply statistics indicate increases in the rate of growth of the nominal money supply in the months after the onset of the financial crisis. In Canada, the (annual) growth rate of the money supply exceeded 11 per cent in every month between November 2008 and July 2010 (with money measured as M1+, CANSIM series V37151).

22 The commodity price index, discussed in Chapter 1, is CANSIM series V52673496.

23 Bank of Canada policy involves setting the target for the overnight rate. But interest rates such as the rates on 1-year and 10-year bonds are determined in the bond market, influenced by both Bank of Canada policy and the actions of the public. See the discussion, for example, by John Crow (1993a).

24 There is an extensive empirical literature, with a variety of approaches and analyses, on the relationship between exchange rates, interest rates, and expectations. See, for example, the literature discussed in Engel et al. (2007) and Engel (2014).

CHAPTER 3

A Fixed Exchange Rate in the Very Short Run

1. INTRODUCTION

Many countries decide to fix, or peg, the value of their currency to a foreign currency. Under a fixed exchange rate, the central bank holds foreign exchange reserves (foreign currency and foreign bonds) and intervenes in the foreign exchange market to keep the exchange rate fixed. While the last worldwide system of fixed exchange rates was the Bretton Woods system between 1946 and 1971, there are many countries today that fix the value of their currency to currencies such as the US dollar or the euro.[1] Some countries operate managed float regimes, which are a combination of fixed and flexible exchange rate regimes. To understand the workings of fixed or quasi-fixed exchange rate regimes, one must master the workings of a standard fixed exchange rate regime.

This chapter analyzes the operation of a fixed exchange rate regime in the very short run. It is assumed that the central bank acts to ensure that the exchange rate remains fixed at the stated level. The purpose is to provide a basic understanding of central bank policy and the workings of financial markets in a small economy with a fixed exchange rate. This chapter addresses the following questions. What factors cause changes in foreign exchange reserves in the very short run? What is the relationship between domestic and foreign interest rates under a fixed exchange rate? Can the central bank influence the domestic interest rate or control the money supply under a fixed exchange rate? How do expectations of a future change in the exchange rate affect financial markets today? Acquiring an understanding of these core issues is an essential prerequisite to a more comprehensive analysis of fixed exchange rate regimes.

2. PRELIMINARIES

Foreign Exchange Reserves, Domestic Credit, and the Money Supply

The nominal money supply is the amount of domestic money held by the public. The nominal money supply, denoted M^s, equals domestic credit, D, plus foreign exchange reserves, denoted R:

$$M_t^s = D_t + R_t,$$

where the subscript t denotes "today" (the subscript t+1 denotes one year into the future).[2] Domestic credit equals the domestic assets of the central bank and includes, for example, domestic government bonds held by the central bank. Foreign exchange reserves are foreign assets (foreign currency and foreign bonds) held by the central bank.

Under a fixed exchange rate regime, the central bank is committed to buying and selling foreign currency at the fixed exchange rate. While the central bank has control of domestic credit, the stock of foreign exchange reserves is an endogenous variable.

Changes in the Money Supply

If the central bank buys domestic bonds from the public in exchange for money, there is an increase in domestic credit and an increase in the money supply (for a given level of foreign exchange reserves). The central bank can also implement a money transfer increase in domestic credit by depositing new money into the private banks.

Foreign exchange operations, or central bank actions that involve changes in foreign exchange reserves, also change the quantity of domestic money in the economy. When the central bank buys foreign currency on the foreign exchange market, it increases the quantity of domestic money held by the public. And when the central bank sells foreign currency in exchange for domestic currency, there is a decrease in both foreign exchange reserves and the domestic money supply.

The Exchange Rate

The exchange rate is defined as the number of units of domestic currency per unit of foreign currency. The exchange rate today is denoted s_t and the expected future exchange rate is denoted s_{t+1}^e. It is assumed that the exchange rate remains fixed in the very short run, but there is no requirement for investors to expect the exchange rate to remain fixed at the same level forever into the future (or even the next year).

Terminology for Fixed but Adjustable Exchange Rate Regimes

Fixed exchange rate regimes are not regimes where the exchange rate is immutably fixed; rather these are regimes of fixed but adjustable exchange rates.[3] The terminology for fixed exchange rates is different from that for flexible exchange rates. Under a fixed exchange rate regime, if the government (along with the central bank) announces that the domestic currency will henceforth be fixed at a lower value in terms of foreign currency, this is called a devaluation of the domestic currency (an increase in s). If the domestic currency is to be fixed at a higher value in terms of foreign currency (a decrease in s), there is a revaluation of the domestic currency.

In the analysis, there are no devaluations or revaluations at time t (the exchange rate remains fixed today). But in section 7, an analysis is conducted of an expected future devaluation, where the public expects the domestic currency to be devalued within the next year.

3. PORTFOLIO EQUILIBRIUM

Portfolio equilibrium requires that domestic residents be content with their existing holdings of domestic bonds, foreign bonds, and domestic money. In equilibrium, there is no incentive to buy or sell domestic or foreign bonds and no incentive to alter the amount of money currently being held. Portfolio equilibrium requires that the interest rate parity condition holds and the money market is in equilibrium.

Interest Rate Parity

The actions of investors ensure that, in equilibrium, the expected returns on domestic and foreign bonds are equalized, so that interest rate parity (IRP) holds:

$$i_t = i_t^* + \frac{s_{t+1}^e - s_t}{s_t},$$

where the time horizon of investors is one year and risk neutrality is assumed to hold. Under a fixed exchange rate, the second term on the right-hand side is called the expected rate of devaluation of the domestic currency.

With respect to the expected rate of devaluation, there are two cases: a credibly fixed exchange rate, where the exchange rate is expected to remain fixed at the current level, and a fixed exchange rate that is expected to change within the next year. In the first case, interest rate parity implies that the equilibrium domestic interest rate equals the foreign interest rate. In the second case, interest rates will not be equal. For example, if investors expect a future devaluation of the domestic currency, the equilibrium domestic interest rate exceeds the foreign rate. While it is convenient to assume that the first case holds for much of the analysis, it is essential to examine how matters change when investors expect a future change in the exchange rate.

Money Market Equilibrium

In equilibrium, the amount of money in existence – the supply of money – equals the amount of money that the public *wants to hold* – the demand for money.[4]

The supply of money, denoted as M^s, is

$$M_t^s = D_t + R_t.$$

Under a fixed exchange rate, the central bank needs to buy or sell foreign currency to hold the exchange rate fixed, and these foreign exchange transactions imply changes in the domestic money supply. While domestic credit is exogenous, the stock of foreign exchange reserves is an endogenous variable.

The public holds money primarily for transactions purposes, but the demand for money is determined within an overall portfolio allocation decision. In terms of transactions demand, the nominal demand for money depends on real income (denoted as y) and the price level (denoted as P). These

Figure 3.1: Portfolio equilibrium

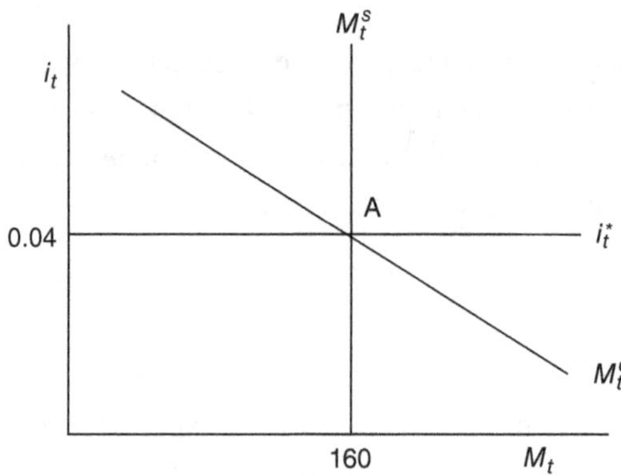

variables are fixed in the very short run, so desired money demand for transactions purposes is constant. But because money earns zero interest, the quantity of money demanded moves inversely with the interest rate on domestic bonds. Portfolio effects on money demand can also arise through various factors incorporated in an exogenous variable, labeled X_t. The nominal demand for money is specified as follows:

$$M_t^d = P\,L\left(y, i_t, X_t\right).$$

This equation for nominal money demand represents the amount of money the public wants to hold, given the variables P, y, i_t, and X_t.

Portfolio Equilibrium

The domestic interest rate and the stock of foreign exchange reserves are determined by portfolio equilibrium, depicted in Figure 3.1.

Assuming that the exchange rate is expected to remain fixed at its current level (an assumption maintained until section 7), the interest rate parity condition implies that the equilibrium domestic interest rate equals the foreign interest rate,

$$i_t = i_t^*,$$

represented by the horizontal line. Nominal money demand, represented by the downward sloping curve M_t^d, equals the nominal money supply, represented by the vertical line M_t^s:

$$D_t + R_t = P\,L\left(y, i_t, X_t\right).$$

In the very short run, the variables P and y are fixed, and i_t^*, D_t, and X_t are exogenous. The endogenous variables are the domestic interest rate and foreign exchange reserves.

Figure 3.2: Increase in foreign interest rate

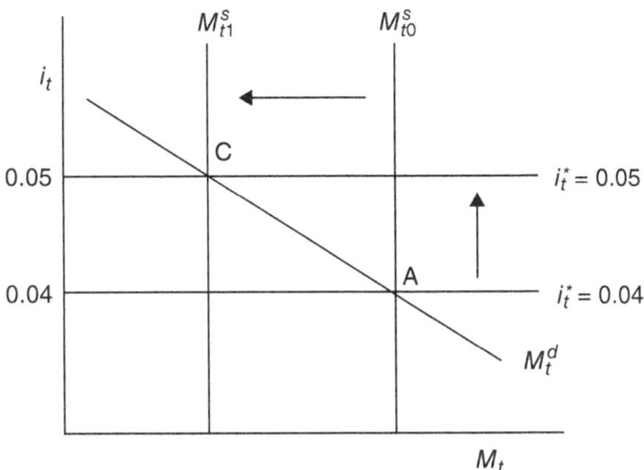

4. EXOGENOUS CHANGES IN THE FOREIGN INTEREST RATE

In the initial equilibrium, domestic and foreign interest rates equal 4 per cent (denoted point A in Figure 3.2). How does an exogenous increase in the foreign interest rate to 5 per cent affect the domestic interest rate and foreign exchange reserves in the very short run? The horizontal line shifts up with the increase in the foreign interest rate, and foreign bonds are a better investment. Domestic residents try to sell domestic bonds, resulting in a decrease in the domestic bond price and an increase in the domestic interest rate. The higher interest rate lowers the quantity of money demanded, so domestic residents want to reduce their money holdings. The public sells domestic currency on the foreign exchange market, acquiring foreign currency from the central bank, and then uses the foreign currency to purchase foreign bonds. The stock of foreign exchange reserves and the domestic money supply fall, shifting the vertical money supply line to the left.

These adjustments occur quickly. In the new equilibrium, domestic and foreign bonds are equally good investments, and the public is content with the lower level of money holdings. The new equilibrium is denoted as point C, with a higher domestic interest rate. In the process, there has been a one-time reduction in both the central bank's holdings of foreign exchange reserves and the domestic money supply.

5. EXOGENOUS CHANGES IN DOMESTIC CREDIT

Under a fixed exchange rate, the exogenous policy variable of the central bank is domestic credit. Suppose there is a "money transfer" increase in domestic credit. The central bank has more domestic assets, and the public is holding more money. This increase in D shifts the vertical money supply line to the right in Figure 3.3, and the public has excess money holdings at point B. Domestic residents can convert the domestic money into foreign currency at the fixed exchange rate, and then acquire foreign bonds that yield a return equal to the fixed foreign interest rate. The public under-

Figure 3.3: Increase in domestic credit

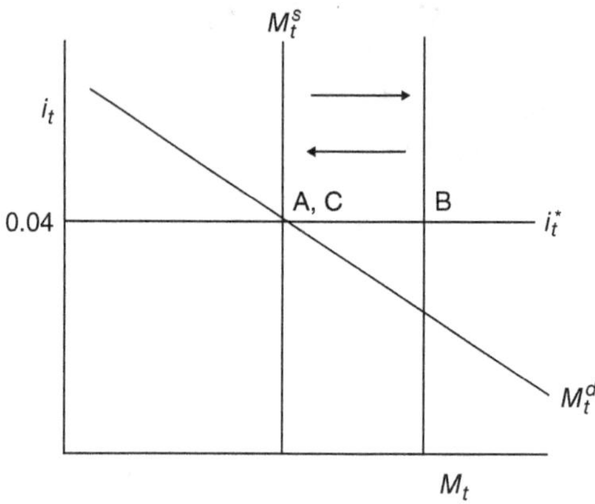

Figure 3.4: Money transfer increase in domestic credit

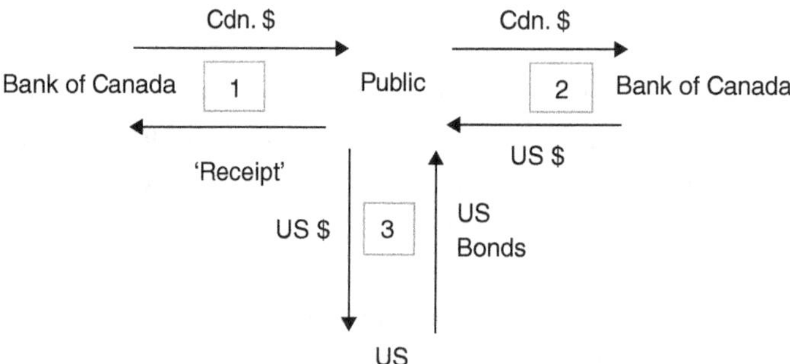

takes these transactions, and the central bank experiences a decrease in foreign exchange reserves. The associated decrease in the money supply shifts the money supply line back to the left. The new equilibrium is at point C, with an unchanged interest rate and an unchanged money supply.

The transactions are summarized in Figure 3.4 (assuming the domestic economy is Canada). The initial increase in domestic credit is shown in box 1. This transaction increases the money supply, with domestic residents now holding more Canadian dollars. The public then sells domestic currency to the central bank in exchange for foreign currency, and with this exchange, the money supply falls back to its original level (box 2). In box 3, the public uses the foreign currency to purchase foreign bonds.

Monetary Independence under a Fixed Exchange Rate

This analysis leads to an important conclusion regarding the operation of a fixed exchange rate regime in small economies. Under a fixed exchange rate, the equilibrium domestic interest rate is determined by the foreign interest rate. If the central bank in the large foreign economy decides to change their interest rate, the domestic interest rate must change with it. The central bank in the domestic economy will not be able to set the domestic interest rate independently of the foreign interest

Figure 3.5: Increase in money demand

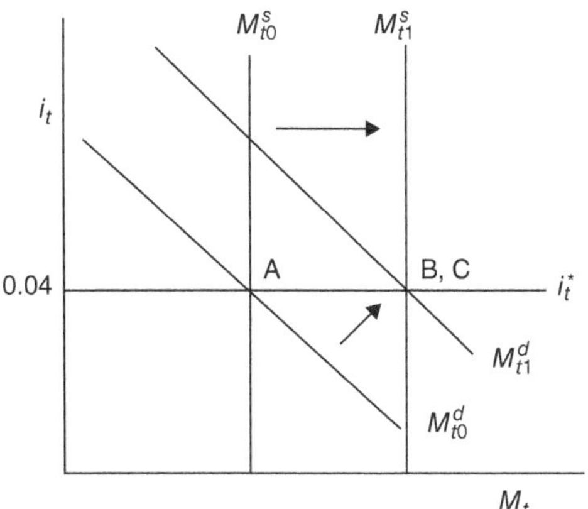

rate. Moreover, the central bank cannot control the money supply and cannot use this mechanism to alter the domestic interest rate. The central bank is said to have "zero monetary independence."

6. EXOGENOUS CHANGES IN THE DEMAND FOR MONEY

Changes in investor expectations can cause shifts in money demand (the exogenous variable X_t changes). Suppose that, all of a sudden, the public wants to hold fewer bonds and more money. The money demand curve shifts to the right and, at the initial interest rate and money supply, there is an excess demand for money (point B in Figure 3.5). The public sells foreign bonds in exchange for foreign currency, and then sells the foreign currency for domestic money. The central bank must supply this domestic currency to maintain the exchange rate fixed at the stated level. Foreign exchange reserves and the money supply increase, shifting the vertical money supply line to the right until a new equilibrium is attained at point C.

In a small economy with a fixed exchange rate, the amount of money in the economy is determined by the public. If domestic residents want to hold more money, the central bank is forced to supply the additional money. The central bank has no control of the money supply.

While the central bank cannot control the money supply, it can influence the level of foreign exchange reserves. If reserves are deemed to be too low, the central bank can replenish reserves by implementing a decrease in domestic credit.[5] And if increases in money demand have caused a high level of reserves, the central bank can always match further increases in money demand with increases in domestic credit.

7. CURRENCY CRISES

When a country adopts a fixed exchange rate, the government and the central bank commit to holding the exchange rate fixed at the announced level. But investors know that a time may come when the authorities regard a change in the exchange rate as the appropriate policy action. For example,

Figure 3.6: Expected future devaluation

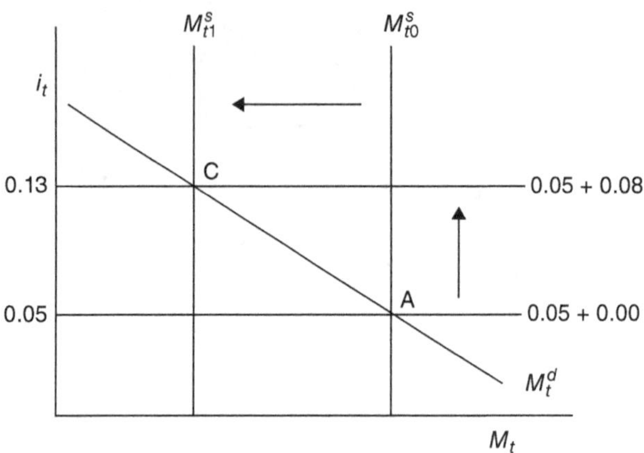

circumstances may arise where investors are confident that a devaluation will occur within the next few months. These periods are referred to as currency crises (or exchange rate crises).

Suppose that, all of a sudden, some news causes an increase in the expected future exchange rate (an increase in s_{t+1}^e from 1.0 to 1.08), but the central bank keeps the exchange rate fixed in the very short run. Though today's exchange rate is unchanged, there is an expected future devaluation (an appendix discusses factors that could cause the change in expectations, such as bad news about the state of the economy).

The initial equilibrium is denoted as point A in Figure 3.6 (the foreign interest rate is fixed at 5 per cent). With an increase in s_{t+1}^e, the horizontal line shifts up. The expected return on foreign bonds increases, and foreign bonds are a better investment than domestic bonds. If domestic investors buy foreign currency at 1.0 today and expect to sell foreign currency in one year for 1.08, there is an 8 per cent expected return strictly from buying low and selling high. The expected return on foreign bonds is 13 per cent – the 5 per cent foreign interest rate plus the 8 per cent that arises from the expected future devaluation. Domestic investors respond immediately, selling domestic currency to the central bank for foreign currency and attempting to sell domestic bonds. These actual and attempted transactions cause a decrease in foreign exchange reserves and an increase in the domestic interest rate. The decrease in the money supply shifts the vertical money supply line to the left, and in the new equilibrium at C, the domestic interest rate equals 13 per cent. In the new equilibrium, domestic residents are holding more foreign bonds and less money.

Currency Crises and Collapsing Fixed Exchange Rate Regimes

Experience with fixed exchange rates indicates that currency crises can cause serious problems. Some well-known cases include the 1992 crises in the European Monetary System, the 1997 Asian crises, and the crisis in Argentina in 2001 and 2002.[6] In many cases, the central bank does initially hold the exchange rate fixed, with a resulting spike in the domestic interest rate and the collapse in the stock of foreign exchange reserves. The currency is soon thereafter devalued, or it depreciates significantly when the exchange rate is floated. The 1992 crisis in the UK provides an interesting example.

In 1990, the British authorities decided to join the European Monetary System (EMS) of fixed but adjustable exchange rates (the EMS, formed in 1979, was a prelude to the European Currency Union that exists today).[7] The British pound was (in effect) fixed to the German mark, the main currency in the EMS. In September 1992, the British economy was in the middle of a prolonged recession, and in conjunction with other factors, investors suddenly came to expect a devaluation of the British pound within the next short while.[8] With the change in expectations, the effect was immediate, and British interest rates rose by almost 300 basis points. The Bank of England initially held the exchange rate fixed, but the rise in interest rates was not what was needed at a time of weakness in the British economy. The British authorities soon decided to return to a floating exchange rate system, whereupon the pound depreciated sharply, and British interest rates returned to lower levels.

An appendix provides further discussion of currency crises, focusing on their underlying causes.

8. CANADA'S FIXED EXCHANGE RATE UNDER BRETTON WOODS

Between 1946 and 1971, the Bretton Woods international monetary system was in place, where most industrialized nations operated under a system of fixed but adjustable exchange rates. While Canada was one of a few countries that had a flexible exchange rate for part of this period, it did have a fixed exchange rate for an eight-year period between May 1962 and May 1970.[9]

Figure 3.7 shows the Canadian–US dollar exchange rate from May 1961 to May 1971, including a year before and a year after the period of the fixed exchange rate regime between May 1962 and May 1970.[10] In 1961 and the beginning of 1962, when the exchange rate was still floating, the value of the Canadian dollar experienced some sharp downward movements.[11] In May 1962, when the Canadian government announced that it was adopting a fixed exchange rate regime, the level of the exchange rate was set at 92.5 cents US with bands of ±1 per cent (with these bands, the Canadian dollar was effectively fixed at a level between 91.575 and 93.425). From May 1962 to May 1970, the Bank of Canada acted to ensure that the exchange rate remained within the narrow bands that had been set (the bandwidth of ±1 per cent was standard under Bretton Woods). After eight years of a fixed exchange rate, the exchange rate was allowed to float in May 1970, whereupon the Canadian dollar appreciated markedly in the first few months of the new regime.

Figure 3.8 shows movements in Canadian and US interest rates over the fixed exchange rate period from May 1962 to May 1970.[12] The Canadian interest rate moved closely with the US interest rate, but for two exceptions. In the first year of the fixed exchange rate regime, the Canadian interest rate exceeded the US rate by 60–250 basis points. In terms of interest rate parity, this differential implies that investors were not convinced that the exchange rate would remain fixed at the 92.5 cent level. Interest rate parity suggests that investors were expecting a devaluation of the Canadian dollar, or a return to floating and a further depreciation. By the spring of 1963, these expectations of devaluation disappeared, and Canadian and US interest rates were fairly similar. Thereafter, the Canadian and US interest rates fluctuated together for most of the period. The other exception is in late 1967 and early 1968, when investors again expected a future devaluation. The British pound had been devalued relative to the US dollar in November 1967, and there was speculation that other currencies would follow suit.

Figure 3.7: Canadian–US dollar exchange rate

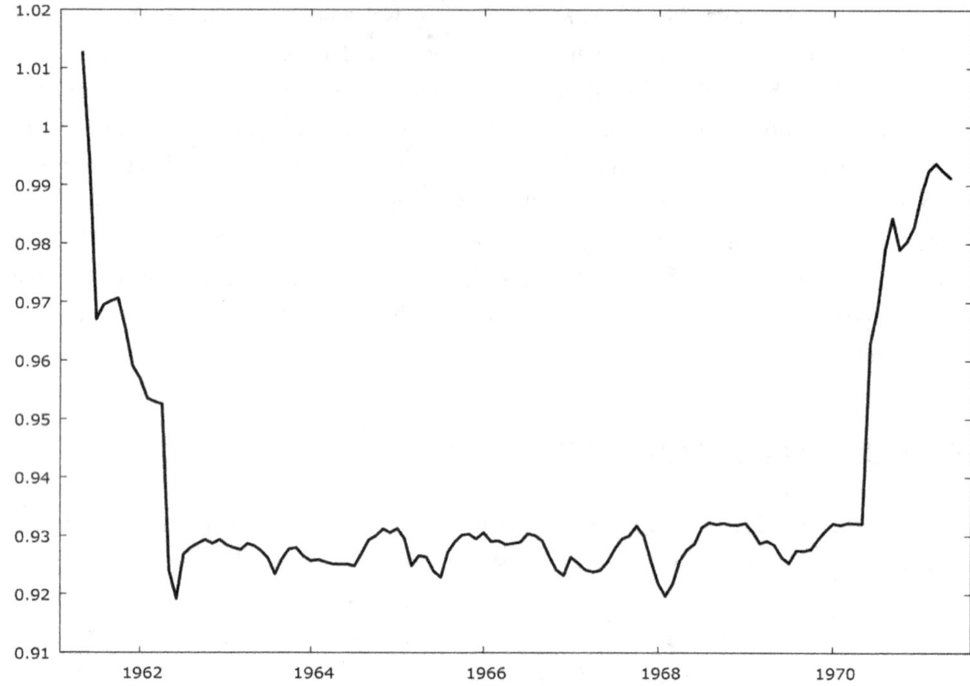

Data source: Statistics Canada

Figure 3.8: Canadian and US interest rates

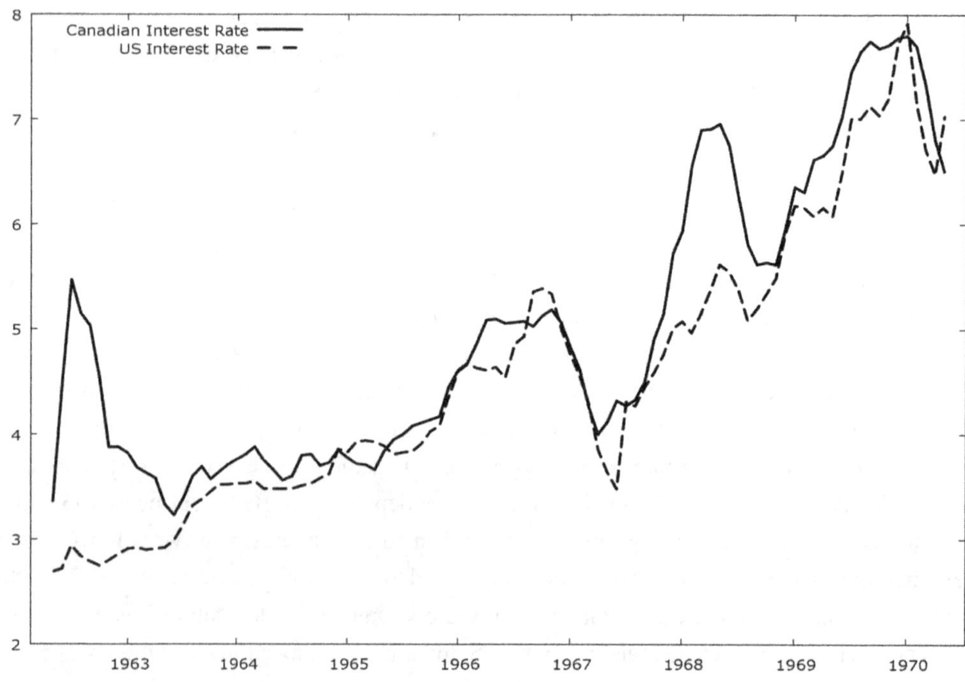

Data sources: Statistics Canada and Board of Governors of the Federal Reserve via FRED

9. CONCLUSION

This chapter examined the operation of a fixed exchange rate regime in the very short run. The main lesson is that a country that adopts a fixed exchange rate loses its monetary independence.[13] If a small economy fixes the value of the domestic currency to the currency in the large foreign economy, the central bank is unable to control the money supply and unable to move the domestic interest rate up or down.[14] The domestic interest rate is determined by the foreign interest rate, and by investors' expectations regarding future changes in the exchange rate.

While the loss of monetary independence and the potential for currency crises under fixed exchange rates are critical issues in the choice of an exchange rate regime, they are not the only relevant issues. Other issues include the ability of the monetary authorities, under the alternative exchange rate regimes, to stabilize short-term fluctuations in production and employment and to control the domestic inflation rate. For any particular nation, the question of the optimal exchange rate regime can only be answered with a comprehensive analysis of the issues.[15]

PRACTICE QUESTIONS

1. Fill in the blanks
   (a) Foreign exchange reserves are ______ held by ______.
   (b) When the central bank buys foreign currency from the public, foreign exchange reserves ______ and the money supply ______.
   (c) When the central bank buys domestic bonds from the public, domestic credit ______.
   (d) Under a permanently fixed exchange rate, movements in the domestic interest rate are caused solely by movements in ______.
   (e) Under a fixed exchange rate, the central bank in a small economy cannot control the nominal ______ supply.
2. Fill in the blanks
   (a) If the central bank increases domestic credit, the new very short-run equilibrium will have a lower level of ______ and ______ level of the domestic interest rate.
   (b) If, all of a sudden, investors come to expect a ______ of the domestic currency in the near future, the domestic interest rate increases in the very short run (the exchange rate remains fixed in the very short run).
   (c) An exogenous increase in the demand for money at each level of the domestic interest rate causes the money demand curve to ______. In the new equilibrium, foreign exchange reserves are ______.
   (d) An increase in the foreign interest rate causes the domestic interest rate to ______ in the very short run, thereby inducing a decrease in the quantity of ______ demanded.

(e) The last time that Canada had a fixed exchange rate was between the years 1962 and _____. The Canadian dollar was fixed to the US dollar at a level of _____ cents US.

3. The exchange rate is fixed (and expected to remain fixed). Using the portfolio equilibrium diagram and numbers, explain how an increase in the foreign interest rate from 2 per cent to 5 per cent affects the domestic interest rate and foreign exchange reserves in the very short run.

4. Assume the exchange rate is permanently fixed. Using the portfolio equilibrium diagram, explain how an exogenous increase in domestic credit affects the domestic interest rate and foreign exchange reserves in the very short run.

5. The exchange rate is fixed in the very short run. Suppose that, all of a sudden, investors come to expect a devaluation of the domestic currency within the next year. Using the portfolio equilibrium diagram, explain how this change in expectations affects the domestic interest rate and foreign exchange reserves in the very short run (the exchange rate remains fixed today, but investors expect a future devaluation).

DATA ANALYTICS

1. Using data available at the European Central Bank, www.ecb.europa.eu, generate a plot of the exchange rate between the Danish krone and the euro over the period since 2000. Comment.

2. A managed float is a combination of fixed and flexible exchange rate regimes. There are many types, with one example being the regime adopted by the Czech National Bank (CNB) in November 2013. The CNB, the central bank, began a policy of not allowing the koruna, denoted as CZK, to be worth more than a particular critical value, namely 27 CZK to the euro (the CNB would not allow the exchange rate 's' to fall below 27, but otherwise would let the exchange rate float). At a June 2015 meeting, the CNB indicated that it would continue this policy at least until the second half of 2016. Using data available at the European Central Bank, www.ecb.europa.eu, generate a plot of the koruna-euro exchange rate between 2013 and 2019. Did the CNB honor the commitment? What actions would the CNB be required to take when the exchange rate approached the critical value? Discuss.

3. In a sovereign debt crisis, foreign and domestic interest rates need not be equal even under a permanently fixed exchange rate (or a currency union, such as the European Currency Union). If a government is in financial difficulty, with investors expecting that the government may not make all future bond payments, investors will demand a higher interest rate to compensate for the higher risk (immediately after the increased riskiness becomes known, investors

try to sell the bonds and the equilibrium interest rate rises to reflect the increase in risk). Using the International Monetary Fund's IFS database, obtain monthly data on government bond yields for Germany and Greece over the period 2006 to 2019. Create a time-series plot. Comment.

APPENDIX: NOTES ON CURRENCY CRISES

Fixed exchange rate regimes are best described as fixed but adjustable exchange rate regimes. The government can, at any time, announce a one-time change in the level of the fixed exchange rate (or move to a flexible rate). When new information generates a significant change in expectation regarding future devaluation, there is the onset of a currency crisis with the jump in the interest rate and the collapse in reserves.[16] But what factors can generate an expectation of future devaluation?

A potential factor is a persistent government budget deficit, with the deficit being financed by continual increases in domestic credit that result in ongoing reserve losses.[17] If the deficits and the associated increases in domestic credit continue for many periods (with relatively small increases in money demand), the central bank will eventually run out of reserves. Unless the government can borrow foreign currency reserves, the central bank will be unable to hold the exchange rate fixed.[18] At some point, investors will come to expect a future devaluation, and a currency crisis will have begun.

In practice, investors must assess whether the government will undertake alternative actions, in the current or future periods, such as borrowing reserves, raising taxes, and reducing spending. Indeed, currency crises can be initiated, as well as tempered, by news that alters expectations regarding future fiscal and financial policy.

A currency crisis can also be initiated by bad news about the current or future state of the economy, such that investors expect that the government will, in the near future, devalue in an attempt to stabilize the economy. If the economy is in a recession, investors may expect government officials to consider devaluation as a policy change that could increase aggregate demand and end the recession (in a model in Chapter 13, a devaluation increases real GDP in the short run). Investor expectations will depend on their assessments of policymakers' views on the costs and benefits of alternative policies, and thus may depend on, among other factors, the state of the economy, the objectives of the government, political factors, announcements, and the credibility of policymakers. Once the crisis has begun, investors will constantly reassess these factors (as well as the possible negative effects of the higher interest rate) as they gauge the likelihood of future devaluation.[19]

A banking crisis can also initiate a currency crisis. Indeed, concurrent banking and currency crises are not uncommon.[20] If the domestic economy has banks in financial difficulty, and investors expect the government to provide financial assistance to the banks, investors may expect the government financing of this assistance to be associated with increases in domestic credit and losses in foreign exchange reserves. The financial assistance could result in a situation where the central bank lacks sufficient reserves to maintain the fixed exchange rate. If investors come to expect that the banking crisis will result in a devaluation in the near future, the currency crisis will have begun. Likewise, a currency crisis (or an actual devaluation) can initiate or exacerbate a banking crisis. If domestic banks borrowed funds in foreign currency, and then converted the foreign currency to domestic currency and loaned out these funds in the domestic economy, a devaluation increases the balance sheet liabilities of the banks (measured in domestic currency). The devaluation could result in negative bank capital, meaning that the banks are technically insolvent.[21]

Of course, any new information that is expected to induce policymakers to consider a devaluation as a possible policy change can cause a currency crisis. Fixed exchange rate regimes are therefore susceptible to currency crises. And while the choice of an exchange rate regime requires an assessment of alternative regimes, the potential for currency crises is a major weakness of a fixed but adjustable exchange rate regime.[22]

NOTES

1 The European Monetary System (1979 to 1999) had fixed exchange rates between various European countries. The IMF's Annual Report on Exchange Arrangements and Exchange Restrictions provides the exchange rate regime and monetary policy framework in each of the 190 member countries (as well as in Hong Kong, a special administrative region of China, and a few other countries).

2 If R is measured in foreign currency, this equation assumes the exchange rate equals 1. The equation abstracts from the banking system and sets the money multiplier equal to 1.

3 Obstfeld and Rogoff (1995a) discuss issues related to the operation of fixed exchange rate regimes, and Rose (2011, 2014) provides useful information on the workings of fixed (and flexible) exchange rates.

4 The approach in this chapter is within the tradition of the monetary approach to the balance of payments (see, for example, Johnson (1972, 1976) and the references in Chapter 9). Purvis (1977), in discussing various policy issues, highlights some implications of the monetary approach. Harry Johnson and Doug Purvis were Canadian-born economists, both widely admired by academic economists and policymakers alike. The Canadian Economics Association offers the Harry Johnson Prize and the Doug Purvis Prize.

5 See, for example, Floyd (2010, 294–5).

6 Bordo and Meissner (2016) discuss banking, sovereign debt, and currency crises. Rose (2014), in discussing the transition of exchange rate regimes in the period that encompasses the global financial crisis, provides a summary of countries that did, and did not, alter their regime between 2006 and 2012.

7 On the workings of the EMS in general, see Eichengreen (2008). The UK, like a few other countries, was allowed wider bands (±6 per cent rather than ±2.25 per cent). But once the band is reached, the central bank must ensure that the exchange rate does not move past the band.

8 Some European countries had begun to institute referenda on the Maastricht Treaty that indicated that (among other policies) the euro was to be created by 1999. Denmark had voted against the ratification of the Treaty, and the French vote was set to be held in a few weeks. See Eichengreen (2008).

9 The Canadian dollar was fixed to the US dollar at the outset of Bretton Woods, but Canada operated under a flexible exchange rate regime between 1950 and 1962. See Schembri (2008).

10 The Canadian–US dollar exchange rate is CANSIM series V37426.

11 In 1961, the Canadian government was in a dispute with James Coyne, Governor of the Bank of Canada. In May, the government requested his resignation but he refused (he resigned in July). This event resulted in some turbulence on the foreign exchange market. The Bank of Canada publication entitled "A History of the Canadian Dollar," written by James Powell, discusses this dispute.

12 The Canadian interest rate is CANSIM series V122484, a Treasury bill rate. The US Treasury Bill rate is from FRED, the Federal Reserve Bank of St. Louis database.

13 For empirical evidence on issues related to monetary independence under a fixed exchange rate, see (for example) Pasula (1994, 1996, 2020), Shambaugh (2004), and Obstfeld et al. (2005).

14 In general, there are two avenues through which the central bank in a small economy may be able to affect the domestic interest rate. The government can impose capital controls that restrict international asset trade (see the discussion in Chapter 9). If the controls cannot be circumvented, the link between domestic and foreign interest rates is severed and the central bank can affect the interest rate (see, for example, Obstfeld et al. 2005). Second, if the interest rate parity relationship incorporates a marginal portfolio adjustment cost or a risk premium, changes in domestic credit may be able to affect the interest rate by affecting the marginal portfolio adjustment cost or the risk premium. See, for example, Flood and Jeanne (2005) and Pasula (2016).

15 Further issues are discussed in Chapters 8, 9, 11, and 13.

16 The seminal literature on currency crises includes Krugman (1979) and Flood and Garber (1984). On the theory and empirics of currency crises, see Obstfeld and Rogoff (1995a), Bordo and Meissner (2016), and Burnside et al. (2016). A "currency crisis" is defined on the basis of an expectation of a future devaluation, without any need for the future devaluation (depreciation) to occur (Hong Kong had a currency crisis in 1997, even though the level of the exchange rate did not change).

17 The government sells domestic bonds to the central bank (the central bank has more domestic assets, an increase in domestic credit). The central bank pays for these bonds with new money and the government uses these funds to pay for the excess spending. Financing budget deficits under a fixed exchange rate regime is discussed further in Chapter 9.

18 Central banks have agreements to swap currencies in times of crisis (Bordo et al. 2015). For an advanced discussion related to defending currencies in crisis, see Flood and Jeanne (2005).

19 In a self-fulfilling crisis, a speculative attack by investors causes the currency crisis and results in a future devaluation, even though devaluation would not have occurred without the attack. The jump in the interest rate may be a factor in self-fulfilling crises, in that the higher rate could result in higher costs of maintaining the exchange rate. The cost–benefit analysis, based on government objectives, may then tend toward devaluation being a better policy and investors may then regard devaluation as a more likely outcome. If investors expect that the speculative attack could result in policymakers altering their view regarding alternative regimes, a self-fulfilling crisis could arise.

20 Sovereign debt, banking, and currency crises can all be intertwined. Bordo and Meissner (2016) provide a discussion, along with the historical evidence, of the different crises and their interrelationships.

21 Government guarantees (promises to bail out banks in financial difficulty) create an incentive for banks to undertake more risky behavior and thus make future government payments more likely.

22 The same analysis applies to "managed float" regimes (which operate like fixed rate regimes near the bands), including crawling peg regimes where the bands change gradually over time to allow for trend depreciation (as in Mexico in the early 1990s). Currency areas, such as the European Currency Area, are not susceptible to this problem.

PART II

The Intertemporal Approach to Net Exports and the Current Account

CHAPTER 4

The Intertemporal Theory of Consumption and Saving

1. INTRODUCTION

Consumer spending is an important component of aggregate demand. What causes consumer spending to rise and fall? Why is the growth rate of consumer spending smooth relative to the growth rate of real income? How do interest rate and tax changes affect consumer spending? These questions are of considerable interest to macroeconomists.

In recent years, macroeconomists have increasingly relied on an intertemporal model of consumption. Because after-tax real income in any period is equal to consumption plus saving (in terms of the real income identity), a theory of consumer spending is also a theory of saving. And because saving is inherently intertemporal, consumer spending is also fundamentally an intertemporal phenomenon.

This chapter outlines the intertemporal theory of consumption and saving.[1] This theory is based on a choice-theoretic framework, with consumption chosen to maximize lifetime utility subject to an intertemporal budget constraint. While open economy issues are not discussed, it is essential to develop a strong understanding of the material. The theoretical analysis serves as a basis for international macroeconomic models formulated in an intertemporal, choice-theoretic framework, including the intertemporal approach to the current account.

2. THE BASIC SETUP AND THE INTERTEMPORAL BUDGET CONSTRAINT

The analysis of consumer spending is based on a relatively simple intertemporal model. There are two periods – the current period and the future period. Variables in the future period are known with certainty in the current period (there is perfect foresight).[2] Consumers act to maximize lifetime utility. Given their opportunities, consumers choose current consumption and future consumption in a way that brings them the most satisfaction over their lifetime. There is one good, with current and future prices fixed at unity. The real income of consumers is exogenous in both periods, and taxes are lump sum (a fixed amount that does not increase with real income).

While macroeconomics focuses on the entire economy, theoretical macroeconomics often relies on the abstraction of a representative agent or a representative firm in developing the basic principles that guide the main actors in the economy. The terms consumer(s) and agent are used interchangeably.

A Note on Notation

In the chapters that analyzed the very short run, *time t* represented a very short period of time, such as one day. In this and subsequent chapters, the notation *period t* is used to represent a period of time such as one year. This notation is standard in dynamic macroeconomics. The current period is denoted as period t, and the future period is denoted as period t+1. While one could assume that there are many periods, the main insights can be garnered in a two-period setup.

Household Budget Constraints

In the current period, the consumer's after-tax real income is denoted as $y_t - T_t$, where y_t denotes real income (and output) and T_t denotes taxes (all variables are measured in real terms). After-tax real income is equal to consumer spending, denoted as c_t, plus private saving, denoted as S_t^{priv}. Private saving equals the accumulation of bonds in period t (the bond is the only asset):

$$S_t^{priv} = B_t - B_{t-1},$$

where B_{t-1} denotes the stock of bonds at the start of period t (carried over from period t-1) and B_t denotes the stock of bonds at the end of period t (or equivalently, the start of period t+1). It is assumed that B_{t-1} equals 0, so the consumer starts the current period with no assets and no debts. The current-period budget constraint is

$$y_t - T_t = c_t + B_t.$$

The variable B_t may be positive (meaning the consumer has acquired bonds) or negative (meaning the consumer has issued a bond or, less formally, has received a loan).

In period t+1, the consumer will earn income and pay taxes, with after-tax real income denoted $y_{t+1} - T_{t+1}$. But the consumer may also receive (or pay) principal plus interest on the bond. The period t+1 budget constraint is[3]

$$y_{t+1} - T_{t+1} + \left(1 + r_t\right) B_t = c_{t+1},$$

where r_t denotes the real interest rate in period t. If B_t equals 10 and the real interest rate equals 0.10 (or 10 per cent), the consumer will have an additional 11 goods in period t+1. Through saving or dissaving, the consumer is able to shift consumption between periods.

Figure 4.1: Intertemporal constraint

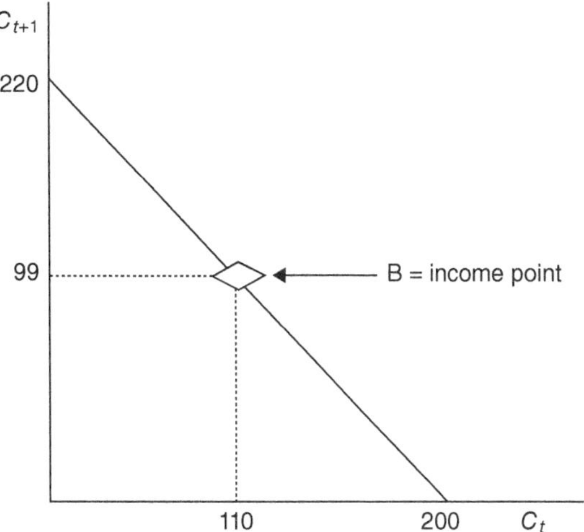

The Intertemporal Budget Constraint

The intertemporal household budget constraint is derived by merging the current and future period budget constraints, yielding

$$c_t + \frac{c_{t+1}}{1+r_t} = y_t - T_t + \frac{y_{t+1} - T_{t+1}}{1+r_t}.$$

The left-hand side represents the present value of lifetime consumption, and the right-hand side represents the present value of lifetime after-tax real income (or lifetime after-tax real income, for short). This intertemporal constraint implies that the agent's consumption is constrained by lifetime after-tax real income (with B_{t-1} equal to 0, the consumer starts period t with no net assets). Consumers can shift consumption between periods, but cannot spend (over their lifetime) more than what they earn over their lifetime.

The intertemporal household budget constraint can be written as

$$c_{t+1} = y_{t+1} - T_{t+1} + \left(1 + r_t\right)\left[y_t - T_t - c_t\right].$$

In Figure 4.1, with c_{t+1} on the vertical axis and c_t on the horizontal axis, the intertemporal budget constraint gives the combinations of current and future consumption that are feasible, given current and future after-tax real income and given the real interest rate. The consumer can consume at any point on the intertemporal constraint.

Suppose $y_t - T_t$ equals 110, $y_{t+1} - T_{t+1}$ equals 99, and the real interest rate equals 10 per cent. The present value of lifetime after-tax real income is then 110 plus the present value of the 99 in the future period. At an interest rate of 10 per cent, this future 99 is worth 90 in present value terms (99/1.1 equals 90).[4] Therefore, the present value of lifetime after-tax real income equals 200 (in real terms, measured as 200 goods).

In Figure 4.1, point B is called the income point, where current after-tax real income equals 110 and future after-tax real income equals 99. The intertemporal constraint goes through the income point, with the slope equal to $-(1+r_t)$. With these numbers, the endpoint on the horizontal axis is 200 (the present value of lifetime after-tax real income), and the endpoint on the vertical axis is 220. The slope of the line equals -1.1 when the real interest rate equals 0.10.

The intertemporal constraint represents the opportunities available to the consumer over the two periods. The consumer can choose to consume at any point along the constraint. The consumer could choose to consume more than the after-tax real income in the current period. For example, the consumer could get a loan of 10 and spend it on consumption, allowing consumption to equal 120 in the current period. In period t+1, the consumer would have to pay back 11 for the loan (principal plus interest) and would be able to consume 88 units. Or the consumer could save in the current period and consume more than 99 in the future period.

3. UTILITY AND LIFETIME UTILITY

The consumer has many feasible combinations of current and future consumption. The combination chosen is based on the consumer's preferences. In economics, consumer choice is based on the idea that consumers make the choices that bring them the greatest satisfaction.

Consumer preferences are represented by a utility function. The utility the consumer obtains from consuming a particular bundle of goods is represented by a number. But the actual numbers for different bundles are meaningless, other than a higher number represents a higher level of utility. The utility function for consumption in the current period is shown in Figure 4.2. Utility, denoted u_t, is measured on the vertical axis, and consumption on the horizontal axis. The shape of the utility function incorporates two principles. First, higher consumption is associated with a higher level of utility. Second, as the consumer obtains more and more consumption, utility increases but increases by smaller and smaller amounts (the future-period utility function has the same shape).

These features are reflected in the marginal utility curve, where marginal utility is the change in utility divided by the change in consumption (the Greek letter delta, Δ, means "the change in")

$$marginal\ utility = \frac{\Delta u}{\Delta c} = u'(c),$$

where $u'(c)$ is notation for the marginal utility of consumption. Marginal utility is always positive because an increase in consumption always increases utility. Marginal utility falls as consumption increases, so there is diminishing marginal utility. Figure 4.3 depicts the curve representing the current-period marginal utility of consumption.

The consumer gets utility from current and future consumption. The objective is to maximize lifetime utility subject to the intertemporal budget constraint. Lifetime utility, denoted as V, is represented by

$$V = u(c_t) + \frac{1}{1+\gamma}\, u(c_{t+1}),$$

Figure 4.2: Utility function

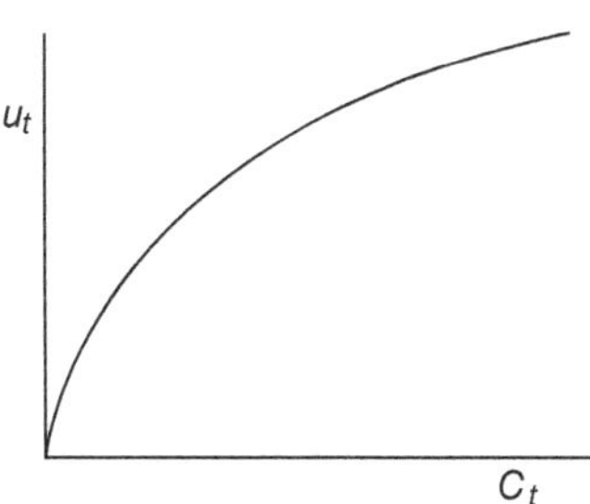

Figure 4.3: Marginal utility

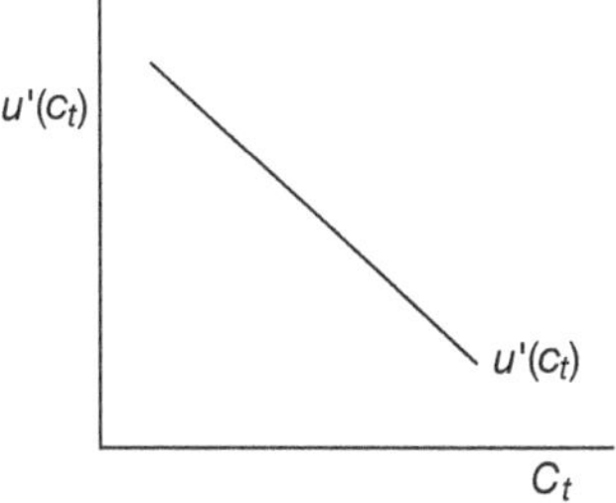

where γ, the Greek letter gamma, represents the fixed marginal rate of time preference. The magnitude of the marginal rate of time preference depends on the tastes of the consumer. If γ is high (say 0.10), the consumer is relatively impatient and has a strong preference for consumption earlier rather than later.[5] If γ equals 0, the consumer is patient and would be indifferent between a given quantity of goods in the current period and the same quantity of goods in the future period.

4. INDIFFERENCE CURVES

The consumer's lifetime utility can be represented by an indifference curve, as shown in Figure 4.4 (the figure also shows a 45° line, along which current and future consumption are equal). On any given indifference curve, lifetime utility, or V, is fixed.

Indifference curves are downward sloping. If one decreases future consumption, the utility of future consumption falls. To hold lifetime utility constant (as along a given indifference curve), current consumption must increase by an amount that increases the utility of current consumption so as to exactly offset the discounted fall in the utility of future consumption. In the figure, V is fixed at some number, say 226. This indifference curve represents the combinations of current and future consumption that yield lifetime utility of 226.

Any given indifference curve is convex to the origin (has the shape shown in the figure). Note that the slope of the indifference curve is as follows:

$$slope = \frac{-(1+\gamma)\,u'(c_t)}{u'(c_{t+1})}.$$

Figure 4.4: Indifference curve

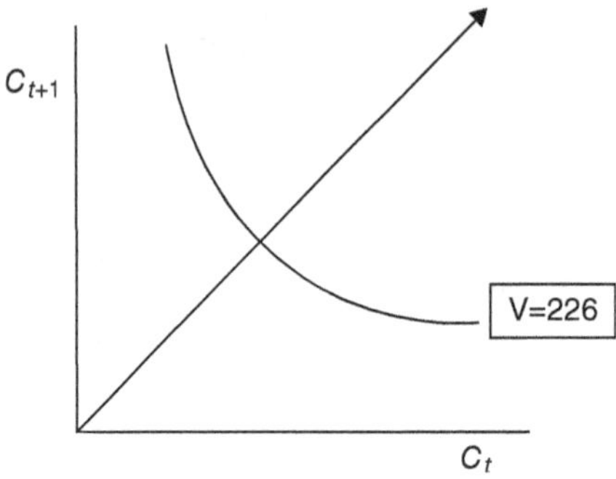

At the point where the indifference curve crosses the 45° line, the slope equals $-(1+\gamma)$. For example, if γ equals 0.02, the slope is -1.02 (current and future consumption are equal on the 45° line, so marginal utility is the same in the two periods). Consider the slope of the indifference curve at points above the 45° line. With a relatively high amount of future consumption, the marginal utility of future consumption is low; likewise, with a relatively small amount of current consumption, the marginal utility of current consumption is high. Therefore the term $u'(c_t)/u'(c_{t+1})$ is larger than 1, say 2. At this point, the slope of the indifference curve equals -2.04. And at points below the 45° line, current consumption is greater than future consumption so that, with diminishing marginal utility, the curve is flatter. For example, at a certain point below the 45° line, the slope could be -0.50.

These different slopes at different points on the indifference curve reflect the change in the consumer's willingness to substitute current for future consumption, when starting from different points on the curve. The indifference curve, by construction, represents willingness to substitute one good for another. If the consumer is indifferent between two different combinations of current and future consumption, the consumer would be willing to exchange (or trade) one bundle for the other.

There is an indifference curve for each level of lifetime utility. In Figure 4.4, an indifference curve further from the origin than the indifference curve with V equal to 226 would have higher levels of both current and future consumption (over a certain range). Therefore, the lifetime utility associated with this indifference curve would be higher than 226. Each spot in the area would have an indifference curve going through it (and indifference curves never cross).

5. MAXIMIZATION OF LIFETIME UTILITY AND THE EULER EQUATION FOR CONSUMPTION

Consumers maximize lifetime utility subject to the intertemporal budget constraint. Consumers choose current and future consumption such that they reach the highest possible indifference curve without spending more than they can afford to spend over their lifetime. This maximum occurs at the point where the indifference curve is tangent to, or has the same slope as, the intertemporal budget constraint.

Figure 4.5: Lifetime utility maximization

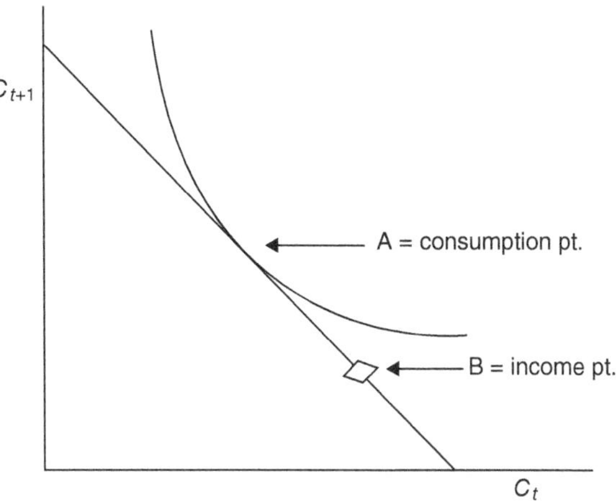

Consider Figure 4.5, where at the consumption point (denoted A), the indifference curve is tangent to the intertemporal budget constraint (note that the income point, denoted as B, is at a different point on the constraint).[6] At the consumption point, the slopes of the indifference curve and budget constraint are equal. Setting the slopes equal to each other, and rearranging, yields a key relationship called the *Euler equation for consumption*:

$$u'(c_t) = \frac{(1+r_t)}{(1+\gamma)} \, u'(c_{t+1}).$$

The agent allocates consumption over time to ensure that the Euler equation is satisfied. This equation is, in effect, a marginal benefit–marginal cost condition. If the agent decreases current consumption, the marginal cost of this action is measured by the marginal utility of current consumption (the left-hand side of the equation). The right-hand side of the Euler equation measures the marginal benefit. The decrease in current consumption allows the agent to purchase bonds, increase future consumption by an amount equal to principal plus interest, and therefore experience a discounted increase in utility from the increase in future consumption. To maximize lifetime utility, marginal benefit and marginal cost must be equal. Otherwise, the agent could reallocate consumption over time and obtain a higher level of lifetime utility.

Suppose, for example, that

$$8 = u'(c_t) < \left[\frac{1+r_t}{1+\gamma}\right] u'(c_{t+1}) = 12.$$

Let r and γ equal 0, and suppose the consumer is in the process of determining the utility-maximizing levels of consumption. With the inequality, the consumer is *not* maximizing lifetime utility. If the consumer cuts current consumption by 1, there is a loss in utility of 8 in the current period: the marginal utility of current consumption equals 8, or $\Delta u/\Delta c_t = -8/-1 = 8$. But the one unit cut in current consumption means that the consumer saves one unit (buys a bond that is worth, in real terms, one unit of the good) and allows for an increase of one unit of future consumption. Future utility increases by 12 because the marginal utility of future consumption equals 12. So by decreasing current consumption by 1 unit and increasing future consumption by 1 unit, lifetime utility has increased by $-8 + 12$, or $+4$. By reallocating consumption, lifetime utility has increased. The consumer could *not* have been maximizing lifetime utility at the initial point. By continuing to reallocate consumption between periods, the consumer will maximize lifetime utility and the Euler equation for consumption will hold as an equality (where, for example, both marginal utilities equal 10).

The consumer always acts to maximize lifetime utility and ensures, given the choices for current and future consumption, that the Euler equation holds.

The Consumption Function

Merging the Euler equation with the intertemporal budget constraint yields the consumption function. This equation determines the lifetime utility-maximizing level of current-period consumption as a function of the key economic variables (an appendix provides an example). Current-period consumer spending depends on current after-tax real income, future after-tax real income, the real interest rate, and the marginal rate of time preference.

6. CONSUMPTION SMOOTHING AND CONSUMPTION TILTING

With diminishing marginal utility, the tendency is for the lifetime utility-maximizing levels of consumption in each period to be fairly close to each other. Whether or not they are equal depends on the magnitude of the real interest rate relative to the marginal rate of time preference.

Consumption Smoothing

Consumption smoothing is defined as equal quantities of consumption in both periods. In the diagram, there is consumption smoothing if the consumption point lies on the 45° line (see Figure 4.6). If the real interest rate, r_t, equals the marginal rate of time preference, γ, the Euler equation implies that there is consumption smoothing:

$$c_t = c_{t+1}.$$

When r_t equals γ, consumption smoothing yields the highest possible level of lifetime utility. Note that the consumer equates consumption in the two periods regardless of the levels of current and future after-tax real income (wherever the income point is located on the constraint).

If r_t and γ both equal 0, the Euler equation implies that the consumer acts to equalize the marginal utilities (ensuring that consumption is the same in the two periods). But if r_t and γ are equal, there is consumption smoothing regardless of the level of the real interest rate.

When the real interest rate equals the marginal rate of time preference, two forces that affect the level of current consumption and saving exactly offset each other. If the real interest rate is high

Figure 4.6: Consumption smoothing

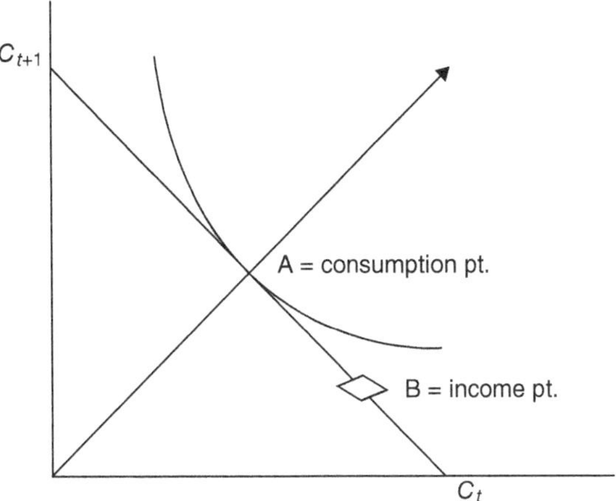

(compared to a real interest rate of zero), the consumer (ceteris paribus) will want to save a larger amount and consume a smaller amount in the current period. A higher real interest rate, in itself, induces an increase in saving. If the marginal rate of time preference is high (so that the consumer heavily discounts future utility relative to current utility), the consumer (ceteris paribus) will want to consume more and save less in the current period, compared to the case where the marginal rate of time preference equals zero. A higher marginal rate of time preference, in itself, implies a lower level of saving. When r_t equals γ, these two forces offset each other exactly and consumption smoothing occurs.

Tastes and Opportunities

The real interest rate represents the rate at which consumption can be shifted between periods – it represents *opportunities*. The marginal rate of time preference is an element of an individual's *tastes*. One must not confound tastes and opportunities.[7]

Consumption Tilting

If the real interest rate is greater than the marginal rate of time preference, the consumer allocates consumption such that

$$c_{t+1} > c_t.$$

With a relatively high real interest rate – high relative to the rate at which the consumer discounts future utility – the consumer has an incentive to move away from a smoothed consumption path. A decrease in current consumption and an increase in current saving generates a relatively large increase in future consumption, and the agent discounts future utility at a relatively low rate. Relative to a smooth consumption path, moving toward this tilted consumption path increases lifetime utility. Consumption will be increasing over time.

Consumption Smoothing, the Real Interest Rate, and Saving

If r_t equals γ, there is consumption smoothing regardless of the location of the income point. Depending on whether current after-tax real income is relatively high or low, the consumer has positive or negative saving so as to allow consumption smoothing.

But would the consumer save if the real interest rate is 0 per cent? To maximize lifetime utility, when r_t equals γ, consumption smoothing must occur. If current after-tax real income is 180 and future after-tax real income is 20, current-period saving will equal 80 so that both current and future consumption equal 100. The consumer saves because smoothed consumption yields higher lifetime utility than any other feasible combination of current and future consumption.

7. EXOGENOUS CHANGES IN CURRENT AND FUTURE REAL INCOME

A number of exogenous changes are examined.[8] The real interest rate is assumed to equal the marginal rate of time preference, so that consumption smoothing holds. For simplicity, r_t and γ are assumed to equal 0 per cent. In the diagrams, the initial consumption and income points are denoted A and B, respectively, and the new consumption and income points are denoted C and D. For convenience, the initial income point is placed on the 45° line.

Temporary Increase in Real Income

A temporary increase in real income (or output) is defined as an increase in current real income with no change in future real income: Δy_t equals 10 and Δy_{t+1} equals 0 (taxes are held fixed). This temporary increase in real income increases lifetime after-tax real income and the intertemporal budget constraint shifts out (with the same slope because the slope equals $-(1+r_t)$ and r_t is fixed). This shift is shown in Figure 4.7, where the income point shifts from B to D. This increase in lifetime after-tax real income causes current consumption to increase. But by how much will it increase? The temporary increase in real income causes current consumption to increase by half of the increase in current real income (the consumption point moves from A to C, with the consumer experiencing a higher level of lifetime utility). Current consumption increases by 5, and the consumer saves one-half of the increase in real income. This increase in private saving of 5 units allows the consumer to increase future consumption by 5 units, thereby ensuring that consumption smoothing continues to hold.[9]

The marginal propensity to consume, defined as $\Delta c_t / \Delta y_t$, is 0.5. Current consumption rises by less than the increase in real income, and the consumer saves the rest. While this result is similar to that in the Keynesian theory of consumption taught in introductory macroeconomics, the following examples demonstrate that this result does not always occur. In the intertemporal theory, the marginal propensity to consume is not a fixed number.

Permanent Increase in Real Income

With a permanent increase in real income, both current and future real income increase by the same amount (for example, Δy_t and Δy_{t+1} equal 10). There is an increase in lifetime after-tax real income, and the intertemporal budget constraint shifts out (the figure for this case is not shown, but

Figure 4.7: Temporary increase in real output

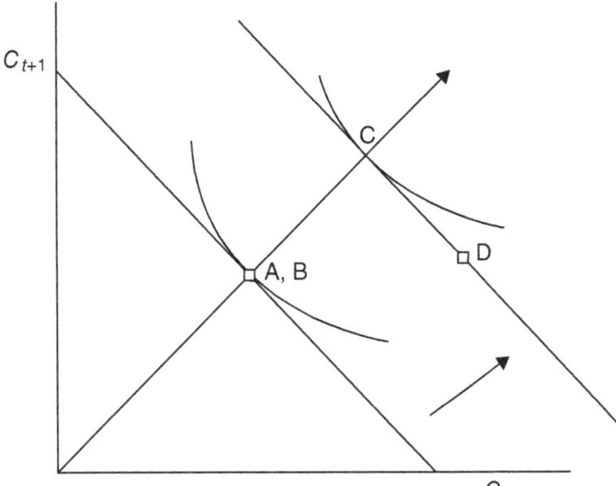

the new income point D would be on the 45° line). The permanent increase in real income causes current consumption to increase by the same amount as the increase in current-period real income, with no change in saving. There is no need to save to smooth consumption, because the future increase in real income will allow for an increase in future consumption. With a permanent increase in real income, the marginal propensity to consume is 1.

Increase in Future Real Income

Consider an increase in future income (with perfect foresight, it is known that future income will increase). There is an increase in future real income, but current real income does not change. Suppose Δy_{t+1} equals 10 and Δy_t equals 0. In Figure 4.8, there is an increase in lifetime after-tax real income and the budget constraint shifts out. The new income point is at point D.

There is an increase in lifetime after-tax real income and current consumption increases. Because the consumer wants to smooth consumption, current consumption increases by 5, equal to one-half of the increase in future real income. The consumer gets a loan (B_t is negative) to increase current consumption (the interest rate equals 0). When the future period arrives, the increase in period t+1 real income allows the consumer to pay off the loan and increase future consumption by 5 (the marginal propensity to consume, in this case, is undefined).

Increases in Current and Future Real Income of Different Amounts

Consider a change where current and future real income increase by different amounts (unlike a permanent increase, where the increases are of the same amount). If Δy_t equals 10 and Δy_{t+1} equals 34, lifetime after-tax real income increases by 44. With r_t and γ equal to 0, the consumer increases current consumption by 22 (to ensure consumption smoothing). The consumer gets a loan of 12 in the current period and spends these funds on goods. In the future period, when future real income increases by 34, the consumer can pay back the loan of 12 and increase future consumer spending by 22.

Figure 4.8: Increase in future real income

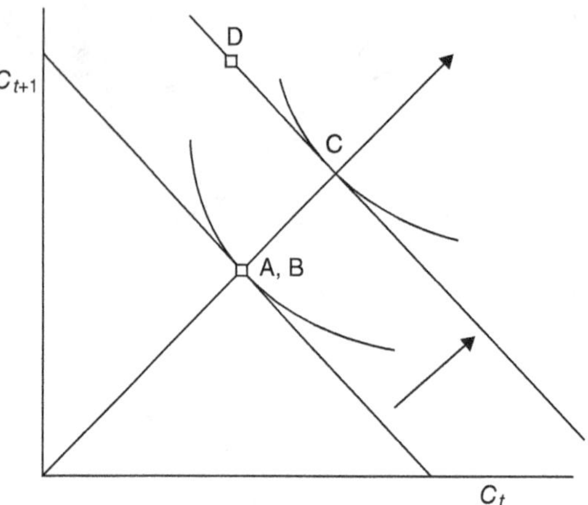

Given that current consumption increases by 22 and current real income increases by 10, the marginal propensity to consume, $\Delta c_t / \Delta y_t$, is 2.2. The marginal propensity is not constant, and it does not have to lie between 0 and 1.

8. EXOGENOUS CHANGES IN CURRENT AND FUTURE TAXES

How do tax cuts affect consumer spending and saving in the current period? Recall that taxes are assumed to be lump-sum taxes.[10] Assume that current and future output are fixed.

A temporary tax cut is a decrease in current taxes, with no change in future taxes. The temporary tax cut increases lifetime after-tax real income and the intertemporal budget constraint shifts out (with the same slope, since r_t is fixed). The diagram is the same as in the case of a temporary increase in real income, where the income point shifts from B to D. This increase in lifetime after-tax real income causes current consumption to increase (the consumption point moves from A to C). With a current-period tax cut of 10, current-period consumption and private saving both increase by 5 units. The increase in saving allows the consumer to increase future consumption by 5 units (if r_t equals γ, lifetime utility is maximized when consumption is smoothed).[11]

The effects of a permanent tax cut are the same as a permanent increase in real income, and the effects of a decrease in future taxes are the same as an increase in future real income. The next chapter discusses tax changes in detail.[12]

9. PRICES, INTEREST RATES, AND THE INTERTEMPORAL CONSTRAINT

The budget constraints in Section 2 did not explicitly incorporate the prices of goods. This section shows that, by using the *real* interest rate, the analysis in effect allowed for different prices over time.

Consider the current-period budget constraint in nominal terms, meaning measured in dollars (ignore taxes for simplicity):

$$P_t\, y_t = P_t\, c_t + B_t,$$

where the variable P denotes the price of goods (the price level) and B is now measured in dollars (rather than goods). The period t+1 constraint is

$$P_{t+1}\, y_{t+1} + \left(1 + i_t\right) B_t = P_{t+1}\, c_{t+1},$$

where the nominal interest rate, denoted i_t, is used since bond payments are paid in dollars. Merging these constraints and dividing through by P_{t+1} yields the intertemporal constraint:

$$y_{t+1} + \left[\frac{\left(1 + i_t\right) P_t}{P_{t+1}}\right]\left(y_t - c_t\right) = c_{t+1}.$$

This intertemporal constraint is identical to the intertemporal constraint in Section 2. The term in square brackets can be rewritten as

$$\frac{\left(1 + i_t\right) P_t}{P_{t+1}} = \frac{1 + i_t}{1 + \pi_t} = \left(1 + r_t\right),$$

where the (forward) inflation rate, π_t, is defined as $\pi_t = \frac{P_{t+1} - P_t}{P_t}$, and the second equality follows from the Fisher equation (named after the Yale University economist Irving Fisher):[13]

$$1 + r_t = \frac{1 + i_t}{1 + \pi_t}.$$

By using the real interest rate in the intertemporal constraint, with all variables measured in real terms, the analysis in effect incorporates both the nominal interest rate and the price levels in the two periods (the effects of real interest rate changes are examined in the next chapter).

10. GROWTH RATES OF CONSUMPTION AND REAL GDP IN CANADA

The analysis assumed that goods are perishable. The best measure of consumer spending on perishable goods is consumer spending on services and non-durable goods (aggregate consumption also includes spending on durables and semi-durables).[14] The intertemporal theory of consumption suggests that consumer spending on services and nondurable goods should follow a relatively smooth path over time. While changes in the real interest rate cause changes in the predicted growth rate of consumption, the theory still predicts a generally smooth growth rate of consumption (even if the growth rate of real GDP is volatile).

Figure 4.9 shows the annual growth rates of Canadian real GDP (denoted as gy) and consumption of services and nondurable goods (denoted as gc1) between 1981 and 2014 (an applied exercise in Data Analytics examines the period since 2014).[15] The growth rate of real GDP is positive, except during the recessions of 1981–1982, 1990–1991, and 2008–2009. While there is some

Figure 4.9: Growth rates of real GDP and consumption

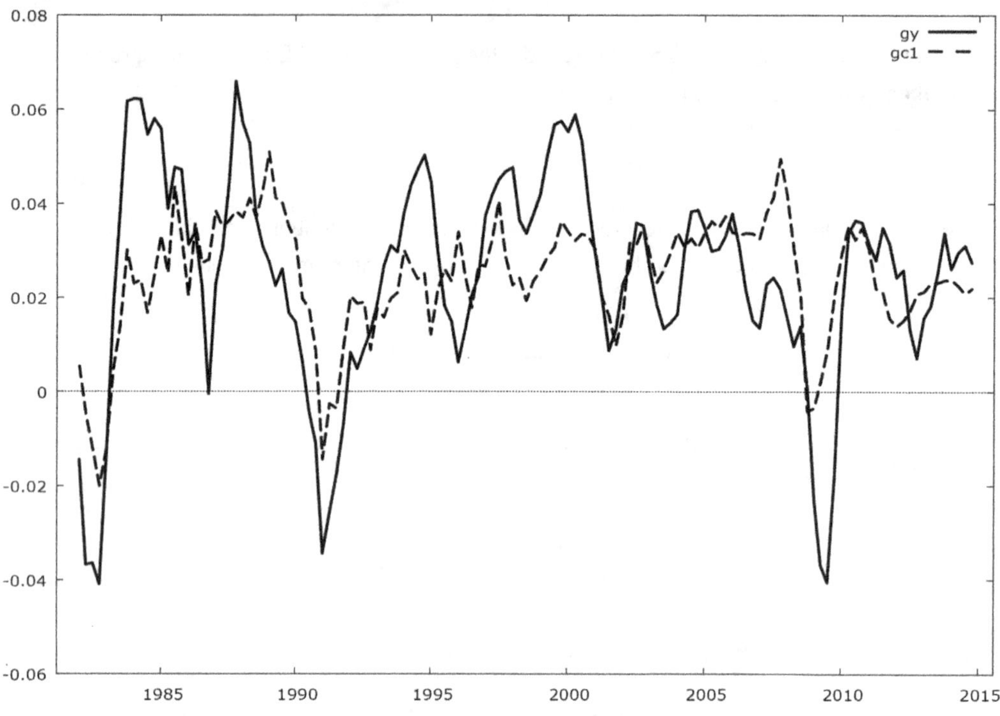

Data source: Statistics Canada

volatility in the growth rate of consumer spending, it is smoother than the growth rate of real GDP. It is interesting that, in the 2008–2009 recession, the level of consumer spending on services and nondurable goods experienced a relatively small decrease. While the growth rate of real GDP is significantly negative, equal to about −4 per cent, the growth rate of consumption is close to 0 per cent. There is similar evidence of consumption smoothing in the US economy during this recession (see Hall 2010).[16]

While the theoretical analysis for durable goods consumption is not covered in this chapter, it is worth noting some evidence. Figure 4.10 compares the growth rate of consumer spending on services and nondurables (denoted as gc1) with the growth rate of consumer spending on durables and semi-durables (denoted as gc2). The latter variable is considerably more volatile, with the annual growth rate ranging from about +12 per cent to −11 per cent.

11. CONCLUSION

The intertemporal theory of consumption is the predominant theory of consumption in advanced macroeconomic analysis.[17] In this theory, current-period consumption depends on current and future real income, current and future taxes, and the real return on bonds relative to the marginal rate of time preference. The distinction between the effects of permanent and temporary changes is highlighted in the theory, as is the tendency for consumption smoothing.

Figure 4.10: Consumption growth rates

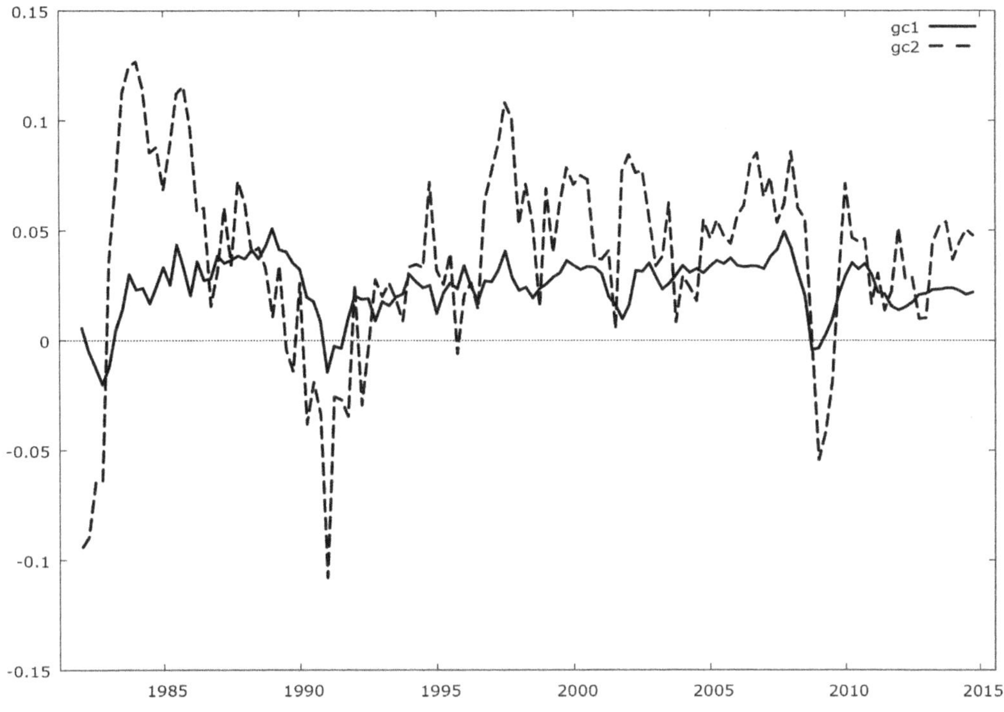

Data source: Statistics Canada

The intertemporal theory of consumption is an integral component of dynamic, choice-theoretic international macroeconomic models, including the intertemporal approach to the current account. The next two chapters analyze movements in trade and current account balances using this framework.

PRACTICE QUESTIONS

1. Fill in the blanks
   (a) As current consumption increases (holding future consumption fixed), lifetime utility ______ and the marginal utility of current consumption ______.
   (b) As one moves down along a given indifference curve (with current consumption on the horizontal axis), lifetime utility ______ and the marginal utility of current-period consumption ______.
   (c) A temporary increase in real income causes saving in the current period to ______, as this change in saving allows future consumer spending to ______.
   (d) With a permanent increase in real income, consumer spending ______ and private saving ______ in the current period.
   (e) If ______ equals ______, the consumer will smooth consumption.

2. Fill in the blanks (the real interest rate and the marginal rate of time preference equal 0).

   (a) If real income increases by 5 in the current period and consumers know that real income will increase by 15 in the future period, lifetime after-tax real income increases by _____ and current-period consumption increases by _____.

   (b) If current after-tax real income equals 140 and future after-tax real income equals 60, private saving in the current period equals _____ (even though the real interest rate equals 0). Assume that the initial net debt equals 0.

   (c) If current real income increases by 10 and future real income increases by 50, lifetime after-tax real income increases by _____ and the marginal propensity to consume in the current period equals _____.

   (d) If current-period taxes increase by 10 but future taxes fall by 30, current-period consumption _____ by _____.

   (e) If current-period real income falls by 10 but future real income increases by 10, lifetime after-tax real income _____ and saving _____ in the current period.

3. (a) How does one calculate lifetime after-tax real income? Write down the equation and explain.

   (b) Write down the Euler equation for consumption. Suppose this equation does not hold as an equality. Explain how consumers reallocate consumption to ensure that the Euler equation holds.

4. Using the intertemporal theory of consumption (with the diagram and numbers), explain how a temporary increase in real income affects consumption and saving in the current period.

5. Using the intertemporal theory of consumption, explain how an increase in current real income of 14 and an increase in future real income of 6 affects consumption and saving (assume that the real interest rate and the marginal rate of time preference equal 0). Use the diagram and numbers.

DATA ANALYTICS

1. Collect quarterly data on Canadian consumption, based on the consumption of services and nondurables, and Canadian real GDP over the period since the start of 2014 (see CANSIM Table 36100104). Calculate the marginal propensity to consume (MPC) and plot MPC over time. Is MPC constant over time or does MPC vary? Comment.

2. Using the same data, plot the quarterly growth rates of consumption and real GDP. Is the growth rate of consumption smoother than the growth rate of real GDP? Are these growth rates ever negative during this period? Comment.

APPENDIX: DERIVING THE CONSUMPTION FUNCTION

With a logarithmic utility function, where utility equals the natural logarithm of consumption, marginal utility (the first derivative of the utility function) equals the inverse of consumption:

$$u'(c) = \frac{1}{c}.$$

This utility function satisfies the two essential features. Marginal utility is positive and marginal utility falls as consumption increases. The Euler equation is

$$\frac{c_{t+1}}{c_t} = \frac{1+r_t}{1+\gamma},$$

so that consumption smoothing holds when the real interest rate equals the marginal rate of time preference. Merging the Euler equation with the intertemporal constraint yields the consumption function:

$$c_t = \frac{1+\gamma}{2+\gamma}\left[y_t - T_t \frac{y_{t+1} - T_{t+1}}{1+r_t}\right].$$

If γ equals 0, current consumption equals one-half of lifetime after-tax real income (an appendix in Chapter 5 derives the consumption function when the initial net debt is not equal to zero).

NOTES

1 For an advanced discussion, with references to the empirical literature, see (for example) Hall (1989) and Abel (1990).
2 A less restrictive assumption would be that the future is uncertain and consumers have "rational expectations," meaning that current-period information and the model are used to generate expectations of future variables.
3 Since t+1 is the final period, B_{t+1} equals 0.
4 If one had 90 in the current period, and invested it in an asset with a 10 per cent rate of return, the 90 in the current period turns into 99 in the future period. Thus, if r equals 0.10, the 99 in the future period is worth 90 in the current period.
5 If γ is positive, the consumer's tastes are such that future consumption of a certain amount of goods provides less lifetime utility than current consumption of the same quantity of goods. Future utility of consumption is discounted, or multiplied by a factor less than 1 (if γ is 0.02, it is multiplied by approximately 0.98).
6 This two-period intertemporal optimization diagram was used (with minor variations) by two of the greatest macroeconomists of the 20th century, Irving Fisher (1930) and Milton Friedman (1957).
7 Epstein and Hynes (1983, 616) briefly discuss this basic point, and a variety of other more advanced issues, in their discussion of the marginal rate of time preference in dynamic models.
8 These exogenous changes are news (were not previously expected to occur). But going forward, there is perfect foresight. The consumers know both current and future real income. Blanchard (2007) adopts the same approach.

9   Letting r_t and γ equal 0 simplifies the calculations. If r_t and γ equal 0.10 with this same exogenous change, current consumption increases by approximately 5.24 and saving equals 4.76. This level of saving yields about 5.24 extra goods in period t+1 (so there is consumption smoothing). These calculations cannot be done easily in your head.

10 In terms of after-tax real income, a lump-sum tax cut of 3 is equivalent to a cut in the income tax rate from 0.20 to 0.17 when real income is 100.

11 Suppose there are 100 periods (with the real interest rate equal to zero). A temporary tax cut means that taxes are cut in the current period, but all future taxes are unchanged. If the current-period tax cut equals 100, current-period consumption increases by 1 and 99 is saved.

12 For survey papers that discuss tax policy and consumption, see Aschauer (1988), Barro (1989), and Abel (1990).

13 This equation is the exact definition of the real rate, rather than the approximation where the real interest rate is defined as the nominal interest rate minus the inflation rate. Chapter 7 provides a detailed discussion.

14 For durable goods, the analysis is more complicated. A durable good provides utility in both the current and future periods, and a durable good can be sold in the future period.

15 The quarterly data are from CANSIM Table 36100104. The series numbers for real GDP, consumption of services, and consumption of non-durables are, respectively, V62305752, V62305729, and V62305728. The series numbers for the consumption of durables and semi-durables used in Figure 4.10 are V62305726 and V62305727.

16 Hall (1978) conducted seminal empirical research based on the Euler equation for consumption. Hall (2010) notes that the small movements in the consumption of services and nondurables in the US during the 2008-2009 recession, when real GDP fell by a large amount, are consistent with intertemporal models that embed consumption smoothing.

17 Survey papers on issues related to the intertemporal theory of consumption (including various extensions) include Abel (1990), Attanasio (1999), and Thimme (2017).

CHAPTER 5

The Intertemporal Approach to the Current Account

1. INTRODUCTION

What determines the current account balance or the balance of trade? What determines net exports, the magnitude of a country's exports relative to imports? This chapter outlines the intertemporal approach to the determination of net exports and the current account balance. This approach, based on the intertemporal theory of consumption, is now the predominant approach used by international macroeconomists.[1]

The intertemporal approach is based on a general equilibrium, small economy macroeconomic model. Output is taken to be exogenous, and investment spending is ignored (the next chapter examines the relationship between investment spending and the current account). Consumers maximize lifetime utility, the government purchases goods and collects taxes, and residents in the domestic economy trade both goods and assets with the foreign economy. With the small economy assumption, foreign variables are exogenous and the analysis focuses on the domestic economy.

The exchange rate regime can be regarded as a flexible exchange rate regime, but as noted below, the exchange rate is not a determinant of the current account balance or net exports. Changes in trade balances are determined by real factors such as temporary and future changes in output and government spending, and changes in the foreign real interest rate.

2. TERMINOLOGY AND A NOTE ON NOTATION

Net exports equal exports minus imports. The term net exports is synonymous with the balance of trade. If net exports are positive, there is a balance of trade surplus. With negative net exports, there is a balance of trade deficit.

The current account balance equals net exports plus the debt service balance (an appendix discusses this identity). When initial net foreign assets of the domestic economy equal zero, the debt service balance equals zero. Net exports then equal the current account balance. If exports exceed imports, the current account is in surplus; if imports exceed exports, there is a current account deficit (or net exports are negative).

In the chapters on the very short run, *time t* represented a very short period of time, such as one day. In the intertemporal approach, the notation *period t* is used to represent a period of time such as one year. This notation is standard in dynamic macroeconomics. The current period is denoted period t, and the future period is denoted period t+1.

3. TWO MACROECONOMIC IDENTITIES

As a prelude, consider two identities widely used in international macroeconomics. In the first identity, the production of goods and services (or "goods" for short) equals sales plus changes in inventory. In the current period, period t, production equals sales (for simplicity, changes in inventory are assumed to equal zero):

$$y_t = c_t^d + I_t^d + g_t^d + EX_t,$$

where y denotes production of the domestic good, c^d denotes consumer spending on domestic goods, I^d denotes investment spending on domestic goods (purchases of domestic goods by domestic firms), g^d denotes government spending on domestic goods, and EX denotes exports. Domestic production is sold to domestic consumers, domestic firms, the domestic government, and foreigners.

Consumer spending, denoted c, includes spending by consumers on both domestic and imported consumer goods (denoted c^f). In this model, domestic and foreign goods are assumed to be identical. Therefore, one can simply add the two components of consumer spending:

$$c_t = c_t^d + c_t^f.$$

Domestic firms and the government also purchase both domestic and foreign goods:

$$I_t = I_t^d + I_t^f,$$

$$g_t = g_t^d + g_t^f.$$

The variables I^f and g^f denote, respectively, imports of foreign goods by domestic firms and imports of foreign goods by the domestic government. Imports, denoted IM, equal the sum of the three categories of imports:

$$IM_t = c_t^f + I_t^f + g_t^f.$$

Using this information, the first identity can be rewritten as (add and subtract IM_t):

$$y_t = c_t^d + I_t^d + g_t^d + EX_t + \left[c_t^f + I_t^f + g_t^f \right] - IM_t,$$

$$y_t = c_t + I_t + g_t + EX_t - IM_t = c_t + I_t + g_t + NX_t,$$

where net exports, denoted NX, equal exports less imports. Production equals the sum of consumer spending, investment spending, government spending, and net exports.

International macroeconomists use this identity as a way to think about the determination of net exports:

$$NX_t = CA_t = y_t - \left[c_t + I_t + g_t \right].$$

Net exports equal total production in the domestic economy less total purchases of goods by domestic consumers, domestic firms, and the domestic government. If production in the domestic economy is 100 units of goods, and domestic consumers, firms, and the government purchase 94 units, the other 6 units are exported.[2]

The second identity is akin to the current-period budget constraint (domestic residents own the domestic firms and, initially, have zero net foreign assets). In terms of macroeconomics, this identity implies that real income, denoted y, equals the sum of consumption, private saving (denoted S^{priv}), and taxes (denoted T):

$$y_t = c_t + S_t^{priv} + T_t.$$

Because production equals real income, merging this identity with the first identity yields

$$c_t + I_t + g_t + NX_t = c_t + S_t^{priv} + T_t.$$

Rearranging the identity yields another way to calculate net exports and the current account:

$$NX_t = CA_t = S_t^{priv} + \left(T_t - g_t \right) - I_t.$$

The term (T-g) is the government budget surplus and is called government saving.[3] Private saving plus government saving is called national saving. Therefore, net exports equal exports minus imports, but net exports also equal national saving less investment spending. Given that saving and investment spending are inherently intertemporal variables, it is evident why the intertemporal approach to the current account is regarded as the predominant approach.

If one simplifies and assumes that the government budget is balanced (T equals g) and investment spending equals zero, then net exports equal private saving. Consider the following example, with the domestic economy as Canada. Assume that all trade is conducted with the United States and all transactions are conducted in US dollars. Suppose Canadian exports to the United States this period generate $140 US, and Canada imports $130 US worth of US goods. The value of Canadian exports exceeds the value of Canadian imports, so Canada has a balance of trade surplus this period. Net exports, or exports minus imports, are positive. Canada has accumulated $10 US from the trade of goods with Americans and, when these US dollars are exchanged for US bonds, Canada has then accumulated $10 US worth of bonds. If this is the only way to save in Canada, the total saving of Canadians in this period is $10 US (the current-period value of the $10 US can be converted to Canadian dollars once the magnitude of the exchange rate is specified, and can be converted to goods once the price level is specified).

4. THE BASIC SETUP

The intertemporal model has a simple structure (with allowance for complications delayed, in large part, until future chapters). There are two periods: the current period, denoted as period t, and the future period, denoted as t+1. Consumers maximize lifetime utility subject to an intertemporal budget constraint. Future variables are known with certainty in the current period. The domestic good is identical to the foreign good, and domestic production is exogenous. The domestic economy is small, with foreign variables taken to be exogenous.

In addition, the following simplifications are added. Government spending and taxes are exogenous, with taxes taken to be lump-sum taxes, and the government budget is balanced in both periods (government deficits are discussed near the end of the chapter). For simplicity, investment spending is assumed to equal zero and the initial net foreign debt is zero. The exchange rate is assumed to be flexible (the central bank holds the money supply fixed).

Macroeconomic analysis often relies on the abstraction of a representative agent in developing the principles that guide consumers in the economy. The terms consumer, consumers, domestic residents, and agent are used interchangeably to represent consumers.

The Exchange Rate

The current-period exchange rate is denoted as s_t and is defined as the number of units of domestic currency (Canadian dollars) required to purchase one unit of foreign currency ($1 US). If s_t equals 1.10, one needs $1.10 Canadian to buy $1 US. An increase in s indicates a depreciation of the domestic currency.

Domestic Goods, Foreign Goods, and the Law of One Price

Because foreign and domestic goods are identical, consumers are indifferent between the two goods if they have the same price when measured in the same currency. Market forces ensure that the two goods have the same price in equilibrium, resulting in a condition called the law of one price condition:[4]

$$P_t = s_t \, P_t^*,$$

where P denotes the domestic price level and P* denotes the foreign price level. If the foreign price level equals $100 US and the exchange rate is 1.10, the Canadian price level must equal $110 Canadian. Competition between foreign and domestic producers, in conjunction with any induced change in the exchange rate, ensures that the law of one price holds (the law of one price and empirical and modeling issues are discussed in an appendix).[5]

It should be emphasized that changes in the equilibrium exchange rate do not affect net exports. The law of one price implies that if the domestic currency depreciates, the equilibrium domestic price level will have also increased (holding the foreign price level fixed). While the depreciation makes foreign goods more expensive for domestic residents, the increase in the domestic price level makes domestic goods more expensive. With the law of one price, these changes offset each other. The changes in the exchange rate and the price level together have no effect on the relative price of goods and thus have no effect on net exports.[6]

Purchasing Power Parity and the Law of One Price

The purchasing power parity (PPP) theory has a long history in international macroeconomics, with the theory asserting that the exchange rate equals the ratio of the domestic price level to the foreign price level (with each price level measured as the consumer price index):[7]

$$ s_t = \frac{P_t}{P_t^*} . $$

Is PPP a valid theory of the exchange rate? If there are non-traded goods, or if foreign and domestic goods are not identical, the PPP condition often does not provide a good indication of exchange rate movements.[8] But in a one-good model where the domestic good is identical to the foreign good, the PPP condition is identical to the law of one price (and therefore holds).

On Saving in the Domestic Economy

Given the assumptions, the only way for domestic residents to save is to buy foreign bonds, and the only way to have negative saving is to get a loan from foreigners.

With a balanced budget, the government is not issuing new bonds, and the central bank is not printing any additional money. In terms of the aggregate economy, the public is not able to save by buying more domestic bonds or holding more money because these variables are fixed. Similarly, with investment spending equal to 0, firms are not issuing any corporate bonds or shares (and are not accumulating capital). The only way to save is to accumulate foreign bonds.

The real interest rate on the foreign bond is denoted as r_t^*. If domestic residents buy a foreign bond in the current period, the payout in real terms in period t+1 is $(1+r_t^*)$. Domestic residents can also get loans from foreigners, with the real interest rate on the loan equal to the foreign real interest rate.

The Real Interest Rate Parity Condition

The interest rate parity condition, together with the PPP conditions and the Fisher equation[9] for each country, implies that the domestic real interest rate equals the foreign real interest rate (the derivation is provided in Chapter 7):

$$ r_t = r_t^* . $$

This condition is called the *real interest rate parity condition*. In a model with these features, domestic and foreign bonds earn the same real return.

5. BUDGET CONSTRAINTS, CONSUMPTION, AND NET EXPORTS

In the budget constraints, domestic bonds and domestic money are ignored (these variables are fixed). The only asset available for saving is a foreign bond, denoted as J. In addition, the analysis abstracts from price and exchange rate changes and writes the constraints in real terms.

In the current period, after-tax real income is denoted as $y_t - T_t$, where y is real income (and output) and T denotes lump-sum taxes.[10] After-tax real income equals consumer spending plus private saving (denoted as S_t^{priv}):

$$y_t - T_t = c_t + S_t^{priv}.$$

Private saving (or simply saving) in period t equals the accumulation of foreign bonds. The period t budget constraint is

$$y_t - T_t = c_t + J_t,$$

where J_t denotes the stock of foreign bonds at the end of period t (J_{t-1} equals 0, meaning that the consumer begins period t with no foreign assets and no foreign debts).[11] The variable J_t may be positive (meaning the consumer has acquired foreign bonds) or negative (meaning the consumer has received a loan from foreigners).

In period t+1, the consumer will earn income and pay taxes, with after-tax real income denoted $y_{t+1} - T_{t+1}$. But the consumer may also have foreign bonds to cash in, or may have to pay back principal plus interest on a foreign loan. The period t+1 budget constraint is

$$y_{t+1} - T_{t+1} + \left(1 + r_t^*\right) J_t = c_{t+1}.$$

If J_t equals 10 and the real interest rate equals 0.10 (or 10 per cent), the consumer will have an additional 11 goods in period t+1 (all variables being measured in terms of goods).[12] Through saving or dissaving, the consumer is able to shift consumption between periods.

The intertemporal budget constraint merges the period t and t+1 budget constraints:

$$c_{t+1} = y_{t+1} - T_{t+1} + \left(1 + r_t^*\right)\left[y_t - T_t - c_t\right].$$

Figure 5.1 depicts this intertemporal budget constraint.

In the figure, $y_t - T_t$ equals 100, $y_{t+1} - T_{t+1}$ equals 110, and the real interest rate equals 0.10 (or 10 per cent). The present value of lifetime after-tax real income equals the sum of 100 and the present value of 110:

$$y_t - T_t + \frac{y_{t+1} - T_{t+1}}{\left(1 + r_t^*\right)} = 100 + \frac{110}{1.1} = 200.$$

In present value terms, the consumer will earn 200 over their lifetime. In the figure, the income point is denoted as B, at the point where $y_t - T_t$ equals 100 and $y_{t+1} - T_{t+1}$ equals 110. The intertemporal budget constraint is a straight line through this point with a slope equal to $-(1 + r_t^*)$.

Figure 5.1: Intertemporal constraint

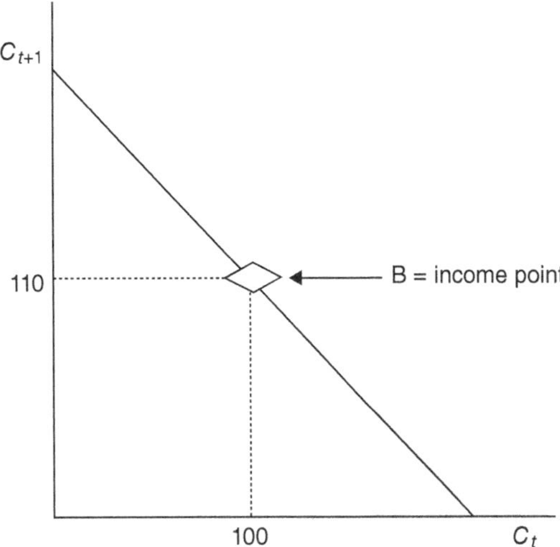

The consumer can choose a point of consumption anywhere on this intertemporal constraint.[13] In the current period, the agent can save by accumulating foreign bonds, and the agent can have negative saving by getting a loan from foreigners. The consumer's choice, based on the maximization of lifetime utility, ensures that the Euler equation for consumption holds:

$$u'(c_t) = \frac{(1+r_t^*)}{(1+\gamma)}\, u'(c_{t+1}),$$

where $u'(c)$ denotes the marginal utility of consumption and γ is the (fixed) marginal rate of time preference. If the foreign real interest rate equals the marginal rate of time preference, the consumer will smooth consumption. When there is consumption smoothing, the highest possible indifference curve (meaning the highest possible lifetime utility of the consumer, given the constraint imposed by the intertemporal budget constraint) is tangent to the intertemporal budget constraint on the 45° line (where c_t equals c_{t+1}).

The case of consumption smoothing is shown in Figure 5.2. Note that the income point is not on the 45° line. In the current period, after-tax real income is higher than consumption. If $y_t - T_t$ equals 100, $y_{t+1} - T_{t+1}$ equals 40, and r_t^* equals 0, the present value of lifetime after-tax real income is 140. With consumption smoothing, consumption equals 70 units in each period (the highest possible indifference curve, denoted V_0 in the figure, is tangent to the intertemporal budget constraint on the 45° line). With [$y_t - T_t$] greater than c_t, and with T_t equal to g_t, production y_t is greater than total domestic spending [$c_t + g_t$]. Net exports are therefore positive, equal to +30. The surplus on the balance of trade means that the domestic economy is accumulating foreign bonds. The domestic economy is saving in the current period, and this saving will allow future consumption to exceed future after-tax real income by 30 units.

Figure 5.2: Consumption smoothing

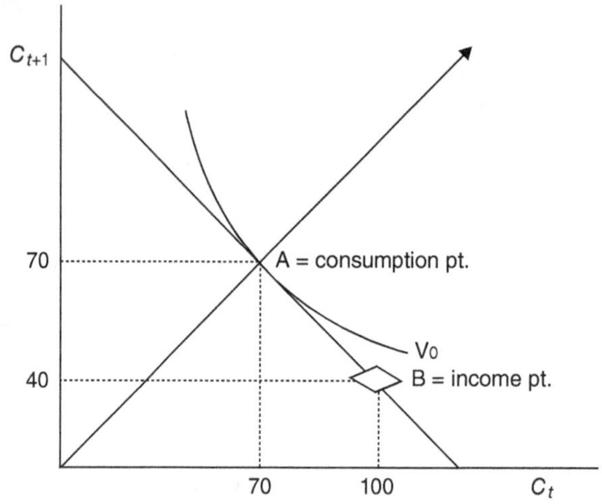

6. NET EXPORTS AND EXOGENOUS CHANGES IN OUTPUT

This section examines how net exports are affected by various exogenous changes: a temporary increase in output, a permanent increase in output, an increase in future output, and an increase in current and future output of different amounts.[14] It is assumed that the foreign real interest rate equals the marginal rate of time preference, so that consumption smoothing holds (for simplicity, r_t^* and γ equal 0). In the diagrams, the initial consumption point is denoted as A, the initial income point is B, the new consumption point is C, and the new income point is D. The initial income point is placed on the 45° line, so that (with the balanced budget assumption) net exports equal 0 in the initial situation.

Temporary Increase in Output

A temporary increase in output (real income) is defined as an increase in current output with no change in future output: Δy_t equals 10 and Δy_{t+1} equals 0 (taxes are held fixed). This temporary increase in real income increases lifetime after-tax real income. The income point changes from point B to point D in Figure 5.3, and the intertemporal budget constraint shifts out. The slope is the same, because the slope equals $-(1+r_t^*)$ and r_t^* is fixed.

The increase in current real income of 10 causes current consumption to increase by 5 units (the consumption point moves from A to C), as consumers will want to save to allow for the increase in future consumption. With current production increasing by 10 units and current consumption increasing by 5 units, the other 5 goods are exported. Net exports increase from 0 to +5, and the domestic economy acquires foreign currency worth 5 goods. Domestic residents convert the foreign currency into foreign bonds (also worth 5 goods). These foreign bonds are carried into period t+1, and allow future consumption to increase by 5 goods.

Figure 5.3: Temporary increase in output

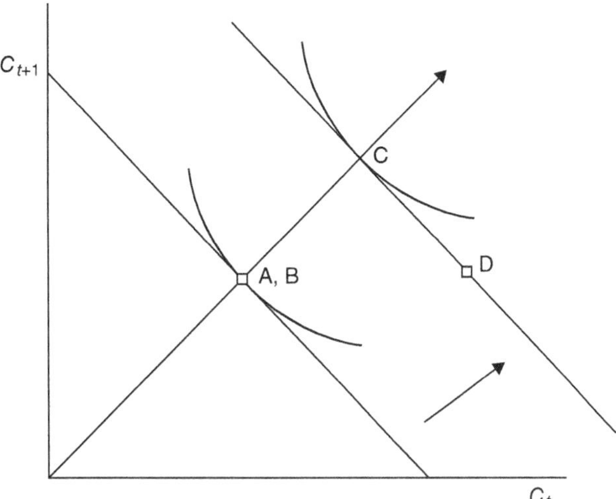

Permanent Increase in Output

A permanent increase in output is defined as an increase in both current and future output, with both variables increasing by the same amount (a diagram is not shown, but the new income point would be on the 45° line). There is an increase in lifetime after-tax real income, and the intertemporal budget constraint shifts out. Current consumption increases by the same amount as current-period real income, with no change in current-period saving. There is no need to save to smooth consumption, because the future increase in real income will allow for an increase in future consumption. Net exports and the current account balance are unchanged.

Increase in Future Output

Suppose there is an increase in future output, but current output does not change (Δy_t equals 0 and Δy_{t+1} equals 10). In Figure 5.4, the increase in lifetime after-tax real income shifts the budget constraint out with the new income point at D. Given the desire to smooth consumption, current consumption increases by 5 units. These goods must be imported, given that production is unchanged in the current period. Consumers get a foreign loan (at a real interest rate equal to 0) to increase current consumption, so that J_t is negative to match the balance of trade deficit. In the future period, the increase in future real income allows consumers to both pay back the loan and increase consumption by 5 units.

Is a Balance of Trade Deficit Bad?

Analysts sometimes regard a balance of trade deficit as bad, implying that the trade deficit must have arisen because domestic producers are not competitive on world markets. In this intertemporal model, this assertion is not correct. With the law of one price always holding in equilibrium,

Figure 5.4: Increase in future output

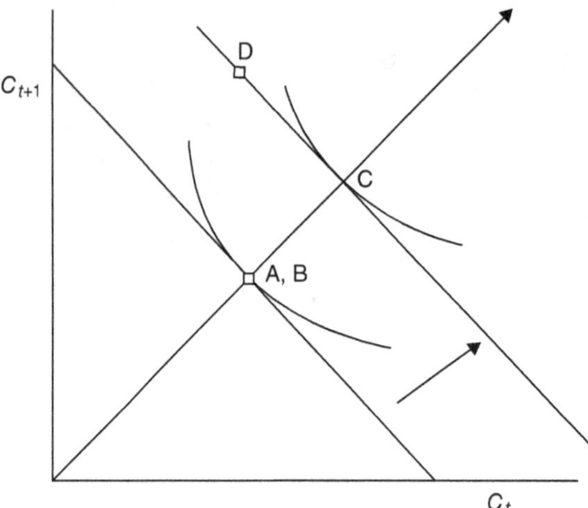

the existing domestic producers are competitive. If domestic prices are too high relative to foreign prices, the markets adjust – and induce changes in the exchange rate, prices, or both – such that the foreign good has the same price as the domestic good, when prices are measured in the same currency.

In the case just examined, the balance of trade deficit has allowed "the consumer" to reach the highest possible indifference curve (to maximize lifetime utility). The domestic economy could have kept current consumption at its initial level, and then increased future consumption by the full amount of the increase in future real income. In this case, the consumer would not have consumed on the 45° line, but at point D in Figure 5.4. If an indifference curve is drawn through point D, this indifference curve is lower than the indifference curve at point C. The balance of trade deficit, and the associated foreign loan, allows consumers to reallocate their consumption over time and thereby attain a higher level of lifetime utility.[15]

Increases in Current and Future Output of Different Amounts

Suppose current and future output increase by different amounts (unlike a permanent increase, where current and future output increase by the same amount). Suppose current output (current real income) increases by 8 and future output (future real income) increases by 32. In Figure 5.5, the new income point is at point D.

Lifetime after-tax real income increases by 40, so consumption increases by 20 in the current period. In the current period, consumers get a foreign loan of 12 units, spending these funds on consumer goods. In the future period, with an increase in future real income of 32, consumers can pay back the loan of 12 and increase future consumer spending by 20 units (consumption smoothing holds). Because current production increases by 8 and current spending increases by 20, these additional goods must be imported. Net exports equal −12 in the current period, and there is a balance of trade deficit.

Figure 5.5: Increase in current and future output

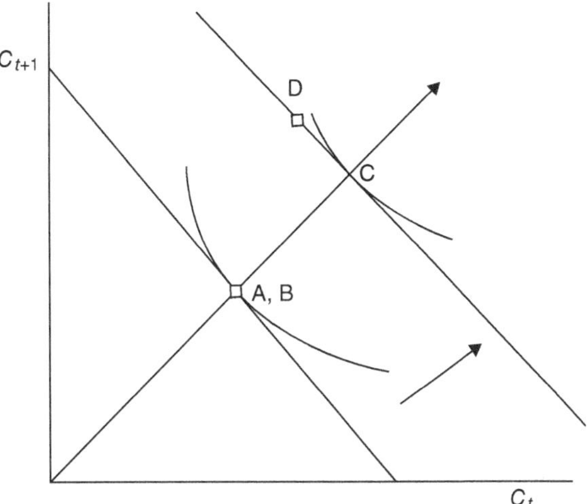

The marginal propensity to consume (MPC), measured as $\dfrac{\Delta c_t}{\Delta y_t}$, is not constant in the intertemporal model. With a temporary increase in output the MPC equals 0.5, whereas with a permanent increase the MPC equals 1. In the case just examined, current consumption increases by 20 and current-period real income increases by 8, so the MPC equals 2.5.

The Balance of Trade as a Shock Absorber

A temporary increase in output improves the balance of trade, and a temporary decrease in output worsens the trade balance.[16] The trade balance acts as a shock absorber. With fluctuations in output, private saving and the trade balance fluctuate but consumption is smoothed.

In a model with many periods, temporary changes in output have a small impact on lifetime after-tax real income and current consumption. With 41 periods and a temporary increase in real output of 123 units, current consumption increases by 3 units (r_t^* and γ equal 0) and the MPC is 0.024. With saving and net exports equal to 120 units in the current period, consumption can increase by 3 units in each of the next 40 periods. In a many-period model, temporary fluctuations in output have a large impact on private saving and the balance of trade.

7. BALANCED-BUDGET CHANGES IN TAXES AND GOVERNMENT SPENDING

Government spending provides benefits, or utility, to consumers. As an example, suppose that part of government spending is on public transit (provided free to users but financed out of taxes). The provision of this service yields utility to consumers. While lifetime utility depends on both consumer spending and government spending, the indifference curves in the diagrams capture only the utility associated with private consumption.[17] To discuss the welfare effects of changes in government spending, the utility that consumers derive from government spending would need to be properly accounted for in the analysis.

As the government budget is assumed to be balanced, any lump-sum tax change is matched by a change in government spending in the same period. The following exogenous changes are examined: a temporary tax cut, a permanent tax cut, and a decrease in future taxes.

Temporary Tax Cut

A temporary tax cut is defined as a decrease in current taxes, with no change in future taxes: ΔT_t equals -10 and ΔT_{t+1} equals 0. The tax cut is matched by a temporary cut in government spending.

The tax cut increases lifetime after-tax real income, and the intertemporal budget constraint shifts out (with the same slope). The diagram for a temporary tax cut is identical to Figure 5.3, the diagram for a temporary increase in output. In the figure, the temporary tax cut moves the income point from B to D. Because consumers want to smooth consumption, current consumption increases by 5 units. Net exports are determined as follows:

$$NX_t = y_t - c_t - g_t.$$

Because current government spending falls by 10 and production is fixed, there are 10 goods available for export. But as consumers increase spending by 5 units, only 5 goods will be exported. There is a balance of trade and current account surplus of 5 goods.

Permanent Tax Cut

Suppose the government cuts both current and future taxes by 10, and matches these tax cuts with cuts in government spending. Consumers experience an increase in lifetime after-tax real income. As lifetime after-tax real income increases by 20, current consumption increases by 10 and offsets the 10 unit decrease in current government spending. In total, the domestic economy is purchasing the same number of goods. Because current production is fixed, net exports and the current account balance are unaffected. Permanent changes in taxes matched by permanent changes in government spending have no effect on net exports or the current account.

Decrease in Future Taxes

Suppose the government holds current taxes and current government spending fixed, but announces cuts in future taxes and future government spending. The decrease in future taxes increases lifetime after-tax real income and shifts the intertemporal budget constraint out (the diagram is the same as in the case of an increase in future output). Consumers increase spending in the current period. As production and government spending are both fixed in the current period, the additional spending by consumers must be imported. Net exports are negative, and J_t is negative. Domestic residents must get a foreign loan to increase spending in the current period. In period t+1, consumers will use the funds associated with the period t+1 tax cut to both repay the loan and allow for the increase in future consumption. Consumers therefore ensure that there is a smoothed consumption path.

8. A DECREASE IN CURRENT TAXES MATCHED BY AN INCREASE IN FUTURE TAXES

Consider a case where the government budget is not balanced. Suppose there is a tax cut in the current period, and assume there is no change in government spending in either period. There is a government budget deficit in the current period, and the government finances this deficit by selling new domestic bonds to the public. In the future period, the government will have to pay principal and interest on the bonds sold in the current period (let the domestic real interest rate, like the foreign real rate, equal 0). Because government spending has been held fixed in both the current and future periods, it follows that future taxes will have to increase. If the government decreases taxes by 10 in the current period, the government will have to increase taxes by 10 in the future period (if the interest rate equals 0.10, a tax cut of 10 in period t implies a tax increase of 11 in period t+1).

These tax changes have no effect on lifetime after-tax real income. The intertemporal budget constraint is

$$y_t - T_t + \frac{y_{t+1} - T_{t+1}}{1 + r_t} = c_t + \frac{c_{t+1}}{1 + r_t}.$$

With lifetime after-tax real income not affected, and with an unchanged real interest rate, consumption is not affected. Consumers save the entire amount of the cut in taxes, to be able to pay for the future tax increase without having to decrease future consumption.[18] This result is known as the Ricardian equivalence theorem.[19]

Are net exports affected? As net exports in the current period are

$$NX_t = y_t - c_t - g_t,$$

net exports are not affected because c_t is unchanged and both y_t and g_t are fixed. Likewise, net exports equal

$$NX_t = S_t^{priv} + T_t - g_t.$$

This identity also indicates that net exports are not affected. While $T_t - g_t$ is negative with the tax cut, meaning the government has a budget deficit, *desired* private saving increases from 0 to 10. The tax cut of 10 increases private saving by 10, meaning all of the tax cut is saved. The consumer willingly purchases the newly issued government bonds to be able to pay for the future tax increase of 10. The decrease in government saving is offset by an increase in private saving.

9. FISCAL POLICY AND NET EXPORTS

How do fiscal policy changes affect consumption and net exports? Is the tax cut a temporary tax cut, a permanent tax cut, a future tax cut, or a current tax cut matched by a future tax increase? Each tax change has a different effect, and any changes in current and future government spending must also be specified. Only when the details are specified can a proper analysis be conducted.

In some other models, income tax cuts (matched by future tax increases) do cause a worsening of both the government budget and current account deficits.[20] But observing "twin deficits" is not necessarily inconsistent with the predictions of the model in this chapter. If there is both a temporary increase in government spending and an income tax cut, the model predicts a worsening of both the government budget and current account deficits. The income tax cut does not affect the current account, but the temporary increase in government spending does.[21] To conduct a proper test of whether tax changes affect the current account, the analysis must account for changes in government spending (as well as the types of tax changes).[22]

Conducting valid empirical testing of economic theories is often wrought with various difficulties. On another problem that arises in many situations, see the appendix on the "Lucas critique."

10. CHANGES IN THE FOREIGN REAL INTEREST RATE

Suppose that, initially, both r_t^* and γ equal 0 per cent, and then r_t^* increases to 10 per cent (with current and future after-tax real income held fixed). The slope of the intertemporal budget constraint becomes steeper, having changed from -1.0 to -1.1, and the line for the constraint goes through the unchanged income point (the diagram is not shown). With the foreign real interest equal to 10 per cent, and greater than the fixed marginal rate of time preference, consumers desire a consumption path that has consumption increasing over time. The higher real return on foreign bonds provides consumers with an incentive to increase current-period saving. Consumers respond by decreasing current-period consumption and increasing saving (the consumption point is no longer on the 45° line). With current output fixed and a decrease in current consumption, net exports increase. The domestic economy moves from a balanced current account to a current account surplus, and domestic consumers accumulate foreign bonds to allow for the future increase in consumption.

11. THE BALANCE OF TRADE IN CANADA, 2007–2011

In the first quarter of 2007, Canada had a balance of trade surplus of about $50 billion (a significant amount, equal to about 3 per cent of Canada's GDP).[23] However, the trade balance moved into a deficit by 2009 and remained in deficit in 2010 and 2011 (see Figure 5.6).

What caused the worsening of the balance of trade over this period? In terms of the model, each of the following changes could have played a role in the decrease in net exports: there was a temporary decrease in real output, associated with the 2009 recession, that caused net exports to fall; the government implemented a temporary policy of increased government spending, and this policy caused net exports to fall;[24] and the fall in the US real interest rate caused the Canadian real interest rate to fall and induced a decrease in Canadian saving and the balance of trade.

While these comments are suggestive of some important factors, a more detailed analysis is required to discriminate between these and other possible factors. This issue is addressed in the next chapter, where a more detailed analysis of trade balance determination is undertaken for this period. In addition, the applied exercise in Data Analytics examines the relationship between output fluctuations and net exports over the period since 2012.

Figure 5.6: Net exports in Canada

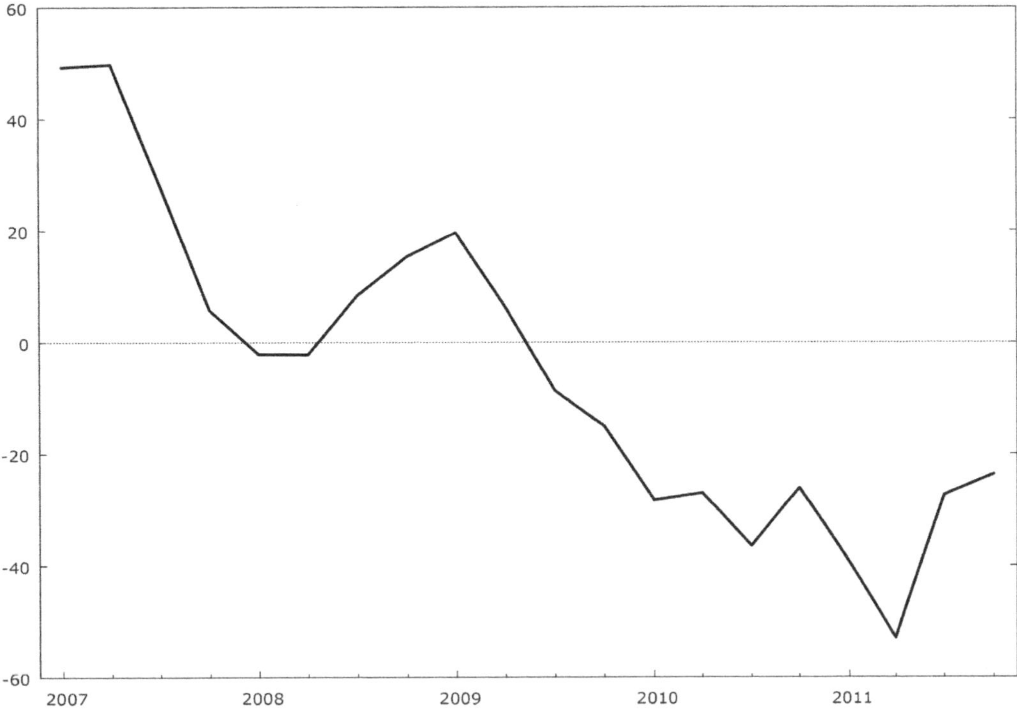

Data source: Statistics Canada

12. INVESTMENT SPENDING, FUTURE OUTPUT, AND NET EXPORTS

While this chapter abstracted from investment spending, this section provides a concise analysis of investment spending and net exports (the next chapter provides a detailed analysis).

Suppose that investment spending increases from zero to a positive number. With positive investment spending in period t, the capital stock (K) increases such that K_{t+1} is greater than K_t (for simplicity, the rate of depreciation on capital is assumed to equal zero). That is, in period t+1, the capital stock is higher (purchases of new machines in the current period are not able to be used in the production process until the future period). With more machines in the future period, production will be higher. Current-period investment spending results in an increase in future production.

How does the increase in I_t and the corresponding increase in y_{t+1} affect net exports in the current period? The identity for net exports is

$$NX_t = y_t - c_t - I_t - g_t.$$

Investment spending and consumer spending increase in the current period. Consumer spending increases because the increase in future output increases lifetime after-tax real income. As production and government spending are fixed, the increases in investment spending and consumer spending must be imported. These changes generate a balance of trade deficit, meaning that net exports are negative.

This trade balance deficit is not bad. The additional imports of consumer goods in the current period are caused by the increase in lifetime after-tax real income. The increased spending allows consumers to smooth consumption and attain a higher level of lifetime utility. Likewise, the imports of machines associated with the increase in investment spending are not bad, as these imports generate the increase in future output.

13. CONCLUSION

The intertemporal approach to net exports and the current account is the predominant approach used by international macroeconomists. In the model depicted in this chapter, net exports and the current account balance are affected by temporary changes in output and government spending, by future changes in output and government spending, and by changes in the foreign real interest rate.[25]

The intertemporal model can be extended by incorporating the production and investment spending decisions of firms (based on the assumption that firms maximize lifetime profit), by including a more realistic tax structure with taxes on goods and factor incomes, and by modeling the demand for money and the central bank's monetary policy framework. The model could also be generalized in terms of the different goods in the economy, by incorporating non-traded goods or multiple traded goods.[26] Such generalizations are undertaken in future chapters.[27] The theoretical analyses, in conjunction with empirical evidence, will allow us to better understand movements in the current account balance and other macroeconomic variables.

PRACTICE QUESTIONS

1. (a) Using identities, show that net exports equal private saving less investment spending (with a balanced government budget and the initial net foreign debt equal to 0).
   (b) Explain why the analysis of net exports is best done in an intertemporal (dynamic) model.
   (c) Explain why a depreciation of the domestic currency has no effect on net exports in this model.
2. Using the intertemporal budget constraint-indifference curve diagram (with income and consumption points), show a case where net exports are positive. Assume that the foreign real interest rate is 0 per cent and the consumer is smoothing consumption. Would it be better for consumption to be at the income point on the diagram? Why does it make sense to save even though the foreign real interest rate is equal to 0 per cent? Explain.

3. Fill in the blanks
   (a) For the domestic good, the quantity produced equals the sum of consumer spending on the domestic good, investment spending on the domestic good, government spending on the domestic good, and ______.
   (b) If initial net foreign assets equal 0, the debt service balance equals 0 and the current account balance equals ______.
   (c) In this one-good model, the current-period exchange rate equals the current-period domestic price level divided by current-period ______. This result is based on the law of ______ condition.
   (d) A temporary increase in output causes consumer spending to ______ and net exports to ______ in the current period.
   (e) With a permanent increase in output, the current account ______. The marginal propensity to consume equals ______.

4. Fill in the blanks
   (a) A future increase in output causes consumer spending to ______ and net exports to fall in the current period. In the new equilibrium, lifetime utility is ______.
   (b) Assume the government budget is always balanced. A temporary decrease in government spending results in ______ lifetime after-tax real income and causes net exports to ______ in the current period.
   (c) The foreign real interest rate and the marginal rate of time preference equal 0 per cent, and trade is initially balanced. If current output increases by 40 and future output increases by 20, current-period consumption increases by ______ and net exports equal ______ in the current period.
   (d) Suppose current taxes fall by 10 and future taxes increase by 10 (let the real interest rate equal 0, and hold current and future government spending fixed). In the current period, private saving ______ and the current account ______.
   (e) Between mid-2008 and mid-2009, net exports in Canada ______. In terms of the intertemporal theory of net exports, this may have been caused by a ______ decrease in output.

5. Using the intertemporal theory of net exports (with the diagram and numbers), explain how a temporary increase in output affects current-period consumption and net exports (also explain what happens to future consumption).

6. Using the intertemporal theory of net exports (with the diagram and numbers), explain how an increase in current real income of 34 and an increase of future real income of 6 affects consumer spending and net exports in the current period.

7. Assuming the government budget is always balanced, how does a decrease in future taxes affect net exports and the foreign debt of consumers in the current period? Explain using the diagram for the intertemporal approach to net exports.

DATA ANALYTICS

1. Access CANSIM Table 380-0064 (now labeled Table 36100104) and download quarterly data on exports, imports, and real GDP over the period since the first quarter of 2012. Create two series – net exports and cyclical real GDP – with the latter defined as real GDP less trend real GDP. Let trend real GDP in 2012:1 equal real GDP in 2012:1, and then let trend real GDP increase by 0.47545 per cent per quarter. Plot real GDP and trend real GDP on the same plot and cyclical real GDP on a separate plot. Comment.
2. Plot net exports and cyclical real GDP on the same plot (but measured on different axes). Comment on whether there is any relationship between the variables.

APPENDIX A: EMPIRICAL AND MODELING ISSUES IN THE LAW OF ONE PRICE

With the domestic good assumed to be identical to the foreign good, and with zero transport costs and no tariffs or other impediments to international trade, the law of one price holds:

$$P_t = s_t \, P_t^*.$$

But many goods and services are non-traded, where the domestic price is not linked to the exchange rate-adjusted foreign price (restaurant meals and haircuts are but two examples). In addition, there are many traded goods where the domestic and foreign goods are not identical (to provide one example, the foreign good could be a lower-quality version of the domestic good).[28] Empirical studies of the law of one price are hampered by various data and measurement problems related to these and other issues. In a study by Statistics Canada, Baldwin and Yan (2004) find that the empirical evidence is supportive of the law of one price for traded goods in the Canadian–US case, when the traded goods closely fit the description identical goods (further comments on sectoral decomposition and empirical studies are provided in Chapter 10).[29]

While the law of one price may hold for identical traded goods, international macroeconomists know that the aggregate price level may not equal the exchange rate-adjusted aggregate foreign price level when these aggregate price levels include the prices of all goods and services. The single-good model, where the price of the single good is the same as the aggregate price level, is adopted as a convenient simplification. But it is essential to develop an understanding of how the economy operates in a world with non-traded goods and multiple traded goods (where domestic and foreign traded goods may be differentiated products). These multi-sectoral models, examined in a series of chapters, are an integral component in the toolkit of international macroeconomists.

APPENDIX B: NET EXPORTS, THE DEBT SERVICE BALANCE, AND THE CURRENT ACCOUNT

If the consumer begins period t with foreign bonds carried over from the previous period, the variable J_{t-1} is positive. If the consumer starts period t with an outstanding foreign debt, J_{t-1} is negative. The current-period budget constraint is

$$y_t - T_t + r^*_{t-1} J_{t-1} = c_t + J_t - J_{t-1}.$$

The consumer earns (or pays) interest on the stock of foreign bonds (or foreign loans) held at the start of period t, with these foreign interest earnings (or foreign interest payments) denoted by $r^*_{t-1} J_{t-1}$. Letting taxes equal government spending and rearranging yields the constraint on the economy in the case of a balanced government budget (and with zero investment spending):

$$[y_t - c_t - g_t] + r^*_{t-1} J_{t-1} = J_t - J_{t-1}.$$

This equation is the balance of payments identity. The term in square brackets is net exports and the term $r^*_{t-1} J_{t-1}$ is the debt service balance (denoted DSB).[30] The left-hand side equals the current account balance. The term on the right-hand side equals the net accumulation of foreign assets by domestic residents, which equals net capital outflows (denoted NCO) in balance of payments accounting.[31] Therefore, this equation is

$$CA_t = NX_t + DSB_t = NCO_t.$$

The theoretical analysis assumed that the agent begins period t with a zero net foreign debt (J_{t-1} equals 0). Suppose, instead, that J_{t-1} equals -60, so the agent begins period t with an obligation to repay foreign debts acquired in earlier periods. In this case, current period consumption is determined as follows (assume that r^*_t and γ equal 0):

$$c_t = \frac{1}{2} \left[J_{t-1} + y_t - T_t + y_{t+1} - T_{t+1} \right].$$

If J_{t-1} equals -60 and the present value of lifetime after-tax real income equals 200, current consumption equals 70 in this two-period model. The agent's lifetime after-tax earnings are 200, but she must repay the foreign debt of 60. Therefore, the consumer only has 140 to spread over the two periods. Based on these numbers, the high net foreign debt places a serious constraint on the magnitude of consumer spending going forward. For example, suppose real income less taxes equals 100 in both periods, and the budget is always balanced. With consumption equal to 70 in each period, net exports are positive in both periods (whereas with zero initial net foreign debt, a trade surplus in one period is matched by a trade deficit in the other period).

And if a country begins the current period with positive net foreign assets (positive J_{t-1}), the country may run trade deficits in both periods. These results need to be considered when examining trade balances in various countries.

APPENDIX C: THE LUCAS CRITIQUE

Robert E. Lucas won the Nobel Prize in Economics in 1995. Professor Lucas made significant contributions to macroeconomics, with many insights derived from analyses in intertemporal, choice-theoretic models. One important insight was that a change in government policy behavior (a change in policy regime) changes private-sector behavior such that statistical models based on one regime may generate incorrect predictions when used in a different regime. This insight is known as the Lucas Critique (Lucas 1976).

Consider a hypothetical example based on consumption (assume that the intertemporal theory of consumption holds). Suppose the existing income tax regime is such that taxes tend to fall one period and increase the next, with no net effect on lifetime after-tax real income. These tax fluctuations are well understood by consumers, and form the basis of their understanding of the current tax regime. Under this regime, consumers do not change spending in response to tax changes since lifetime after-tax real income is not affected.

But suppose a new government comes to power and announces a permanent cut in income taxes (along with a permanent cut in government spending). And suppose the public believes that the government will implement this tax change. Under this new regime, consumers will increase spending in response to the cut in taxes, because the tax change is regarded as permanent. The regime change will change consumer behavior.

Consider the hazards of using a statistical (or econometric) analysis, along with an older-style Keynesian consumption function where consumer spending depends only on current-period real income and current-period taxes. When the parameters of the model are estimated using the existing data (all from the previous regime), the statistical results will suggest that tax changes have no effect (or a small effect) on consumer spending. If the model is used to predict future consumer spending under the new regime, the predictions will underestimate consumer spending. The model will not have accounted for the regime change and the change in behavior.

The change in behavior is incorporated *within* the intertemporal theory of consumption, so that an empirical analysis based on it would work well. But an older-style model of consumption would generate incorrect predictions of future levels of consumer spending.

NOTES

1   The intertemporal approach to the current account is discussed in Obstfeld and Rogoff (1995b) and Gourinchas and Rey (2014). The seminal literature includes, among others, Sachs (1981), Stockman (1983), and Greenwood (1983). The approach is based on dynamic models with optimizing agents but encompasses many alternative specifications. The model in this chapter is a relatively simple version within this family of models.

2   Exports and imports could be 8 and 2, 27 and 21, or any combination where the difference, net exports, is 6.

3   Government debt is assumed to equal 0, so there is no interest on the debt in the period.

4   There are no transport costs, tariffs, or sales taxes.

5   If the domestic good is cheaper, everyone will want to buy it. Foreigner consumers will try to buy domestic currency, and the domestic currency appreciates. Or domestic firms realize they can increase

the domestic price and still sell their production. These changes continue until the law of one price holds as an equality.

6 Real income, or nominal income divided by the price level, is fixed. If the price level changes and real income is fixed, nominal income has also changed to keep real income unchanged.

7 See, for example, Rogoff (1996).

8 For example, changes in the price of non-traded goods can cause the consumer price index to change yet there may be no effect on the exchange rate. These matters are discussed in Chapters 10, 11, 12, and 14. For the Canadian-US dollar exchange rate, and indeed many exchange rates, the deviations from PPP are large and persistent.

9 The Fisher equation links the nominal interest rate to the real interest rate and the inflation rate.

10 All variables are measured in real terms, so taxes denote real taxes. Real taxes are taxes in dollars divided by the price level, and measure the number of goods that could be purchased with the dollars.

11 With this assumption, net exports equal the current account balance in the current period.

12 This equation sets J_{t+1} equal to 0, since t+1 is the final period.

13 This chapter assumes that the reader has an understanding of utility, lifetime utility, indifference curves, and the Euler equation. These topics are discussed in Chapter 4, Sections 3, 4, and 5.

14 These exogenous changes are news, in that they were not previously expected to occur. But going forward, there is perfect foresight. The consumer knows the levels of real income and taxes in both the current and future periods. The same approach is adopted by, for example, Blanchard (2007).

15 The trade deficit may be regarded as bad because of the implied increase in foreign debt of domestic residents. But, in this model, these increases in foreign debt are undertaken on a rational basis and allow domestic consumers to undertake a desired increase in current-period consumption. For an advanced analysis of current account imbalances and lifetime utility, see (for example) the discussion in Blanchard (2007).

16 This sentence uses the verbs improves and worsens. This terminology is standard in international economics, but the words increases and decreases may be more appropriate.

17 Lifetime utility, denoted V, depends on consumption (denoted c) and real government expenditure (denoted g): $V = u\left(c_t\right) + u\left(g_t\right) + \dfrac{u\left(c_{t+1}\right) + u\left(g_{t+1}\right)}{1+\gamma}$. Preferences are assumed to be separable, implying that changes in g affect utility through u(g) but have no direct effect on the utility of consumption (have no effect on the u(c) function).

18 If current consumption did increase, future consumption would have to fall. Lifetime utility would be lower.

19 On Ricardian equivalence and the effects of tax changes on consumption in general, see (for example) Aschauer (1988), Barro (1989), and Abel (1990). For an advanced quantitative analysis of Ricardian equivalence, see Barczyk (2016).

20 The current account falls because the tax cut does increase consumer spending. See, for example, the discussion in Obstfeld and Rogoff (1995b).

21 For empirical studies on the effects of fiscal policy changes on consumption and the current account balance, see (for example) Leiderman and Razin (1988, 1991). Boothe and Reid (1989) examine the effects of fiscal and monetary variables on asset returns in Canada.

22 One may need to not only account for aggregate government spending, but to differentiate between government spending on traded and non-traded goods (see Chapter 14). Likewise, different tax changes can have very different effects. Changes in sales taxes affect consumption, and temporary or future changes in sales taxes cause changes in the current account balance. Suppose the government cuts the current-period sales tax rate, and raises the future-period sales tax rate such that there is no effect on the present value of lifetime taxes. Holding other factors fixed, these sales tax changes decrease the relative price of the current-period good, inducing an increase in current consumption and a fall in future consumption. For an empirical study that examines a temporary sales tax change, see Agarwal et al. (2017).

23 Export and import data (chained 2007 dollars) are from CANSIM Table 380-0064, now Table 36100104.

24 The government was attempting to stimulate the economy during the recession. In this intertemporal model, increases in government spending do not affect production.

25 Empirical studies based on a model similar to that in this chapter include Ahmed (1986), Pasula (1997), and Hoffmann (2013). See also Obstfeld and Rogoff (1995b) and the empirical references in Chapter 6.

26 Chapters 10, 11, 12, and 14 outline a macroeconomic approach based on modeling the economy in a multi-sectoral framework.

27 For an advanced discussion of issues related to sovereign debt, see Aguiar and Amador (2014).

28 Some goods may be transformed from traded goods to non-traded goods when services or other non-traded components are encompassed within the product. For example, cattle may be regarded as a traded good, but a steak in a restaurant becomes a non-traded good (with no tight link to the price of steak in foreign restaurants). That many retail goods have this feature was emphasized by Harrod (1939, 55). For related comments by contemporary international economists, see (for example) Obstfeld and Rogoff (2000, 373) and Crucini and Landry (2019, 86-87).

29 John Maynard Keynes (1923, 74) made the following point a century ago: "If we restrict ourselves to articles entering into international trade and make exact allowance for transport and tariff costs, we should find that the theory is always in accordance with the facts, with perhaps a short time-lag." Keynes' views on the PPP hypothesis, based on aggregate price levels, are discussed in Chapter 8.

30 For further discussion of the debt service balance, see Chapters 5 and 6 in Frenkel and Razin (1987).

31 The current account balance equals net capital outflows plus the balance of payments, where the latter variable equals changes in the central bank's stock of foreign exchange reserves. Under a flexible exchange rate, with no central bank intervention in the foreign exchange market, the balance of payments equals zero.

CHAPTER 6

Investment Spending, Production, and the Intertemporal Approach to the Current Account

1. INTRODUCTION

What determines the current account balance or the balance of trade in a small open economy? This chapter extends the intertemporal approach to the current account by incorporating investment spending into the analysis. The setup of the model is the same, except for two important changes. First, investment spending is introduced, meaning that domestic firms (owned by domestic residents) can accumulate capital over time. Second, production is an endogenous variable, and changes in production are caused by exogenous changes in total factor productivity and other exogenous changes that induce changes in the capital stock (the quantity of labor is assumed to be fixed). Apart from that, the structure is unchanged. There are two periods with perfect foresight of future variables, consumers maximize lifetime utility, domestic and foreign goods are identical, and the domestic economy is small.[1]

An implication of the model is that, in equilibrium, both the domestic marginal product of capital and the domestic real interest rate equal the real interest rate in the large foreign economy. This condition implies that fluctuations in domestic saving and domestic investment spending have no effect on the domestic real interest rate. With a fixed real interest rate, fluctuations in domestic saving and investment affect the balance of trade and current account balance.

The exchange rate can be regarded as being flexible, but the determinants of the current account balance are the same whether the exchange rate is fixed or flexible.[2] With the law of one price holding, the nominal exchange rate is not a determinant of the current account. Movements in the current account balance are caused strictly by real variables, such as changes in total factor productivity, government spending, and the foreign real interest rate.

It should be noted that the model forms the basis of both the neoclassical model of long-term growth and the one-sector real business cycle (RBC) model. Researchers may also model labor supply and demand to generate variable employment and real wage rates. This core setup, which embeds lifetime utility maximization for consumers and lifetime profit maximization for firms, is now a standard framework in both open-economy macroeconomics and macroeconomics in general. Learning this material may therefore improve understanding of other topics in macroeconomics.[3]

2. PRELIMINARIES

Representative Agent and Representative Firm

Macroeconomic analysis often relies on the abstraction of a representative agent in developing the principles that guide consumers in the economy. The terms consumer, consumers, and agent are used interchangeably to represent consumers. Likewise, the analysis of the competitive firm applies to all firms in the domestic economy.

Net Exports and the Current Account Balance

Net exports equal exports minus imports. The term net exports is synonymous with the balance of trade. The current account balance equals net exports plus the debt service balance. When the initial net foreign assets of the domestic economy equal zero, the debt service balance equals zero and net exports equal the current account balance.

Notation for Stocks

Variables that are stocks can be measured at a point in time. Money and bonds are examples of *financial* stock variables, and the quantity of machines (or capital) is a *real* stock variable.

The following notation is used throughout the book. For financial variables like foreign bonds (denoted as J), the agent starts period t with J_{t-1}, chooses J_t in period t, and carries J_t into period t+1. The same timing convention is used for other financial variables, such as domestic bonds and money. For real variables like the capital stock (denoted K), a different convention is used. The agent (or the firm the agent owns) starts period t with K_t, chooses K_{t+1} in period t, and carries K_{t+1} into period t+1.

3. PRODUCTION, INVESTMENT SPENDING, AND CAPITAL ACCUMULATION

The quantity of goods and services produced (or real GDP, denoted as y) depends on the factors of production, labor and capital, as well as on the level of total factor productivity. Labor (denoted as L) is measured as the number of workers or the number of hours worked. The stock of capital (denoted as K) represents the number of machines (or, in general, represents machines, equipment, buildings, and so on). Total factor productivity (denoted as A) depends on other factors that affect production besides capital and labor, such as the skills of workers, the quality of machines, and a number of other factors.

The production function represents the maximum amount of production that can be derived from given quantities of the two factors of production, at a fixed level of total factor productivity. In general, the production function is written as follows (where f means "is a function of"):

$$y_t = f\left(A_t, K_t\right),$$

where labor is assumed to be fixed and is omitted. The variable A is exogenous (fixed, but can change exogenously). The capital stock is given in period t but can be adjusted over time.

Firms choose the capital stock so as to maximize lifetime profit. The capital stock evolves over time because of investment spending and depreciation. The change in the capital stock is

$$K_{t+1} - K_t = I_t - \delta K_t,$$

where I is investment spending and the parameter δ denotes the constant depreciation rate. If δ equals 0.10, 10 per cent of existing machines are discarded at the end of the period (they are worn out and can no longer be used in production). For simplicity, δ is assumed to equal 0, so that investment spending equals the change in the capital stock.

For the economy as a whole, the accumulation of machines provides an additional avenue to shift consumption into the future period. By decreasing consumer spending and increasing investment spending in the current period, the economy has higher future production and higher future consumption.

The production function exhibits the property of a diminishing marginal product for each factor. As one factor increases – holding the other factor fixed – production always increases, but the increase in production becomes smaller as that factor increases to higher levels. The marginal product of capital is denoted $f'(K)$ and is defined as

$$f'(K) = \frac{\Delta y}{\Delta K}.$$

As capital increases, $f'(K)$ falls. Capital, like labor, experiences a diminishing marginal product.[4] In addition, the marginal product of capital depends on the level of total factor productivity. At any given level of the capital stock, an increase in total factor productivity increases the marginal product of capital.

4. BUDGET CONSTRAINTS

For simplicity, domestic bonds and domestic money are ignored (these variables are assumed to be fixed). The only financial asset available for saving is a foreign bond, denoted as J, but domestic residents can also save through the accumulation of the real asset "capital." The analysis abstracts from price and exchange rate changes and writes the budget constraints in real terms. The relative price of investment goods, in terms of consumer goods, is assumed to equal 1.[5] For simplicity, it is assumed that the domestic capital stock is owned by domestic firms, and domestic firms are owned by domestic residents. Likewise, domestic residents do not own any capital located in the foreign economy.

While one could formally model the investment decisions of firms, it is convenient to add the investment spending decision to the consumer's problem (an appendix outlines the case where a representative firm chooses capital to maximize the present value of lifetime profit).

Current-Period Household Budget Constraint

After-tax real income in the current period is denoted as $y_t - T_t$, where y denotes real income (and output) and T denotes (real) lump-sum taxes. If the stock of foreign bonds at the start of period t, denoted as J_{t-1}, is nonzero, the consumer may have foreign interest earnings or foreign interest payments. The consumer can purchase consumer goods (denoted as c_t) and investment goods (denoted as I_t), and can increase or decrease the quantity of foreign bonds holdings:

$$y_t - T_t + r^*_{t-1} J_{t-1} = c_t + I_t + J_t - J_{t-1},$$

where J_t denotes the stock of foreign bonds at the end of period t and r* denotes the foreign real interest rate. From the perspective of the consumer (who owns the domestic firms), there are two ways to save. The consumer can save by acquiring foreign bonds, and the consumer can save by acquiring investment goods (new machines). A decrease in consumption in the current period allows the consumer to purchase an asset, either foreign bonds or capital, and therefore allows for higher future consumption. The consumer can also get a loan to spend more than after-tax real income. Since "the consumer" represents all domestic residents, the only way to get a loan is to get one from foreigners.[6]

The variables c and I include both domestic purchases and imports. Domestic and foreign goods are assumed to be identical, so domestic goods and imported goods have the same price (when measured in the same currency).

This household budget constraint can be written as

$$f\left(A_t, K_t\right) - T_t + r^*_{t-1} J_{t-1} = c_t + K_{t+1} - K_t + J_t - J_{t-1},$$

where real income has been replaced with the production function and investment spending has been replaced by the change in the capital stock (with the rate of depreciation equal to 0). Note the different notation for the stock variables:

- at the start of period t, the agent has J_{t-1} units of foreign bonds and K_t units of capital;
- the agent chooses J_t and K_{t+1} in period t and carries these stocks into the start of t+1.

In the analysis, the following simplifications are adopted: all domestic capital is owned by domestic residents, domestic residents do not own any foreign capital, and the variable J_{t-1} equals 0. With these assumptions, consumers begin period t with no foreign assets and no foreign debts. Net exports equal the current account balance in the current period, and domestic production equals domestic real income.

Future Household Budget Constraint

In period t+1, the consumer earns after-tax real income $[y_{t+1} - T_{t+1}]$. But the consumer may also earn interest on the foreign bond or pay interest on a foreign loan. The period t+1 constraint is[7]

$$f(A_{t+1}, K_{t+1}) - T_{t+1} + \left(1 + r_t^*\right) J_t = c_{t+1} + K_{t+2} - K_{t+1},$$

where r_t^* is the foreign real interest rate and y_{t+1} has been replaced with the production function $f(A_{t+1,} K_{t+1})$. If J_t equals 10, for example, and the real interest rate equals 0.10 (or 10 per cent), the principal and interest will allow for the purchase of an additional 11 goods in period t+1 (there is no tax on interest earnings). Through saving or dissaving, the consumer is able to shift consumption between periods. Likewise, the agent carries K_{t+1} units of capital into the start of period t+1. This capital is used to produce goods in period t+1, so that purchasing additional capital in period t (an increase in K_{t+1}) allows for more future consumption.[8]

Government Budget Constraints

The government follows a balanced budget, with lump-sum taxes always adjusting to equal government spending in the period:

$$g_t = T_t,$$

$$g_{t+1} = T_{t+1}.$$

Intertemporal Constraints

The intertemporal household budget constraint merges the current and future period household budget constraints:

$$c_{t+1} = y_{t+1} - T_{t+1} - I_{t+1} + \left(1 + r_t^*\right)\left[y_t - T_t - c_t - I_t\right].$$

Using the government budget constraints, the production functions, and the link between investment spending and capital accumulation yields the intertemporal constraint on the economy:[9]

$$c_{t+1} = f\left(A_{t+1,} K_{t+1}\right) - g_{t+1} + K_{t+1} + \left(1 + r_t^*\right)\left[f\left(A_t, K_t\right) - g_t - c_t - \left(K_{t+1} - K_t\right)\right].$$

5. THE CURRENT-PERIOD CONSTRAINT ON THE ECONOMY

Merging the current-period government and household budget constraints yields the current-period constraint on the economy:

$$y_t - c_t - I_t - g_t = J_t.$$

The left-hand side of this equation equals net exports (NX) and the current account balance (CA). This equation is the balance of payments identity, and can be rewritten as

$$NX_t = CA_t = y_t - c_t - I_t - g_t = S_t^{priv} + \left[T_t - g_t\right] - I_t = J_t,$$

where private saving is defined as

$$S_t^{priv} = y_t - c_t - T_t,$$

and where government saving equals taxes less government spending. Private saving plus government saving, or national saving, equals

$$S_t^{nat} = \left[y_t - c_t - T_t\right] + \left[T_t - g_t\right] = y_t - c_t - g_t.$$

The current account balance equals three different items: domestic production minus total spending (the sum of consumer spending, investment spending, and government spending in the domestic economy);[10] private saving plus government saving less investment spending (or national saving less investment spending); and the net accumulation of foreign assets by domestic residents.

With the assumption of a balanced budget, the identity becomes

$$NX_t = CA_t = S_t^{priv} - I_t = J_t.$$

The current account balance (net exports) in the current period equals the accumulation of foreign bonds, or J_t when J_{t-1} is equal to 0. The current account balance equals private saving less investment spending. Movements in the current account balance can be interpreted as being caused by factors that cause changes in saving and changes in investment. Domestic residents can save by accumulating foreign bonds ($J_t > 0$) or by accumulating machines ($I_t > 0$).

The current account balance is an intertemporal phenomenon. Both saving and investment spending are inherently intertemporal in nature. Given this identity, one can argue that a valid theory of the current account balance must be based on an *intertemporal* analysis.[11]

6. THE DEMAND FOR CAPITAL

The capital stock at the start of period t, K_t, is given, determined by conditions in previous periods. In the current period, firms choose investment spending, the number of new machines to purchase, which means that firms are choosing K_{t+1} (the amount of capital taken into period t+1). Current-period purchases of capital can only be used in production in the following period.

The competitive firms maximize lifetime profit. A condition of lifetime profit maximization is that firms choose capital such that the marginal product of capital equals the foreign real interest rate (a derivation is provided in an appendix):

Figure 6.1: Future marginal product

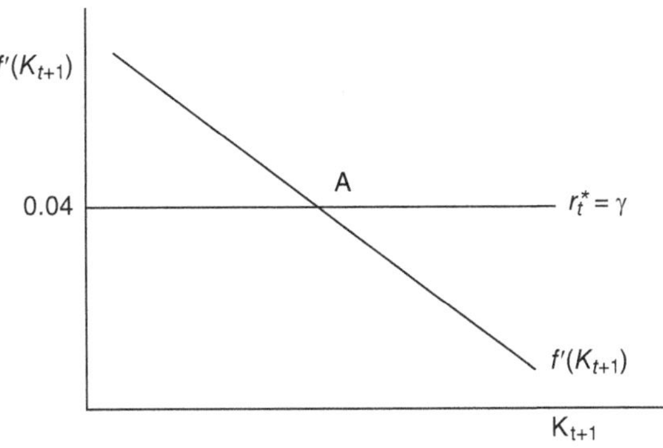

$$f'\left(K_{t+1}\right) = r_t^*.$$

A firm can borrow at the foreign real interest rate (say 4 per cent) and use the funds to purchase new machines. If the marginal product exceeds 4 per cent, the increase in future production generates a real return for the firm that is greater than 4 per cent. The firm would therefore have an incentive to increase the capital stock and would continue doing so until the marginal product of capital is reduced to a level equal to the foreign real interest rate. Thus, in equilibrium, the equality holds.[12]

All domestic firms are owned by domestic residents, and the maximization of lifetime utility by consumers is also consistent with a choice of K_{t+1} where the marginal product of capital equals the foreign real interest rate. The optimal choice of K_{t+1} is the same whether one focuses on a representative firm (owned by consumers) or on consumers. This optimal choice of capital is at point A in Figure 6.1, where it is assumed that the marginal rate of time preference (denoted γ) equals the (initial) foreign real interest rate.

While the model abstracts from domestic bonds, their inclusion would result in another equilibrium condition in which the real interest rates on domestic and foreign bonds would be equal. This condition is the *real interest rate parity condition* (a derivation is provided in Chapter 7). In this perfect foresight environment, all three assets – domestic bonds, foreign bonds, and capital – would earn the same real return in equilibrium.

7. KEY EQUATIONS

The key equations in the model are as follows:

$$u'(c_t) = \frac{(1+r_t^*)}{1+\gamma} u'(c_{t+1}) \rightarrow c_t = c_{t+1} \ \text{if} \ r_t^* = \gamma$$

$$f'\left(K_{t+1}\right) = r_t^*$$

$$CA_t = f\left(A_t, K_t\right) - c_t - \left(K_{t+1} - K_t\right) - g_t$$

$$c_{t+1} = f\left(A_{t+1},\ K_{t+1}\right) - g_{t+1} + K_{t+1} + \left(1 + r_t^*\right)\left[f\left(A_t,\ K_t\right) - c_t - \left(K_{t+1} - K_t\right) - g_t\right].$$

The first equation is the Euler equation for consumption. If the foreign real interest rate equals the marginal rate of time preference, there is consumption smoothing. In the second equation, the future marginal product of capital equals the foreign real rate (this marginal product is a function of, or depends on, the future capital stock and future total factor productivity). The third equation is the identity that the current account balance equals domestic production less total purchases by domestic consumers, firms, and government. The last equation is the intertemporal constraint on the economy.

The endogenous variables are c_t, c_{t+1}, K_{t+1}, and CA_t. These endogenous variables are determined by the economics that underlies these four equations. The exogenous variables are A_t, A_{t+1}, g_t, g_{t+1}, r_t^*, *and* γ. The capital stock at the start of period t, K_t, is given. The exogenous variables are fixed, and only change if it is indicated that they changed exogenously.

8. EXOGENOUS CHANGES IN TOTAL FACTOR PRODUCTIVITY

Any change in production, for a given level of capital and labor, is a change in total factor productivity. Exogenous increases in total factor productivity are caused by an increase in the skills of workers, an innovation, and a number of other factors (examples are discussed below).

This section examines temporary, permanent, and future increases in total factor productivity. It is assumed that the foreign real interest rate is fixed and equal to the marginal rate of time preference.[13] The current account balance is initially equal to zero.

Temporary Increase in Total Factor Productivity

With a temporary increase in total factor productivity, ΔA_t is positive but ΔA_{t+1} equals zero. For example, with an agricultural good, the temporary increase in total factor productivity could be due to a one-time improvement in the weather.[14] Because the exogenous change is temporary, there is no effect on the future marginal product of capital. Investment spending is unchanged, remaining at zero, and the period t+1 capital stock remains at the initial level. The equilibrium remains at point A in Figure 6.1.

The temporary increase in total factor productivity increases production and real income in the current period. Consumers experience an increase in lifetime after-tax real income and increase spending. But consumers know that the increase in real income is temporary and therefore spend around half of the increase in real income. As consumption increases less than production, and investment and government spending are unchanged, the current account balance improves (net exports are now positive). Private saving increases and the current account moves from a balance to a surplus. The domestic economy exports the surplus production, and domestic residents accumulate foreign bonds. In period t+1, the foreign bonds will be redeemed, allowing for the desired increase in future consumption so as to smooth consumption.

Permanent Increase in Total Factor Productivity

With a permanent increase in total factor productivity, ΔA_t and ΔA_{t+1} are both positive (and the same amount). This increase could be caused, for example, by an increase in the skills of workers or an innovation (production increases even though factor inputs are fixed).[15] This permanent increase in total factor productivity increases production in both periods.

Investment spending increases in the current period. Firms recognize that the increase in productivity is permanent and that this change increases the marginal product of capital in the future period. In Figure 6.2, the increase in the future level of total factor productivity shifts the marginal product of capital curve upward to the right. At the initial level of the period t+1 capital stock, the marginal product of capital (at point B) exceeds the fixed foreign real rate of interest. Firms increase investment spending in the current period, as accumulating capital in this period is required to allow them to fully take advantage of the higher level of the productivity of capital in the future period. Firms increase their current-period purchases of new machines until the amount of capital they will carry into the future period is at point C, where the future marginal product is again equal to the foreign real rate of interest.

The permanent increase in total factor productivity also increases lifetime after-tax real income and consumer spending. Current consumption, in fact, rises more than the induced increase in current-period production and real income. As there is consumption smoothing, future consumption rises by an equivalent amount (in the future, production is higher because of both higher total factor productivity and a higher capital stock).

Given these changes in investment and consumer spending in the current period, the current account balance deteriorates (there is a current account deficit, matched by a negative J_t).[16] While production increases, total spending increases more. In the future period, the associated increase in production will allow consumers to both repay the foreign loan and increase consumption (to ensure consumption smoothing).[17]

Is the current account deficit bad? Part of the deficit is due to the increase in spending by consumers, who are doing so on a rational basis in response to the increase in lifetime after-tax real income. And part of the deficit arises because firms have increased investment spending and are importing machines that will allow for an increase in future production. These actions serve to maximize the lifetime profit of domestic firms and the lifetime utility of domestic residents.

Increase in Future Total Factor Productivity

With a future increase in total factor productivity, ΔA_t is zero but ΔA_{t+1} is positive. With perfect foresight, domestic firms and consumers know that this future change will occur.

Investment spending increases in the current period. Firms recognize that this increase in future total factor productivity will increase the marginal product of capital in period t+1. In the figure (the diagram is the same as in Figure 6.2), the marginal product of capital curve shifts upward so that, at the initial capital stock, the marginal product exceeds the foreign real interest rate. Firms are thereby induced to increase their investment spending in the current period. Firms must buy the capital in the current period, so that it can be used in the future period. To maximize lifetime profit,

Figure 6.2: Increase in future marginal product

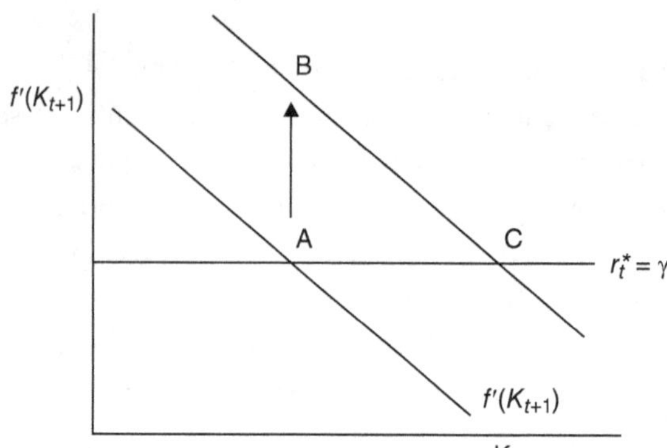

firms increase investment spending such that the future marginal product is driven back down to a level equal to the foreign real interest rate.

The increase in future total factor productivity increases lifetime after-tax real income. Consumption in the current period therefore rises by an amount equivalent to the increase in consumption in the future period. Consumers spread the associated potential increase in spending over the two periods so that consumption smoothing holds.

Given these changes in consumer and investment spending, the current account decreases. With no change in current-period production, the additional spending must be on imported goods. The current account deficit allows consumers to smooth consumption and firms to take advantage of the future increase in the marginal product of capital.

A Note on Decreases in Total Factor Productivity

Decreases in total factor productivity have the opposite effects of the equivalent (permanent, temporary, and future) increases in total factor productivity. For example, a temporary fall in total factor productivity causes the current account balance to fall. But how can total factor productivity fall?

It is true that, in general, total factor productivity tends to be increasing over time. Increases in skills and innovation both cause it to be increasing as time passes. But other factors can cause total factor productivity to decrease. A random shock such as bad weather causes total factor productivity to fall when the good being produced is an agricultural product (there are the same number of machines and the same number of workers, so a fall in production is necessarily a fall in total factor productivity).

Other factors, such as increases in government regulation, can also cause a decrease in total factor productivity.[18] Suppose the government increases the regulatory burden on firms, such that more workers are needed to handle the regulatory requirements and fewer workers are involved in the production of goods. The total number of workers is the same, but more workers are involved in the process of complying with the regulation (conducting tests, completing paperwork, and so on). So labor and capital are unchanged, but the production of goods is lower. This fall in production, with fixed levels of factor inputs, means that total factor productivity has decreased.

Likewise, structural changes that cause reallocations between sectors of the economy may result in less production (with fixed inputs) during the transition period. These times would be associated with a decrease in total factor productivity.[19]

9. FISCAL POLICY

In this model, government purchases of goods and services are assumed to provide benefits, or utility, to consumers. For example, the government purchases health care services and then provides these services to consumers free of charge (though consumers pay a lump-sum tax that finances government spending). But it is assumed that the government does not purchase any "capital" that could have an effect on the economy's production function.[20] In this framework, the effects of fiscal policy can be summarized as follows. Tax changes have no effect on investment spending, but do affect consumer spending if the tax change alters the present value of lifetime after-tax real income. Changes in government spending have no direct effect on consumer or investment spending, but may affect consumer spending indirectly given that a change in government spending may imply a change in the present value of lifetime taxes.[21]

To take one example, consider a temporary decrease in government spending matched by a temporary tax cut. The change in government spending has no effect on the real interest rate, investment spending, the capital stock, or the production function. Net exports rise since the decrease in government purchases is only partially offset by the increase in current consumption. The domestic economy exports the surplus production and accumulates foreign bonds, allowing for the desired increase in future consumption.

10. CHANGES IN THE FOREIGN REAL INTEREST RATE AND TOTAL FACTOR PRODUCTIVITY

Small economies are confronted with various disturbances, including exogenous changes in the foreign real interest rate. For example, fluctuations in the US real interest rate impact the real interest rate and macroeconomic variables in countries such as Canada.[22]

Changes in the Foreign Real Interest Rate

An exogenous decrease in the foreign real interest rate causes a decrease in the domestic real interest rate and induces an increase in both investment spending (see Figure 6.3) and consumer spending in the current period.[23] In addition, the associated increase in future production and real income generates a further increase in consumer spending in the current period. With r_i^* less than γ, the consumer desires a tilted path that has consumer spending falling over time. With production and government spending fixed in the current period, these increases in consumer and investment spending cause the current account balance (net exports) to fall.

Figure 6.3: Decrease in foreign real rate

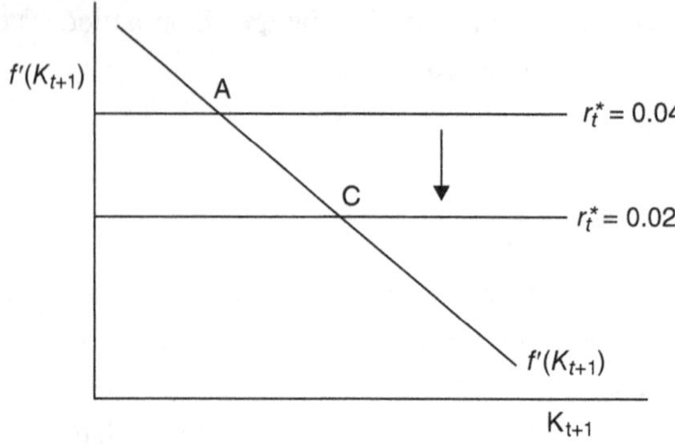

Figure 6.4: Two exogenous changes

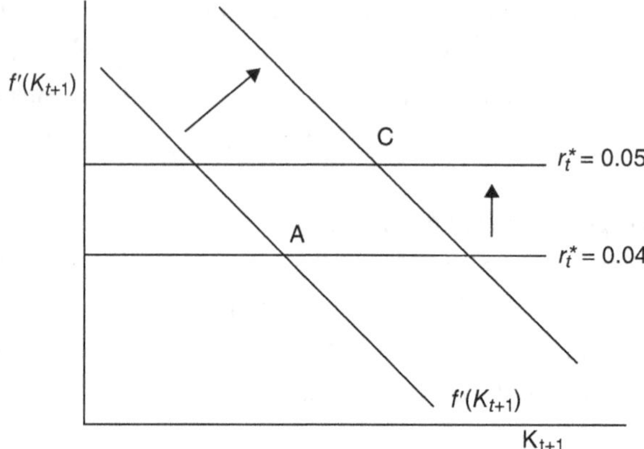

Changes in Total Factor Productivity and the Foreign Real Interest Rate

Suppose two exogenous changes occur at once: a permanent increase in total factor productivity and an increase in the foreign real interest rate. Both the marginal product curve and the foreign real interest rate line shift upward; assume that, at the initial capital stock, the marginal product of capital exceeds the now higher foreign real interest rate. There is an increase in investment spending in the current period, such that the new equilibrium period t+1 capital stock is at point C in Figure 6.4. In this case, there is an increase in investment spending even though the real interest rate has increased. This result is important because there are occasions when investment spending does increase in the same period in which the real interest rate has risen (and vice versa).

The increases in total factor productivity and the capital stock cause lifetime after-tax real income and consumption to increase, but the increase in the real interest rate induces a decrease in current consumption. If the former effect is larger, consumer spending increases. Current production increases with the increase in current-period total factor productivity, but the increases in current-period consumer and investment spending moderate any movement in the current account.

11. THE CANADIAN TRADE BALANCE, 2007–2011

Movements in Canada's balance of trade (net exports) between 2007 and 2011 provide an interesting case study, as the period includes the 2008–2009 recession (the quarterly data are measured in real terms, in billions of chained 2007 dollars).[24] In the first quarter of 2007, Canadian exports exceeded imports by about 50 billion (see Figure 6.5). The magnitude of this trade surplus was significant, equal to about 3 per cent of real GDP.[25] But the trade balance moved into a deficit in 2009 and remained in deficit in 2010 and 2011. In terms of the intertemporal model, what is the interpretation of the movements in net exports and other macroeconomic variables during this period?

The intertemporal approach focuses on national saving and investment spending. National saving is defined as

$$S_t^{nat} = y_t - c_t - g_t,$$

where y is measured as real GDP, so national saving measures domestic production relative to consumer and government spending.[26] The net export balance equals

$$NX_t = y_t - c_t - g_t - I_t = S_t^{nat} - I_t.$$

Figure 6.6 plots investment spending and national saving. In the first quarter of 2007, national saving exceeded investment spending, generating the trade surplus. National saving fell in 2007 because the increases in production were smaller than the sum of the increases in consumer and government spending (Figure 6.7 shows changes in y, c, and g). The relatively large increases in consumer spending suggest that consumers were expecting future increases in real income associated with future increases in total factor productivity. In conjunction with increases in investment spending, also caused by the "expected" future increases in total factor productivity, these changes deteriorated the balance of trade. By the end of 2007, the trade surplus had been eliminated.

Both national saving and investment spending collapsed in the recession, falling by more than 20 per cent between 2008:3 and 2009:2. The fall in national saving was due to decreases in production during the recession, along with small increases in government spending and the smoothing of consumption.[27] In terms of the model, the decreases in production are caused by decreases in total factor productivity (the model abstracts from changes in labor). With investment spending falling *before* the fall in production (see Figure 6.6), it is evident that decreases in "expected" future total factor productivity played a role in the decrease in investment spending (as discussed below, investment spending fell even though there was a decrease in the real interest rate).[28] During the recession, national saving fell slightly more than investment spending, and the balance of trade deteriorated.

In the period after the recession, investment spending increased in response to renewed increases in expected future total factor productivity. While national saving also increased with the increases in current production in the recovery period, the magnitude of the increase in national saving was dampened by moderate increases in consumer spending and some large increases in government spending in late 2009. In total, investment spending increased more than national saving, and the balance of trade deteriorated further.[29]

Figure 6.5: Net exports, 2007:1 to 2011:4

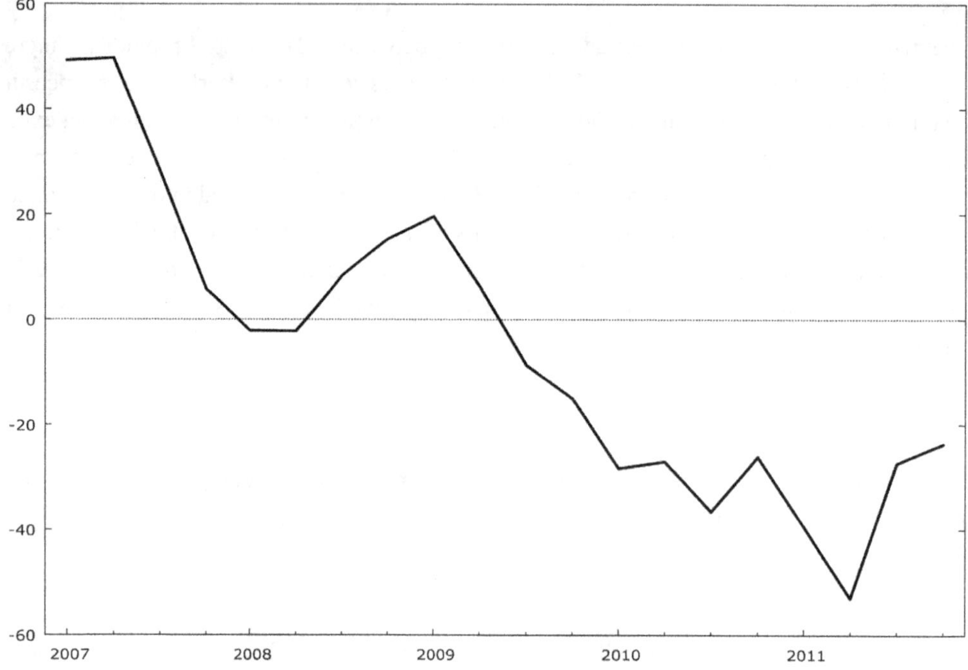

Data source: Statistics Canada

Figure 6.6: Investment spending and national saving

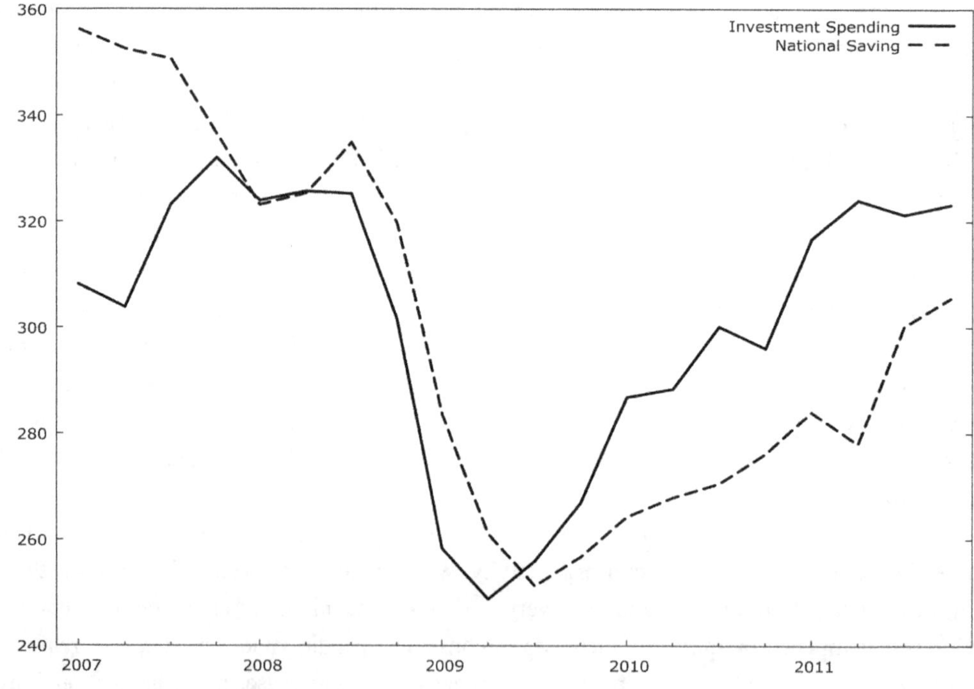

Data source: Statistics Canada

Figure 6.7: Changes in output and spending

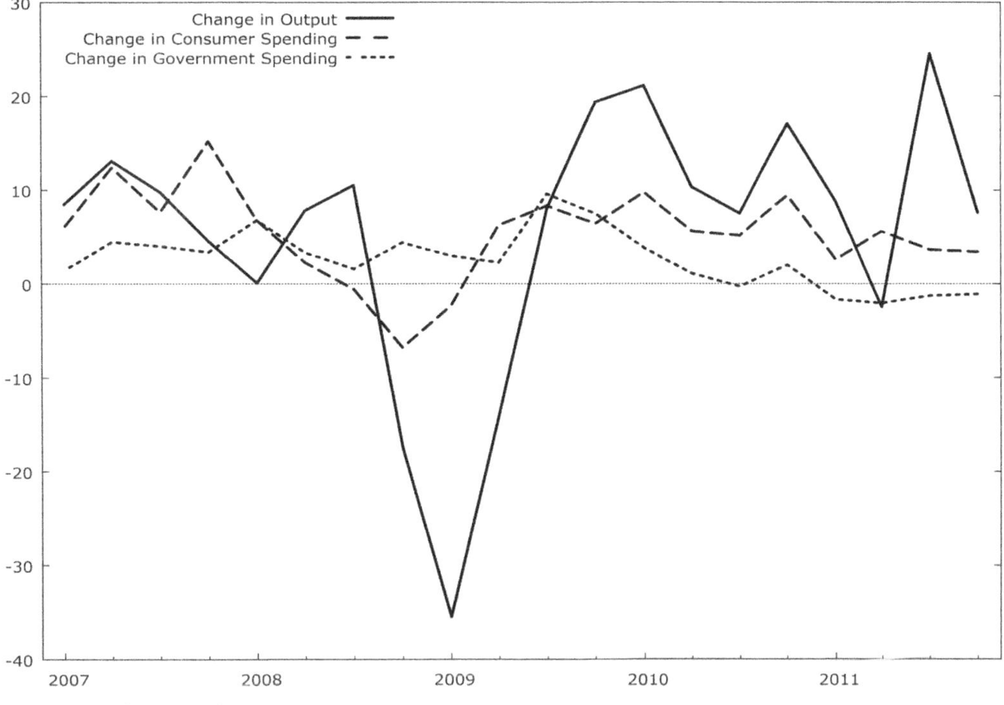

Data source: Statistics Canada

The large volatility of production, in conjunction with the relative smoothness of consumer and government spending, highlights the role of saving in trade balance fluctuations. This fact is evident in Figure 6.7 and is consistent with the prediction of the intertemporal model that temporary changes in production can have a large effect on the balance of trade. But movements in investment spending are also important. Given that investment spending is both a relatively volatile component of aggregate expenditure and a significant proportion of aggregate imports, fluctuations in investment spending play a critical role in trade balance fluctuations (an appendix provides statistical information on the relative volatility of output and the components of aggregate expenditure).

An applied exercise in Data Analytics examines the determination of the Canadian balance of trade over the period since 2012.

Investment Spending and the Real Interest Rate

Increases in future total factor productivity can cause investment spending to rise even though the real interest rate has increased. Investment spending can fall even though the real interest rate has decreased, provided that future total factor productivity has also dropped. The period examined here provides examples of these points.

Figure 6.8 depicts movements in investment spending and the Canadian real interest rate over the five-year period.[30] At the start of the period, investment spending increases even though the

Figure 6.8: Investment spending and the real rate

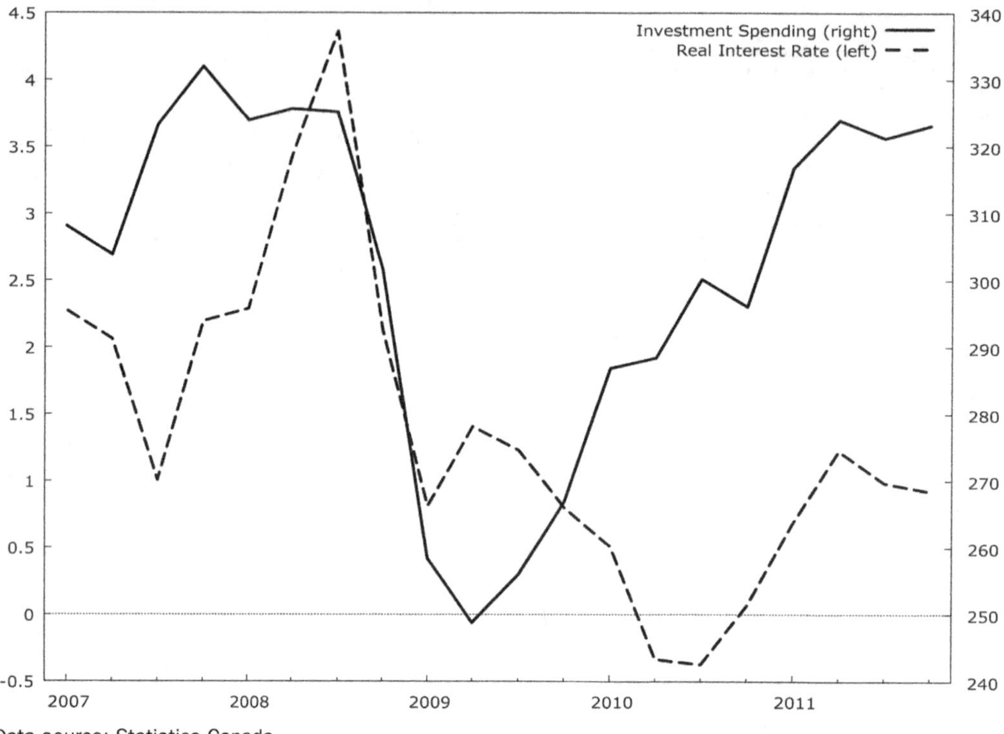

Data source: Statistics Canada

real interest rate moved higher, and then investment spending collapses during the recession, even though the real interest rate decreases from 4 per cent to 1 per cent. With fluctuations in "expected" future total factor productivity, investment spending need not move in the direction suggested by the change in the real interest rate.[31]

12. NOTES ON REAL BUSINESS CYCLE THEORY

A prominent theory of the business cycle is the real business cycle (RBC) theory, where short-term fluctuations in aggregate production are caused by real factors such as cyclical fluctuations in total factor productivity.[32] The model in this chapter provides the basis for a simple one-good RBC model (with a fixed quantity of labor). Proponents of RBC theory regard long-term growth as being driven by trend increases in total factor productivity,[33] and regard the business cycle as arising out of a dynamic process whereby changes in total factor productivity do not occur smoothly over time. Sometimes there are large increases in total factor productivity and the economy grows at a high rate, whereas at other times the economy grows slowly since the increases in total factor productivity are more modest. Occasionally, forces within the economy result in a decrease in total factor productivity and recession ensues. These cyclical movements in total factor productivity generate cyclical movements in real GDP and cause the business cycle.[34]

On the Decomposition into Trend and Cyclical Components

For business cycle analysis, economists have found it useful to decompose variables into trend and cyclical components, where the trend component reflects the longer-term (or growth-related) changes in the variable. A simple approach to the decomposition of a variable into trend and cyclical components is to assume that the trend component grows at a constant rate each year (using the average growth rate over the full period). An alternative approach is the Hodrick–Prescott (or HP) decomposition, in that it allows the trend component to have a variable growth rate.[35] For any time-series variable z, the cyclical component (denoted as z^c) is the deviation of the actual variable from the trend component (denoted as z^{Trend}):

$$z_t^c = z_t - z_t^{Trend}.$$

In the implementation of the technique, one typically takes the logarithm of each variable and then does the decomposition. The change in the logarithm of a variable is measured as a percentage change, allowing a straightforward assessment of the magnitude.

Figure 6.9 plots Canadian real GDP and trend real GDP over the period 1981:1 to 2013:3, with trend real GDP constructed using the HP decomposition (an applied exercise in Data Analytics examines trend and cyclical real GDP over the more recent period). Trend real GDP is fairly smooth, whereas real GDP is variable (with recessions in Canada in 1981–1982, 1990–1991, and 2008–2009).

Figure 6.10 depicts the cyclical component of real GDP in Canada, along with a measure of cyclical total factor productivity. The cyclical component of real GDP reflects the business cycle, meaning the short-term fluctuations in real GDP relative to trend.[36] In RBC theory, an important factor causing fluctuations in real GDP is fluctuations in cyclical total factor productivity (RBC models also embed labor demand and labor supply decisions that determine cyclical fluctuations in employment, and incorporate other factors such as changes in the marginal income tax rate). While there are various issues with respect to the measurement of total factor productivity,[37] the conventional calculation is widely used (an appendix provides an explanation of this approach). There is a strong positive co-movement between cyclical total factor productivity and cyclical real GDP, with the correlation coefficient equal to 0.91 for this period. In terms of RBC theory, this evidence may be regarded as being supportive of the hypothesis that fluctuations in total factor productivity are an important determinant of short-term fluctuations in real GDP.[38]

Alternative Models of the Business Cycle

The RBC theory is a supply-side theory of the business cycle, where shifts in aggregate demand have no effect on real GDP. But in other open-economy models, shifts in aggregate demand due to monetary policy, fiscal policy, changes in expectations, or exogenous shifts in export demand can cause short-term fluctuations in production. An open-economy model that stresses demand-side factors is discussed in Chapter 13. And the RBC approach is touched on again in Chapter 14, where dynamic multi-sectoral models are discussed.

Figure 6.9: Real GDP and trend real GDP

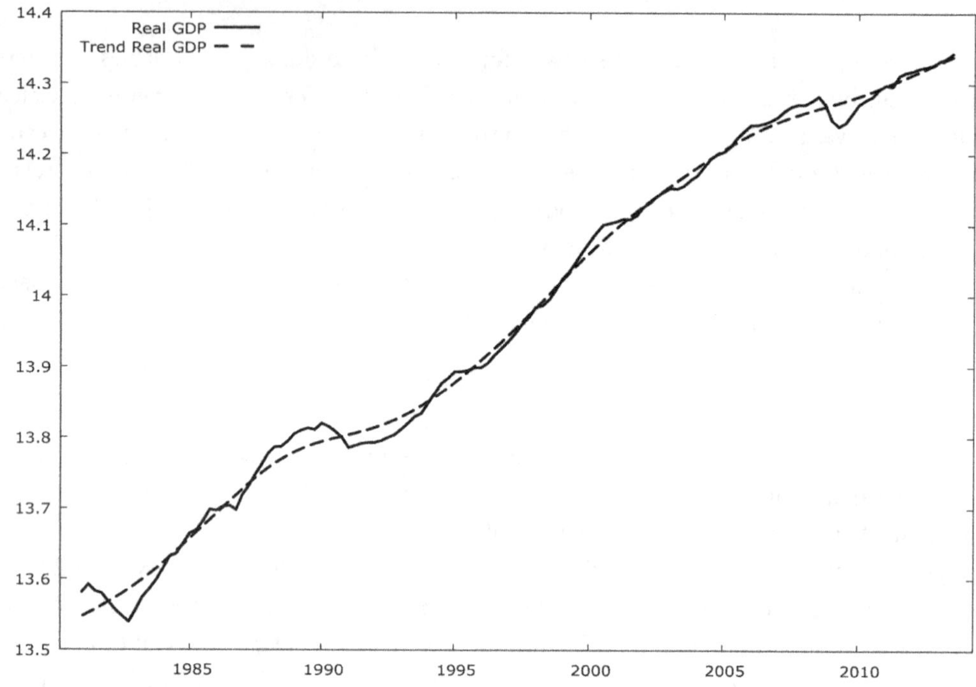

Data source: Statistics Canada (with the author's derivation of trend real GDP)

Figure 6.10: Cyclical production and total factor productivity

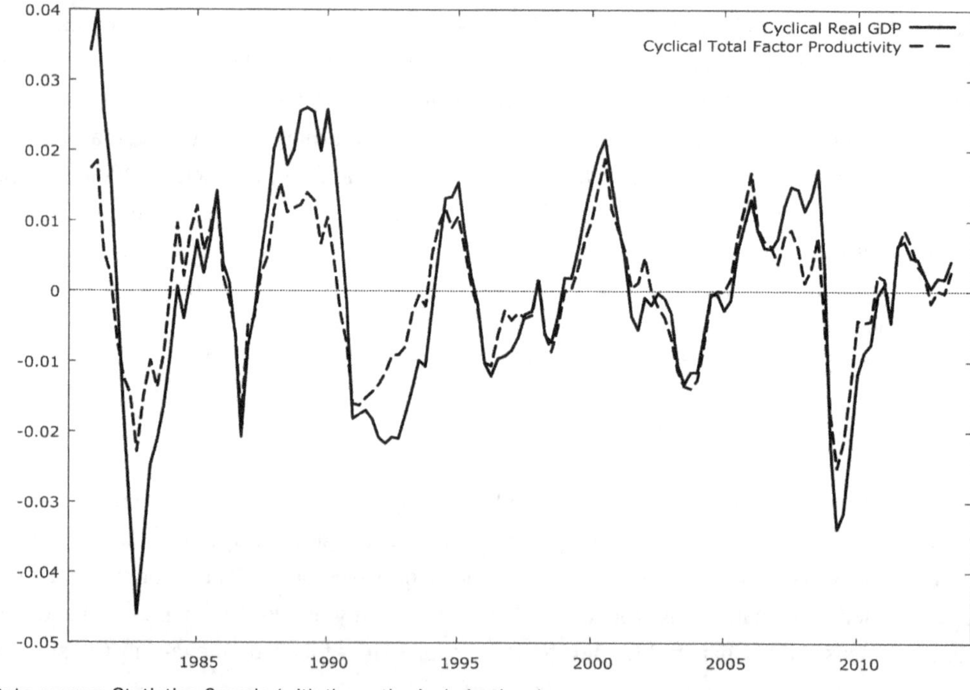

Data source: Statistics Canada (with the author's derivations)

13. CONCLUSION

Trade and current account imbalances are an intertemporal phenomenon. The intertemporal approach to the current account is now the predominant approach used by international macroeconomists.[39] In the small-economy model in this chapter, net exports and the current account balance are affected by real shocks to total factor productivity, as well as by changes in real government spending and the foreign real interest rate.

While this model allows one to analyze movements in the current account balance, extensions to this core structure are required to address other macroeconomic issues.[40] The one-good nature of the model does not allow for an analysis of real exchange rate determination, or of the relationship between the real exchange rate and the current account. A framework that incorporates traded and non-traded goods or multiple traded goods (export goods and import goods) is needed to address these issues.[41] In addition, while abstracting from monetary factors simplifies the analysis, it limits the applicability of the model. One must incorporate both money and the monetary policy regime to analyze the determination of the aggregate price level and the nominal exchange rate, and to provide a valid comparison of alternative exchange rate regimes. While the one-good RBC model is a useful tool in business cycle analysis, both multi-sectoral models and monetary models provide significant insights into the determination of business cycles in open economies.

PRACTICE QUESTIONS

1. Fill in the blanks
   (a) Net exports equal private _____ less investment spending (assume a balanced government budget). The current account balance equals _____ when the debt service balance equals zero.
   (b) As capital increases (holding other factors fixed), the marginal product of capital _____.
   (c) If total factor productivity increases, production _____ for given levels of _____ and labor.
   (d) In equilibrium, the domestic marginal product of _____ equals the foreign _____ interest rate.
   (e) The change in the capital stock, $K_{t+1} - K_t$, equals _____ minus depreciation.
2. Fill in the blanks
   (a) A temporary increase in total factor productivity causes investment spending to _____ and net exports to _____ in the current period.
   (b) A temporary increase in total factor productivity causes net exports to _____ in the current period, whereas a permanent increase in total factor productivity causes net exports to _____ in the current period.

    (c) An exogenous future increase in total factor productivity causes lifetime after-tax real income to increase, inducing an increase in _____ in both periods; the exogenous increase also increases _____ in the current period, by generating an increase in the future marginal product of capital.

    (d) A decrease in current-period net exports could be caused by a temporary _____ in total factor productivity or a future _____ in total factor productivity.

    (e) A permanent increase in total factor productivity causes the future marginal product of capital to increase, and therefore causes _____ to increase in the current period. Net exports fall in the current period, as domestic expenditure rises more than current-period _____.

3. (a) Explain why a depreciation of the domestic currency (relative to the foreign currency) has no effect on net exports in this model.

    (b) Write down the equation in which net exports equal domestic production less total domestic spending. Explain the meaning of this equation.

    (c) Using identities, show the relationship between net exports, saving, and investment spending. Assume the government budget is balanced, domestic production equals domestic real income, and the initial net foreign debt equals zero.

    (d) What causes total factor productivity to increase? List two factors and explain.

    (e) Is it possible for total factor productivity to decrease? Provide an example and explain.

4. Using equations and the diagram for the marginal product of capital (with a fixed foreign real interest rate), explain how an exogenous temporary increase in total factor productivity affects consumption, investment spending, and net exports in the current period.

5. Using equations and the diagram for the marginal product of capital (with a fixed foreign real interest rate), explain how an exogenous permanent increase in total factor productivity affects consumption, investment spending, and net exports in the current period.

6. Is a trade balance deficit, caused by a future increase in total factor productivity, bad? Explain.

7. Suppose there is both an exogenous permanent increase in total factor productivity and an exogenous increase in the foreign real interest rate. What happens to investment spending? Explain using a diagram.

8. (a) What factors cause the business cycle in the RBC framework? Explain.

    (b) With quarterly data, a recession occurs when there is a fall in real GDP for at least two consecutive quarters. Consider the Hodrick–Prescott decomposition of real GDP into trend and cyclical components. Explain how it is possible to have a series of consecutive negative cyclical components even though the economy is not in a recession.

DATA ANALYTICS

1. Access CANSIM Table 380-0064, and collect the quarterly data needed to replicate Figures 6.5, 6.6, and 6.7 for the period 2012:1 to 2019:4. See that section for details on the construction and manipulation of the data. Comment on the results.
2. Using the same data, calculate the trend and cyclical components of real GDP over the same time period using the Hodrick–Prescott filter. Plot real GDP and trend real GDP on the same plot and cyclical real GDP on a separate plot. Explain whether there was a recession between 2014 and 2016.

APPENDIX A: PROFIT MAXIMIZATION AND INVESTMENT SPENDING BY FIRMS

Lifetime profit, in nominal terms, equals current-period profit plus the present value of future profit (discounted using the nominal interest rate, denoted as i_t):

$$P_t f\left(K_t,\ L_t,\ A_t\right) - w_t L_t - P_t^K\left[K_{t+1} - K_t\right]$$

$$+ \frac{P_{t+1} f\left(K_{t+1},\ L_{t+1},\ A_{t+1}\right) - w_{t+1} L_{t+1} - P_{t+1}^K\left[K_{t+2} - K_{t+1}\right]}{\left(1 + i_t\right)},$$

where P is the price level (the price of goods), L denotes the quantity of labor, w is the nominal wage rate, and P^K is the price of capital. The rate of depreciation is assumed to equal 0. The firm chooses K_{t+1} such that the following condition holds:[42]

$$\frac{P_{t+1} f'\left(K_{t+1}\right) + P_{t+1}^K}{1 + i_t} = P_t^K.$$

The marginal cost of an extra unit of capital is P_t^K. The marginal benefit of the extra unit of capital is the present value of the extra production in period t+1, $\dfrac{P_{t+1} f'\left(K_{t+1}\right)}{1 + i_t}$, plus the present value of the extra unit of capital in period t+1, $\dfrac{P_{t+1}^K}{1 + i_t}$.

This chapter assumed that the relative price of goods in terms of capital was equal to 1.[43] Adopting this assumption, the equation can be rewritten as

$$\frac{f'(K_{t+1})+1}{\dfrac{(1+i_t)\,P_t}{P_{t+1}}} = 1.$$

Using the definition of the forward inflation rate, denoted π_t, and the Fisher equation,

$$\pi_t = \frac{P_{t+1}-P_t}{P_t} = \frac{P_{t+1}}{P_t} - 1,$$

$$1+r_t = \frac{1+i_t}{1+\pi_t} = \frac{(1+i_t)\,P_t}{P_{t+1}},$$

the equation can be rewritten as

$$f'(K_{t+1}) = r_t.$$

APPENDIX B: MEASUREMENT OF TOTAL FACTOR PRODUCTIVITY

The Cobb–Douglas production function is specified as

$$y_t = A_t\,K_t^{\alpha}\,L_t^{1-\alpha},$$

where α is a parameter that lies between 0 and 1. In constructing a measure of A, researchers sometimes simplify and assume that the capital stock is fixed.[44] With K set equal to 1, α set at 0.30, and using employment to measure L,[45] total factor productivity is calculated as

$$A_t = \frac{y_t}{L_t^{0.7}}.$$

APPENDIX C: VARIABILITY AND CROSS CORRELATIONS OF CYCLICAL VARIABLES

Business cycle analysis often includes estimates of the standard deviation of the output and expenditure variables, as a measure of the variability of these variables, and estimates of the cross-correlation between any two variables. These statistical measures provide information on how the economy tends to operate, and can be useful for both assessing a given theory and discriminating between alternative theories.

Table 6.1 provides a summary of relevant statistical information on the cyclical variables, using data for Canada. Cyclical exports and imports are about three times more variable than cyclical output, and national saving and investment spending are about four or five times more variable. Consumption and government spending are less variable than output.[46]

The table also provides the correlation coefficient between cyclical total factor productivity and each of the other cyclical variables. The correlation coefficient lies between $+1$ and -1 and provides an indication of the direction and size of the correlation. Cyclical total factor productivity is positively correlated with all variables except government spending and net exports relative to output (NX/y). Some other cross-correlations of the cyclical variables may be of interest: the correlation between national saving and investment spending is 0.81, between national saving and net exports relative to output is 0.04, and between investment spending and net exports relative to output is -0.54.

Table 6.1: Statistical information on cyclical variables

	Standard Deviation	Relative Standard Deviation	Correlation with A^c
y^c	0.0149	1.00	0.91
A^c	0.0095	0.64	1.00
c^c	0.0115	0.78	0.63
I^c	0.0753	5.07	0.76
g^c	0.0111	0.75	-0.19
EX^c	0.0378	2.54	0.80
IM^c	0.0494	3.33	0.74
NX/y	0.0067	0.45	-0.02
$S^{nat,c}$	0.0556	3.74	0.89

Data source: Statistics Canada and the author's derivations

Note: All variables, except NX/y, are in logarithms. All variables are HP-filtered to create the cyclical component. Relative standard deviation is the ratio of that variable's standard deviation to the standard deviation of cyclical output. The sample period is 1981:1 to 2013:3.

NOTES

1 Chapter 15 extends the model to the case of two "large" economies. At advanced levels, the models are infinite period models, with an allowance for uncertainty. For survey papers that discuss the intertemporal approach to the current account, see Baxter (1995), Obstfeld and Rogoff (1995b), and Gourinchas and Rey (2014). The literature includes both models with complete asset markets and models with incomplete asset markets. The models in this book are akin to incomplete asset market models.
2 In this intertemporal model, monetary factors have no effect on real variables. Monetary neutrality holds.
3 References to the RBC literature are provided in this chapter and Chapter 14. Turnovsky (2009) provides an advanced discussion of both one-good and multi-sectoral small-economy models of economic growth. Jones (2016) summarizes empirical evidence related to long-term growth.
4 In general, there are many different measures of productivity: labor productivity (average and marginal), capital productivity (average and marginal), and total factor productivity.
5 This assumption is a common simplification. See, for example, Obstfeld and Rogoff (1996, 15).
6 The consumer could sell foreign bonds or capital to foreigners, but these possibilities are ruled out below.
7 This equation has set J_{t+1} equal to 0, since t+1 is the final period.

8   In addition, the K_{t+1} will be "consumed" by the agent; K_{t+2} is set equal to 0, as period t+1 is the last period.

9   For simplicity, the government budget is assumed to be balanced in each period. But, in general, consumers are assumed to understand the details and implications of the intertemporal government budget constraint. Consumers know that any change in government spending (current or future) affects lifetime taxes and thereby affects consumer spending, irrespective of whether or not bond financing is used.

10 The absorption approach to the balance of trade used this identity. The sum of total spending by domestic consumers, domestic firms, and the domestic government was called absorption. See Alexander (1952).

11 See, for example, the discussion in Sachs (1981).

12 Many studies (for example, Engel and Wang 2011) assume that there are adjustment costs associated with changing the capital stock.

13 On the diagram, it is typically assumed that the foreign real interest rate is positive. If the real rate is zero, one must then assume that there is a level of K where $f'(K)$ falls to zero. With certain production functions, the marginal product only approaches zero as the capital stock becomes large.

14 Even though the firm (in this case, the farm) has the same number of machines (plows, tractors, and so on) and the same number of hours worked, production is higher because of the better weather. This increase in production, with fixed K and L, corresponds to an increase in total factor productivity.

15 In neoclassical growth theory, total factor productivity is exogenous. Endogenous growth theory regards total factor productivity as endogenous and explains why it changes. For example, why do workers improve skills and how does this skill acquisition affect growth? Why do firms innovate and how does innovation affect growth? For a non-technical discussion, see Grossman and Helpman (1994) and Helpman (2004).

16 For an advanced analysis, see Glick and Rogoff (1995).

17 In the model with investment spending, a permanent increase in total factor productivity reduces the current account. In the model in Chapter 5, a permanent increase in output has no effect on the current account.

18 For a related argument, see Hansen and Prescott (1993). Hansen and Ohanian (2016) provide extensive discussion of decreases in total factor productivity.

19 Workers released in one sector are hired by firms in other sectors, but it may take time before the new workers are trained and able to add production at the normal level.

20 Aschauer (1988) discusses the effects of fiscal policy in a framework that nests within it the model in this chapter. The framework also allows government capital in the production function, various tax regimes, and so on.

21 Backus et al. (2008) discuss the theory and empirics of the relationship between taxes and capital–output ratios.

22 Chapter 15 extends the model to allow both the foreign and domestic economies to be "large."

23 To analyze an increase in the foreign real interest rate, one could incorporate depreciation. If firms do not purchase new machines to replace the machines discarded at the end of the period, the capital stock is reduced.

24 The GDP and expenditure variables are taken from CANSIM Table 380-0064, now labeled Table 36100104. The statistical discrepancy that arises in national income accounting is ignored in the calculations.

25 Canadian exports were equal to about 540 billion (35 per cent of real GDP), and imports were equal to about 490 billion.

26 On issues related to the measurement of saving, see Backus et al. (1992). If one uses domestic real income rather than production, then national saving less investment spending equals the current account

balance. Net exports and the current account move together over time, because the debt service balance reflects interest flows arising from net foreign assets acquired in previous periods.

27　Consumers may have regarded a large fraction of the decrease in production as temporary, so that the fall in consumer spending was limited.

28　The fall in the real interest rate moderated, but did not prevent, the fall in investment spending.

29　Abstracting from changes in total factor productivity and lifetime after-tax real income, the downward trend in the real interest rate over the period would reduce saving, increase investment spending, and decrease the trade balance.

30　The annual real interest rate, with quarterly data, is measured as $r_t = \dfrac{(1 + i_t) P_t}{P_{t+4}} - 1$, where the nominal interest rate is measured as the interest rate on medium-term government bonds and the price level is the consumer price index (CANSIM series V122486 and V41690973, respectively).

31　The Business Outlook Survey, available at the Bank of Canada website, has information on (among other things) business investment intentions.

32　The seminal research on the RBC model was conducted by Kydland and Prescott (1982) and Long and Plosser (1983). The panel discussion summarized in Altug and Young (2015) provides commentary by these researchers.

33　While capital accumulation increases production, the diminishing marginal product means that growth cannot be sustained if total factor productivity is not increasing. The underlying factors that increase total factor productivity, such as innovation and skill improvement, must be integral components of long-term growth theory.

34　Baxter (1995) discusses the RBC approach from the perspective of open-economy models. Applications to Canada include studies by Mendoza (1991, 1995) and Blankenau et al. (2001). Costa Junior and Garcia-Cintado (2018) discuss teaching RBC models in an advanced undergraduate course in macroeconomics.

35　See Hodrick and Prescott (1997). The HP filter and other filters are typically included in the statistical packages used by economists.

36　Cyclical real GDP is negative not only in recessions but also in periods when real GDP is below trend real GDP (for example, in 1986). Note that the drop in cyclical real GDP in 1981-1982 is larger than in 2008-2009.

37　See the discussion, for example, in Baxter (1995), Glick and Rogoff (1995), Amaral and MacGee (2002), and Hansen and Ohanian (2016).

38　On the possible mismeasurement of real GDP, total factor productivity, and the intellectual property products component of investment spending, see (for example) McGrattan and Prescott (2014), Hansen and Ohanian (2016), and Prescott (2016).

39　Interesting empirical studies are conducted by, among many others, Leiderman and Razin (1991), Glick and Rogoff (1995), and Engel and Wang (2011). The survey papers by Baxter (1995), Obstfeld and Rogoff (1995b), and Gourinchas and Rey (2014) provide extensive references to the empirical literature.

40　Gourinchas and Rey (2014) provide a summary of the literature on valuation effects and current account imbalances.

41　Incorporating a more realistic structure for the real sector of the economy adds other insights. For example, in a dynamic model with a non-traded good, exogenous changes in total factor productivity in the non-traded sector may not affect the current account. See Chapter 14 and the academic literature cited therein.

42　The same solution is obtained when lifetime profit is written in real terms (advanced analyses often incorporate adjustment costs). The firm also chooses L_t and L_{t+1} such that, in each period, the marginal product of labor equals the real wage rate.

43　Under a more realistic set of assumptions, such as a constant relative price of goods in terms of capital and equal forward inflation rates for goods and capital, the resulting equation is similar to that derived in the text.

44 See, for example, Backus et al. (1992).

45 It can be shown that α equals capital's share of real income. Backus et al. (1992) set α equal to 0.36 in their US study, and Mendoza (1991) sets α equal to 0.32 in his Canadian study. The employment data are seasonally adjusted (CANSIM number V2062811). The variable L can also be measured as total hours worked.

46 Consumer spending includes all components of consumer spending, including spending on durables and semi-durables, so that aggregate consumer spending is more volatile than spending on services plus nondurables.

PART III

Intertemporal Monetary Models of the Price Level, the Exchange Rate, and the Balance of Payments

CHAPTER 7

An Intertemporal, Choice-Theoretic Model with Money

1. INTRODUCTION

While certain issues in international macroeconomics can be analyzed in purely real models, issues such as the determination of the aggregate price level are inherently monetary in nature. Under a flexible exchange rate, the price level and the nominal exchange rate are influenced by monetary policy. Indeed, in extreme cases like hyperinflations, these nominal variables are determined predominantly by the nominal money supply. Under a fixed exchange rate, the determination of the balance of payments (flows in foreign exchange reserves) is fundamentally a monetary phenomenon.

This chapter outlines a general equilibrium, maximizing model of a small open economy, where money is modeled by adding real money balances to the utility function.[1] The general equilibrium framework allows for the interaction between the real and monetary sectors. The choice-theoretic approach ensures that the model has strong micro-foundations and allows one to discuss the welfare (or utility) effects of macroeconomic policies.

This chapter provides some background and summarizes the key relationships in the model. Chapter 8 examines the determination of the endogenous variables, both nominal and real, under a flexible exchange rate, and Chapter 9 examines the variables when the exchange rate is fixed.

2. THE BASIC SETUP

The model is similar to the model used in the intertemporal approach to the current account. A representative agent is assumed to maximize lifetime utility subject to an intertemporal budget constraint (the terms consumers, domestic residents, and agent are used interchangeably). Utility depends on consumption, government spending, and real money balances.[2]

In concise terms, the setup incorporates the following aspects. There are two periods: the current period (period t) and the future period (period t+1). There is perfect foresight. Production and lump-sum taxes are exogenous, and investment spending equals zero. There is one good in the domestic economy, with this good identical to the foreign good, and the domestic economy is small (foreign variables are exogenous). There are three assets: money, a domestic bond, and a foreign bond. Consumers understand government budgets and issues related to the tax, bond, and money financing of government expenditure.

3. THE EXCHANGE RATE AND THE LAW OF ONE PRICE

The exchange rate in the current period is denoted s_t, and is defined as the amount of domestic currency required to purchase one unit of foreign currency. The variable s represents the price of foreign currency for domestic residents. An increase in s, for example, indicates a depreciation of the domestic currency (relative to the foreign currency).

Foreign and domestic goods are identical, with zero tariffs and transport costs. The law of one price holds, which in a one-good model is equivalent to the purchasing power parity (PPP) condition:[3]

$$P_t = s_t P_t^*,$$

where P is the domestic price level and P* is the foreign price level.[4] Competition between foreign and domestic producers ensures that the law of one price holds. Similarly, the law of one price holds in the future period:

$$P_{t+1} = s_{t+1} P_{t+1}^*.$$

While monetary policy in the domestic economy affects the exchange rate, it also affects the price level. With identical foreign and domestic goods and the law of one price, monetary policy has no effect on the real exchange rate, denoted as q, defined as

$$q_t = \frac{s_t P_t^*}{P_t}.$$

The real exchange rate equals the relative price of goods (foreign and domestic). In a more general framework, changes in the real exchange rate may induce residents to shift their expenditure toward the good that has become relatively cheaper. But with identical goods and the law of one price, the real exchange rate is always equal to 1. Monetary policy causes the exchange rate and the domestic price level to change proportionately and therefore cannot affect net exports through this channel.

4. LIFETIME UTILITY AND REAL MONEY BALANCES IN THE UTILITY FUNCTION

Lifetime utility, denoted as V, depends on consumption (denoted c), real government expenditure (denoted g), and real money balances (denoted m) in both periods. Lifetime utility is represented by[5]

$$V = u\left(c_t\right) + u\left(g_t\right) + v\left(m_t\right) + \frac{u\left(c_{t+1}\right) + u\left(g_{t+1}\right) + v\left(m_{t+1}\right)}{1+\gamma},$$

where the parameter γ is the fixed marginal rate of time preference. The utility functions u(·) and v(m) need not have the same functional form. However, in each case, marginal utility is positive and there is diminishing marginal utility.

Money and the Utility of Real Money Balances

Money acts as a medium of exchange, and allows transactions to be conducted in an efficient manner. Individuals and firms accept money in exchange for goods, services, and financial assets because they know that they, in turn, can use money to purchase items that they want to purchase. In a well-functioning monetary system, these transactions occur smoothly and seamlessly. These benefits of money are incorporated into the model by assuming that real money balances yield utility.[6]

Nominal money – the quantity of money measured in dollars – is typically defined as currency held by the public plus checkable deposits at financial institutions (which allow for the transfer of money through written checks and the processing of debit card transactions). Money is used for conducting transactions, and though it earns zero interest, money is an asset. Not counting the marginal transactions benefits of money, money can have a negative real return if the prices of goods and services are rising over time. But even in economies with a high inflation rate, the public still holds money (though inflation does affect the amount of money the public wants to hold). The public continues to hold money because money provides benefits – associated with money as a medium of exchange.

The agent obtains utility from holding *real* money balances, where real money balances are defined as nominal money M divided by the price level P. For example, if nominal money equals \$140 and the price of the good equals \$7 per good, real money balances equal 20 goods. The \$140 can purchase 20 goods.

There is a shopping-time rationalization for putting real money balances into the utility function.[7] Suppose that utility depends on leisure, and the total time available (equal to 1) is split between leisure (denoted as ℓ), labor (denoted as L), and shopping (denoted as h):

$$1 = \ell + L + h.$$

With labor time L assumed to be fixed (given that output is exogenous), any decrease in shopping time implies an increase in leisure time. Shopping time is assumed to depend negatively on the quantity of real money balances and positively on consumption, with the shopping time function written as

$$h = h\left(m, c\right).$$

An increase in real money holdings is assumed to reduce shopping time, and an increase in consumer spending implies an increase in shopping time. The utility of consumption and leisure can be written (approximately) as

$$u(c) + u(\ell) = u(c) + u(1 - L - h(m,c)) \equiv u(c) + v(m).$$

Consumption affects utility directly through the consumption of goods, and indirectly in that a higher level of consumption implies a higher level of shopping time and therefore less leisure. The first effect dominates, so that the marginal utility of consumption is positive. Higher levels of real money balances are associated with more time available for leisure and therefore higher utility. For convenience, the utility from consumption and real money is defined as $u(c) + v(m)$.

The agent's utility depends on the amount of real money balances, because the benefits received from holding nominal money depend on how many goods these dollars allow the agent to buy. Given the level of consumption, a higher level of real money balances implies less shopping time, more leisure, and higher utility.

5. HOUSEHOLD BUDGET CONSTRAINTS

In the current period, the agent's budget constraint is

$$P_t\, y_t - T_t = P_t c_t + B_t + s_t\, J_t + M_t.$$

The left-hand side represents after-tax nominal income, where y denotes real income (and output) and T denotes nominal taxes. The right-hand side equals, in nominal terms, consumer spending plus the net acquisition of assets in period t. For simplicity, the period t-1 asset variables are set equal to zero, so the consumer starts period t with no assets and no debts. The variables B, J, and M denote the agent's holdings of, respectively, domestic bonds, foreign bonds, and nominal money. To buy foreign bonds, the agent must first purchase foreign currency at the exchange rate s_t.

The term $P_t\, c_t$ captures consumer spending on both domestic goods (denoted c^d) and foreign goods (denoted c^f). The variable c is a measure of consumer spending (the number of goods purchased), as calculated in the national income accounts. But because the two goods are identical and because the law of one price (PPP) holds, consumer spending can be written as

$$P_t\, c_t^d + s_t\, P_t^*\, c_t^f = P_t \left[c_t^d + c_t^f \right] = P_t\, c_t.$$

The future period budget constraint is

$$P_{t+1}\, y_{t+1} - T_{t+1} + \left(1 + i_t\right) B_t + \left(1 + i_t^*\right) s_{t+1} J_t = P_{t+1} c_{t+1} + M_{t+1} - M_t,$$

where i denotes the domestic nominal interest rate and i* is the foreign nominal interest rate. In period t+1, the agent earns after-tax nominal income, denoted $P_{t+1} y_{t+1} - T_{t+1}$, but also has earnings (or payments) on domestic and foreign bond holdings (the variable J can be positive or negative). The only taxes are lump-sum taxes T (there are no taxes on domestic or foreign interest earnings and no taxes on capital gains). Foreign bond payments (principal plus interest) are converted to domestic currency amounts at the future exchange rate s_{t+1}.

In period t+1, the agent can spend the proceeds (both nominal income earnings and payoffs from domestic and foreign bond holdings) on the consumption good and on the accumulation of money balances. The change in nominal money balances, $M_{t+1} - M_t$, can be positive or negative (the agent needs money to conduct transactions). As period t+1 is the last period, the agent does not purchase any bonds in period t+1 (B_{t+1} and J_{t+1} equal 0).

The agent's lifetime, or intertemporal, budget constraint merges the current-period and future-period budget constraints.

6. INDIVIDUAL BEHAVIOR AND MARKET BEHAVIOR

The model is based on a representative agent that represents a typical consumer in the economy. There are, in effect, many consumers in the economy. In macroeconomics, one must distinguish between actions taken by an individual and actions taken by all individuals at once. This distinction is important in the analyses of many economic issues, but it is critically important in issues pertaining to monetary economics.

Consider an analogy that highlights this point. Suppose that an investor realizes that the expected return on an asset has increased substantially. This one investor, acting alone, would attempt to buy the asset at the initial market price. But if all investors experienced the same increase in expected return, all individuals will not be able to purchase the asset. The market behavior of investors will lead to investors bidding higher and higher prices, with no investors willing to sell the asset. At some point, the price will be bid up to a level such that the bidding stops and in fact no trades have been made (assuming identical expectations).

A similar issue arises in goods markets. For example, an increase in the money supply causes the individual to want to increase purchases of the domestic good. But if the supply of domestic goods is fixed, an actual increase in purchases is not possible. Both individual and market behavior must be analyzed to examine the effects of any exogenous change, accounting for the equilibrium conditions in the general equilibrium model.

7. KEY RELATIONSHIPS

The agent chooses consumption, money, and domestic and foreign bond holdings to maximize lifetime utility subject to the budget constraints. There are six key relationships: the Euler equation for consumption; the interest rate parity condition; the definition of the real interest rate (the Fisher equation); the real interest rate parity condition; the current-period real money demand function; and the future-period real money demand function.

Euler Equation for Consumption

To maximize lifetime utility, the agent allocates consumption between periods such that the Euler equation holds:

$$u'(c_t) = \frac{(1+r_t)}{1+\gamma} u'(c_{t+1}),$$

where $u'(c)$ denotes the marginal utility of consumption. If the agent decreases current consumption by 1 unit, allowing a unit increase in domestic bonds, the marginal cost is $u'(c_t)$. The bond pays off $(1+r_t)$ in real terms in period t+1, allowing a $1+r_t$ increase in future consumption. The marginal benefit, in real terms, is $(1+r_t)$ times the discounted gain in future utility.

Suppose the Euler equation does not hold, where for example

$$u'(c_t) < \frac{(1+r_t)}{1+\gamma} u'(c_{t+1}).$$

Assume, for simplicity, that r_t and γ equal 0. The marginal cost of a decrease in current consumption is less than the marginal benefit of this action. If the agent reduces consumption by 1 unit (and saves this amount instead), the marginal cost is $u'(c_t)$. The marginal benefit is the gain in utility from the increase in future consumption, $u'(c_{t+1})$. Given the inequality, this reallocation has increased lifetime utility. Therefore, the inequality implies that the agent has not yet completed the necessary reallocations to *maximize* lifetime utility. But the agent does maximize lifetime utility. So reallocation continues until marginal benefit and marginal cost are equal. As current consumption falls, current-period marginal utility rises; as future consumption rises, future-period marginal utility falls. Both changes serve to reduce, and then eliminate, the inequality as the reallocation in consumption occurs.

Interest Rate Parity Condition

For the agent to willingly hold both domestic and foreign bonds, these two assets must be equally good investments. The interest rate parity (IRP) condition must hold:

$$(1+i_t) = \frac{(1+i_t^*)\, s_{t+1}}{s_t}.$$

This equation is the exact specification of IRP, rather than the approximation typically used:

$$i_t = i_t^* + \frac{s_{t+1} - s_t}{s_t},$$

where the second term on the right-hand side of this approximation represents the rate of appreciation of the foreign currency (relative to the domestic currency).[8]

Consider a numerical example where the agent has $100 Canadian to invest. If they invest in Canadian bonds, the payoff in period t+1 equals $121 Canadian when the interest rate equals 21 per cent. If the $100 Canadian is invested in US bonds, the agent must first convert the Canadian dollars to US dollars. If s_t equals 1.25, the $100 Canadian is exchanged for $80 US, which is then used to purchase a US bond. If the US interest rate equals 10 per cent, the US bond has a payoff of

$88 US in period t+1. If the exchange rate in period t+1 equals 1.375 (meaning that the US dollar has appreciated by 10 per cent since period t), the $88 US can be sold on the foreign exchange market for $121 Canadian. Given these numbers, both Canadian and US bonds have a 21 per cent return.

If the returns on domestic and foreign bonds are not equal, the actions of traders will, without delay, cause the exchange rate or interest rates to change to ensure that the equality holds. In equilibrium, the interest rate parity condition holds.

Definition of the Real Interest Rate: The Fisher Equation

The Fisher equation is an identity that defines the real rate of interest on the domestic bond, denoted as r, in terms of the nominal interest rate and the (forward) inflation rate, denoted as π:[9]

$$1 + r_t = \frac{1 + i_t}{1 + \pi_t}, \text{ where } \pi_t = \frac{P_{t+1} - P_t}{P_t} = \frac{P_{t+1}}{P_t} - 1.$$

This definition of the real interest rate is exact (rather than the approximation, where the real interest rate is defined as the nominal interest rate less the inflation rate). The nominal interest rate measures the percentage return on bonds in terms of dollars, whereas the real interest rate measures the percentage return on bonds in terms of goods. Investors are interested in the real return on a bond (or are interested in both the nominal interest rate and the forward inflation rate).

Suppose the nominal interest rate equals 16 per cent and the inflation rate is 14 per cent. If one invests $100 in a bond today, the bond holder obtains $116 in period t+1. This individual could have purchased $100 worth of goods today, or 100 goods if the price level equals 1.0 in the current period. What is the return on the bond in terms of goods? In period t+1, the $116 can buy 101.754 goods if P_{t+1} equals 1.14 (the inflation rate equals 14 per cent). The real return, or the percentage return in terms of goods, equals

$$r_t = \frac{101.754 - 100}{100} = 0.01754 = 1.754 \text{ per cent.}$$

The nominal return on the bond is 16 per cent, but the real return is 1.754 per cent. The real interest rate on foreign bonds is defined analogously.

Real Interest Rate Parity Condition

Using the PPP conditions and the Fisher equation for both economies, the interest rate parity condition implies that real interest rates are equal in the two countries. The PPP conditions, along with the definitions of inflation, imply that

$$\frac{s_{t+1}}{s_t} = \frac{\dfrac{P_{t+1}}{P_{t+1}^*}}{\dfrac{P_t}{P_t^*}} = \frac{\dfrac{P_{t+1}}{P_t}}{\dfrac{P_{t+1}^*}{P_t^*}} = \frac{1 + \pi_t}{1 + \pi_t^*}.$$

This result, the IRP condition, and the Fisher equations together imply that

$$1+r_t = \frac{1+i_t}{1+\pi_t} = \frac{\left(1+i_t^*\right)\frac{S_{t+1}}{S_t}}{1+\pi_t} = \frac{1+i_t^*}{1+\pi_t^*} = 1+r_t^*$$

$$r_t = r_t^* \,.$$

In this model, the domestic real interest equals the foreign real interest rate.[10] This condition is called the real interest rate parity condition. With identical foreign and domestic goods, the equalization of nominal returns on domestic and foreign bonds (with both returns measured in terms of the same currency) implies the equalization of real returns on the two bonds.

An important implication is that, in a small economy, the central bank is unable to affect the domestic real interest rate. The domestic real interest rate is determined solely by the real interest rate in the large foreign economy.

Current-Period Real Money Demand

In terms of individual behavior, the agent chooses nominal money balances (an individual takes the price level as given). But the equation is expressed in terms of the variables m (real money balances) and P (the price level).

The agent holds money because money is needed to purchase goods. The services provided by money are the reason that money yields utility. When the agent is maximizing lifetime utility, the following condition holds:

$$u'\left(c_t\right) = v'\left(m_t\right) + \frac{P_t}{P_{t+1}} \frac{u'\left(c_{t+1}\right)}{\left(1+\gamma\right)},$$

where $v'\left(m\right)$ denotes the marginal utility of real money balances. Why does this equation hold? For simplicity, let P_t and P_{t+1} equal 1. Suppose the agent decreases current consumption by 1 unit and adds 1 unit of money: decrease c_t by 1 unit and increase m_t by 1 unit (the price of consumption equals 1). The marginal cost is $u'\left(c_t\right)$, the loss in utility from the unit decrease in consumption. What is the marginal benefit? Money is a *durable good*, so there are benefits in both the current and future periods. In the current period, the agent gains $v'\left(m_t\right)$, representing the benefits of holding an additional dollar of money.[11] More money yields extra benefits because it reduces the shopping time costs associated with purchasing goods during the period. Then the agent carries the extra money into the future period, and this extra dollar allows the agent to purchase an extra unit of consumption (the price of period t+1 consumption is $1 per good). The extra consumption generates a discounted gain in utility,[12] equal to $\frac{u'\left(c_{t+1}\right)}{\left(1+\gamma\right)}$. The marginal cost of the extra $1 of money is $u'\left(c_t\right)$ and the marginal benefit is $v'\left(m_t\right) + \frac{u'\left(c_{t+1}\right)}{\left(1+\gamma\right)}$.

Now consider the case where the price level increases from one period to the next. If P_t equals $4 per good and the agent decreases current consumption by 1 unit, $4 is added to money holdings. But the real quantity of money, or M_t/P_t, is $4 divided by $4 per good, or 1 good. So the agent decreases c_t by 1 and increases m_t by 1. The marginal cost is $u'(c_t)$. What is the marginal benefit? In period t, the agent gains $v'(m_t)$, representing the benefits of holding an additional real dollar of money in the current period (reduced shopping time costs). Then the agent carries the extra $4 into period t+1, allowing the purchase of additional goods. If P_{t+1} equals $6 per good, the agent can buy 4/6 of one period t+1 good. This consumption generates a discounted gain in utility that equals

$2/3 \dfrac{u'(c_{t+1})}{(1+\gamma)}$. Thus, the marginal cost is $u'(c_t)$, and the marginal benefit is $\left[v'(m_t) + \dfrac{P_t\, u'(c_{t+1})}{P_{t+1}(1+\gamma)} \right]$.

With a higher future price level, the marginal benefit of the additional money is lower than if the price level had remained unchanged between periods.

Using the Euler and Fisher equations, this equation can be rewritten such that the current-period marginal utility of money is linked to the nominal interest rate and current-period consumption:

$$u'(c_t) = v'(m_t) + \frac{P_t u'(c_{t+1})}{P_{t+1}(1+\gamma)} = v'(m_t) + \frac{u'(c_t)}{(1+i_t)}.$$

Collecting terms and rearranging yields the relationship:

$$\frac{v'(m_t)}{u'(c_t)} = \left[\frac{i_t}{1+i_t} \right].$$

The ratio of marginal utilities, or the marginal rate of substitution between real money balances and consumption, depends on the nominal interest rate. This equation defines the agent's real money demand as a function of the nominal interest rate and consumption.

This real money demand function is shown in Figure 7.1. Along the curve, consumption is held fixed. This function is downward sloping because, as real money balances increase, the marginal utility of real money falls. With a decrease in the interest rate on bonds, the opportunity cost of holding real money decreases and the agent willingly decides to hold more real balances. An increase in consumption increases real money demand (in this model, money demand depends on consumption rather than real income). As consumption increases, the marginal utility of consumption falls and the real money demand function shifts to the right. An increase in the price level (all else held fixed) causes a proportional increase in nominal money demand (with real money demand unchanged).

Future-Period Real Money Demand

In period t+1, the agent holds an amount of money that ensures that

$$v'(m_{t+1}) = u'(c_{t+1}).$$

If the utility functions have a logarithmic functional form, one obtains (where the parameter α is positive):[13]

Figure 7.1: Real money demand

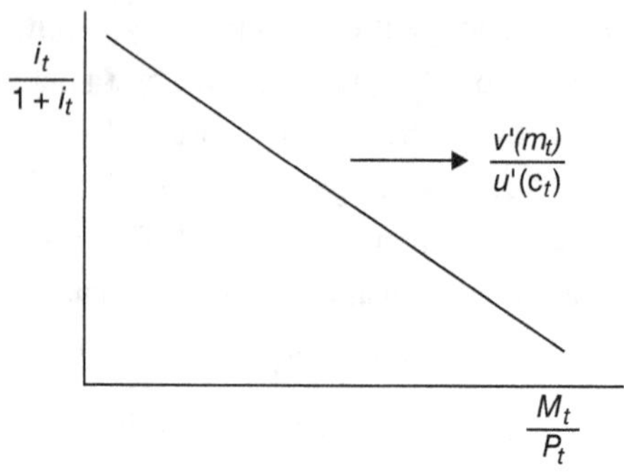

$$m_{t+1} = \frac{M_{t+1}}{P_{t+1}} = \alpha\, c_{t+1}.$$

Real money demand in period t+1 depends only on consumption (the agent will not hold bonds since t+1 is the last period). Letting nominal money supply (M^{s}_{t+1}) equal nominal money demand (M_{t+1}) yields

$$P_{t+1} = \frac{M^{s}_{t+1}}{\alpha\, c_{t+1}}.$$

In perfect foresight models, as in rational expectations models with uncertainty, the model is used to determine expectations regarding future endogenous variables.[14] The agent knows that the model implies that the future price level is related to the future money supply and future consumption, and uses this knowledge in developing the expectation regarding this future variable (one cannot simply assume, for example, that forward inflation equals zero if this assumption violates the prediction of the model).[15]

And it is important to highlight that the determination of the future price level depends on the exchange rate regime. Under a flexible exchange rate, the equation above is used to determine the future price level, and the future exchange rate is determined with the future law of one price (or PPP) condition. But under a fixed exchange rate regime, the future domestic price level is determined by the future foreign price level. The equation above then determines the money supply in the future period (with a fixed exchange rate, the nominal money supply is endogenous). These mechanisms are discussed in detail in the next two chapters.

8. THE INTEREST RATE AND REAL MONEY DEMAND IN CANADA

A prediction of the analysis is that an increase in the domestic interest rate results in a lower level of desired real money balances (for a given level of consumer spending), and vice versa. This theoretical relationship is shown in Figure 7.1.

Figure 7.2: The interest rate and money demand

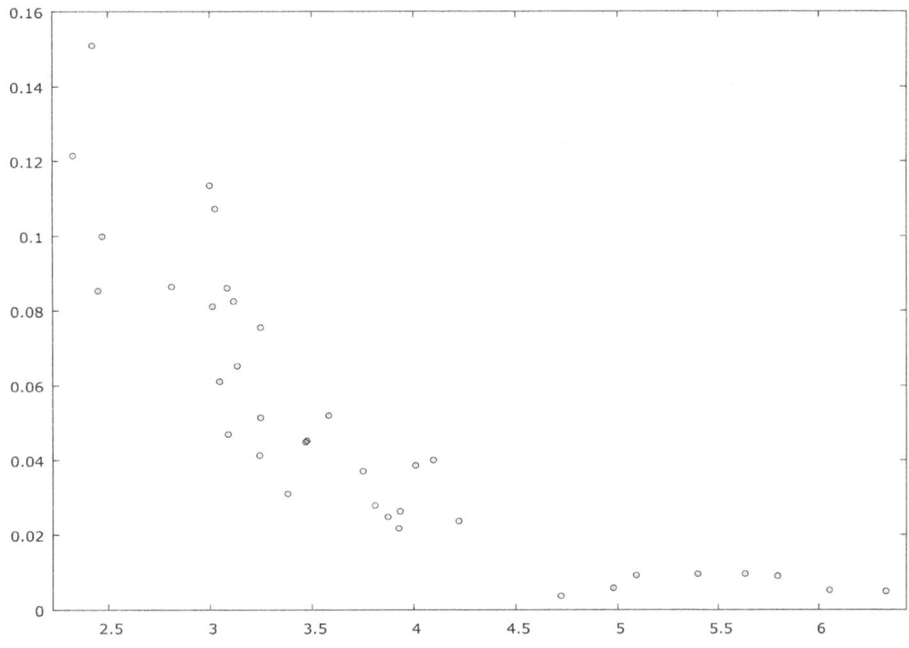

Data source: Statistics Canada

Figure 7.2 plots data points for $\dfrac{i_t}{1+i_t}$ (on the vertical axis) and $\dfrac{M_t}{P_t\, c_t}$ (on the horizontal axis) using annual Canadian data from 1981 to 2016. By including consumption in the variable $\dfrac{M_t}{P_t\, c_t}$, changes in consumption are in effect accounted for in this empirical relationship (if the consumption elasticity of real money demand equals 1.0, any change in consumption causes a proportional change in real money balances, so that the variable M/Pc is unchanged). The interest rate is the 91-day Treasury bill interest rate, money is the monetary aggregate M1+, the price level is the consumer price index, and consumption is aggregate consumer spending.[16] The negative relationship between the two variables is evident in the figure. Given the financial innovation that could potentially have affected the desired amount of real money balances for any level of the interest rate, the relationship appears to hold fairly well.[17]

This real money demand relationship plays an integral role in the analysis in Chapters 8 and 9. The exercise in Data Analytics examines another relationship: the real interest rate parity condition.

9. CURRENT-PERIOD CONSTRAINT ON THE ECONOMY

The domestic economy consists of households and the "consolidated" government, meaning the government and the central bank together. Merging the current-period household budget constraint (from section 5) with the current-period consolidated government budget constraint yields the current-period constraint on the economy.

Current-Period Government Budget Constraint

The current-period consolidated government budget constraint is[18]

$$P_t g_t + s_t R_t = T_t + B_t^s + M_t^s.$$

In terms of nominal spending (the left-hand side), the government purchases goods (denoted as g) and the central bank may purchase foreign exchange reserves (denoted as R). It is assumed that foreign exchange reserves are held as foreign bonds (interest earnings on reserves are part of government revenues in the future period). The right-hand side represents nominal tax revenue (denoted as T) plus the net issues of money and government bonds in the current period (as with the household constraint, period t−1 asset variables are ignored for simplicity).[19] The variable B[s] denotes government bond supply, and the nominal money supply, denoted as M[s], consists of domestic credit (denoted as D) and foreign exchange reserves:[20]

$$M_t^s = D_t + s_t R_t.$$

Domestic credit and government spending are the exogenous policy instruments of, respectively, the central bank and the government (under a flexible exchange rate, domestic credit equals the money supply because R equals 0).

Current-Period Constraint on the Economy and the Balance of Payments Identity

The current-period household and government budget constraints together yield the current-period constraint on the economy:[21]

$$P_t \left[y_t - c_t - g_t \right] - s_t J_t = s_t R_t.$$

This constraint is also called the balance of payments identity and consists of three components: net exports (the current account balance), net capital inflows, and the balance of payments. The first term represents net exports in nominal terms, where net exports in real terms are denoted as NX_t and defined as (investment spending equals zero)

$$NX_t = CA_t = y_t - c_t - g_t.$$

The current account is denoted as CA_t and equals net exports as the domestic economy has zero net foreign assets at the start of the current period (the debt service balance equals zero).[22] The second term, denoted as $-s_t J_t$, equals net capital inflows (in nominal terms). If the agent has a net acquisition of the foreign bond, so that J_t is positive, then net capital inflows are negative. There are net capital outflows. If J_t is negative, there are net capital inflows. The sum of the current account and net capital inflows equals the balance of payments, denoted as $s_t R_t$. The balance of payments is the net accumulation of foreign exchange reserves by the central bank (reserves equal zero at the start of period t, so R_{t-1} is zero). Under a flexible exchange rate, the balance of payments is zero and net exports are

$$NX_t = y_t - c_t - g_t = \frac{s_t J_t}{P_t} = \frac{J_t}{P_t^*}.$$

Net exports equal the net accumulation of foreign bonds by domestic residents, with all variables measured in real terms.

10. INTERTEMPORAL CONSTRAINT ON THE ECONOMY

The agent internalizes the intertemporal government budget constraint into the intertemporal household budget constraint.[23] The merging of these constraints yields the intertemporal constraint on the economy (an appendix provides details on all the intertemporal constraints):

$$c_{t+1} = y_{t+1} - g_{t+1} + \left(1 + r_t\right)\left[y_t - c_t - g_t\right].$$

Because the real interest rate parity condition holds, r_t could be replaced with $r_t{}^*$. This intertemporal constraint can be rewritten as

$$c_t + \frac{c_{t+1}}{\left(1 + r_t\right)} = y_t - g_t + \frac{y_{t+1} - g_{t+1}}{\left(1 + r_t\right)}.$$

The present value of lifetime consumption is constrained by the present value of lifetime output less the present value of lifetime government spending. The agent knows that the present value of lifetime consumption is determined by this equation. Merging the Euler equation with this intertemporal constraint on the economy yields the consumption function. Current-period consumption depends on the present value of lifetime output less the present value of lifetime government spending (as well as on the real interest rate and the marginal rate of time preference).

An important implication is that a tax cut in the current period, holding both current and future government spending fixed, has no effect on current-period consumer spending. Ricardian equivalence holds.[24] In addition, monetary policy does not affect the intertemporal constraint on the economy.[25] Money is neutral, in that changes in the nominal money supply have no effect on real variables such as consumer spending (further discussion on monetary neutrality is provided in Chapters 8 and 9).

11. A MODEL WITH MANY PERIODS

In a multiple-period model, current consumption depends on the present value of lifetime output less government spending over all future periods. Likewise, the agent uses the equilibrium conditions in conjunction with the law of one price conditions in determining future endogenous variables such as future exchange rates and future price levels. And for any two adjacent periods, the Euler equation for consumption, the interest rate parity condition, and the real money-consumption marginal rate of substitution condition continue to hold. The two-period setup is adopted for convenience, but the insights garnered from the two-period model are similar to those that arise in a multiple-period model.

12. CONCLUSION

This chapter outlined the basic structure and explained the key equations of the intertemporal model with money. The next two chapters provide a detailed discussion of various exogenous changes and related policy issues, first under a flexible exchange rate and then under a fixed exchange rate.

PRACTICE QUESTIONS

1. Provide a summary of the Euler equation for consumption, interest rate parity, the Fisher equation, real interest rate parity, and the condition that the current-period marginal rate of substitution between real money and consumption depends on the nominal interest rate.

2. Fill in the blanks
   (a) If the money supply equals \$100 and the price level equals \$20 per good, the real money supply equals _____ goods.
   (b) In the exact specification of interest rate parity, $(1+i_t)$ equals _____.
   (c) Consider the exact specification of the Fisher equation. If the inflation rate equals 14 per cent and the _____ interest rate equals 16 per cent, the _____ interest rate equals 1.75 per cent.
   (d) The real interest rate in the domestic economy is determined by _____.
   (e) If the foreign real interest rate equals the marginal rate of time preference, the marginal utility of consumption in the current period equals _____.

3. When the consumer decreases current-period consumption, allowing for an increase in real money balances, the marginal cost of this action is the marginal utility of current-period consumption. What is the marginal benefit over their lifetime? Explain in terms of the marginal utility of current-period real money balances and the marginal utility of future consumption (let the price level equal 1 in both periods).

4. Draw the diagram for the real money demand function in the intertemporal model of money. Label the axes. Explain why the real money demand function is downward sloping.

DATA ANALYTICS

1. (a) Collect data on the interest rate and the consumer price index, beginning in 1981. CANSIM numbers are provided in section 8. Convert the original monthly data to annual data. Calculate the forward annual inflation rate and the ex-post real interest rate (the real interest rate based on the actual forward inflation rate). Create a plot of the nominal interest rate and the inflation rate and another plot of the real interest rate. Comment.

(b) Using the Federal Reserve Bank of St. Louis FRED database, collect data on the US interest rate and the US consumer price index. Begin the sample in 1981. Calculate and plot the ex-post US and Canadian real interest rates. Comment.

APPENDIX A: INTERTEMPORAL CONSTRAINTS

Intertemporal Household Budget Constraint

Merging the current and future household constraints (by eliminating B_t) yields the intertemporal budget constraint, where TX denotes real taxes measured as nominal taxes divided by the price level:

$$y_{t+1} - TX_{t+1} + \frac{\left(1+i_t\right)P_t}{P_{t+1}}\left[y_t - TX_t - c_t\right] + \frac{J_t}{P_{t+1}}\left[\left(1+i_t^*\right)s_{t+1} - \left(1+i_t\right)s_t\right]$$

$$= c_{t+1} + \frac{M_t\left(1+i_t\right)}{P_{t+1}} + \frac{M_{t+1} - M_t}{P_{t+1}}.$$

The term in square brackets at the end of the upper line equals zero, because interest rate parity holds in equilibrium. With perfect foresight, there are no unanticipated capital gains or losses from the holding of foreign bonds. Using the Fisher equation and rearranging yields[26]

$$y_t - TX_t + \frac{y_{t+1} - TX_{t+1}}{\left(1+r_t\right)} = c_t + \frac{c_{t+1}}{\left(1+r_t\right)} + \frac{M_t}{P_t} + \frac{M_{t+1} - M_t}{P_{t+1}\left(1+r_t\right)}.$$

Intertemporal Government Budget Constraint

The current and future consolidated government budget constraints are as follows:

$$P_t\,g_t + s_t\,R_t = T_t + B_t^s + M_t^s.$$

$$P_{t+1}\,g_{t+1} + \left(1+i_t\right)B_t^s = T_{t+1} + \left(1+i_{t+1}^*\right)s_{t+1}\,R_t + M_{t+1}^s - M_t^s.$$

The current-period constraint was discussed in the chapter. In the future period, the government must pay principal plus interest on domestic bonds that were issued, or sold, in period t (there is now "interest on the debt"). And the government earns interest on the central bank's holdings of foreign exchange reserves.[27] In principle, there could be capital gains or losses on foreign exchange reserves through changes in the exchange rate (but capital gains will not arise if the exchange rate is permanently fixed; capital gains do not arise under a flexible exchange rate when reserves are zero). In addition, the government can finance future-period spending by printing money. In a two-period model, B^s_{t+1} and R_{t+1} are set equal to 0.

Consider the case of a flexible exchange rate, so that the variable R equals 0. Merging the period t and period t+1 government budget constraints (by eliminating domestic bonds) yields the intertemporal government budget constraint:

$$g_t + \frac{g_{t+1}}{(1+r_t)} = TX_t + \frac{TX_{t+1}}{(1+r_t)} + \frac{M^s_t}{P_t} + \frac{M^s_{t+1} - M^s_t}{P_{t+1}(1+r_t)}.$$

Over the lifetime, government spending can be financed by taxes and by printing money.[28]

Intertemporal Constraint on the Economy

Merging the intertemporal household budget constraint with the intertemporal government budget constraint yields the intertemporal constraint on the economy:

$$c_{t+1} = y_{t+1} - g_{t+1} + (1+r_t)[y_t - c_t - g_t],$$

where it is assumed that domestic money and domestic bonds are held only by domestic residents:

$$M^s_t = M_t, \; M^s_{t+1} = M_{t+1}, \; B^s_t = B_t.$$

APPENDIX B: ALTERNATIVE MODELS OF MONEY

There are models of money that do not put real money balances into the utility function, motivating the demand for money in other ways. Two widely used models are the transactions costs model and the cash in advance (CIA) model.[29]

The transactions costs model includes real money in the budget constraints. For example, current-period production net of transactions costs can be specified as $y_t(1-v(x_t))$, where $v(x)$ measures real transactions costs (for example, Greenwood 1983). The function $v(x)$ lies between 0 and 1, with x_t equal to M_t/P_ty_t. Increases in M/P relative to y cause $v(x)$ to decrease and increase $y(1-v(x))$. This approach is similar to putting real money balances into the production function.

The CIA model assumes that consumers need money to purchase goods. The current-period cash in advance constraint is

$$M_t = P_t \, c_t.$$

Nominal money demand in this model depends on the price level and consumption, but not on the interest rate (more sophisticated CIA models allow the demand for money to depend negatively on the nominal interest rate).

NOTES

1 This setup has a long history, dating back at least to the closed-economy models in Patinkin (1965) and Sidrauski (1967). Open-economy models along these lines experienced a resurgence in the 1980s, with contributions by Stockman (1983), Obstfeld (1986), and others.
2 On government spending yielding benefits, or utility, to consumers, see the discussion in Chapters 5 and 6.
3 Rogoff (1996), among other things, surveys the origins of PPP, including the contribution of Gustav Cassel.
4 For example, if the foreign price level equals $100 US and the exchange rate s_t equals 1.10, so that $1.10 Canadian is required to buy $1 US, the equilibrium Canadian price level must equal $110 Canadian.
5 Preferences are assumed to be separable. This assumption means that g affects utility through u(g) and m affects utility through v(m), but changes in g and m have no direct effect on the u(c) function.
6 Macroeconomists understand, in general, the benefits that money provides, but there is dispute on how best to model monetary economies. An appendix summarizes alternative approaches to modeling money.
7 See the discussion, for example, in Brock (1974) and McCallum and Goodfriend (1989).
8 The approximation ignores the cross-product term $\left[i_t^* \left(\dfrac{s_{t+1} - s_t}{s_t} \right) \right]$, which is relatively small.
9 The equation is named after Irving Fisher, whose book *The Theory of Interest* (1930) was one of the most important macroeconomic books of the century. Note that the equation is often specified under uncertainty, using the expected inflation rate and the expected real interest rate.
10 With uncertainty, the IRP condition may include a risk premium related to consumption covariance risk or to default risk (see Chapter 2). Domestic and foreign real interest rates then differ by the risk premium. And domestic and foreign real rates may differ when the PPP condition is not valid. See Chapters 14 and 15.
11 The money may circulate through the economy a number of times in the period, and returns to the agent.
12 If the money is held, the gain is $v'(m_{t+1})/(1+\gamma)$. But $u'(c_{t+1})$ equals $v'(m_{t+1})$, so the expressions are equal.
13 For a function f(x) = ln x, $f'(x)$ equals x^{-1}. Let u(c) = ln c, and v(m) = α ln m.
14 On rational expectations, see the comments in Hall and Sargent (2018).
15 On solving backward in dynamic models, see Brock (1975). LeRoy (1984a, 1984b) discusses the money-in-the-utility-function model with uncertainty. The seminal literature on two-period, open-economy models with uncertainty includes Helpman and Razin (1982), Stockman (1983), and Greenwood (1983).
16 CANSIM numbers are in parentheses: M1+ (V37151), consumer price index (V41690973), aggregate consumption (the sum of V62305724 and V62305730), and the interest rate (V122484). These annual data are averages of the original monthly or quarterly data.
17 See Lucas (2000) and Alvarez and Lippi (2014) for similar plots, based on US data with real GDP, rather than consumption, as the scale variable.
18 For simplicity, initial net government debt is zero.
19 Budget deficits can be financed by selling new domestic government bonds, by printing money, or by selling foreign exchange reserves (as noted in Chapter 9, financing deficits is constrained under a fixed exchange rate).
20 The money multiplier is assumed to equal 1, so the money supply equals the monetary base.

21 Domestic bonds and money are held only by domestic residents, so $\left[B_t - B_t^s\right]$ and $\left[M_t - M_t^s\right]$ equal zero.
22 An appendix in Chapter 5 discusses the debt service balance.
23 In effect, the agent understands the details of government budget constraints and uses this knowledge in determining how current and future taxes are affected by government and central bank policy.
24 Ricardian equivalence is discussed in Chapter 5, as well as in Chapters 8, 9, 14, and 15. Stockman (1983) discusses this result in a similar but more advanced model that incorporates uncertainty and a non-traded good.
25 Brock (1975) and LeRoy (1984a, 1984b) discuss various advanced, technical issues related to models that have real money balances in the utility function.
26 The term M_t/P_t would be $[M_t\text{-}M_{t-1}]/P_t$ if the agent started period t with money equal to M_{t-1}.
27 The agent understands the consolidated budget and knows that these interest earnings, all else held fixed, allow for lower taxes (either current or future).
28 Bond sales do not allow for higher lifetime government spending. The principal and interest of any current-period sale of government bonds must be paid fully in the future period.
29 For an advanced discussion of these models, see Walsh (2010). Another model, the overlapping-generations model, is discussed in Champ et al. (2011).

CHAPTER 8

Money, the Price Level, and the Exchange Rate

1. INTRODUCTION

What factors cause long-term movements in the nominal exchange rate? This question is one of the fundamental issues in international macroeconomics. In general, both real and monetary factors influence the nominal exchange rate in the long run. This chapter abstracts from a number of important real factors in exchange rate determination by assuming that domestic and foreign goods are identical. This setup embeds the following assumptions: there are no non-traded goods, and the domestic traded good is identical to the foreign traded good. In this framework, the nominal exchange rate is determined strictly by the factors that affect the aggregate domestic and foreign price levels.[1]

This chapter examines a flexible exchange rate regime, using the intertemporal model with money. The discussion focuses on a range of questions. Does monetary policy affect any real variables? How do changes in the money supply affect the price level, the exchange rate, and the nominal interest rate? How do changes in output affect these nominal variables? What is the relationship between the exchange rate and the current account? What is the optimal monetary policy under a flexible exchange rate? In addition, this chapter presents and discusses some evidence regarding long-term movements in money, the price level, and the exchange rate.

2. THE INTERTEMPORAL MODEL WITH MONEY

This section provides an overview of the intertemporal model with money (the model is discussed in detail in Chapter 7). There is a current period (period t) and a future period (period t+1), with perfect foresight of future variables. Consumers maximize lifetime utility subject to an intertemporal budget constraint (the terms consumers, consumer, and agent are used interchangeably). Lifetime utility depends on consumption (denoted as c), real government expenditure (denoted as g), and real money balances (denoted as m) in both the current and future periods. Real money balances yield utility because "money" allows transactions to be conducted in an efficient manner. In a shopping-time rationalization of the model, a higher level of real money balances implies less shopping time and therefore more leisure and a higher level of utility.

Domestic production (denoted as y) is exogenous, and the good produced in the domestic economy is identical to the foreign good. The domestic economy is small, with foreign variables taken to be exogenous. The exchange rate, denoted as s, is flexible (an increase in s represents a depreciation of the domestic currency).

Key Relationships

In equilibrium, foreign and domestic bonds are equally good investments. The interest rate parity condition holds, and given that foreign and domestic goods are identical, this condition implies that domestic and foreign real interest rates are equal. These conditions are specified as

$$\left(1+i_t\right) = \frac{\left(1+i_t^*\right) s_{t+1}}{s_t},$$

$$r_t = r_t^*,$$

where i_t is the domestic nominal interest rate, r_t denotes the domestic real interest rate, and the corresponding foreign variables are denoted with an asterisk (*). The model also incorporates the Fisher equation, an identity that defines the real interest rate in terms of the nominal interest rate and the forward inflation rate (denoted as π_t):

$$1+r_t = \frac{1+i_t}{1+\pi_t}, \; where \; \pi_t = \frac{P_{t+1} - P_t}{P_t}.$$

The lifetime utility-maximizing consumer allocates consumption between periods in a way consistent with the Euler equation for consumption:

$$u'\left(c_t\right) = \frac{\left(1+r_t\right)}{1+\gamma} u'\left(c_{t+1}\right) \; \rightarrow \; c_t = c_{t+1} \; if \; r_t = \gamma,$$

where $u'\left(c\right)$ is the marginal utility of consumption and the parameter γ denotes the fixed marginal rate of time preference. If r_t equals γ, the agent ensures that consumption smoothing holds (regardless of the levels of current and future after-tax real income). Current-period consumption is determined by the Euler equation and the intertemporal constraint on the economy:

$$c_t + \frac{c_{t+1}}{\left(1+r_t\right)} = y_t - g_t + \frac{y_{t+1} - g_{t+1}}{\left(1+r_t\right)}.$$

This constraint implies that, over the lifetime, consumer spending is constrained by the present value of lifetime output less the present value of lifetime government spending.[2]

The current account balance, denoted as CA_t, equals domestic production less total spending by consumers and the government (the model abstracts from investment spending):

$$CA_t = y_t - c_t - g_t.$$

As the domestic good is identical to the foreign good, competition between domestic and foreign firms ensures that the law of one price holds in each period. Letting P denote the domestic price level and P* denote the foreign price level, the law of one price conditions are

$$P_t = s_t P_t^*,$$

$$P_{t+1} = s_{t+1} P_{t+1}^*.$$

In this one-good model, the law of one price conditions are identical to the purchasing power parity (PPP) conditions.

The demand for real money balances in the current period, denoted as m_t or $\dfrac{M_t}{P_t}$, is based on a relationship that links the current-period marginal utility of real money, denoted as $v'(m_t)$, with the current-period marginal utility of consumption and the nominal interest rate (an appendix provides further explanation). More generally, this condition means that the demand for real money balances depends positively on consumer spending and negatively on the domestic nominal interest rate (and an increase in the price level causes a proportional increase in the nominal demand for money). In equilibrium, the current-period nominal demand for money, M_t, equals the current-period nominal supply of money, M_t^s (and real money demand equals the real money supply). The equilibrium condition is

$$v'\left(\frac{M_t^s}{P_t}\right) = \left[\frac{i_t}{1+i_t}\right] u'(c_t),$$

and is shown diagrammatically in Figure 8.1.

The curve denoted $\dfrac{v'(m_t)}{u'(c_t)}$ represents the amount of real money balances the agent *wants to hold* at different levels of the domestic interest rate (holding current-period consumption fixed). This curve is downward sloping because the agent wants to hold fewer real money balances when the interest rate increases. An increase in current-period consumption increases money demand and shifts the curve to the right. The vertical line RM_t^s represents the real money supply, denoted as $\dfrac{M_t^s}{P_t}$. The central bank controls the nominal money supply, but the price level is an endogenous variable that responds to exogenous shocks. The RM_t^s line shifts to the left (for example) if the current-period nominal money supply falls or if the current-period price level rises.

In addition, there is a future-period money market equilibrium condition:

$$v'\left(\frac{M_{t+1}^s}{P_{t+1}}\right) = u'(c_{t+1}) \;\rightarrow\; P_{t+1} = \frac{M_{t+1}^s}{\alpha\, c_{t+1}},$$

Figure 8.1: Money market equilibrium

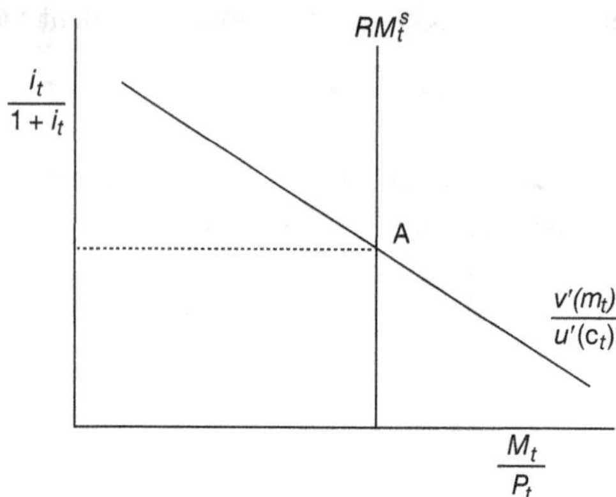

where α is a constant parameter.[3] As explained below, this condition plays an integral role in generating "expectations" (or the perfect foresight value) of the future price level.

Endogenous and Exogenous Variables

The endogenous variables are the four real variables c_t, c_{t+1}, r_t, and CA_t and the six nominal variables i_t, s_t, s_{t+1}, P_t, P_{t+1}, and π_t. With a flexible exchange rate, the central bank controls the nominal money supply. The exogenous variables are M_t^s, M_{t+1}^s, y_t, y_{t+1}, g_t, g_{t+1}, i_t^*, r_t^*, P_t^*, P_{t+1}^*, and γ. These variables are fixed but can change exogenously.

The Long Run and the Short Run

The model assumes that the domestic price level is flexible in the current period. The model does not explicitly incorporate firms or labor and capital markets, but it assumes that production is exogenous. This assumption implies that the supply curve for domestic goods is vertical. Many economists would describe this flexible-price setup as being consistent with the long run. Other economists, such as proponents of real business cycle theory, may regard the setup as being consistent with the short run. These economists regard goods and factor prices as being flexible even in the short run (reflecting a period such as a quarter or a year).[4] Whether the current-period equilibrium is regarded as a long-run or short-run equilibrium is not a matter of concern with respect to the theoretical analysis.[5]

3. MONETARY POLICY AND REAL VARIABLES

Changes in the nominal money supply have no effect on the real interest rate. The domestic real interest rate is determined by the exogenous foreign real interest rate:

$$r_t = r_t^*.$$

The central bank, in a small open economy, is unable to influence the real interest rate. The domestic real interest rate can fluctuate, but these fluctuations are caused solely by changes in the foreign real interest rate.

Likewise, changes in the nominal money supply have no effect on consumption. The Euler equation for consumption, in conjunction with the intertemporal constraint on the economy, implies that current consumption is determined by the real interest rate (relative to the fixed marginal rate of time preference) and the present value of lifetime output less the present value of lifetime government spending. Because central bank policy has no effect on these variables, there is no effect on consumer spending.

Moreover, from the current account identity, net exports and the current account balance are not affected by monetary policy if consumer spending is unaffected (in this model, output and government spending are exogenous, and investment spending equals zero). Because changes in the money supply do not affect consumer spending, they do not affect net exports.

Even the relative price channel is not operative in this model. An increase in the money supply causes a depreciation of the domestic currency, which in itself makes the domestic good relatively cheaper. But the increase in the money supply also causes a proportionate increase in the domestic price level. Through the law of one price, these two changes offset each other and net exports are unaffected.

If a change in the level of the money supply has no effect on real variables, monetary neutrality holds. If a change in the rate of growth of the money supply has no effect on real variables, super-neutrality holds. Both neutrality and super-neutrality hold in this model.[6]

4. SOLVE THE INTERTEMPORAL MODEL BACKWARD

Because changes in future variables can potentially affect current-period variables, one must first solve for the effects on the future variables and work backward. The agent adopts this perspective in determining the effects of any exogenous change.

Under a flexible exchange rate, the future domestic price level is determined by the future money market equilibrium condition:

$$P_{t+1} = \frac{M_{t+1}^s}{\alpha\, c_{t+1}}.$$

The future exchange rate is then determined by the future law of one price (or PPP) condition:

$$S_{t+1} = \frac{P_{t+1}}{P_{t+1}^*}.$$

With perfect foresight, the magnitudes of these future variables are known.[7]

Monetary Changes

The next four sections examine the effects of monetary policy actions on the price level, the exchange rate, and the nominal interest rate.[8] The exogenous changes are permanent, temporary, and future changes in the nominal money supply, as well as an exogenous change in the foreign price level (caused by a change in the foreign money supply).[9]

5. PERMANENT CHANGES IN THE MONEY SUPPLY

Suppose there is a permanent increase in the nominal money supply, where both M_t^s and M_{t+1}^s increase from 100 to 110. What are the effects of this policy action on the endogenous nominal variables in the model?

The agent must solve backward, first determining how this exogenous change affects variables in period t+1. The future price level is determined by

$$P_{t+1} = \frac{M_{t+1}^s}{\alpha c_{t+1}}.$$

The increase in the future nominal money supply will cause the future price level to increase. Given that the change in the future money supply has no effect on future consumption, a 10 per cent increase in the future money supply causes a 10 per cent increase in the future price level. And through the law of one price condition, the agent infers that the domestic currency will be worth less (in terms of foreign currency) in period t+1. That is, the agent knows that an increase in M_{t+1}^s causes s_{t+1} to rise. Having worked out the future effects, the agent decides on the appropriate actions to be taken in the current period.

With the rise in s_{t+1}, the interest rate parity condition no longer holds:

$$\left(1+i_t\right) < \frac{\left(1+i_t^*\right) s_{t+1}}{s_t}.$$

At the initial current exchange rate and the initial interest rates, the return on foreign bonds exceeds the return on domestic bonds. The representative agent (and all individuals, because everyone has the same information) attempts to buy foreign currency. As the agent bids higher and higher prices for foreign currency, the return on the foreign bond is reduced. At the new equilibrium point, the increase in s_{t+1} is matched by the increase in s_t, a current-period depreciation of the domestic currency. The interest rate parity condition again holds (with no change in the domestic interest rate), so that foreign and domestic bonds are equally good investments.

The depreciation of the domestic currency in the current period implies that the law of one price does not hold:

$$P_t < s_t P_t^*.$$

At the initial domestic price level, the domestic good is cheaper. As domestic residents attempt to increase their purchases of the domestic good, the domestic price level rises (production is fixed, and firms can sell their production at the higher price level). While one does not want to overemphasize the timing of changes in the endogenous variables, some may argue that it is plausible that the depreciation of the domestic currency occurs first and induces an increase in the domestic price level.[10]

While the permanent increase in the money supply causes an increase in the price level, the current and future price levels both rise by 10 per cent and the inflation rate remains at zero (where it was initially). There is a one-time increase in the price level, but (going forward) the inflation rate

Figure 8.2: Permanent increase in the money supply

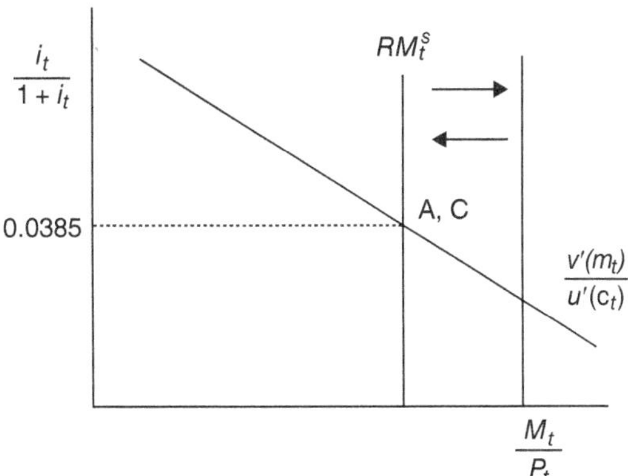

equals 0 per cent. The current and future exchange rate also both increase by 10 per cent, and the rate of appreciation of the foreign currency equals 0 per cent. As this change in the money supply has no effect on the real interest rate or the inflation rate, the nominal interest rate is unchanged (an appendix examines this case in further detail).

In Figure 8.2, the initial domestic interest rate equals 0.04 and $[i_t/1+i_t]$ equals 0.0385 (denoted as point A). The increase in the nominal money supply shifts the vertical real money supply line RM_t^s to the right, but the increase in the domestic price level shifts the line back to the left. The new equilibrium is at point C, with no net shift in the real money supply line and no change in the nominal interest rate.

6. TEMPORARY CHANGES IN THE MONEY SUPPLY

With a temporary increase in the money supply, the current money supply increases and the future money supply is unchanged. Solving backward, the agent infers that there is no change in the future price level or the future exchange rate. In Figure 8.3, the increase in the nominal money supply, for a given price level, shifts the RM_t^s line to the right and reduces the domestic nominal interest rate to point B. With the return on domestic bonds less than the return on foreign bonds, the actions of the agent cause the domestic currency to depreciate in the current period. And through the law of one price condition, the increase in s_t implies that P_t increases and shifts the RM_t^s line back to the left (the higher price level increases nominal money demand, causing residents to try and sell domestic bonds, pushing the interest rate back up). In the new equilibrium at point C, the domestic interest rate has been reduced from the initial equilibrium at A.

The rate of appreciation of the foreign currency, $\dfrac{s_{t+1}-s_t}{s_t}$, is negative in the new equilibrium because s_{t+1} is unchanged and s_t has increased. Likewise, the fall in the nominal interest rate is consistent with a decrease in the inflation rate. There is now going to be deflation as the economy moves forward into period t+1. The rise in the exchange rate and the price level are temporary, like the increase in the money supply, with these nominal variables falling as the economy moves forward into the future period.

Figure 8.3: Temporary increase in the money supply

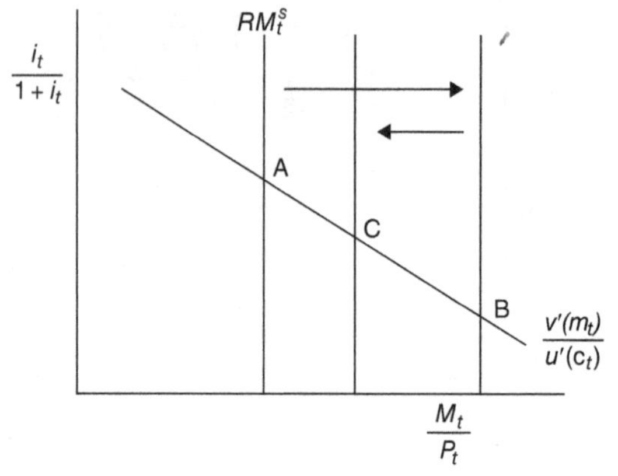

Consumer Spending and the Interest Rate

For a given inflation rate, a decrease in the nominal interest rate increases desired spending, but a decrease in the inflation rate acts to decrease desired spending. With an unchanged real interest rate, these two effects offset each other. Consumer spending is unchanged.

7. CHANGES IN THE "EXPECTED" FUTURE MONEY SUPPLY

"Expectations" of future exogenous changes are important, resulting in changes in current-period endogenous variables. Suppose the current money supply is unchanged, but the central bank announces that the future money supply will be increased (this change is similar to an increase in the rate of growth of the money supply). The agent infers that the future price level and the future exchange rate will both increase. The increase in s_{t+1}, through the interest rate parity condition, induces the agent to try and buy foreign currency and causes the domestic currency to depreciate in the current period. To maintain the law of one price, the domestic price level increases. The increases in the current price level and exchange rate are less than the corresponding increases in the future price level and exchange rate, so there are increases in both the forward inflation rate and the rate of depreciation of the domestic currency.

The diagram for money market equilibrium is shown in Figure 8.4, where the induced increase in the current-period price level decreases the real money supply and shifts the RM_t^s curve to the left. The new equilibrium is at point C. The increase in the future money supply results in an increase in the current-period nominal interest rate.

A Note on Difficulties in Conducting Empirical Analyses

This exogenous change highlights one of the difficulties of analyzing the causes of changes in the exchange rate, the price level, and the nominal interest rate. With an increase in the (expected) *future* money supply, the current-period exchange rate, price level, and nominal interest rate increase

Figure 8.4: Increase in the future money supply

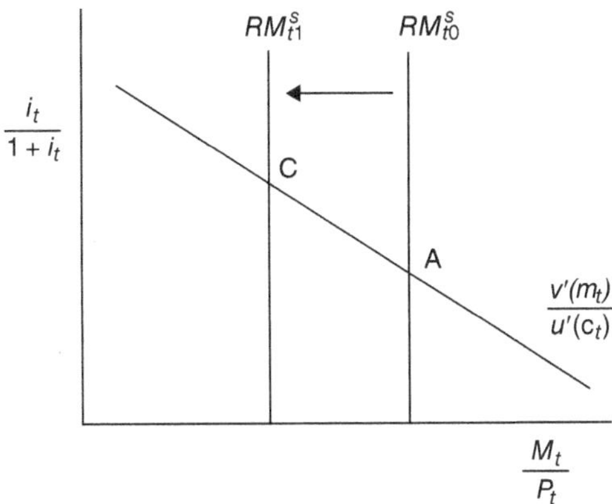

without any change in current-period exogenous variables. The endogenous variables in the current period are affected by expectations about future variables. Economists analyzing data must be aware of this possibility, so as to not be misled with respect to the causes of exchange rate, price level, and interest rate movements.[11]

8. CHANGES IN THE FOREIGN PRICE LEVEL

Monetary changes in the foreign country have no effect on the domestic price level, but they do cause changes in the exchange rate. Suppose there is a permanent increase in the foreign price level (with no change in the foreign nominal interest rate or the foreign real interest rate). The agent solves backward. The future domestic price level is unaffected because it is determined by the period t+1 domestic money supply and consumption (which are unchanged). But the increase in the future foreign price level will, through the law of one price, cause a future appreciation of the domestic currency. The fall in s_{t+1} induces the agent to try and sell foreign currency in the current period and therefore causes the domestic currency to appreciate. The fall in s_t offsets the increase in the foreign price level in period t, so as to maintain the law of one price. Under a flexible exchange rate, changes in the foreign price level result in exchange rate movements but do not affect the domestic price level.

A Note on Policy

If the foreign price level continues to rise period after period in a multiple-period environment, the domestic currency appreciates in each period.[12] The domestic central bank can maintain a zero-inflation policy even though the foreign economy has the price level rising over time. The flexible exchange rate insulates the domestic economy from the price level changes occurring in the foreign economy.

The appreciation of the domestic currency does not cause the domestic economy to become uncompetitive on world goods markets. The zero-inflation policy of the domestic central bank does result in a continual appreciation of the domestic currency (holding other exogenous factors fixed), but the appreciation in any period simply offsets the rise in the foreign price level in that period. In this model, there is no negative effect on the competitiveness of domestic firms.

9. THE EXCHANGE RATE AND PRICE LEVELS: SOME EMPIRICAL EVIDENCE

The theoretical analysis on the effects of changes in the money supply on the exchange rate and the price level continues to hold in more complicated models (for example, in models where PPP does not hold and the real exchange rate changes in response to real factors). But when applying the model, it is convenient to focus on cases where monetary policy in the countries was very different and overrides any real factors that may also be affecting the exchange rate (the Canadian–US dollar exchange rate is not a good case because of the similarity of Canadian and American monetary policy).[13] The following subsections examine two interesting cases where monetary policies differed substantially.

The French Franc Relative to the US Dollar after World War I

While the classical gold standard (a fixed exchange rate regime) operated before World War I, the French economy moved to a flexible exchange rate after the war (France would return to a gold standard regime in the latter half of the 1920s). By April 1920, the franc had depreciated substantially relative to the US dollar, such that the franc was worth less than one-third of its prewar rate.

John Maynard Keynes, in his monograph *A Tract on Monetary Reform* (1923), examined the validity of the PPP theory as an explanation of the movements in the French franc–US dollar exchange rate.[14] In general, Keynes (1923, 74) was skeptical of the PPP theory based on aggregate price levels, noting that the prices of non-traded goods need not move similarly in the two countries: "... the theory requires a further assumption for its validity, namely, that in the long run the home prices of the goods and services which do not enter into international trade, move in more or less the same proportions as those which do."[15] But Keynes (1923, 75) noted that if monetary factors are the predominant factor in causing changes in the exchange rate, the PPP prediction may be expected to hold.[16]

Figure 8.5 shows movements in the franc relative to the US dollar (indexed such that the pre-war value is 100) and in the ratio of a US price index to a French price index, over August 1919 to June 1923 (the data are taken from Keynes 1923). The solid line represents the exchange rate, with a fall in the line representing a depreciation of the franc. From mid-1919 to mid-1920, the franc depreciated by more than 40 per cent (and this fall was after an earlier 35 per cent depreciation). The dotted line represents the US price level divided by the French price level. The two lines move closely together. As Keynes (1923, 86) noted, "the purchasing power parity theory, even in its crude form, has worked passably well."

In the period between April 1920 and May 1921, the value of the franc (relative to the US dollar) rose by over 30 per cent, fell by almost 30 per cent, and then rose again by over 40 per cent.

Figure 8.5: The franc–dollar exchange rate and the relative price level

Data source: Keynes (1923)

This variability over a 13-month period is phenomenal. Expectations were undoubtedly a factor in this variability, as investors paid attention to news with respect to current and future policy.[17] And the pronounced variability may have played a role in convincing policymakers to return to a gold standard system in the second half of the 1920s.

Italy and Germany in the Late 1970s

In the 1970s, many industrialized countries had much higher inflation rates than they do today. Among G7 countries, Italy had the highest inflation rate and Germany the lowest. Italy's annual inflation rate ranged from 10 per cent to 22 per cent from 1976 to 1979, whereas the German inflation rate moved between 2 per cent and 6 per cent. Given that Germany was a large trading partner of Italy, did this divergence in inflation rates cause problems for the Italian economy?

Figure 8.6 shows the exchange rate and the ratio of price levels in the two countries, indexed to allow for a straightforward comparison.[18] The solid line depicts the index of the Italian lira–German mark exchange rate from 1976 to 1979, where an upward movement represents a depreciation of the lira. The dotted line represents the index of the Italian price level relative to the German price level, with each price level based on the consumer price index that include the prices of both traded and non-traded goods. With the Italian price level increasing about 60 per cent more than the German price level over this period, an observer may think that Italian goods would have become too expensive compared to German goods. But the inflationary monetary policy in Italy

Figure 8.6: The lira–mark exchange rate and the relative price level

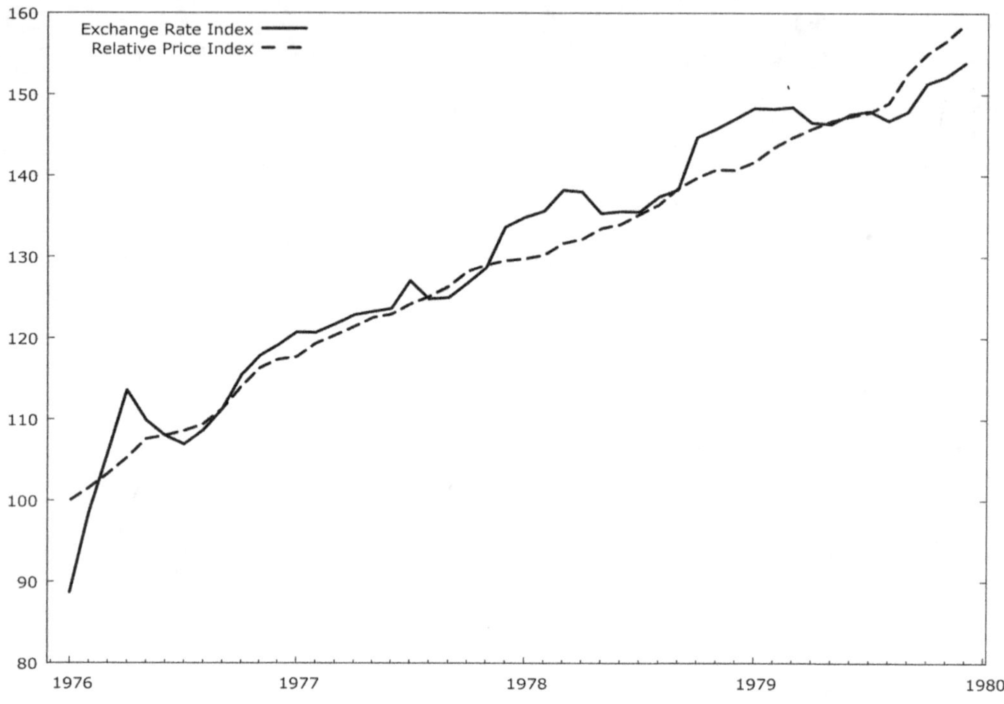

Data source: International Monetary Fund

also caused a significant depreciation of the lira, and the relative increase in the Italian price level was offset by the change in the exchange rate. The depreciation of the lira served to maintain the international competitiveness of Italian products.

10. CHANGES IN OUTPUT

Changes in output also affect the exchange rate and the price level. This section examines exogenous changes in output, holding the money supply and other exogenous variables fixed (fiscal policy changes are discussed in an appendix).

It is important to note that the variable in the money demand function is consumption, not real income (or output).[19] Any change in output causes a change in consumption, so the results will be similar to a model where money demand depended on output. An important difference is that, with consumption smoothing, current consumption will change in response to any change in output, current or future. For simplicity, it is assumed that the consumption elasticity of money demand equals 1.0 in both periods. Given that the different changes in output (permanent, temporary, or future) have similar effects on the price level and the exchange rate, this section examines just one case.

With a temporary increase in output, y_t increases but y_{t+1} is unchanged. But with consumption smoothing, any increase in output causes both current and future consumption to increase. The

Figure 8.7: Increase in consumption

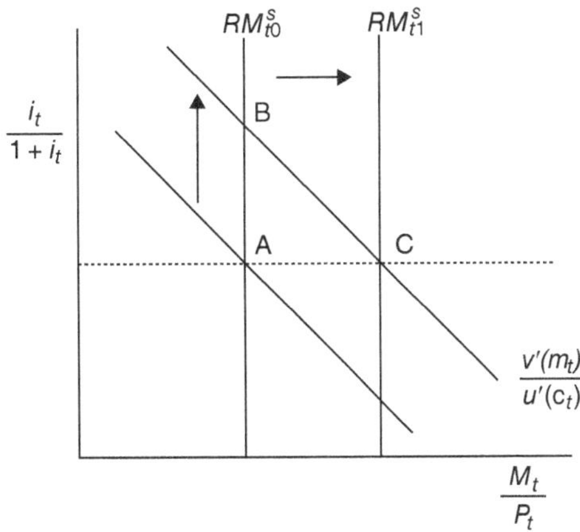

associated increase in future consumption increases future money demand and decreases the future price level (see the equation for the future price level specified in Section 2). Even though future output is unchanged, the future price level falls. Through the law of one price, the agent infers that the domestic currency will appreciate in period t+1. Having determined the future effects, the agent takes actions in the current period. The reduction in s_{t+1} reduces the return on foreign bonds, so the agent tries to sell foreign currency in the current period. The domestic currency appreciates relative to the foreign currency, and through the law of one price condition, the current-period price level falls.

Because money demand depends on consumption and both current and future consumption increase, P_t and P_{t+1} both fall in response to the temporary increase in output. The inflation rate and the nominal interest rate remain unchanged (P_t and P_{t+1} fall by the same amount). In Figure 8.7, the increase in current consumption shifts the $\dfrac{v'(m_t)}{u'(c_t)}$ curve upward to the right, representing an increase in real money demand. As the current-period price level falls, the real money supply increases and the real money supply curve shifts to the right. The new equilibrium is at point C.

11. THE CURRENT ACCOUNT AND THE EXCHANGE RATE

In the model, changes in monetary variables have no effect on real variables, and the determination of the current account balance is a real phenomenon. The discussion in this section is brief (current account determination was discussed in Chapters 5 and 6, and is discussed further in Chapter 14). For simplicity, the debt service balance is assumed to equal zero, so that net exports (denoted NX) equal the current account balance (denoted CA).

In real terms, the current-period balance of payments identity is as follows:

$$NX_t = CA_t = \left[y_t - c_t - g_t \right] = \frac{J_t}{P_t^*}.$$

With positive NX_t, J_t is positive and the agent has saved by accumulating foreign bonds. The real variable $\dfrac{J_t}{P_t^*}$ measures the number of foreign goods that the foreign bonds are able to purchase. If J_t equals \$10 US and P_t^* equals \$5 US per good, this variable is 2 goods. Foreign goods are assumed to be identical to domestic goods.

There is no simple relationship between movements in the current account and the exchange rate.[20] In the intertemporal model with money, any increase in output (holding the nominal money supply fixed) results in an increase in consumption, a fall in the price level, and an appreciation of the domestic currency. In the current period, an appreciation of the domestic currency can be associated with an improving current account, a deteriorating current account, or no change in the current account (in response, respectively, to temporary, future, or permanent increases in output).[21] And of course, exogenous changes in the nominal money supply will move the exchange rate but leave the current account balance unchanged.

12. THE OPTIMAL INFLATION RATE

Under a flexible exchange rate, the central bank can control the supply of money and can therefore control the price level. In this intertemporal model where real money balances yield utility, what is the inflation rate that maximizes the lifetime utility of the agent?

While the central bank controls the nominal money supply, the public chooses the *real* quantity of money. Real money balances measure the number of goods that the money held will buy, and this quantity is determined by the public.[22] If the central bank has a zero-inflation policy and the real interest rate equals 0.04, the nominal interest rate also equals 0.04 and $\dfrac{i_t}{1+i_t}$ equals 0.0385. The public then chooses to hold the quantity of real money balances at point A in Figure 8.8. The agent, given the conditions, is maximizing lifetime utility. But is the central bank's zero-inflation policy optimal, or is there some other policy that will generate a higher level of lifetime utility?

The demand curve for real money balances, represented by $\dfrac{v'(m_t)}{u'(c_t)}$, is akin to the marginal benefit curve for real money balances, and the opportunity cost of holding real money depends on the nominal interest rate.[23] But given that the marginal social cost of real money is zero, the marginal benefit of real money at point A exceeds the marginal social cost. This creates a deadweight loss to society, a loss that can be eliminated by conducting the appropriate policy. If the central bank implements a policy of deflation, such that the nominal interest rate falls to zero, the new equilibrium is at point C in the figure (the announcement of a decrease in the future money supply causes the price level in the current period to fall, shifting the RM_{t0}^s line to the right). The deflationary policy induces the agent to hold a higher level of real money balances. Because this monetary policy action has no effect on consumption, and therefore has no effect on the lifetime utility associated with consumer spending, the increase in real money balances associated with the move from point A to point C generates an increase in lifetime utility.

This policy rule, where the central bank sets the inflation rate (approximately) equal to the negative of the real rate of interest,

Figure 8.8: Optimal inflation policy

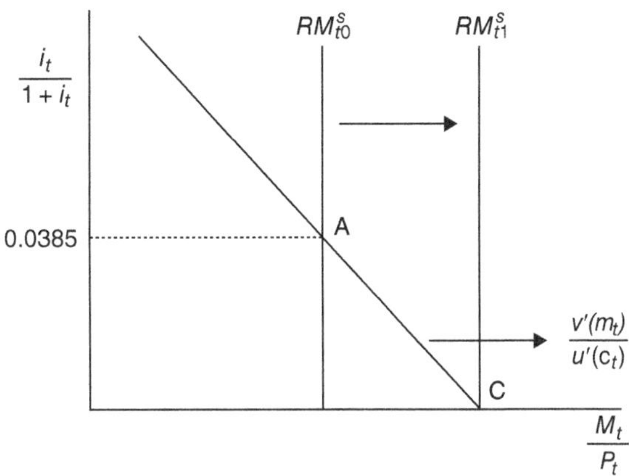

$$\pi_t = \frac{-r_t}{1+r_t},$$

is called the "Friedman rule" (Friedman 1969). Based on the numbers in the figure, the optimal rate of inflation is −0.0385, or −3.85 per cent. At the new equilibrium at point C, the marginal social benefit of money and the marginal social cost of money are equal. This deflationary monetary policy makes domestic residents better off. Given the setup of the model, this policy is the optimal monetary policy of the central bank.[24]

Note that the initiation of this policy causes the price level to fall in the current period, and the domestic currency also appreciates in this period. As the economy moves forward into the future period, the price level will fall further and the domestic currency will appreciate further. In a setup with multiple periods, with other factors fixed, the domestic currency appreciates at an annual rate equal to 3.85 per cent. But with a zero foreign inflation rate, the trend appreciation of the domestic currency is offset by the trend fall in the domestic price level.

13. CONCLUSION

This chapter focused on how changes in the nominal money supply affect nominal variables such as the price level, the nominal exchange rate, and the nominal interest rate. The importance of understanding how monetary factors affect the exchange rate and other nominal variables has long been at the center of the study of international economics, and this understanding is critical in the analysis of cases both when inflation is high and when inflation is low.

The intertemporal model with money was also used to discuss other issues, including the question of the optimal monetary policy under a flexible exchange rate regime.[25] Indeed, one of the benefits of a macroeconomic model formulated in terms of the utility of domestic residents is that it allows an assessment of the welfare (or utility) effects of alternative policies.

The next chapter continues this modeling approach, using the model to analyze the determination of the price level and the balance of payments under a fixed exchange rate regime.

PRACTICE QUESTIONS

1. Fill in the blanks. Use the intertemporal model with money.
   (a) The domestic real interest rate is determined by _____.
   (b) If the domestic nominal interest rate is equal to the foreign nominal interest rate, the interest rate parity condition implies that _____ is equal to _____.
   (c) Suppose the foreign real interest rate is unchanged, so that the domestic real interest rate is constant. A higher domestic nominal interest rate is consistent with _____ (forward) inflation rate (through the Fisher equation) and with _____ equilibrium return on foreign bonds for domestic investors (through the interest rate parity condition).
   (d) The law of one price implies that, in equilibrium, the domestic price level equals _____ times the foreign price level.
   (e) With the Friedman rule, the central bank sets the nominal interest rate equal to _____. The lifetime utility of domestic residents under the Friedman rule is _____ than when the central bank follows a zero-inflation policy (assume that the real interest rate is greater than zero).

2. Fill in the blanks. Use the intertemporal model with money.
   (a) A temporary increase in the money supply causes the current-period domestic currency to _____ (relative to the foreign currency) and the current-period _____ interest rate to fall.
   (b) A permanent increase in the money supply causes the current-period price level to _____ and the current-period nominal interest rate to _____.
   (c) An increase in the future money supply causes the current-period exchange rate (denoted as s_t) to _____ and the current-period nominal interest rate to _____.
   (d) An exogenous permanent increase in the foreign price level causes the current-period exchange rate (denoted as s_t) to _____ and the current-period price level to _____.
   (e) A temporary increase in output causes net exports to _____ in the current period, even though the domestic currency _____ (relative to the foreign currency).

3. Suppose there is a temporary increase in the money supply.
   (a) Is the future price level or the future exchange rate affected? Explain.
   (b) Explain how the current-period nominal interest rate and the current-period exchange rate are affected. Use the money market equilibrium diagram.

4. Does an increase in the money supply affect net exports in the current period? Explain (discuss how changes in the money supply affect the domestic real interest rate, lifetime after-tax real income, the exchange rate, and the domestic price level).

5. Explain how a permanent increase in the money supply affects the future price level, the future exchange rate, and the exchange rate and the price level in the current period (for a given interest rate). And using the diagram, explain how the current-period nominal interest rate is affected.

6. Suppose the central bank announces that there will be an increase in the future money supply, and the public realizes that this change will increase the future price level.
   (a) Explain how the future exchange rate and the current-period exchange rate are affected (for a given interest rate).
   (b) Explain how the current-period price level is affected.
   (c) Does the nominal interest rate rise, fall, or remain the same? Explain using the diagram.

7. A temporary increase in the money supply causes the domestic interest rate to fall. Is this fall in the interest rate consistent with the interest rate parity condition? What happens to the expected rate of appreciation of the foreign currency? Explain.

8. Suppose there is a temporary increase in output. Explain how the future price level and exchange rate are affected. Note that this "temporary" change does cause future variables to change. Explain how the current-period exchange rate and price level are affected.

9. In the intertemporal model with money under a flexible exchange rate, what is the optimal inflation rate? Explain.

DATA ANALYTICS

1. Since the path-breaking research by Kydland and Prescott (1982), it has become common for macroeconomists to use a technique known as calibration analysis.[26] In simple cases, the technique begins with a key equation (the model), calibrates the parameters in the equation, collects data on the variables, simulates the model, and compares the predictions of the model with actual movements in the variable.[27]

   Consider an example based on the model of the price level (the derivation uses calculus and a logarithmic transformation, but understanding the model requires no additional analysis). The real money demand relationship is

$$v'(m_t) = \left[\frac{i_t}{1+i_t}\right] u'(c_t).$$

A common specification for utility is

$$u(c) + v(m) = \frac{c^{1-\sigma}}{1-\sigma} + \frac{m^{1-\eta}}{1-\eta},$$

where the parameters σ and η are both positive. Using calculus, $u'(c_t)$ equals $c_t^{-\sigma}$ and $v'(m_t)$ equals $m_t^{-\eta}$ (both marginal utilities are positive).[28] Substituting these results into the equation, letting nominal money demand equal nominal money supply, and taking logarithms yields an equilibrium condition for the logarithm of the price level, $\ln P_t^{model}$:

$$\ln P_t^{model} = \ln M_t^s + \frac{1}{\eta}\ln\left[\frac{i_t}{1+i_t}\right] - \frac{\sigma}{\eta}\ln c_t.$$

This equation is a model of the (logarithm of the) price level, where the price level depends on the nominal money supply, the nominal interest rate, and consumption. If one sets σ equal to 6 and η equal to 5, this calibration results in the equation[29]

$$\ln P_t^{model} = \ln M_t^s + 0.2\ln\left[\frac{i_t}{1+i_t}\right] - 1.2\ln c_t.$$

Given data for the right-hand side variables, the model generates predicted values that can be compared with the actual logarithm of the price level.

Collect Canadian data between 1981 and 2014 (use averaging to convert the original monthly or quarterly data to annual data). Use the following variables: the consumer price index (CANSIM series V41690973), the M1+ money supply (V37151), the interest rate (V122484), and aggregate consumption (the sum of V62305724 and V62305730).

Use a software package to generate the predicted values for $\ln P_t^{model}$ for all periods from 1981 to 2014 (adjust the model, by adding or subtracting a constant, so that the model and the actual variable are equal in 1981). Create a time-series plot of the predicted and actual logarithms of the price level. Confirm that, for this calibration, the plot appears as shown in Figure 8.9. Based on the underlying theory and a visual inspection of the figure, provide comments on the strengths and weaknesses of the model in tracking the movements in the logarithm of the price level. It is beneficial to create plots of the other variables, to improve understanding of their movements.

2. Using the same model and data as question 1, do a calibration that sets σ equal to 1.44 and η equal to 1.20. Plot the actual and predicted logarithms of the price level. Comment.

3. Using the Euler equation for consumption, with the utility function specified in question 1, it can be shown that the forward growth rate of consumption depends on the real interest rate (and the fixed marginal rate of time preference):

Figure 8.9: Actual and predicted values

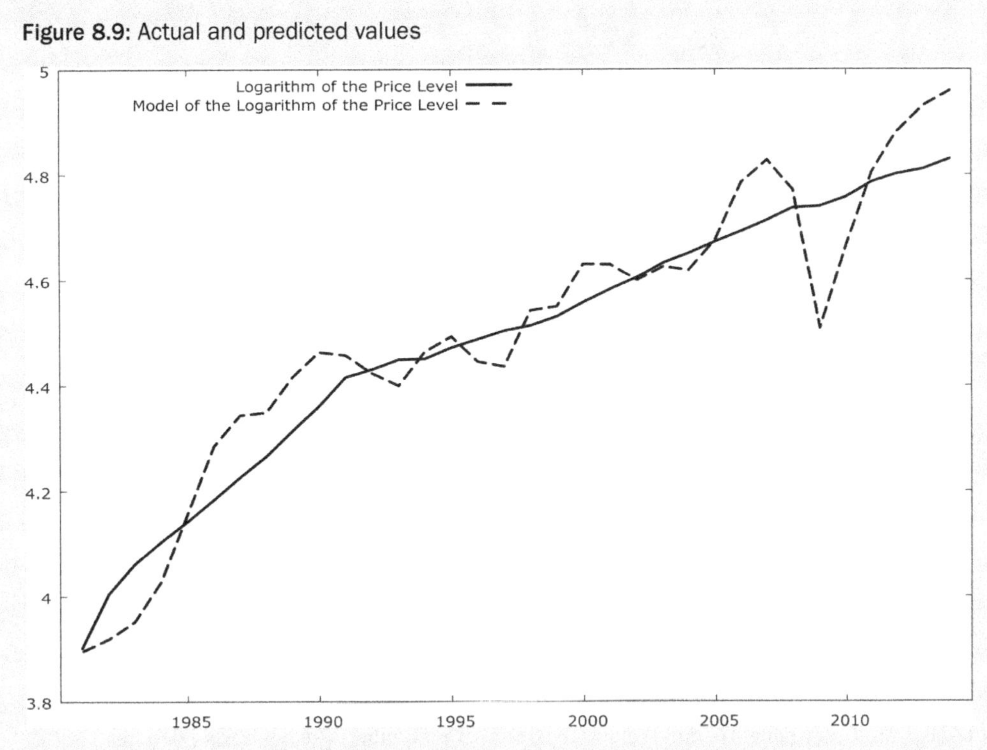

Data source: Statistics Canada, with the predictions of the model

$$\frac{c_{t+1} - c_t}{c_t} = \frac{1}{\sigma}\left[r_t - \gamma \right].$$

Using the data from question 1, calculate the real interest rate (using the Fisher equation) and conduct calibration analyses for the cases where σ equals 2 and σ equals 6. Let γ equal 0.01. Ensure that the real interest rate and consumption growth are measured as decimals. Create plots of the predicted and actual variables. Comment.

APPENDIX A: AN ALTERNATIVE DERIVATION OF REAL MONEY DEMAND

Chapter 7 discussed the derivation of the condition that links the marginal rate of substitution between real money and consumption to the nominal interest rate. This appendix provides an alternative derivation, but of course it arrives at the same result. Suppose the agent decreases money holdings by 1 unit and uses the proceeds to purchase a domestic bond (for simplicity, assume that nominal and real interest rates are the same, with the current and future price levels both equal to 1). The marginal cost of holding fewer money balances is equal to

$$v'\left(m_t\right)+\frac{v'\left(m_{t+1}\right)}{1+\gamma}.$$

As money is a durable good, the agent loses the benefits associated with the services of money in both the current and future periods. The marginal benefit of the additional bond holding is the discounted gain in utility from the additional future consumption that arises in period t+1:

$$\frac{\left(1+r_t\right)u'\left(c_{t+1}\right)}{1+\gamma}.$$

To maximize lifetime utility, marginal benefit must equal marginal cost (both properly measured):

$$v'\left(m_t\right)+\frac{v'\left(m_{t+1}\right)}{1+\gamma}=\frac{\left(1+r_t\right)u'\left(c_{t+1}\right)}{1+\gamma}.$$

Using the following condition,

$$v'\left(m_{t+1}\right)=u'\left(c_{t+1}\right),$$

as well as the Euler equation and the assumption that r_t equals i_t, the equation becomes

$$v'\left(m_t\right)=u'\left(c_t\right)-\frac{u'\left(c_t\right)}{1+r_t}=u'\left(c_t\right)\left[1-\frac{1}{1+r_t}\right]=u'\left(c_t\right)\left[\frac{r_t}{1+r_t}\right],$$

$$\frac{v'\left(m_t\right)}{u'\left(c_t\right)}=\left[\frac{i_t}{1+i_t}\right].$$

APPENDIX B: PERMANENT MONEY SUPPLY CHANGES AND THE INTEREST RATE

A permanent increase in the money supply has no effect on the nominal interest rate. The domestic real interest rate equals the fixed foreign real interest rate, but how does one know that the inflation rate is unchanged? The future price level must rise by 10 per cent. Can the current price level increase by less than 10 per cent? If the current price level rises by less than 10 per cent, the (forward) *inflation rate will be positive*. Is this possible? No, but suppose it is and see what happens (a contradiction arises). If the current price level rises by less than 10 per cent and the money supply increases by 10 per cent, the real money supply increases. As current consumption is unchanged, an increase in real money balances is only consistent with money market equilibrium if the nominal interest rate falls (the agent will only hold more real money balances at a lower interest rate). But consider the Fisher equation, the identity that defines the real rate of interest:

$$1 + r_t = \frac{1 + i_t}{1 + \pi_t}.$$

If the nominal interest rate falls, with a fixed real rate of interest, the Fisher equation implies that the *inflation rate will be negative*. But this is a contradiction. Therefore, a permanent increase in the money supply must cause both the current and future price levels to rise by 10 per cent, with no effect on the inflation rate or the nominal interest rate.

APPENDIX C: THE EFFECTS OF FISCAL POLICY CHANGES

Any increase in government spending, current or future, increases the present value of lifetime taxes and decreases current and future consumption. The associated fall in nominal money demand causes the price level to increase (in each period). Through the law of one price condition, there is an induced depreciation of the domestic currency (in each period).[30]

Suppose the government cuts taxes in the current period, finances the budget deficit by selling domestic bonds to the public (current and future government spending are fixed), and plans to increase future taxes such that there is no effect on lifetime after-tax real income. These tax changes have no effect on consumption or the current account balance.[31] With consumption and the money supply unchanged, the price level and the exchange rate do not change.

APPENDIX D: THE QUANTITY THEORY OF MONEY

The effects of monetary changes on the price level can be analyzed in terms of the quantity theory of money. This theory dates back at least to the analysis of David Hume in the mid-1700s. The modern version is a theory of the price level based on the demand for and supply of money as articulated, for example, by Friedman (1969). The discussion in this appendix uses consumption as the scale variable (rather than transactions or real income), so as to explain the quantity theory in a framework consistent with the intertemporal model with money (for a detailed discussion of the quantity theory, see Friedman 2008).[32]

The inverse of the price level measures the number of goods that \$1 can purchase. If the price level equals \$0.50 per good, 1/P equals 2 goods per \$1. The inverse of the price level therefore measures the value of money. It is straightforward to argue that the value of money is determined by the demand and supply of money.

This approach is depicted in Figure 8.10, with the value of money on the vertical axis and the quantity of nominal money on the horizontal axis. The money supply curve is the vertical line, where the initial stock of money equals \$100. The nominal demand for money, denoted M^d, depends on the price level, as well as on consumer spending and the interest rate. As the price level rises and 1/P falls, the demand for money increases proportionally (so that real money balances are unchanged). Along any given money demand curve, consumer spending and the nominal interest rate are fixed (changes in these variables cause shifts in this money demand curve).

Figure 8.10: Quantity theory of money

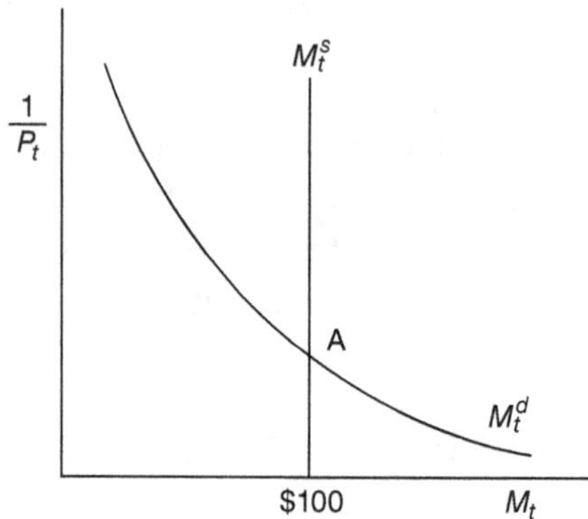

An increase in the money supply from $100 to $200 shifts the nominal money supply curve to the right (not shown in the figure). The increase in money supply, with an unchanged demand curve, reduces the value of money. The doubling of the money supply cuts the value of money in half, falling from 2 goods per dollar to 1 good per dollar. The price level increases from $0.50 per good to $1.00 per good. With an increase in the supply of money, the price level rises as residents reduce their excess money balances by attempting to purchase more goods. In the new equilibrium, the nominal money supply is higher but the quantity of real money balances is unchanged.[33]

The quantity theory can be derived from the intertemporal model with money. Consider the money market equilibrium condition in the intertemporal model:

$$v'\left(\frac{M_t^s}{P_t}\right) = \left[\frac{i_t}{1+i_t}\right] u'(c_t).$$

Given that consumption is determined by real variables and the nominal interest rate is determined according to the Fisher equation, this equilibrium condition determines the current-period price level. If the utility functions u(c) and v(m) are specified, an equation like the quantity theory equation can be derived:

$$M_t^s V_t^m \left(i_t, \alpha\right) = P_t\, c_t,$$

where α is a fixed parameter that enters the utility function and V^m denotes the function that represents the velocity of money (defined as Pc/M). If M equals $100, P equals $10 per good, and c equals 20 goods per year, Pc equals $200 per year and the velocity of money is 2 per year. The $100 in the economy allows for the purchase of $200 worth of goods in the year, so the money must circulate through the economy (on average) 2 times during the year.

The theory of the price level in the quantity theory is

$$P_t = \frac{M_t^s V_t^m \left(i_t, \alpha\right)}{c_t}.$$

The price level depends on the money supply, the velocity of money, and consumer spending. For given velocity and consumption, an increase in the money supply increases the price level. If the money supply increases from \$100 to \$200, the price level doubles.

An increase in consumption increases nominal money demand. With a fixed money supply, there is a decrease in the current price level. In the diagram for the quantity theory, the demand curve for money shifts out when consumption increases. The increase in the demand for money increases the value of money, meaning that the price level decreases.[34]

Future changes in the money supply affect the current-period price level through the nominal interest rate. If the future money supply increases, with no change in the current money supply, the nominal interest rate rises because of the rise in the forward inflation rate. With a higher interest rate, individuals want to hold fewer real money balances and try to increase purchases of goods (the velocity of money increases). In the diagram, an increase in the interest rate shifts the money demand curve down and increases the price level.

NOTES

1 Multi-sectoral models that examine movements in real and nominal exchange rates are discussed in Chapters 10, 11, 12, and 14.
2 The agent internalizes the intertemporal government constraint into the intertemporal household constraint, meaning the agent understands the details of the consolidated government budget constraints and uses this knowledge in determining how current and future taxes and transfers are affected by government and central bank policy. In effect, decisions are based on the intertemporal constraint on the economy.
3 The derivative of a function $f(x) = \ln x$ equals x^{-1}. The condition assumes that $u(c) = \ln c$, and $v(m) = \alpha \ln m$.
4 Real business cycle theory, discussed in Chapter 6, has a vertical short-run aggregate supply curve, with the supply curve shifting in response to factors such as changes in total factor productivity and income tax rates.
5 Models that incorporate nominal rigidities, such as sticky wages and prices, are widely used in the literature. For analyses based on small-economy models with money in the utility function, see (for example) Kollmann (2001) and Bergin (2003).
6 An increase in the rate of growth of nominal money increases inflation and reduces real money balances. But super-neutrality means that there are no effects on real variables other than real money balances. In an advanced analysis, Epstein and Hynes (1983) examine dynamic models with capital where the rate of time preference depends on future consumption; in a version with real money in the utility function, the rate of growth of the money supply affects real variables like consumption and capital.
7 On solving backward, see Brock (1975). In an uncertain environment, the agent would generate rational expectations of the future variables, based on current-period information and the model of the economy. See, for example, Greenwood (1983).
8 Some economists use the quantity theory of money to examine the effects of exogenous monetary changes. An appendix summarizes this theory and discusses its relationship to the intertemporal theory with money.

9   These exogenous changes are news, in that they were not previously expected to occur. But going forward, there is perfect foresight. Consumers know the levels of both current and future exogenous variables.

10 Frenkel (1976), in discussing the post-World War I literature on PPP, briefly discusses related points.

11 The intertemporal model with money encapsulates this type of effect, but some models may not. Brock (1975, 142), among others, has emphasized the difficulties in interpretation that may arise.

12 With the foreign price level increasing each period, there is an increase in the foreign nominal interest rate.

13 An applied exercise in "Data Analytics" undertakes a calibration analysis to assess the model's predictions regarding movements in the Canadian price level between 1981 and 2014.

14 In the preface, Keynes (1923) writes as follows: "It is often argued that the franc cannot fall in value because France is a wealthy, thrifty, and industrious country or because her balance of trade is prima facie satisfactory… The value of a country's monetary unit is not a function of its wealth or even of its trade policy… What, then, has determined and will determine the value of the franc? First, the quantity, present and prospective, of the francs in circulation. Second, the amount of purchasing power which it suits the public to hold in that shape." Professor Friedman (1997) noted that, in his view, *The Tract on Monetary Reform* was Keynes' best book.

15 Keynes (1923, 74) was supportive of the law of one price for traded goods. Pigou (1922, 64–6) also provides interesting comments on non-traded goods, PPP, and the exchange rate.

16 In the *Tract*, Keynes (1923) also discussed the monetary causes of the hyperinflations that occurred in Germany, Austria, and Russia in the early 1920s.

17 Yeager (1976, 326) notes that the French public closely tracked movements in the government budget deficit and talks regarding war reparation payments, and monitored the financial statements of the Bank of France.

18 The data are from the International Monetary Fund's International Financial Statistics (IFS) database. The mark–US dollar and lira–US dollar exchange rates are used to generate the lira–mark exchange rate. The price levels are consumer price indexes.

19 In this regard, the money demand relationship has similarities with Professor Friedman's (1959) model, where money demand depends on permanent income.

20 Greenwood (1983) and Stockman (1988), among others, have emphasized this point.

21 The phrase "deteriorating current account" means that the current account has decreased, but this terminology should not be interpreted as having a negative connotation. In fact, the associated increases in consumption and real money balances result in an increase in lifetime utility.

22 If the public has too much money, the public will attempt to reduce money holdings by increasing their spending on goods. This action will increase the price level, and thereby reduce real money balances.

23 It is assumed that the curve denoting $\dfrac{v(m_t)}{u'(c_t)}$ falls to 0 at a finite level of real money balances, touching the horizontal axis. Note that, with some utility functions, $v'(m_t)$ only approaches 0 as m_t increases to higher levels.

24 The model assumes that the government can finance spending with a lump-sum tax. In general, taxation may itself be a source of distortions. Since money finance is an alternative to taxation, the welfare effects of fiscal and monetary policy are best examined in a general equilibrium model. For an advanced discussion of the optimal inflation rate, see, for example, Phelps (1973) and Lucas (2000).

25 On the Bank of Canada's inflation targeting policy, see Melino (2012) and Beaudry and Ruge-Murcia (2017).

26 Excellent references include Hansen and Prescott (1993), Kydland and Prescott (1996), Kydland (2006), Prescott (2006), and Hansen and Ohanian (2016). On some differences in approaches within the framework, see the discussion in Hansen and Ohanian (2016, 2063–4).

27 In advanced calibration exercises, the model is a dynamic, stochastic, general equilibrium model. There are multiple equations, with allowance for expectations of future variables. See, for example, McCandless (2008).

28 Using calculus, $u''(c_t)$ equals $[-\sigma\, c_t^{-\sigma-1}]$. The term in brackets is negative, implying that the marginal utility of consumption is diminishing. Likewise, the marginal utility of real money falls as real money increases.

29 Researchers use various techniques to assist with calibration. Empirical studies on money demand can be used to suggest plausible values for σ and η (see, for example, Lucas 2000 and Alvarez and Lippi 2014).

30 It is not uncommon for fiscal policy changes to have different effects in different models. In the IS-LM-IRP model with a fixed price level and variable output (see Chapter 13), an increase in government spending causes the domestic currency to appreciate.

31 While a budget deficit caused by a tax change has no effect on the current account, a budget deficit caused by a temporary increase in government spending decreases the current account (on "twin deficits," see Chapter 5). To work out the effects of any change, one must specify how the budget deficit is financed and what happens in the future. Is the deficit financed by selling bonds or printing money? In the future, is there a cut in government spending or an increase in taxes?

32 Lucas (2014) provides an interesting discussion, along with a summary of related empirical evidence, of the relationship between money growth and inflation.

33 While the central bank determines the nominal money supply, the public determines real money balances. For an excellent discussion, see Friedman (1959, 330–1).

34 If current consumption increases by 2 per cent, the current price level falls by 2 per cent. In terms of the quantity equation, $P_t\, c_t$ is unchanged (velocity and the money supply are unchanged).

CHAPTER 9

Money, Reserves, and the Price Level under a Fixed Exchange Rate

1. INTRODUCTION

Many nations decide to fix the value of their currency to a foreign currency. Under a fixed exchange rate, the central bank holds foreign exchange reserves (foreign currency and foreign bonds) and intervenes in the foreign exchange market to keep the exchange rate fixed.

While certain aspects of economic performance can be the same whether the exchange rate is fixed or flexible, there are other aspects where the differences are profound. This chapter uses the intertemporal model with money to analyze the workings of a permanently fixed exchange rate regime. The analysis focuses on some fundamental issues. What factors cause changes in foreign exchange reserves (the balance of payments)? In a fixed exchange rate regime, can the central bank in a small economy influence the domestic interest rate or control the nominal money supply? What are the determinants of the domestic price level and inflation rate in a small economy operating under a fixed exchange rate? Does a fixed exchange rate regime lead to a lower level of welfare (or lifetime utility) than a flexible exchange rate regime? The chapter includes applications of the model, including a discussion of reserve flows in China during the period the yuan was rigidly fixed to the US dollar.

2. THE BASIC SETUP

There are two periods, the current period (denoted as t) and the future period (denoted as t+1). The domestic economy is small, and the domestic good is identical to the foreign good. The representative agent maximizes lifetime utility subject to an intertemporal budget constraint (consumers are synonymously referred to as domestic residents, the public, and the agent). Lifetime utility depends on consumption and real money balances, with real balances yielding utility because money allows transactions to be conducted in an efficient manner.[1]

The current-period endogenous variables are the price level, the nominal interest rate, the real interest rate, foreign exchange reserves, consumption, and the current account balance. The exogenous variables are as follows: the monetary variables, domestic credit (denoted as D) and the nominal exchange rate (denoted as s); real output, y_t and y_{t+1}, and real government spending, g_t and g_{t+1}; the foreign nominal interest rate i_t^*, the foreign real interest rate r_t^*, and the foreign price level variables P_t^* and P_{t+1}^*; and the marginal rate of time preference γ. These exogenous variables are held fixed but can change exogenously.

The exchange rate is permanently fixed, and this fact is known by the public.

3. KEY RELATIONSHIPS

Determination of the Price Level and Interest Rates

With identical foreign and domestic goods and the exchange rate fixed at 1, the domestic price level in each period equals the foreign price level (the purchasing power parity condition holds):

$$P_t = P_t^*,$$

$$P_{t+1} = P_{t+1}^*.$$

If the foreign price level is not changing, the domestic price level will not change, and the domestic inflation rate equals zero. In this model, the domestic inflation rate is determined completely by the foreign inflation rate under a fixed exchange rate. International macroeconomists refer to this phenomenon as imported inflation.[2]

With a permanently fixed exchange rate, there are no exchange rate-related capital gains or losses on foreign bond holdings.[3] Domestic and foreign bonds are perfect substitutes, and the interest rate parity condition implies that the equilibrium domestic nominal interest rate equals the foreign nominal rate:

$$i_t = i_t^*.$$

The central bank is therefore unable to affect the domestic nominal interest rate. With identical goods, the interest rate parity condition implies that real interest rate parity holds:

$$r_t = r_t^*.$$

The domestic real interest rate is determined solely by the exogenous foreign real interest rate.

Determination of Foreign Exchange Reserves

The nominal money supply, denoted as M^s, equals domestic credit, D, plus foreign exchange reserves, denoted as R (the money multiplier is assumed to equal 1):

$$M_t^s = D_t + R_t.$$

Domestic credit equals the domestic assets of the central bank, and foreign exchange reserves are foreign assets (foreign currency and foreign bonds) held by the central bank.[4] Under balance of payments accounting, changes in the central bank's foreign exchange reserves equal the balance of payments (the sum of the current account balance and net capital inflows).

The central bank is committed to buying and selling foreign currency at the fixed level to keep the exchange rate fixed. While the central bank has control of D, the variable R is an endogenous variable. Real money demand in the current period, denoted as m_t or $\dfrac{M_t}{P_t}$, is determined by

$$v'\left(\frac{M_t}{P_t}\right) = \left[\frac{i_t}{1+i_t}\right] u'(c_t),$$

where $v'(m)$ denotes the marginal utility of real money balances and $u'(c)$ is the marginal utility of consumption. Nominal money demand depends on the price level, consumption, and the interest rate. Setting money demand equal to money supply yields the money market equilibrium condition. Foreign exchange reserves, and reserve flows, are thus determined by domestic credit and the variables that affect nominal money demand.

The analysis focuses on portfolio equilibrium, which embeds the conditions representing money market equilibrium and interest rate parity. Portfolio equilibrium implies that domestic residents are willingly holding the existing quantity of domestic bonds, foreign bonds, and domestic money. Portfolio equilibrium is depicted in Figure 9.1. Real money demand, represented by the downward sloping curve, $\dfrac{v'(m_t)}{u'(c_t)}$, equals the real money supply (the vertical RM^s line); and the domestic interest rate equals the foreign interest rate, so that $\dfrac{i_t}{1+i_t}$ equals $\dfrac{i_t^*}{1+i_t^*}$ (as represented by the horizontal line).

Determination of Consumption and the Current Account Balance

The intertemporal constraint on the economy can be written as

$$c_t + \frac{c_{t+1}}{(1+r_t)} = y_t - g_t + \frac{y_{t+1} - g_{t+1}}{(1+r_t)},$$

where the right-hand side represents the present value of lifetime output less the present value of lifetime government spending. It is known that consumption is limited by this constraint, including the implication that increases in government spending, current or future, increase lifetime taxes.[5] Current-period consumption is determined jointly by this intertemporal constraint and the Euler equation for consumption, with the latter specified as

$$u'(c_t) = \frac{(1+r_t)}{1+\gamma} u'(c_{t+1}) \ \rightarrow \ c_t = c_{t+1} \ \text{if} \ r_t = \gamma.$$

Figure 9.1: Portfolio equilibrium

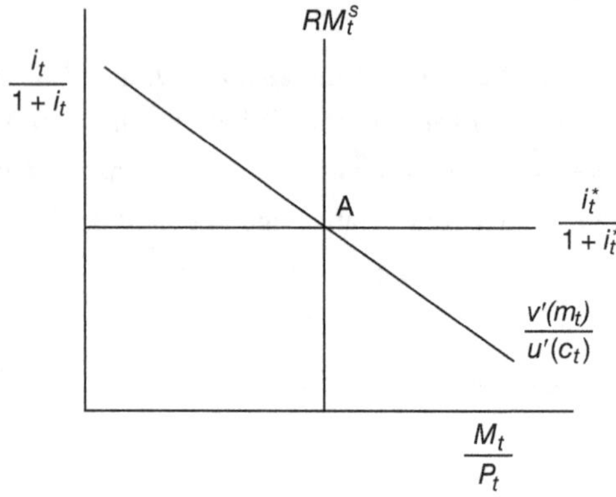

The current account balance, measured in real terms, is defined as

$$CA_t = y_t - g_t - c_t.$$

Current account fluctuations are caused by exogenous changes in output and government spending, in addition to other exogenous factors (such as changes in the foreign real interest rate) that induce changes in consumer spending.

4. FOREIGN EXCHANGE RESERVES AND THE MONETARY APPROACH TO THE BALANCE OF PAYMENTS

The balance of payments is a monetary phenomenon, meaning that changes in foreign exchange reserves are caused by exogenous changes in domestic credit and exogenous changes that induce changes in variables that affect the demand for money. These results are within the tradition of the monetary approach to the balance of payments.[6]

Changes in Domestic Credit

Under a fixed exchange rate, the exogenous policy variable of the central bank is the stock of domestic credit. The central bank can increase domestic credit in two ways: an open market operation where the central bank buys domestic government bonds from the public (in exchange for new money), or a money transfer where the central bank gives the public some new money balances (in exchange for a receipt that the money was received).[7] In either case, the central bank has more domestic assets (either the government bonds or the "receipt") and the public is holding more money.

Suppose there is an exogenous increase in domestic credit implemented as a money transfer (assume that i_t^* equals 0.04, so that $\dfrac{i_t^*}{1+i_t^*}$ equals 0.0385). This increase in domestic credit shifts the vertical real money supply line to the right in Figure 9.2, and the public has excess money hold-

Figure 9.2: Increase in domestic credit

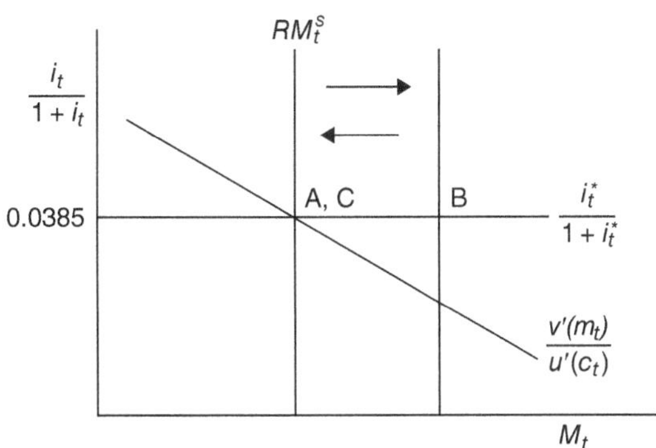

ings at point B (the nominal money supply exceeds nominal money demand at the initial interest rate). The excess cash balances can be eliminated by purchasing assets. The public knows that it can convert domestic money into foreign currency at the fixed exchange rate, and then purchase foreign bonds with the foreign currency (because the domestic economy is small, this transaction has no effect on the foreign interest rate). The public acquires the foreign currency, which the domestic central bank must supply to keep the exchange rate fixed, and then purchases foreign bonds. When the central bank sells foreign currency in exchange for domestic currency, the money supply falls and the vertical real money supply line shifts back to the left. In the new equilibrium at point C, the domestic interest rate and the real money supply are unchanged.

Because these monetary actions have no effect on consumption, the real money demand curve, denoted as $\frac{v'(m_t)}{u'(c_t)}$, does not shift. The increase in domestic credit has no effect on the domestic interest rate or consumption, but it simply results in a portfolio adjustment that causes a proportionate fall in foreign exchange reserves. The nominal money supply is unchanged.

The transactions are summarized in Figure 9.3 (with Canada as the domestic economy). The initial increase in domestic credit is shown in Box 1. This transaction increases the money supply, as the public is now holding more Canadian dollars. In Box 2, the central bank sells foreign bonds so as to have the necessary foreign currency on hand to conduct the foreign exchange transaction (the central bank is assumed to hold all foreign assets in the form of interest-earning foreign bonds, as foreign currency can be purchased or sold instantaneously at zero cost). The central bank sells the foreign currency in exchange for domestic currency in Box 3, and therefore decreases the money supply. In Box 4, the public uses the foreign currency to purchase foreign bonds. The central bank is now holding fewer foreign bonds than at the start of the period, so that foreign exchange reserves are lower.

Changes in Output and Government Spending

An exogenous increase in output increases current consumption, shifting the real money demand curve to the right (because money demand depends on consumption, the increase in output can be

Figure 9.3: Asset adjustment diagram

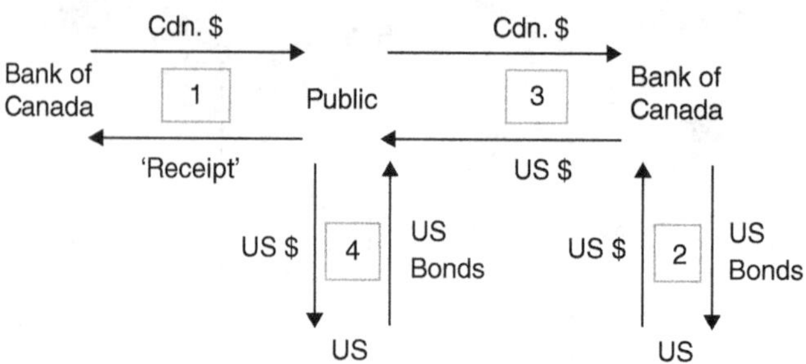

a temporary increase, a permanent increase, or a future increase). With real money demand at point B in Figure 9.4 but the real money supply still at A, there is an excess demand for money. The public can sell assets to acquire money balances. The public sells foreign bonds and then sells foreign currency in exchange for domestic currency. The central bank must buy the foreign currency and supply the domestic money, shifting the RM_{t0}^s line rightward to RM_{t1}^s. In the process, the public has acquired the desired amount of money and the foreign exchange reserves of the central bank have increased. The portfolio adjustment results in a balance of payments surplus (the transactions are shown in Figure 9.5).

A booming economy, due either to a cyclical or a permanent increase in output, is associated with a balance of payments surplus. Increases in output generate increases in the demand for money that cause the central bank to accumulate foreign exchange reserves. In practice, an economy with a high growth rate of real GDP would experience ongoing balance of payments surpluses, provided that domestic credit is not increasing too much.

A decrease in government spending decreases the present value of lifetime taxes and increases current consumption. The real money demand curve shifts to the right, generating an excess demand for money. The portfolio adjustment and the associated increases in the money supply and foreign exchange reserves are the same as in the case of an exogenous increase in output (the diagram is the same as Figure 9.4).

Changes in Foreign Interest Rates

Suppose there is an exogenous increase in the foreign real interest rate from 4 per cent to 5 per cent (let foreign and domestic inflation be fixed at 0 per cent). The associated increase in the foreign nominal rate shifts the horizontal line up in Figure 9.6, and the foreign nominal rate exceeds the domestic rate. The attempted selling of domestic bonds reduces the domestic bond price and increases the domestic nominal rate. The resulting higher domestic real interest rate decreases current consumption, shifting the real money demand curve to the left. Both effects reduce nominal money demand. The higher interest rate results in a lower quantity of money demanded, and the decrease in consumption reduces nominal money demand at each level of the interest rate. The public sells domestic currency on the foreign exchange market and acquires foreign currency to be able to purchase foreign bonds. The central bank must supply this foreign currency. Therefore,

Figure 9.4: Increase in output

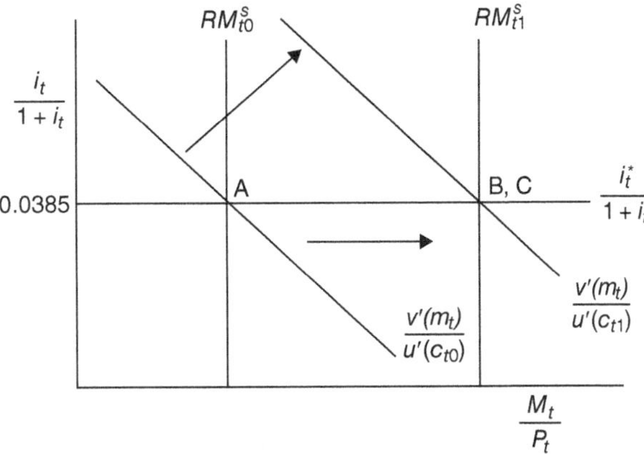

Figure 9.5: Asset adjustment diagram

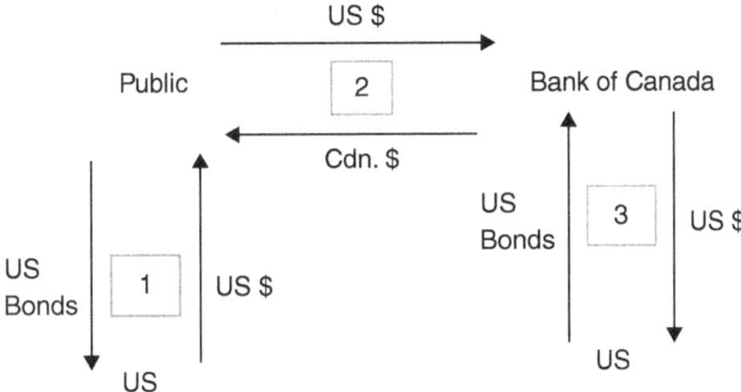

Figure 9.6: Increase in the foreign real rate

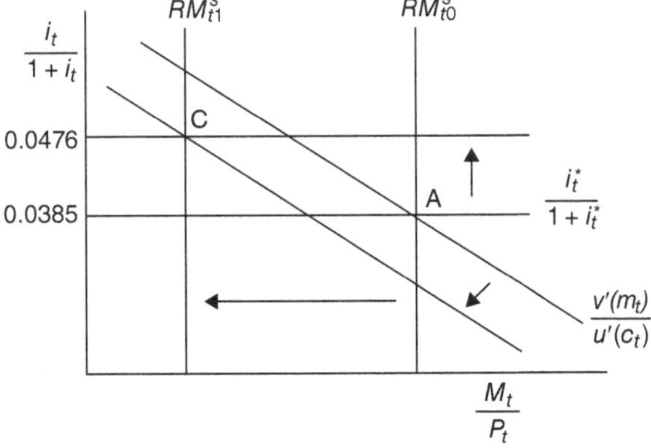

reserves and the money supply fall. The decrease in the money supply shifts the vertical real money supply line leftward, with the new equilibrium at C. The domestic interest rate is higher, and real and nominal money balances are lower.

5. ON THE LACK OF MONETARY INDEPENDENCE UNDER A FIXED EXCHANGE RATE

Under a fixed exchange rate, the central bank cannot control the nominal money supply or influence the macroeconomic variables in the economy. Changes in domestic credit have no effect on the domestic interest rate, because interest rate parity implies that the domestic interest rate equals the foreign interest rate. Changes in domestic credit do not generate any effects on lifetime after-tax real income or the domestic real interest rate, so consumer spending is not affected. And changes in domestic credit have no effect on the price level, because the domestic price level is determined solely by the foreign price level.

Because an increase in domestic credit has no effect on the interest rate, consumption, or the price level, foreign exchange reserves fall proportionately. The offset coefficient, measured as $\dfrac{\Delta R_t}{\Delta D_t}$ and accounting for all general equilibrium effects, equals -1. An increase in domestic credit causes a one-for-one decrease in foreign exchange reserves, with no effect on the nominal money supply.[8] This also means that the central bank cannot prevent the money supply from changing when other factors are changing.[9] Exogenous changes that induce changes in nominal money demand (such as changes in output or government spending) cause both reserves and the nominal money supply to change. The central bank is unable to prevent these changes in the money supply, as the induced changes in reserves are required to keep the exchange rate fixed.

The central bank loses control of the money supply and has "zero monetary independence."[10] Under a fixed exchange rate, the central bank must take an active role in keeping the exchange rate fixed, but the central bank is unable to influence either the domestic interest rate or the nominal money supply.[11]

6. IMPORTED INFLATION

In this one-good model, with identical foreign and domestic goods, the domestic price level is determined solely by the foreign price level under a fixed exchange rate. Likewise, domestic inflation is determined by foreign inflation, so that any inflation is imported inflation.[12]

Changes in the Foreign Price Level

A permanent increase in the foreign price level (with foreign real and nominal interest rates unchanged) causes the domestic price level and reserves to increase, but leaves the domestic interest rate unchanged.[13] The increase in the foreign price level, through the law of one price, increases the domestic price level. For a given nominal money supply, the increase in the price level shifts the vertical real money supply line to the left in Figure 9.7. The higher price level generates an increase in the nominal demand for money. The public sells foreign bonds in exchange for foreign currency and offers this newly acquired foreign currency for sale on the foreign exchange market. The central bank must purchase this foreign currency to ensure that the exchange rate remains

Figure 9.7: Increase in foreign price level

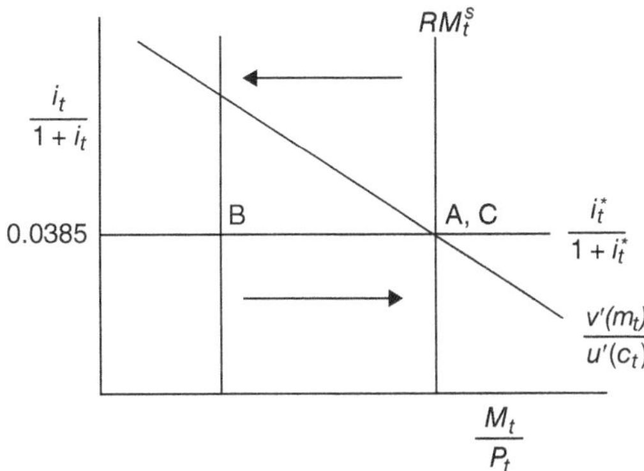

fixed. When the central bank sells domestic currency in exchange for the foreign currency, reserves increase. The public has acquired the additional domestic money, and this increase in the nominal money supply shifts the real money supply line back to the right. While the nominal money supply and reserves have increased, the domestic interest rate and the real money supply are unchanged (at the new equilibrium point C).

Money and the Price Level: The Direction of Causality

The direction of causality under a fixed exchange rate is not from "money to the price level," but rather from "the price level to money." An increase in the foreign price level causes the domestic price level to increase and the higher price level causes a higher level of money demand and money supply (as the central bank holds the exchange rate fixed).[14] The direction of causality depends on the exchange rate regime. Under a flexible exchange rate, a change in the quantity of money causes the price level to change. But under a fixed exchange rate, a change in the price level causes the quantity of money to change.[15]

Changes in the Foreign Inflation Rate

Suppose the foreign inflation rate increases exogenously from 0 per cent to 10 per cent (for simplicity, with an increase in the future foreign price level from 1.0 to 1.1 but no change in the current-period foreign price level). Through the Fisher equation in the foreign country, the foreign nominal interest rate increases (but the foreign real interest rate is unchanged). The law of one price condition implies that the future domestic price level must also increase by 10 per cent, generating a 10 per cent (forward) inflation rate in the domestic economy. Domestic bonds will be regarded as unattractive at the initial nominal interest rate, and residents will attempt to sell domestic bonds. This attempted selling causes the domestic nominal interest rate to increase by the same amount as the foreign nominal rate. In addition, the higher nominal interest rate generates a decrease in the quantity of money demanded. The public sells domestic currency to the central bank in exchange for foreign currency and uses these funds to purchase foreign bonds. Foreign exchange reserves and the nominal money supply are correspondingly reduced.[16]

The increase in the foreign inflation rate causes an increase in the domestic inflation rate. There is imported inflation.

7. THE BALANCE OF PAYMENTS IDENTITY

Merging the current-period household and consolidated government constraints yields the balance of payments identity. Assuming that J_{t-1} and R_{t-1} equal 0, the identity is as follows (measured in nominal terms, in terms of domestic currency):

$$P_t\left[y_t - c_t - g_t\right] - s_t J_t = s_t R_t.$$

There are three subaccounts: the current account balance (in nominal terms) equal to $P_t\left[y_t - c_t - g_t\right]$; net capital inflows equal to $[-s_t J_t]$; and the net accumulation of foreign assets by the central bank (the balance of payments) equal to $s_t R_t$.[17]

Of course, the identity can also be written as

$$P_t\left[y_t - c_t - g_t\right] = s_t\left[J_t + R_t\right],$$

so that a current account surplus, for example, implies that the domestic economy as a whole is accumulating foreign assets.[18] Under a fixed exchange rate, a positive current account balance implies that the public is accumulating assets, either foreign bonds or domestic money. In the case where the public has accumulated domestic money, the central bank has increased its holdings of foreign bonds.[19]

With an increase in domestic credit, the public accumulates foreign bonds, and the central bank loses foreign exchange reserves, so that J_t increases and R_t falls (the current account is unaffected). With real shocks such as output changes, all three accounts may be affected (these changes are discussed in an appendix). In these cases, there is often both a portfolio adjustment and a flow adjustment, the latter being the public's net asset accumulation associated with current account imbalances.

8. RESERVES AND RESERVE FLOWS IN CHINA, 1996–2005

The intertemporal model predicts that, holding other factors fixed, increases in domestic credit result in decreases in foreign exchange reserves, and increases in nominal income (GDP) increase the demand for money and therefore increase reserves. These predictions are assessed informally, by examining China's balance of payments.

Between 1996 and 2005, the Chinese currency – the renminbi (the yuan) – was fixed at the rate of 8.28 yuan to 1 US dollar.[20] Over this period, the average annual growth rate of nominal GDP was 11.2 per cent, with a low of 6.1 per cent in 1999 (after the Asian crisis) and a high of 16.3 per cent in 2004.[21] These large continued increases in nominal GDP are associated with increases in real GDP and increases in the price level, both of which cause the demand for money to increase. The monetary approach predicts that a high-growth country like China should have had continued balance of payments surpluses, provided that increases in domestic credit were not unduly large.[22]

Figure 9.8: China, nominal GDP and reserves

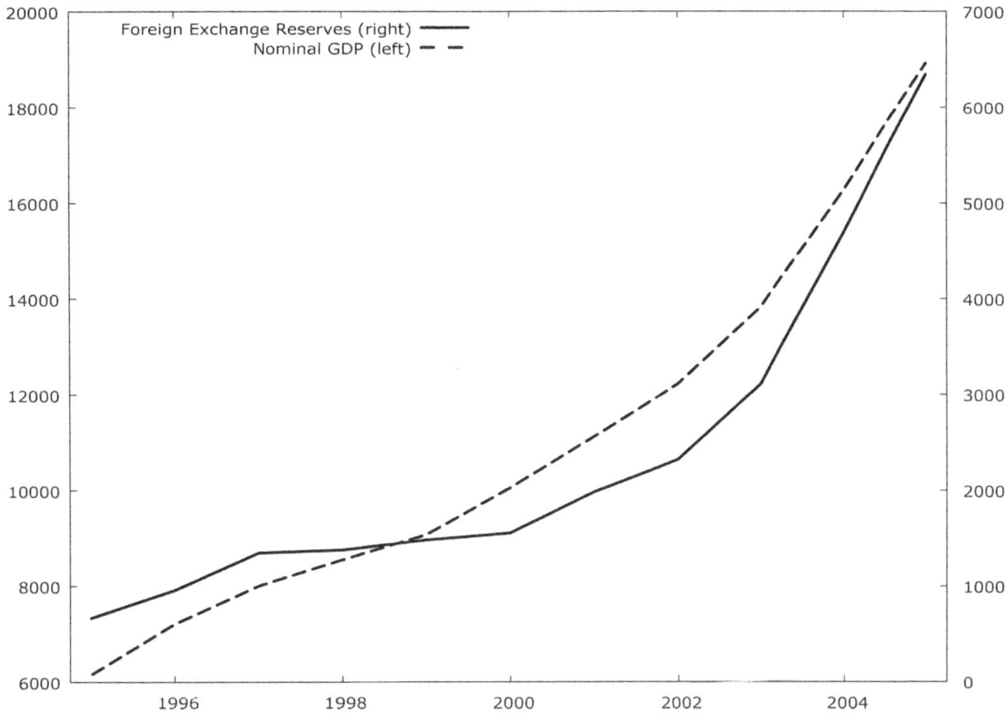

Data source: International Monetary Fund

Figure 9.8 depicts nominal GDP and foreign exchange reserves, with both variables measured in billions of yuan. The increases in nominal GDP are associated with a continued increase in foreign exchange reserves. Figure 9.9 shows the balance of payments (changes in foreign exchange reserves) and changes in domestic credit. Even though there were, in some years, substantial increases in domestic credit, the high-growth Chinese economy had a balance of payments surplus in every year between 1996 and 2005. In 2004 and 2005, there were large decreases in domestic credit, which added to the balance of payments surplus in these years.

An applied exercise in Data Analytics compares the movements in China's exchange rate and foreign exchange reserves in the periods before and after 2005.

9. INFLATION AND WELFARE

Optimal Inflation and the Exchange Rate Regime

In this model, the optimal inflation rate, equal to $\dfrac{-r_t}{1+r_t}$, is negative (as discussed in Chapter 8).[23] Under a flexible exchange rate, the central bank can control the money supply and can therefore achieve the optimal inflation rate. But under a fixed exchange rate, the domestic central bank has no control of the money supply, and the domestic inflation rate equals the foreign inflation rate.

Figure 9.9: Monetary flows in China

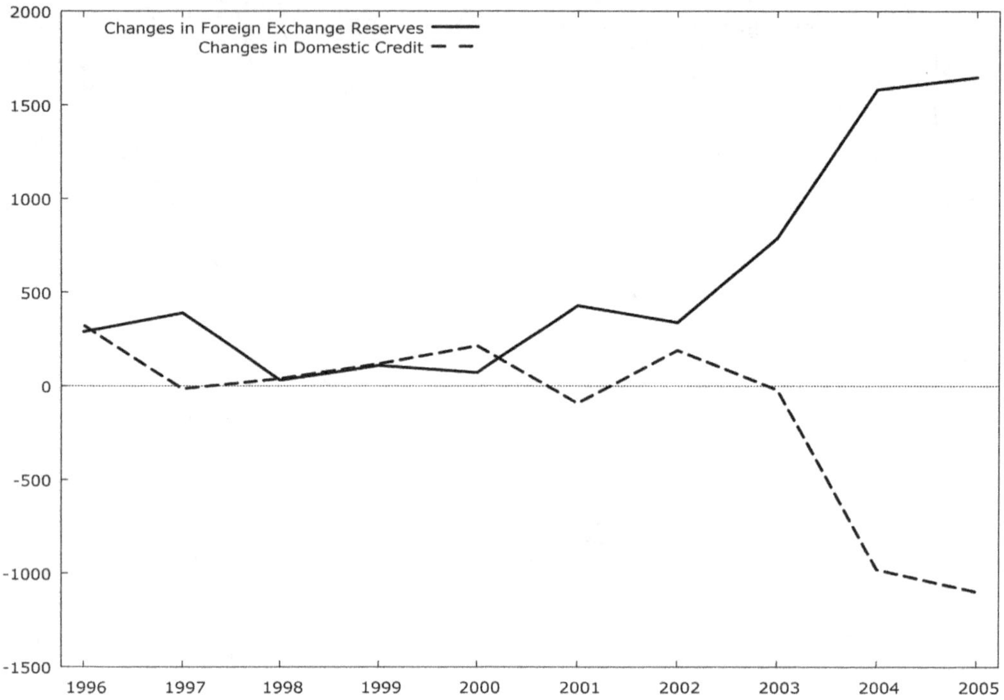

Data source: International Monetary Fund

Unless the foreign central bank is implementing the optimal deflation, there is a deadweight welfare loss. Relative to a flexible exchange rate regime with the optimal monetary policy, lifetime utility is lower under a fixed exchange rate regime.

In this intertemporal model, the best exchange rate regime on welfare grounds may be a flexible exchange rate. But this result depends, of course, on the assumption that the central bank strives to achieve the optimal inflation rate under a flexible exchange rate.

Stopping a Hyperinflation

Some countries have experienced very high inflation rates under flexible exchange rates. An extremely high inflation, such as 50 per cent per month or higher, is called a hyperinflation. In these cases, there is a link to fiscal policy and, in particular, to government budget deficits. Nominal government expenditure exceeds tax revenue, and the government budget deficit is being financed by printing money.

The welfare losses experienced by the public in a high inflation environment can be substantial. Although the rate of growth of the nominal money supply is high, the equilibrium level of real money balances is low. The high inflation rate generates a high nominal interest rate, increasing the opportunity cost of holding money, and the public responds by taking actions that result in a low level of real money balances (for a given level of consumption, there is a large increase in the velocity of money). In this environment, there is a welfare loss associated with the reduction in real money balances.

Empirically, the countries that have suffered very high inflation rates have had flexible exchange rates. An interesting policy question therefore arises. Can a move from a flexible to a fixed exchange rate help to end a hyperinflation? Fixing the value of the domestic currency to a foreign currency, such as the US dollar, can work to reduce the domestic inflation rate to the inflation rate being experienced in the foreign (US) economy. Through the law of one price, a permanently fixed exchange rate implies that increases in the equilibrium domestic price level will match increases in the foreign (US) price level. If the United States has an inflation rate equal to 5 per cent, the domestic inflation rate will, in equilibrium, also equal 5 per cent.[24]

In the intertemporal model with money, fixing the exchange rate imposes discipline on the monetary and fiscal authorities. Under a fixed exchange rate, the central bank can only increase the money supply when money demand increases. Therefore, the ability to finance a government budget deficit by printing new money is limited, and the government must adopt other measures to ensure that the government budget is close to being balanced.[25] In moving from a flexible exchange rate (with money financing of budget deficits) to a fixed exchange rate, the government may have to reduce government expenditures and increase taxes.

The applied exercises in Data Analytics examine two cases where a switch from a flexible to a fixed exchange rate resulted in a collapse of the inflation rate: Bolivia in the mid-1980s and Argentina in the early 1990s.

10. CONCLUSION

The balance of payments is a monetary phenomenon. Changes in foreign exchange reserves are caused by exogenous changes in domestic credit and exogenous changes that induce changes in the demand for money. In a small economy, exogenous changes in domestic credit cause offsetting changes in foreign exchange reserves. The central bank is unable to control the nominal money supply and unable to affect the domestic interest rate or the domestic price level. The central bank has "zero monetary independence."

In the intertemporal model with money, the domestic inflation rate is determined by the foreign inflation rate under a fixed exchange rate. If the foreign inflation rate does not equal the optimal inflation rate, a move to a flexible exchange rate regime can increase the welfare of domestic residents. But the desirability of any regime depends on the actual policy implemented by the authorities. In certain cases, a fixed exchange rate regime may be the better regime on welfare grounds (as when there is a high inflation under the flexible exchange rate).[26]

The intertemporal model with money is a one-good model, with identical domestic and foreign goods. While this assumption was adopted for convenience, the analysis of certain issues requires a multi-sectoral model, where each sector produces a distinct good or service. For example, the macroeconomic model could incorporate three sectors, representing the manufacturing, resource, and service sectors. This multi-sectoral approach to international macroeconomics is examined in subsequent chapters, where a variety of issues are examined under flexible and fixed exchange rates.

PRACTICE QUESTIONS

1. Fill in the blanks
   (a) Changes in foreign exchange reserves, or the _____, are caused by changes in domestic credit and changes in the variables that affect the _____.
   (b) An exogenous increase in domestic credit results in _____ in foreign exchange reserves and _____ in the public's holdings of foreign bonds.
   (c) In a one-good model with a fixed exchange rate, the domestic inflation rate is determined exclusively by the _____. This phenomenon is called _____.
   (d) A permanent increase in the foreign price level causes the current-period domestic price level to _____, and this change results in _____ in the central bank's foreign exchange reserves.
   (e) A temporary increase in output, by increasing current-period consumption and money demand, results in _____ in foreign exchange reserves.
2. Using the portfolio equilibrium diagram, as well as the asset adjustment diagram, explain how an exogenous increase in domestic credit affects the domestic interest rate, foreign exchange reserves, and the quantity of foreign bonds held by domestic residents.
3. Using the portfolio equilibrium diagram, explain how a permanent increase in output affects foreign exchange reserves and the interest rate.
4. Using the intertemporal model with money under a fixed exchange rate, list three factors that could have caused the large increases in China's foreign exchange reserves from 1996 to 2005.
5. Does a fixed exchange rate regime result in lower lifetime utility than a flexible exchange rate regime? Comment using the intertemporal model with money.

DATA ANALYTICS

1. Using the Federal Reserve Bank of St. Louis FRED database, collect annual data on the following variables between 1985 and 2005: the Argentine peso–US dollar exchange rate; the consumer price index for Argentina; the US consumer price index; and inflation rates for Argentina, the United States, and Brazil.

   For part of the period between 1985 and 2005, the Argentine peso was fixed to the US dollar at an exchange rate equal to 1.0.[27] When did this fixed exchange rate regime occur? Split the 1985–2005 period into three sub-periods: the initial period when the exchange rate was flexible; the period when the exchange rate was fixed at 1.0; and the period after the large devaluation of the Argentine peso, when the exchange rate regime returned to a flexible rate regime.

   Using plots, show the Argentine inflation rate during each sub-period and during the transitions from one regime to another. Is the evidence consistent with imported inflation? Given that Brazil was Argentina's largest trading partner, why did the government decide to fix to the US dollar and not the Brazilian currency? Comment.

2. Bolivia experienced a hyperinflation in the mid-1980s, with inflation at times exceeding 50 per cent per month. The exchange rate was flexible, the government budget was in deficit, and there were large increases in the money supply. In the summer of 1985, the government introduced a managed exchange rate regime.[28] Using the International Monetary Fund's IFS database, collect monthly data on the exchange rate (relative to the US dollar), the price level, and the M1 money supply from November 1984 to October 1985. Create plots of the price level and the exchange rate, the (monthly) inflation rate and percentage change in the exchange rate, and the inflation rate and the M1 growth rate. Discuss in general, and comment on the movements near the end of the period.

3. Access the International Monetary Fund's IFS database and collect data (beginning in 1996) on the Chinese yuan–US dollar exchange rate and the central bank of China's foreign exchange reserves. Create time-series plots of the exchange rate and foreign exchange reserves, with the sample period beginning in 1996. How has the exchange rate moved in the period after 2005? Has the accumulation of foreign exchange reserves continued in the period after 2005? Comment.

APPENDIX A: INTEREST-EARNING FOREIGN EXCHANGE RESERVES AND MONETARY POLICY

In the intertemporal model with money, consumption is constrained by the present value of lifetime real income less the present value of lifetime government spending. Monetary policy has no effect on this intertemporal constraint on the economy. This result hinges on assumptions that the central bank holds all foreign exchange reserves as interest-earning foreign bonds and that the intertemporal government budget constraint is internalized into the intertemporal household constraint. This appendix provides a concise discussion of this more advanced topic.

In this framework, the public regards central bank assets as their own. In terms of the consolidated government budget constraint, the money transfer increase in domestic credit is equivalent to a decrease in current taxes (in nominal terms). But the associated reduction in foreign exchange reserves in the current period means that the central bank will have lower interest earnings on foreign bonds as the economy moves into period t+1. The lower foreign interest earnings imply an increase in the period t+1 tax, with all else fixed. Thus, the equivalence of a tax cut in the current period associated with the money transfer is matched by a future tax increase. In total, there is no effect on the intertemporal constraint that outlines the lifetime possibilities available to consumers. Therefore, consumption is unchanged.

When the central bank conducts an open market purchase of domestic bonds, there are fewer domestic bonds held by investors. In period t+1, the government will experience smaller interest payments on their debt. But the open market operation also decreases the central bank's foreign exchange reserves (foreign bonds), so the government will experience lower interest earnings on foreign bonds held by the central bank. These two effects offset each other, and the present value of the public's tax liability is unchanged. The monetary policy action, thus, has no effect on consumer spending.[29]

APPENDIX B: OUTPUT CHANGES, THE CURRENT ACCOUNT, AND THE BALANCE OF PAYMENTS

Exogenous changes in output affect both the current account and the balance of payments. Is an improvement in the current account balance always associated with an improvement in the balance of payments? This appendix examines some exogenous changes (assume that the real interest rate and the marginal rate of time preference equal 0, the exchange rate and prices equal 1, and the current account is initially balanced).

With a temporary increase in output, the public saves to allow for consumption smoothing. The domestic economy exports the surplus production, the current account improves, and the domestic economy, as a whole, accumulates foreign bonds to allow for the desired increase in future consumption. But the increase in current consumption increases the demand for money, and a portfolio adjustment takes place. Domestic residents sell foreign bonds to acquire additional money balances. For example, if the increase in output in the current period is +10, the current account balance improves to a surplus of +5. Net capital inflows are negative (for example, equal to −4), representing the net accumulation of foreign bonds by domestic residents. And there is a balance of payments surplus (in this case, equal to +1), representing the accumulation of domestic money by residents and the accumulation of foreign bonds by the central bank.

With a permanent increase in output, the public consumes all the extra production in the current period. The current account does not change. But the increase in consumption increases the demand for money. In the portfolio adjustment, the public reduces their holdings of net foreign assets and increases their holdings of domestic money.[30] In this adjustment process, central bank reserves increase. There is a balance of payments surplus matched by net capital inflows.

With an increase in future output, the current account balance deteriorates. But the corresponding increase in current consumption generates an increase in money demand and an increase in foreign exchange reserves. The balance of payments improves. If future output increases by 10, the current account balance deteriorates from 0 to −5. Residents get a foreign loan of 6, so that net capital inflows equal +6. The balance of payments, the increase in foreign exchange reserves, and the increase in money holdings equal +1 in this numerical example.

Under a flexible exchange rate, there is no simple relationship between the exchange rate and the current account. Likewise, under a fixed exchange rate, there is no simple relationship between the current account balance and the balance of payments.[31] An improvement in the balance of payments can be associated with an improving current account, a deteriorating current account, or no change in the current account. Of course, these co-movements depend on the other exogenous variables being held fixed. If the central bank is implementing large increases in domestic credit in each period, the balance of payments could be in deficit regardless of the level of the current account.

APPENDIX C: CAPITAL CONTROLS AND THEIR CIRCUMVENTION

Governments sometimes impose capital controls to provide the central bank with some monetary independence under a fixed exchange rate.[32] To implement the regime, the government creates a law that makes it illegal to acquire foreign exchange for the purpose of acquiring foreign assets (without special permission from the government). This control on capital outflows breaks the link between the expected returns on domestic and foreign assets. The IRP condition does not hold, and the central bank is able to influence the interest rate.[33]

There are often loopholes within the capital control regime that hamper the effectiveness of the controls. For example, the law may include an exemption for the financing of international trade, including trade credit (changes in trade credit are referred to as "leads and lags"). This exemption is allowed so as to not interfere with the normal procedures in the international trade of goods, such as early payment for goods (where payment is made before the goods are delivered) or delayed payment for goods (where the firm selling the goods allows delayed payment and charges interest on accounts receivable).

These practices are normal in business operations, so the government implementing the capital control regime may regard the exemption as acceptable. But in terms of monetary independence, the exemption provides domestic residents with an avenue through which the controls can be circumvented.

Consider some examples. A domestic importer could lead, meaning that the payment for the imports (in foreign currency) is provided in advance. If the foreign company offers the domestic importer a discount for early payment, the importer has effectively acquired a foreign asset and earned interest (and will, in relative terms, experience a benefit akin to a capital gain if the domestic currency happens to be devalued). Likewise, a domestic exporter could allow delayed payment for goods sold (referred to as a lag). If the exporter charges interest at a rate equivalent to the foreign interest rate, this domestic firm has circumvented the controls by acquiring the equivalent of an interest-earning foreign asset.

These processes may work to limit the monetary independence of the central bank. Suppose the central bank increases domestic credit, putting more domestic currency in the hands of the public. The intent of the central bank is to induce domestic residents to purchase domestic bonds and generate a reduction in the domestic interest rate. With no exemptions in the capital control regime, the domestic interest rate will fall. But with the exemption, the domestic interest rate may remain unchanged. If domestic residents unload the domestic currency on the foreign exchange market in exchange for foreign currency, the domestic bond market will be unaffected. In the capital control regime, this acquisition of foreign currency must be for the purchase of foreign goods (the domestic residents are acquiring the foreign currency now to pay for some foreign goods to be delivered in the next period). In this case, the increase in domestic credit results in a proportional fall in foreign exchange reserves in this period, with no net effect on the money supply and no effect on the domestic interest rate. The exemption has allowed the controls to be circumvented, and the central bank is unable to influence the domestic interest rate.

In practice, capital controls are implemented for various reasons, some unrelated to monetary independence, and the structure of regimes varies from case to case.[34]

NOTES

1 The seminal literature on the operation of fixed exchange rate regimes from the perspective of dynamic, choice-theoretic models includes Helpman and Razin (1982), Stockman (1983), Persson (1984), Greenwood (1984), and Obstfeld (1986).

2 Imported inflation occurs only under a fixed exchange rate. With a flexible exchange rate, the central bank can generate any inflation rate it desires.

3 Currency crises are discussed extensively in Chapter 3, and Chapter 13 also provides some discussion.

4 The central bank is assumed, at the end of the period, to convert all foreign currency into foreign bonds. By holding foreign bonds, the consolidated government (the government and the central bank together) ensures that taxes are lower than if the central bank held foreign currency.

5 The agent internalizes the intertemporal government budget constraint into the intertemporal household budget constraint. An appendix provides related discussion on the importance of the central bank holding all foreign exchange reserves as interest-bearing foreign bonds (rather than foreign currency).

6 While the monetary approach to the balance of payments has a long history, monetary factors were downplayed for part of the twentieth century. In the 1960s and 1970s, Harry Johnson and Robert Mundell played predominant roles in revitalizing both the interest in and the acceptance of the monetary approach. See, for example, the articles in Frenkel and Johnson (1976).

7 The money transfer increase in domestic credit is similar to the case where the central bank deposits new money into private banks.

8 The trilemma asserts that a country cannot enjoy all three: a fixed exchange rate, unrestricted international asset trade, and monetary independence (Obstfeld et al. 2005). The trilemma holds in the model in this chapter, with the offset equal to -1. But the offset may or may not equal -1 in more general models, even with unrestricted international asset trade. A non-neutrality may allow some monetary independence. In addition, with transactions costs or uncertainty, changes in domestic credit may alter the interest rate by affecting the marginal portfolio adjustment cost or the risk premium (see, for example, Stockman 1983, Flood and Jeanne 2005, and Pasula 2016). For empirical estimates of the offset, see (for example) Kouri and Porter (1974), Pasula (1994, 1996, 2020), and Ouyang et al. (2010).

9 A "sterilization policy" is not effective. Suppose an exogenous change increases reserves and the central bank decreases domestic credit in an attempt to hold the money supply fixed. The initial exogenous change increases reserves and the money supply, and the decrease in domestic credit increases reserves but leaves the money supply unchanged. The initial change increases the money supply, and the attempted sterilization cannot overturn this result.

10 Since changes in domestic credit have an offsetting effect on reserves, the central bank can control the level of foreign exchange reserves. To increase reserves, the central bank can implement a decrease in domestic credit.

11 Capital controls often accompany fixed exchange rates, in an attempt to restrict international asset trade and allow some monetary independence (an appendix discusses capital controls and their circumvention).

12 When there are non-traded goods, and when domestic and foreign traded goods are not identical, the domestic inflation rate is also affected by domestic real variables. This issue is addressed in Chapter 11.

13 A permanent, one-time devaluation of the domestic currency has the same effects.

14 For an examination of various issues related to Canada under the gold standard, including the direction of causality, see Dick and Floyd (1992). For a general discussion of the gold standard, see (for example) Eichengreen (2008).

15 Under a flexible exchange rate, causality may be bidirectional (a higher price level, caused by other factors, may cause the central bank to change the money supply). For causality studies based on small

economies, international macroeconomists may recommend that the data not be pooled across exchange rate regimes.

16 In period t+1, the higher foreign price level results in a higher domestic price level, generating an endogenous increase in the period t+1 money supply.

17 The current account balance equals net exports, because the debt service balance is zero. In general, the balance of payments equals $[s[R_t - R_{t-1}]]$. Like the variable J, R_t can be negative when the central bank obtains a loan from foreigners (see, for example, the discussion in Obstfeld 1986).

18 In balance of payments accounting, the net acquisition of foreign assets is included in the financial account.

19 If exports exceed imports and the public has accumulated foreign currency, it can be converted to foreign bonds or domestic currency. In the latter case, the central bank accumulates foreign exchange reserves as domestic residents sell foreign currency for domestic currency. Because the central bank holds all reserves as foreign bonds, the central bank will sell the foreign currency for foreign bonds.

20 Mussa (2008) provides an interesting discussion of the Chinese economy over this period, including an interpretation of China's reserve flows in terms of the monetary approach to the balance of payments.

21 The Chinese data on foreign assets of the central bank, reserve money (the monetary base), and nominal GDP are taken from the International Monetary Fund's IFS database.

22 That an increase in output improves the balance of payments and that controlling domestic credit is critical in influencing the balance of payments were emphasized by economists at the IMF during the Bretton Woods era (see Polak 1998).

23 The optimal inflation rate may be positive in an environment with distortionary taxes. A higher inflation rate may allow for a reduction of taxes (on labour and goods) that increases lifetime utility more than the reduction in utility associated with the higher inflation rate. See the discussion in Phelps (1973) and Lucas (2000).

24 In a model with traded and non-traded goods, as shown in Chapter 11, domestic real shocks affect the inflation rate under a fixed exchange rate. But adopting a fixed exchange rate still aids in reducing the inflation rate.

25 Likewise, for a government within a currency union (such as the European Currency Union), there can be no money financing of budget deficits. If investors begin to expect that a government may have difficulty making future bond payments, the interest rate on that government debt will rise relative to rates for other countries within the currency union. Moreover, the higher interest rate will exacerbate the financial conditions faced by the government and could result in a sovereign debt crisis. See Bordo and Meissner (2016).

26 The analysis abstracted from issues important in assessing the desirability of alternative regimes, such as the potential for exchange rate crises under a fixed exchange rate and the extent to which an exchange rate regime acts as an automatic stabilizer in response to the real and monetary shocks that impact the economy. These issues are discussed in Chapters 3 and 13. For an excellent discussion of regime choice, see Stockman (1999).

27 Edwards (2003) discusses Argentina's currency board.

28 Sachs (1987) and Morales (1988) discuss this period in Bolivian economic history.

29 On neutrality and non-neutrality in these monetary models, see the discussion in Stockman (1983), Obstfeld (1981, 1986), Persson (1994), and Pasula (1996, 2016).

30 Given that domestic residents are assumed to begin the current period with zero net foreign assets, domestic residents get a loan from foreigners. In the new equilibrium, the variable J_t is negative.

31 In this intertemporal model, the effects of a temporary decrease in government spending are the same as the effects of a temporary increase in output, and likewise for permanent and future changes. A tax cut, matched by an equivalent future tax increase, has no effect on the current account or the balance of payments.

32 See, for example, the discussion of Eichengreen (2008) on the Bretton Woods era.
33 Edwards (1999) discusses both controls on capital outflows and controls on capital inflows.
34 Interesting references on capital controls include Edwards (1999), Obstfeld et al. (2005), and Eichengreen and Rose (2014). On issues related to British capital controls under Bretton Woods, see Einzig (1968), Cumby (1983), Cairncross and Eichengreen (2003), and Pasula (2020).

PART IV

Multi-Sectoral Models of Real and Nominal Exchange Rates

CHAPTER 10

Traded Goods, Non-Traded Goods, and the Exchange Rate

1. INTRODUCTION

Non-traded goods and services constitute a large fraction of aggregate production in industrialized nations. The non-traded sector consists predominantly of service sectors, whereas the traded sector is comprised largely of goods-producing sectors such as the manufacturing and resource sectors. If aggregate production is decomposed into the production of the traded and non-traded sectors, non-traded goods and services make up more than 50 per cent of production in industrialized economies. Given the significance of the non-traded sector, international macroeconomists have long recognized the importance of modeling the economy in a multi-sectoral framework.[1]

The large and persistent movements in the real exchange rate (the nominal exchange rate adjusted for the aggregate price levels in the two countries) suggest that sectoral changes may be important factors influencing movements in the nominal exchange rate. If two countries have similar movements in aggregate price levels but there are large long-term changes in the nominal exchange rate, real factors within the different sectors are likely to be causing the movements in the nominal exchange rate. Starting with this chapter, the chapters in Part IV use multi-sectoral models to analyze exchange rate determination and other macroeconomic issues.

The model is a long-run model in which the main real variables that cause changes in the exchange rate are productivity variables (the model is in the tradition of the Harrod–Balassa–Samuelson model).[2] If productivity growth differs between the sectors of the economy, the exchange rate will typically be changing. But while productivity is given significant emphasis, the model incorporates other factors, such as terms of trade changes and monetary changes, that can also cause long-run changes in the exchange rate.

The basic model is a two-sector model, with a non-traded sector and a traded sector. This structure is analyzed in detail, examining different exogenous shocks that impact the exchange rate in

Figure 10.1: The production of goods and services

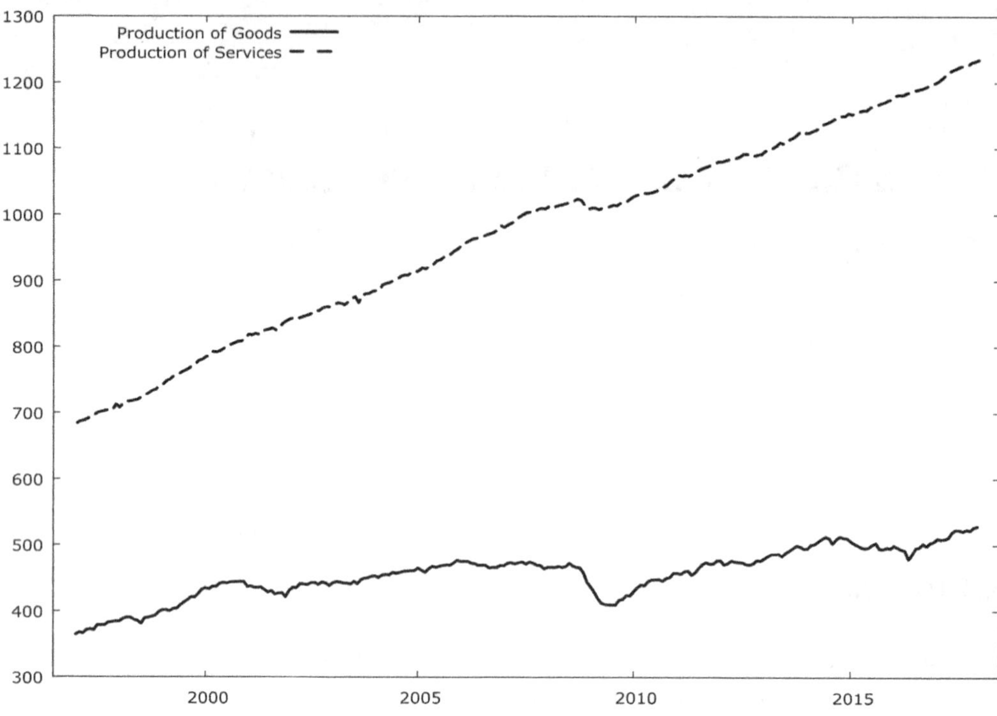

Data source: Statistics Canada

the long run. For simplicity, the two-sector model assumes that marginal products of labor are exogenous. A three-sector model is also analyzed, where there is one non-traded sector and two traded sectors representing the manufacturing and resource sectors. The three-sector model is also differentiated from the two-sector model in that it incorporates diminishing marginal products. The three-sector model is appropriate for countries like Canada, where resource products play a prominent role in the macroeconomics of the economy. Indeed, this three-sector model performs well in explaining aspects of the Canadian economy, including the substantial appreciation of the Canadian dollar between 2002 and 2007.

2. SECTORAL PRODUCTION IN CANADA

The sectoral decomposition of the economy into traded and non-traded sectors is not always a straightforward exercise. A simple approach regards the production of *goods* as production of the traded sector and the production of *services* as production of the non-traded sector. Figure 10.1 provides these data series using Canadian monthly data from 1997 to 2017 (measured at annual rates, in billions of chained 2007 dollars).[3] Based on this decomposition, the fraction of production in the non-traded sector has ranged from about 64 per cent to 71 per cent of the aggregate economy (an appendix summarizes existing multi-sectoral databases and discusses various measurement issues).[4]

3. THE TWO-SECTOR MODEL

The model includes the following features (the analysis focuses on the domestic economy, holding foreign factors fixed): there are two goods, a non-traded good and a traded good; the traded good in the domestic economy is identical to the traded good in the foreign economy; there is competition in the goods and labor markets; there is full employment of the labor force, and all workers are identical.

The model is a long-run model with flexible wages and prices, and it does not focus on intertemporal issues. In effect, the analysis is in terms of long-run, or steady-state, changes in the variables.

Two Sectors: a Traded Sector and a Non-Traded Sector

The domestic economy produces two goods: a traded good and a non-traded good (the foreign economy has the same structure). The traded good represents goods such as manufactured goods and resource products that are typically involved in international trade. The non-traded good represents services (for example, medical, restaurant, education, legal, and financial services), which are typically not traded, as well as products that are not traded because of high transport costs. While the non-traded goods in the two economies can have very different prices, the prices of the traded goods in the two countries are closely linked.

There are many firms in each sector, and all firms behave competitively.

The Law of One Price for the Traded Good

The traded good in the domestic economy is assumed to be identical to the traded good in the foreign economy. The prices of the domestic and foreign traded goods are tightly linked (for simplicity, transport costs, tariffs, and sales taxes are assumed to equal 0):

$$P^T = s\, P^{T*},$$

where P^T is the domestic price of the traded good, P^{T*} is the foreign price of the same good, and the variable s denotes the nominal exchange rate (an increase in s represents a depreciation of the domestic currency). This equation is called the law of one price condition.[5]

Because domestic and foreign traded goods are identical, the prices must be the same once there is due allowance for the exchange rate (or when the goods are measured in the same currency). Otherwise, with zero transport costs, consumers in both countries would buy the product from the firms that had the lower price. Competition therefore ensures that the law of one price holds.

Suppose the exchange rate equals 1.20, so that $1 US equals $1.20 Canadian. If the US price of the traded good equals $100 US, a Canadian would pay $120 Canadian to purchase it. The price of the traded good in Canada must equal $120 Canadian, or else everyone would buy from the country with the lower price (competition ensures that firms within a country have the same price). Of course, the firms with lower prices cannot produce enough to satisfy the entire market and would be overwhelmed with business. Market forces come into play, with either prices or the exchange rate adjusting to restore the law of one price.

Full Employment

The number of workers in the domestic economy is fixed. Since the model is a long-run model with flexible prices and wages, it is assumed that all workers are employed in one of the two sectors. There is full employment. If a sector is attempting to add workers, it must obtain these workers from the other sector.

Profit Maximization

The competitive firms maximize profit. In choosing the number of workers, firms ensure that the value of marginal product equals the wage rate. In the traded sector, the condition is

$$P^T f_L^T = w^T,$$

where f_L^T and w^T denote, respectively, the marginal product of labor and the nominal wage rate in the traded sector. The marginal product of labor f_L^T equals $\Delta y^T / \Delta L^T$, or the change in production in the traded sector divided by the change in labor in that sector.

Suppose the value of marginal product exceeds the wage rate in the traded sector. With this inequality, hiring an additional worker adds more to revenue than to cost. For example, if the price equals \$4 per good and the marginal product equals 7 goods per hour, the additional worker generates additional revenue of \$28 per hour. If the wage rate is less than \$28 per hour, the extra worker will generate an increase in profit. Competitive firms will therefore add this worker and keep adding workers until it is no longer profitable to do so (when the equation holds as an equality).

There are different forces that can work to eliminate this inequality. Price may fall to sell the additional production; firms may increase the wage rate to entice workers into this sector; and the marginal product of labor could fall as the quantity of labor increases (but in the two-sector model, marginal products are exogenous). In equilibrium, the value of the marginal product of labor equals the wage rate.

A similar condition holds in the non-traded good sector:

$$P^N f_L^N = w^N,$$

where f_L^N is the marginal product of labor in the non-traded good sector, measured as $\Delta y^N / \Delta L^N$, and w^N is the nominal wage rate paid by firms in the non-traded sector.

Workers are assumed to be identical, so the wage rates in the two sectors must be the same. The two conditions for profit maximization imply that

$$P^T f_L^T = w^T = P^N f_L^N = w^N.$$

This equation, called the labor market equilibrium condition, is a key equation in analyzing the effects of exogenous changes.

Exogenous Marginal Products of Labor

In the two-sector model, the marginal product of labor in each sector is assumed to be exogenous.[6] That is, the variables f_L^T and f_L^N are held fixed but can change exogenously. Exogenous increases in a sectoral marginal product could be caused by, among other things, an innovation in the sector or changes in the skills of workers in the sector.

The Price Level and a Zero Inflation Monetary Policy Rule

The consumer price index, or the price level, is a weighted average of the prices of the two goods, where the weights represent the fraction of a typical consumer's expenditure on that good:

$$P = 0.4\ P^T + 0.6\ P^N.$$

Under a flexible exchange rate, the central bank can influence the price level. For simplicity, it is assumed that the central bank acts to keep the price level, P, fixed. While P^T and P^N can and will change, the central bank will ensure that the aggregate price level P remains constant. This policy is a zero-inflation policy, which the central bank can achieve by altering the money supply. This assumption simplifies the analysis, as it implies that the two individual prices must always move in opposite directions. If the equilibrium price of the traded good falls, the equilibrium price of the non-traded good must rise (and vice versa).[7]

Solving the Model

The two marginal products of labor and all foreign variables are exogenous. In addition, the consumer price level is fixed. The endogenous variables will, in response to an exogenous change, adjust to maintain equilibrium in the different markets.

4. EXOGENOUS CHANGES IN PRODUCTIVITY

Increase in the Marginal Product of Labor in the Traded Sector

Suppose there is an exogenous increase in the marginal product of labor in the traded sector, for example, due to an innovation in the traded sector. Hold all other exogenous variables fixed, including the marginal product of labor in the non-traded sector. How does this exogenous change affect the price of the traded good, the price of the non-traded good, the wage rate, and the exchange rate in the long run?

Consider the labor market equilibrium condition where, with the exogenous increase in f_L^T, the value of marginal product exceeds the wage rate in the traded sector. At the initial wage rates and prices,

$$P^T f_L^T > w^T = P^N f_L^N = w^N.$$

Figure 10.2: Exogenous increase in f_L^T

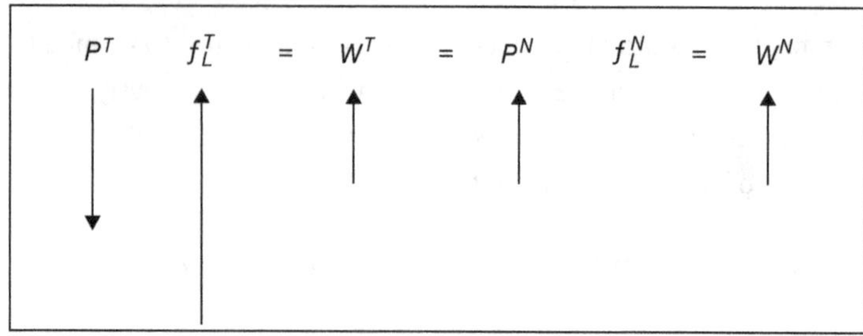

As domestic firms react to this condition, several changes occur. With the increase in productivity, traded-good firms can produce at a lower average and marginal cost. With competition, the price of the traded good falls. With the value of marginal product greater than the wage rate in the traded sector, there is an incentive to increase the number of workers. Traded-sector firms increase the wage rate to attract workers currently employed in the non-traded sector. Firms in the non-traded sector will not want to lose their workers, so they increase their wage rate to match the traded-sector wage rate. And because firms in the non-traded sector have not experienced a change in productivity, the increase in wages requires a higher price to cover the increased costs. The price of the non-traded good therefore increases.

In the new equilibrium, wage rates in the two sectors are equal and the value of the marginal product of labor is equal to the wage rate in both sectors. The following changes will have occurred in response to an exogenous increase in f_L^T of 10 per cent: a decrease in P^T of 6 per cent, increases in w^T and w^N of 4 per cent, and an increase in P^N of 4 per cent. With these changes, depicted in Figure 10.2, the different equalities all hold in the new equilibrium.

The consumer price index is unchanged, with the given weights in the index, in that the 6 per cent decrease in P^T offsets the 4 per cent increase in P^N.[8]

What happens to the exchange rate? With the fall in the domestic price of the traded good, the exchange-rate adjusted price of the foreign traded good is too high: $P^T <_S P^{T*}$. Consumers in both economies would want to purchase the traded good from domestic firms (but domestic firms will not be able to satisfy this huge demand). In the process, foreign consumers demand domestic currency on the foreign exchange market. This increase in demand for domestic currency causes the domestic currency to appreciate, so that the variable s falls. This process continues until the law of one price holds. Thus, the exogenous increase in the marginal product of labor in the traded sector causes an appreciation of the domestic currency.

Increase in the Marginal Product of Labor in the Non-Traded Sector

Suppose there is an exogenous increase in f_L^N, holding other exogenous variables and the aggregate price level fixed. With the increase in f_L^N, price times marginal product exceeds the wage rate in the non-traded sector. As firms react to this condition, there are changes in the various markets. The increase in productivity implies that firms in the non-traded sector can produce the good more cheaply. Through competition, the price of the non-traded good falls. And with the value of marginal product greater than the wage rate in the non-traded sector, firms in the non-traded sector increase the wage rate. In the traded sector, firms increase the wage rate to match the higher wage in the other sector and increase the traded-good price to cover the increase in costs.

The exogenous increase in f_L^N of 10 per cent has resulted in a decrease in P^N of 4 per cent, increases in w^N and w^T of 6 per cent, and an increase in P^T of 6 per cent. The three equalities hold in the new equilibrium. The 4 per cent fall in the price of the non-traded good offsets the 6 per cent increase in the traded-good price, leaving the price level unchanged.

With the rise in the price of the traded good, the law of one price does not hold. Consumers in both economies would want to purchase the traded good from foreign firms. In the process, domestic residents demand foreign currency on the foreign exchange market, causing the domestic currency to depreciate. This process continues until the law of one price holds. In this long-run model, the exchange rate adjusts to maintain the competitiveness of the traded-goods sector.

Note that in this general equilibrium model, exogenous shocks that originate in the non-traded sector affect the exchange rate.

5. PRODUCTIVITY CHANGES AND REAL AND NOMINAL EXCHANGE RATES

Consider the real exchange rate q, defined as $\dfrac{s\,P^*}{P}$, an aggregate measure of the relative price of foreign to domestic goods (including the prices of both traded and non-traded goods). With exogenous productivity changes, which are "real shocks," nominal and real exchange rates move together (assuming the inflation rates of the two countries are similar).[9] With an increase in the marginal product of labor in the traded sector, for example, there is a permanent decrease in both the nominal and real exchange rate. This positive co-movement does not occur when there are "monetary shocks" (discussed below), where the nominal exchange rate changes but the real exchange rate does not. Therefore, economists may be able to determine the type of shocks predominantly hitting an economy by examining how nominal and real exchange rates move over time. If they move closely together in the long run, real shocks are likely to be the predominant factor causing the nominal exchange rate to change.

The PPP Theory

The purchasing power parity (PPP) theory tends to work well if the prices of all goods move in the same direction. With the price of non-traded goods not moving in the same direction as the price of traded goods, the PPP theory of the exchange rate does not hold:

$$s \neq \frac{P}{P^*}.$$

With exogenous productivity changes and similar inflation rates, the nominal and real exchange rates move together. And the change is permanent, without any forces causing the nominal exchange rate to revert to a point equal to P/P*.

Long-run Growth and the Exchange Rate

If there are productivity increases in each period, there is continued growth in production in the economy. But there is no simple relationship between long-run growth and the real exchange rate. While higher growth in the domestic economy (relative to the foreign economy) may be associated with a depreciating currency in real terms, this is not always true. While it is true for growth in the non-traded sector, it is not true for growth in the traded sector. With balanced growth (the same growth rate in the two sectors), the real exchange rate remains unchanged.

Interest Rate Parity in the Very Short Run

In the very short run, the exchange rate is determined by the interest rate parity condition. The expected future exchange rate $\left(s_{t+1}^{e} \right)$ is the exchange rate investors expect to hold in one year (for simplicity, assume the long-run equilibrium is attained by time t+1). Exogenous changes in productivity are factors that can cause changes in the expected future exchange rate. Suppose that, today, investors come to expect an increase in the traded-sector marginal product of labor in the near future. This change causes the expected future exchange rate to fall *today*, and the attempt by investors to sell foreign currency causes the domestic currency to appreciate *today*.[10]

6. PRODUCTIVITY GROWTH AND THE YEN–DOLLAR EXCHANGE RATE IN THE 1970S

The two-sector model is most appropriate for explaining exchange rate movements in countries where traded-sector productivity growth has been significantly higher than in the United States (the foreign country), such as in Japan in the 1970s. Figure 10.3 shows the movements in traded and non-traded productivity indexes in Japan between 1971 and 1979 (with both indexes set equal to 100 in 1971), using data from the Groningen Growth and Development Centre (GGDC) 10 Sector database (see Timmer et al. 2015). The traded sector includes manufacturing, agriculture, and mining, whereas the non-traded sector consists of seven sectors (the appendix provides details). The average annual growth rate of traded-sector productivity was 5.6 per cent, compared to 2.3 per cent in the non-traded sector. This differential is quite large. By the end of the decade, traded-good productivity had increased 30 per cent more than non-traded productivity.[11]

The nominal and real yen–dollar exchange rates are shown in Figure 10.4.[12] At the start of 1971, the exchange rate was still being fixed at a level of 360 yen to 1 US dollar (this regime was the Bretton Woods era of fixed exchange rates that was near its end, having been in place since 1946). The yen appreciated, in both nominal and real terms, throughout most of the next eight years, before beginning a period of depreciation in late 1978. By the end of the decade, the yen was 33 per cent higher in nominal terms and over 40 per cent higher in real terms.[13]

Figure 10.3: Productivity in Japan in the 1970s

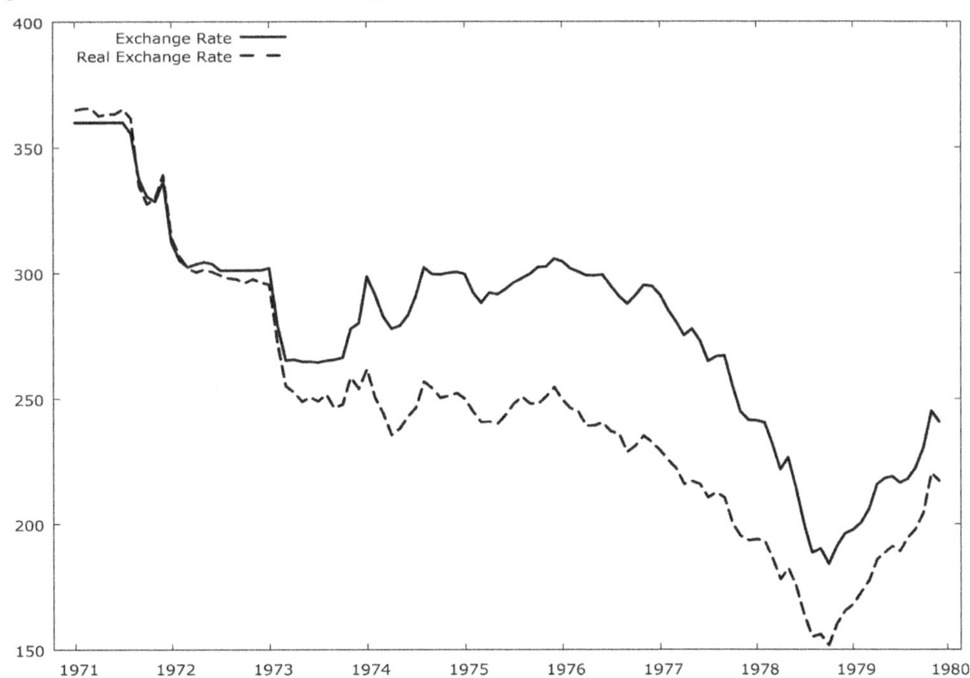

Data source: Groningen Growth and Development Centre (with the author's calculations)

Figure 10.4: Nominal and real exchange rates

Data source: International Monetary Fund

7. MONETARY FACTORS

Increase in the Money Supply

In the previous sections, the central bank was assumed to be implementing monetary policy so as to hold the price level fixed. For this subsection, this assumption is dropped and the effects of an exogenous change in the money supply are analyzed.

In this long-run analysis, the public holds money solely for the purpose of purchasing goods (the analysis is based on a one-period framework, so one abstracts from interest rates). The demand for money is therefore influenced by the price level and real income. In an initial equilibrium, the public is willingly holding a quantity of money determined by the amount of spending in the period.

When the central bank increases the nominal money supply, the public initially has more money than they want to hold (the demand for money has not changed). The public will attempt to reduce their money holdings by spending the additional money. With the supply of each good unchanged, the action by domestic residents to eliminate their excess cash balances causes the prices of both traded and non-traded goods to increase. As these prices increase, firms try to increase the number of workers, and the nominal wage rate increases to match the higher prices. The increase in the domestic traded-good price means that, at the initial exchange rate, the foreign traded good is cheaper. As residents attempt to shift their spending to the foreign traded good, they demand foreign currency and cause a depreciation of the domestic currency. This process continues until the law of one price holds.

With this "monetary shock," the nominal exchange rate moves together with the price level, but the real exchange rate is unchanged. If there are large changes in the nominal exchange rate and the domestic price level (relative to the foreign price level), with no or very small changes in the real exchange rate, one can infer that "monetary factors" are the main cause of the movement in the nominal exchange rate.

Implementing a Zero-Inflation Policy

Suppose, again, that the central bank is acting to hold the price level fixed. If a real shock occurs, such as an exogenous change in a marginal product of labor, the prices of both traded and non-traded goods begin to change. In general, these prices may not change in a way consistent with zero inflation. Suppose, for example, that an exogenous increase in f_L^T causes P^T to decrease by 3 per cent, but P^N is unchanged. The central bank will then have to increase the money supply to ensure that all prices increase by 1.2 per cent from this level. In total, the price of the traded good will fall by 1.8 per cent and the price of the non-traded good will increase by 1.2 per cent. With the given weights in the consumer price index, the price level is unchanged, and the central bank has effectively taken the correct action to keep the consumer price index fixed.

Increase in the Price of the Foreign Traded Good

Suppose there is an exogenous increase in the price of the foreign traded good (hold other exogenous variables fixed), and continue assuming that the central bank is acting to hold the price level fixed. Immediately after the exogenous change, the domestic traded good is cheaper. As foreign residents try to acquire domestic currency to be able to purchase the cheaper domestic traded good, the domestic currency appreciates (s falls) until the law of one price holds.

The exogenous increase in the price of the foreign traded good is exactly offset by the appreciation of the domestic currency, without any change in the prices of domestic goods. How does one know that the domestic price of the traded good does not increase? If the price of the traded good increases, there would also be pressure for the price of the non-traded good to increase and inflation would not equal zero.[14] Because the domestic central bank is following the zero-inflation policy, the domestic prices will not change. The flexible exchange rate, with the zero-inflation policy, allows the domestic economy to be insulated from the effects of increases in the foreign price level.

8. THE THREE-SECTOR MODEL

In this model, there is one non-traded and two traded sectors. The non-traded sector is denoted as N and the traded sectors are denoted as R for the resource good and as M for the manufactured good. Because the resource good is traded and identical in the two countries, the domestic price of the resource good equals the exchange rate-adjusted price of the resource good sold by foreign producers. Likewise, the law of one price holds for the manufactured good. These conditions are

$$P^R = s\, P^{R^*},$$

$$P^M = s\, P^{M^*}.$$

With three sectors, labor market equilibrium implies that

$$w = P^R f_L^R = P^M f_L^M = P^N f_L^N,$$

where w denotes the equilibrium nominal wage rate. Unlike in the two-sector model, the three-sector model assumes that the marginal product of labor for each sector is *diminishing*. When labor is induced to move between sectors, the marginal product in each sector will change *endogenously*. In addition, each sector has an upward sloping supply curve for goods, so the quantity of each good produced depends positively on the (relative) price of that good. While the domestic prices of the traded goods are linked to the foreign prices, the price of the non-traded good is determined by domestic demand and supply in the market for the non-traded good.[15]

The central bank acts to keep the price level fixed, with P specified as

$$P = 0.2\, P^R + 0.2\, P^M + 0.6\, P^N.$$

Increase in the Foreign Price of the Resource Good

Suppose there is an exogenous 10 per cent increase in P^{R^*} due, for example, to an exogenous increase in foreign demand for resource products. Immediately after the change, the law of one price does not hold for the resource good:

$$P^R < s\, P^{R*}.$$

The resource good in the domestic economy is cheaper, inducing foreign residents to try and acquire domestic currency for the purpose of buying the resource good from domestic firms. These actions cause the domestic currency to appreciate, so the exchange rate s falls. While it is possible that the domestic currency could appreciate to exactly offset the increase in the foreign price of the resource good, it is also possible that the domestic price of the resource good increases to some extent. For this section, it is assumed that the following changes occur to ensure that the law of one price holds after the 10 per cent increase in P^{R*}: the exchange rate s falls by 7 per cent, and the equilibrium P^R rises by 3 per cent (as outlined below, these changes are consistent with the fixed price level assumption).

In the domestic manufacturing sector, the appreciation of the domestic currency (with an unchanged foreign price of the manufactured good) initially results in a violation of the law of one price:

$$P^M > s\, P^{M*}.$$

Domestic manufactured goods are overpriced. The appreciation of the domestic currency has decreased the price of foreign manufactured goods for domestic residents and increased the amount that foreign residents have to pay, in terms of foreign currency, for the domestic manufactured good. The price of the domestic manufactured good must fall. As the exchange rate, s, falls by 7 per cent, the equilibrium price of the manufactured good falls by 7 per cent.

As the price of the manufactured good falls and the price of the resource good rises, there are changes in production in these two sectors. In the new long-run equilibrium, production of the manufactured good is lower.[16] As the domestic economy moves down along the long-run supply curve for the manufactured good, high-cost manufacturing firms exit the industry and production falls. With the increase in the price of the resource good, production of the resource good increases.

When the domestic economy exports resource products and imports manufactured goods, the exogenous increase in the foreign price of the resource good implies that there is an increase in the terms of trade (denoted as TOT), defined as the price of exports relative to the price of imports:

$$TOT = \frac{P^R}{P^M} = \frac{s\, P^{R*}}{s\, P^{M*}} = \frac{P^{R*}}{P^{M*}}.$$

The domestic economy is now exporting the resource good at a higher price and importing the manufactured good at a lower price.[17] This increase in the terms of trade is equivalent to an increase in real income, as it allows domestic residents to purchase more goods than before the exogenous change (the domestic economy's opportunity set has expanded).

The price of the non-traded good is determined by demand and supply in the market for the non-traded good. Because the rise in the foreign resource price increases both the terms of trade and domestic real income, domestic residents increase their spending. If all goods are normal goods, this income effect increases spending on all goods, including the non-traded good.[18] The demand curve for the non-traded good shifts to the right. With an upward sloping supply curve, there is an increase in both the price and production of the non-traded good.

Recall that the central bank is acting to hold the price level fixed. The domestic price of the manufactured good falls by 7 per cent, the domestic price of the resource good rises by 3 per cent, and the price of the non-traded good rises. Consider the consumer price index,

$$P = 0.2 \; P^R + 0.2 \; P^M + 0.6 \; P^N.$$

If the price of non-traded goods rises by 1.33 per cent, the price level will remain unchanged. While this is not guaranteed to occur on its own, the central bank will take any necessary action to ensure that P remains fixed (assume that the numbers used in fact occur).

Sectoral Employment Reallocation

In response to the exogenous increase in the foreign price of the resource good, the induced changes in domestic prices and production result in sectoral changes in employment. As the manufacturing sector contracts, it releases workers. Both the resource sector and the non-traded sector are expanding and adding workers (given the assumptions, the only way to increase production in a sector is to increase the number of workers). With the assumption of full employment, all workers laid off in manufacturing find employment in the expanding sectors.

As labor rises in the resource and non-traded sectors and falls in manufacturing, the marginal products change *endogenously* (falling in the two expanding sectors and rising in the manufacturing sector). In conjunction with the price changes, the actions of profit-maximizing firms ensure that the equalities hold. The equilibrium changes are depicted in Figure 10.5.[19] If the wage rate increases by 1 per cent, the marginal product of labor in the manufacturing sector rises by 8 per cent and the marginal product of labor in the resource and non-traded sectors falls by 2 per cent and 0.33 per cent, respectively.

The Dutch Disease

The term *Dutch disease* refers to the case where the domestic currency is appreciating, the resource sector is booming, and the manufacturing sector is contracting. The Dutch economy experienced these changes in an earlier period, and the term is now used more generally when these changes are occurring in any economy (as in Canada between 2002 and 2007, or in Colombia in the mid-1970s, when world coffee prices skyrocketed).[20]

The disease part of the term arises from the fact that the manufacturing sector is contracting. Is the contraction in manufacturing bad? The rise in the relative price of the resource good is a signal that the resource industry needs to expand, and it does expand in response to the increase in foreign demand for resource products. The economy appears to be allocating resources properly. Unless there is some market failure in the economy, the decrease in the size of the domestic manufacturing sector need not be a matter of concern.

Figure 10.5: Exogenous increase in P^{R*}

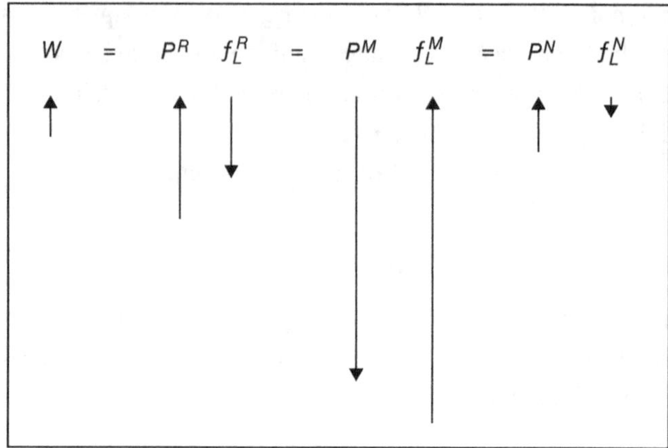

9. COMMODITY PRICES, THE EXCHANGE RATE, AND SECTORAL EMPLOYMENT: 2002–2007

World resource prices rose sharply between 2002 and 2007. The commodity price index, a weighted average of the US dollar prices of resource products important to the Canadian economy, rose by more than 140 per cent over this period (see Figure 10.6).[21] The Canadian dollar also appreciated substantially, rising from the low 60s to a level above par. This strong positive correlation between world commodity prices and the Canadian–US dollar exchange rate is evident in the figure (the exchange rate is measured as 1/s so that an increase in the line is an appreciation of the Canadian dollar). The positive relationship between the two variables is predicted by the theoretical analysis in section 8.

The three-sector model also provides an explanation of the profound structural changes within the Canadian economy during this period. While manufacturing struggled, the resource industry was booming, and the service sectors were expanding. Between 2002 and 2007, manufacturing employment fell from 2.21 million to 1.96 million, a drop of more than 11 per cent. This drop in manufacturing employment occurred in an environment where the aggregate economy was expanding at a relatively high rate. Indeed, employment in the rest of the economy increased by more than 16 per cent during this period, rising from 12.26 million to 14.25 million.[22]

These trends in sectoral employment are summarized in Figure 10.7, which depicts indexes of employment in manufacturing and the other sectors of the economy (each variable is set equal to 100 at the start of the period to allow a straightforward comparison). While employment in the rest of the economy increased strongly throughout the period, employment in manufacturing fell. These changes in sectoral employment are consistent with the prediction regarding changes in world resource prices and the Dutch disease.[23]

An applied exercise in Data Analytics examines sectoral employment between 2013 and 2016, when world commodity prices trended downward.

Figure 10.6: Commodity prices and the exchange rate

Data source: Statistics Canada

Figure 10.7: Sectoral employment

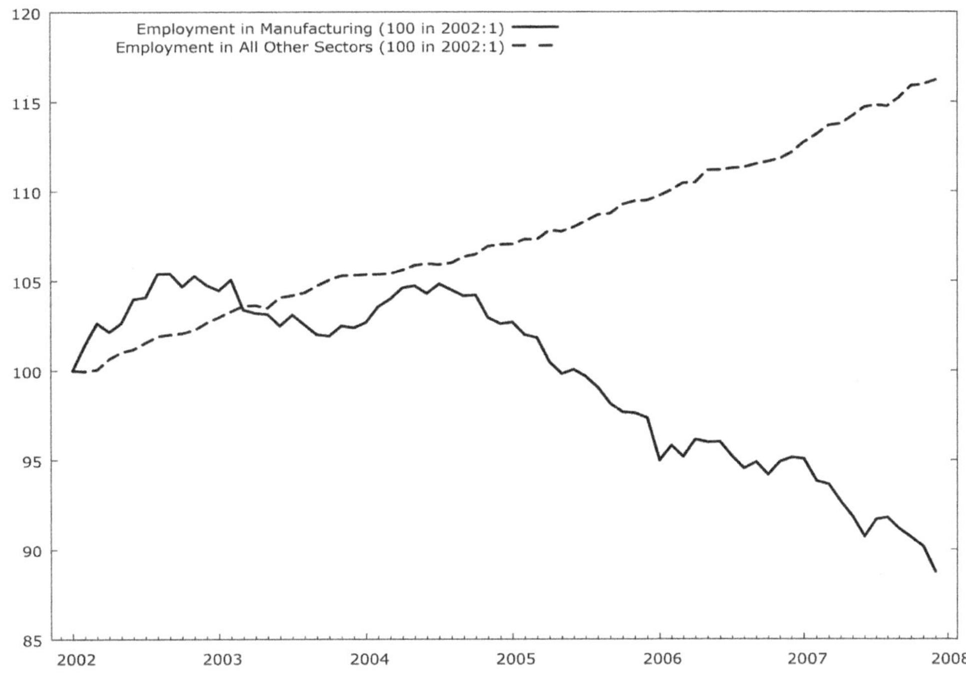

Data source: Statistics Canada, with the author's calculations

10. NOMINAL AND REAL EXCHANGE RATES SINCE 1980

The equation that defines the real exchange rate implies that

$$\frac{1}{s} = \frac{P^*}{P}\frac{1}{q}.$$

A rise in $1/s$ is a nominal appreciation of the domestic currency, which occurs if there is a rise in the foreign price level relative to the domestic price level (an increase in P^*/P) or if there is a real appreciation of the domestic currency (an increase in $1/q$). A real appreciation implies that there has been an increase in the relative price of domestic "goods," where the prices of both traded and non-traded goods and services are included in the aggregate price indices.[24]

In the long run, the real exchange rate is determined solely by real variables. Monetary policy in each country affects the domestic price level under a flexible exchange rate, but monetary policy has no effect on the real exchange rate.[25]

Nominal and Real Exchange Rates

From 1980 to 2016, Canadian–US dollar nominal and real exchange rates moved closely together (more recent data are examined in a Data Analytics exercise). In Figure 10.8, the positive correlation between the two variables is striking.[26] This suggests that the predominant longer-term forces impacting the nominal exchange rate have been real factors.

Canadian and US monetary policies have tended to be similar, with the Bank of Canada and the US Federal Reserve acting in a way that results in similar inflation rates in the two countries. Figure 10.9 plots the exchange rate as $1/s$ and the ratio of aggregate price levels measured as P^*/P. The Canadian inflation rate was marginally higher in the 1980s (so P^*/P fell) and then slightly lower in the following decades (so P^*/P rose moderately). But while the differences in price level movements were small, the nominal exchange rate moved substantially.

The Canadian–US dollar nominal exchange rate does not move in a way consistent with the PPP theory of the exchange rate. If the PPP theory held, the nominal exchange rate would have closely tracked the ratio of aggregate price levels. Starting at 86 cents US in 1980, the exchange rate would have fluctuated in a range between 75 and 88 cents. But the Canadian dollar depreciated to a level below 63 cents and appreciated to a level above par. Of course, the PPP theory has worked well in cases where monetary factors overwhelmed real factors (to name an example from Chapter 8, the Italian lira–German mark exchange rate in the late 1970s). But the PPP theory does not provide a good explanation of movements in the Canadian–US dollar exchange rate, because real factors have tended to play a predominant role.

World Commodity Prices and the Exchange Rate

Consider again the changes that occurred between 2002 and 2007. Figure 10.10 shows the nominal exchange rate (measured as $1/s$), the real exchange rate (measured as $1/q$), and the ratio of the US price level to the Canadian price level (P^*/P). The world price of oil skyrocketed during this period,

Figure 10.8: Nominal and real exchange rates

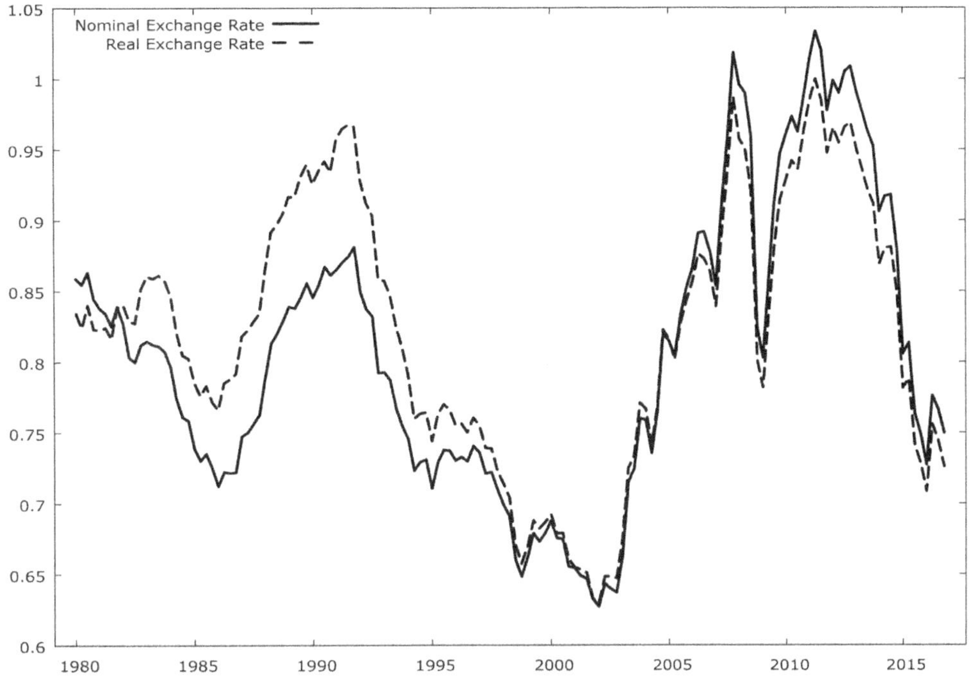

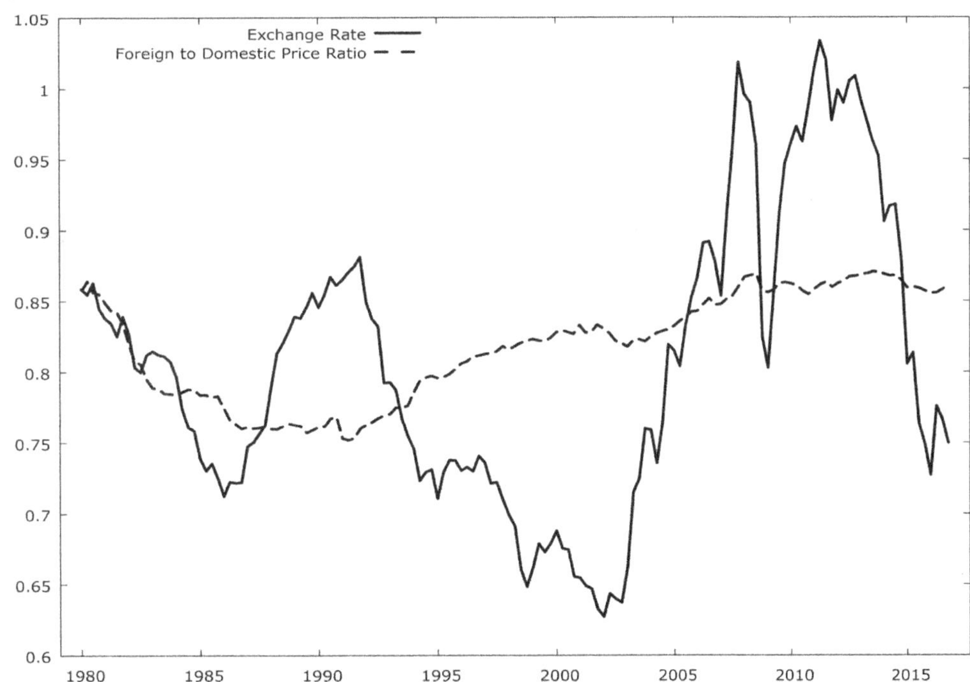

Data sources: International Monetary Fund and Statistics Canada

Figure 10.9: The exchange rate and the price ratio

Data sources: International Monetary Fund and Statistics Canada

Figure 10.10: The appreciation, nominal and real

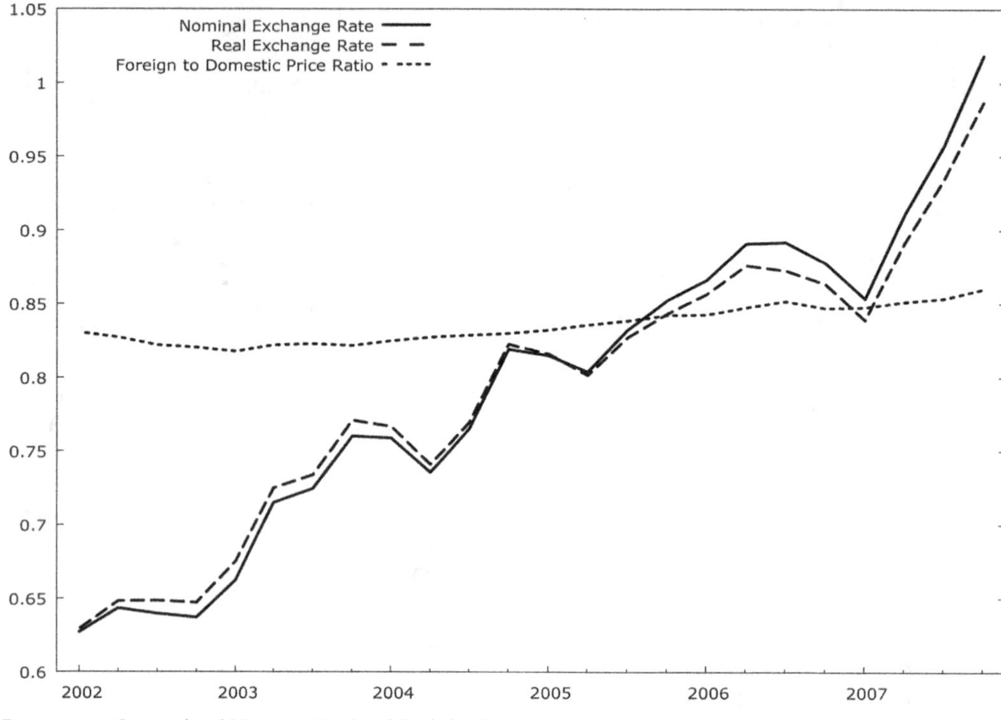

Data sources: International Monetary Fund and Statistics Canada

and most other commodity prices also rose sharply (as reflected in the substantial upward movement in the commodity price index depicted in Figure 10.6). The Canadian dollar appreciated by 60 per cent during this six-year period, an unprecedented magnitude in terms of the historical movements in the Canadian–US dollar exchange rate. Given the similarity of the movements in Canadian and US consumer price indices, the real exchange rate moved almost one-for-one with the nominal exchange rate. Substantial market forces impacting world commodity markets caused the large increase in the relative price of resource products. These shocks in the world economy then fed through and, in conjunction with the low inflation rate policies of the Bank of Canada and the Federal Reserve, resulted in the large nominal appreciation of the Canadian dollar relative to the US dollar.

If the world behaved as implied by the PPP theory, the Canadian–US dollar exchange rate would have hardly moved at all during this six-year period.

11. CONCLUSION

Real shocks can generate long-term changes in the relative price of non-traded goods and long-term changes in the terms of trade.[27] These changes in real factors are transmitted through the economy and, with low inflation policies of central banks, result in movements in the nominal exchange rate and the real exchange rate.[28] To understand the impact of these factors, international macroeconomists need to use multi-sectoral models of the economy.[29]

This chapter has used both two-sector and three-sector models to examine how various exogenous changes affect nominal and real exchange rates. The next chapter examines the effects of these factors when the nominal exchange rate is fixed.

PRACTICE QUESTIONS

1. Fill in the blanks
   (a) The marginal product of labor in the traded sector is calculated as ______ divided by ______.
   (b) In the two-sector model, the equilibrium wage rate in the traded sector equals the price of the traded good times ______ in the traded sector.
   (c) The central bank is holding the price level fixed. In the two-sector model, an exogenous increase in the foreign price of the traded good causes the domestic currency to ______ (relative to the foreign currency) and results in ______ in the wage rate in the domestic economy.
   (d) In the two-sector model, an exogenous increase in the marginal product of labor in the non-traded sector causes the price of the non-traded good to ______ and the exchange rate (denoted s) to ______ (assume that the central bank is holding the price level fixed).
   (e) The domestic traded-good price equals ______ times the foreign price of the traded good. Because the domestic and foreign traded goods are identical, with zero transport costs, the two goods must have the same price when measured in the ______.
2. Fill in the blanks
   (a) When a country experiences the Dutch disease, the domestic currency ______ (relative to the foreign currency) and production in the ______ sector falls.
   (b) In the three-sector model, an increase in demand for the non-traded good results in an increase in the number of workers in this sector. The marginal product of labor ______.
   (c) The commodity price index is a weighted average of the US dollar prices of products from four sectors of the Canadian economy: forestry, ______, metals and minerals, and ______.
   (d) Consider the three-sector model with a flexible exchange rate (and a fixed price level). An exogenous increase in the foreign price of the resource good causes employment in the domestic non-traded sector to ______ and the marginal product of labor in this sector to ______.
   (e) From 2002 to 2007, the Canadian dollar ______ relative to the US dollar. Over the same time period, the commodity price index ______.

3. In the two-sector model, explain how an exogenous increase in the marginal product of labor in the traded sector affects prices and the exchange rate in the long run. Assume that the central bank is acting to hold the price level fixed.

4. Using the two-sector model, explain how an exogenous increase in the foreign price of the traded good affects prices and the exchange rate in the long run. Assume that the central bank holds the price level fixed.

5. (a) The two-sector model and the three-sector model make different assumptions regarding productivity and supply. Provide a summary of the differences.

   (b) What does the commodity price index measure? Explain.

   (c) In the three-sector model, what determines the terms of trade? Explain using equations.

6. Consider the three-sector model (with a fixed price level). Explain how an exogenous increase in the foreign price of the resource good affects the exchange rate and the domestic price of the manufactured good.

7. Fill in the blanks. Consider the three-sector model with a flexible exchange rate (with the standard assumptions). The domestic economy exports the resource good, and the central bank holds the price level fixed. An exogenous 10 per cent increase in the foreign price of the resource good causes the domestic currency to appreciate by 7 per cent, and the following changes also occur: the domestic resource price __________ by ______ per cent, the domestic price of the manufactured good __________ by ______ per cent, the marginal product of labor in the resource sector ________, the terms of trade of the domestic economy ________, and non-traded production ____________.

DATA ANALYTICS

1. Collect data on the commodity price index, the Canadian–US dollar exchange rate, employment in manufacturing, and employment in the rest of the economy for the period since 2013 (the CANSIM numbers for these series are provided in sections 9 and 10). Comment on the full period, but include a comment on the period between 2013 and 2016.

2. Read the discussion of the NAICS in Appendix A. Access CANSIM Table 36100434 and collect monthly production data on any two sectors over the period 2015 to 2019. Plot these measures of production on the same plot (measure each sector's production on a separate axis), and comment on the extent to which sectoral production moved together over this period.

3. Collect monthly data on the Canadian–US dollar exchange rate and Canadian and US price levels, beginning with data in 2017 (see section 10 for data sources). Convert the monthly data to quarterly data. Examine whether the movements in the exchange rate since 2017 are consistent with the PPP theory. Comment.

APPENDIX A: DATABASES AND DECOMPOSITIONS

This appendix provides information on existing multi-sectoral databases and on the decomposition of the aggregate economy into traded and non-traded sectors.

The North American Industry Classification System

Statistics Canada has collaborated with American and Mexican government statistical organizations to develop statistics on sectoral production and so on. The North American Industry Classification System (NAICS) is a system that, at the two-digit level, has 20 sectors.

For international economists, a useful disaggregation is the decomposition into a traded sector and a non-traded sector. As an example, consider Table 10.1 that shows production in each sector (measured in billions of chained 2007 dollars) for February 2012.[30] These sectoral production numbers are rounded off, with aggregate production equal to 1541, but there is little discrepancy as the "All Industries" statistic (CANSIM series V41881175) equals 1551.

The non-traded sectors are predominantly service sectors.[31] The construction sector is also regarded as non-traded because a large fraction of production is conducted on a local basis. Based on these numbers and this decomposition, the traded sector comprises 36 per cent of the Canadian economy and the non-traded sector 64 per cent. Note that, based on the national accounts data for Canada, about 30 per cent of real GDP was exported in 2012.

Difficulties in Allocating Sectors to a Category

The determination of whether a given sector is traded or non-traded is not a straightforward exercise. For example, the finance and insurance sector does export some services; and in the educational services category, university education services are traded. Nonetheless, the large majority of output in these sectors is regarded as non-traded, and these sectors have been uniformly defined as belonging to the non-traded sector. But there are a few sectors that have been designated as traded in some studies and non-traded in others (similar issues arise with the databases listed below). In particular, the transportation sector is sometimes taken to be non-traded, and some studies assign both wholesale trade and retail trade to the non-traded sector. For a discussion of issues with respect to decomposing the data into traded and non-traded sectors, see Marston (1987), De Gregorio et al. (1994), Stockman and Tesar (1995), Spence and Hlatshwayo (2012), and Devereux and Hnatkovska (2012).

A More Direct Dichotomy

Another dichotomy that Statistics Canada uses is to split industries into goods-producing and service-producing industries.[32] For February 2012, the numbers were 470 and 1082 for a total of 1552. On this basis, the service-producing industries make up 70 per cent of the total economy.

Given the difficulties of determining the proper assignment of various sectors to either sector, a simpler approach may be to assume that the traded sector consists of the goods-producing industries and the non-traded sector consists of the service-producing industries. For example, Chen and Rogoff (2003) use this approach in their construction of US variables.[33]

Table 10.1: Sectoral and aggregate production

Traded Sectors	
Agriculture, forestry, fishing, and hunting	23
Mining, quarrying, and oil and gas extraction	126
Manufacturing	168
Transportation and warehousing	65
Wholesale trade	87
Retail trade	80
Production in the Traded Sector	**549**

Non-Traded Sectors	
Utilities	35
Construction	115
Information and cultural industries	50
Finance and insurance	101
Real estate and rental and leasing	193
Management of companies and enterprises	11
Professional, scientific, and technical services	83
Administrative and support, waste management, and remediation services	40
Educational services	82
Health care and social assistance	105
Arts, entertainment, and recreation	11
Accommodation and food services	31
Other services	30
Public administration	105
Production in the Non-Traded Sector	**992**
Aggregate Production	**1541**

Data source: Statistics Canada

The OECD STAN (Structural Analysis) Database

The OECD Structural Analysis (STAN) database is a widely used cross-country, multi-sectoral database. For each nation in the OECD, the database includes statistics on a variety of economic variables for nine broad sectors (as well as for subsectors within each sector). One approach (for example, Devereux and Hnatkovska (2012)) regards five sectors (manufacturing; agriculture, hunting, forestry and fishing; mining and quarrying;[34] wholesale and retail trade- restaurants and hotels; transport, storage and communications) as "traded" and four sectors (electricity, gas and water supply; finance, insurance, real estate, and business services; construction; community, social, and personal services) as "nontraded."

GGDC 10 Sector Database

The Groningen Growth and Development Centre (GGDC) database, for more than forty countries, decomposes data into 10 sectors. The data are annual, including (for each sector) value added, the output deflator, and total number of persons employed (see Timmer et al. 2015). The 10 sectors are agriculture, mining, manufacturing, construction, public utilities, retail and wholesale trade, transport and communication, finance and business services, other market services, and government services. The first three sectors could be regarded as traded, and the next seven sectors as non-traded.

APPENDIX B: DIFFERENTIATED TRADED GOODS

When domestic and foreign traded goods are not identical, the goods need not have the same price (when measured in the same currency):

$$P^T = \lambda \, s \, P^{*T},$$

where the parameter λ is exogenous. In this setup, λ is the terms of trade. When this condition holds as an equality, the markets for the two traded goods are in equilibrium.

Suppose that, in the initial equilibrium, the price of the foreign good equals $1 US, the exchange rate s equals 1.5, λ equals 2, and the price of the domestic good equals $3 Canadian. The Canadian dollar price of the US good is $1.5 Canadian. At these prices, both Canadians and Americans regard the two goods as equally good (based on the characteristics of the goods). The price of the Canadian traded good is higher, but this is an equilibrium situation. Given the fixed production of both goods, these quantities are willingly purchased by domestic and foreign consumers. Demand equals supply for each good.

Suppose an exogenous change increases λ from 2 to 3. With fixed supplies, this change in λ is due to a shift in relative demand. All of a sudden, everyone increases their demand for the domestic good and decreases their demand for the foreign good (at the initial prices and the initial exchange rate). With the increase in λ, it is now the case that

$$P^T < \lambda \, s \, P^{*T}.$$

The goods markets are not in equilibrium in that, immediately after the change, everyone wants to buy the domestic good. Suppose that, given zero-inflation policies, only the exchange rate changes. The increase in λ from 2 to 3 causes the exchange rate s to fall from 1.5 to 1.0, where a new equilibrium situation has been established. The exogenous increase in relative demand for the domestic good results in an appreciation of the domestic currency relative to the foreign currency.

NOTES

1   On the historical background on non-traded goods in macroeconomic models, see Viner (1937, chapter VI), Oppenheimer (1974), and Asea and Corden (1994).
2   See Harrod (1939), Balassa (1964), and Samuelson (1964).

3   The CANSIM series are V65201211 and V65201212 in Table 379-0031 (now labelled Table 36100434). In Pasula (2017) and Chapter 14, the sectoral decomposition is based on the 20 sectors in the North American Industry Classification System.

4   Many retail goods have significant non-traded components and may need to be regarded as non-traded. An appendix to Chapter 5 also discusses measurement issues.

5   Baldwin and Yan (2004) conduct an empirical analysis of the law of one price condition using Canadian and US data. Some researchers modify the condition by incorporating trade costs; see, for example, Obstfeld and Rogoff (2000) and Engel and Wang (2011). In addition, the condition is altered when domestic and foreign traded goods are differentiated products (this case is discussed in an appendix).

6   In the academic literature, applications of the two-sector model typically incorporate diminishing marginal products. The assumption of exogenous marginal products is adopted for pedagogical reasons. But see, for example, the empirical study by Hsieh (1982). An appendix to Chapter 11 outlines a widely used diagram for a two-sector model with diminishing marginal products.

7   Lecturers may find it convenient to assume that the consumer price index has equal weights of 0.5, so that an x per cent increase in one price requires an x per cent decrease in the other price.

8   The assumption of a fixed aggregate price level ensures a unique equilibrium. Without this restriction, there are multiple solutions. For example, if the traded-good price fell by 10 per cent, the wage rate and the non-traded price would not change. Or if wage rates and the non-traded price rose by 10 per cent, the traded-good price would not change.

9   In this model, any long-term change in the real exchange rate is caused by a real factor, such as an exogenous change in productivity. But the condition of similar inflation rates is also needed to generate the prediction that nominal and real exchange rates move together.

10 Bond traders have an incentive to accurately predict future factors, both real and monetary. If only a few investors correctly foresee a future change, these investors will be able to trade foreign currency at the existing exchange rate and earn higher returns than others. But if a future change is widely foreseen, there is a rapid adjustment of today's exchange rate to account for the expected change.

11 The US growth rates and sectoral differences were smaller than in Japan. For interesting empirical studies, see Hsieh (1982) and Marston (1987). In a multi-country study, Duarte and Restuccia (2010) provide information on relative price changes and sectoral productivity growth (for agriculture, industry, and services).

12 These monthly exchange rate and price level data are from the International Monetary Fund's IFS database.

13 The average inflation rate was higher in Japan which, in itself, would induce a nominal depreciation of the yen. The yen appreciated another 40 per cent in the 1980s, ending the decade at 144 yen to 1 US dollar.

14 If the traded-good price rises, these firms would increase the wage rate. Non-traded firms would match the wage increase and increase prices. The zero-inflation target would be violated.

15 On three-sector models, see (for example) Corden and Neary (1982) and Neary and Purvis (1983).

16 One interpretation of an upward sloping long-run aggregate supply curve is that different points on the curve represent different firms (or different plants) with different cost structures. At low prices, there is production by low-cost firms. At higher points on the curve, the extra production comes from higher cost firms (or higher cost plants). There is competition, but different firms have different cost structures.

17 With no asset accumulation, the value of exports and imports are equal: $P^R \left[y^R - c^R \right] = P^M \left[c^M - y^M \right]$, where y is production and c is consumption. When P^{R*} increases, production of R increases and production of M decreases. With standard changes in consumption, both exports, $y^R - c^R$, and imports, $c^M - y^M$, increase.

18 There may also be relative price effects, as demands change in response to changes in relative price. Income and relative price effects are examined in detail in the multi-sectoral models in Chapters 12 and 14.

19 These changes are assumed to be consistent with full employment. The slopes of the marginal product curves may be different in the manufacturing, resource, and non-traded sectors.

20 On the Dutch disease, see (for example) Corden and Neary (1982). Sachs and Larrain (1993) discuss the effects of increases in world coffee prices on various sectors in Colombia.

21 The commodity price index includes US dollar prices of forestry products, agricultural products, metals and minerals, and energy products. The CANSIM numbers for the commodity price index and the Canadian-US dollar exchange rate are, respectively, V52673496 and V37426.

22 The sectoral employment data are from CANSIM Table 282-0088. These data are used in Figure 10.7.

23 There may be other factors that affected sectoral employment during this period. See Leung and Cao (2009) and Iscan (2015). Macdonald (2007) also discusses issues related to the Dutch disease in Canada.

24 There is an extensive empirical literature on the PPP relationship, the law of one price condition for traded goods, and the relationship between prices and the exchange rate in general, where the empirics are based strictly on exchange rate and price data. See the survey papers by Froot and Rogoff (1995), Rogoff (1996), Taylor and Taylor (2004), and Burstein and Gopinath (2014). Readers need to be aware of both the underlying assumptions and the measurement issues that arise. Interesting empirical studies are conducted by, among many others, Baldwin and Yan (2004), Burstein et al. (2006), Betts and Kehoe (2017), and Crucini and Landry (2019).

25 The model is a long-run model with flexible wages and prices. Monetary policy may have a temporary, or transitory, effect on the real exchange rate, but does not have a permanent, long-run effect.

26 The data are quarterly (averages of monthly data). The exchange rate is CANSIM V37426 and the Canadian consumer price index is V41690973. The US consumer price index data are from the International Monetary Fund's IFS database.

27 Real shocks could be due to (among other things) increases in the skills of workers or innovations that allow for increased production with the same number of workers. For an interesting economic and historical discussion of various issues related to production, innovation, and the labor time required to produce a car chassis at Ford in the early 1900s, see Eli et al. (2025).

28 It may be beneficial in empirical work to decompose the economy into two non-traded sectors, representing services and construction, and two traded sectors, representing manufacturing and resources (including agriculture).

29 For related empirical literature, see, for example, Hsieh (1982), Froot and Rogoff (1995), Canzoneri et al. (1999), Chinn (2000), Floyd (2010), Ricci et al. (2013), and Choudhri and Schembri (2014).

30 The data are from CANSIM Table 379-0031 (now labelled Table 36100434). Statistics Canada provides detailed descriptions of the various sectors in the NAICS. There is also a three-digit level that splits each sector into subsectors.

31 Statistics Canada provides information on Canada's international trade in services.

32 These data are also available in CANSIM Table 379-0031 (now labelled Table 36100434).

33 This approach can also be used in allocating consumer spending to sectors. For example, Stockman and Tesar (1995) assume that consumption of the non-traded good equals the consumption of services and consumption of the traded good equals the consumption of nondurables. And depending on the purpose of the study, the consumption of durables and semi-durables could be regarded as traded-good consumption.

34 Note that the sector "mining and quarrying" includes the subsector called "extraction of crude petroleum and natural gas and related services."

CHAPTER 11

Traded Goods, Non-Traded Goods, and the Price Level under a Fixed Exchange Rate

1. INTRODUCTION

Under a fixed exchange rate, the domestic prices of traded goods are linked very closely to the foreign prices of the same goods. In effect, these prices are determined by world demand and supply conditions. The prices of goods and services in the non-traded sector, however, are determined by demand and supply conditions in the domestic economy. Given this sharp dichotomy in the determination of prices in the different sectors of the economy, international macroeconomists have long recognized the importance of modeling the economy in a multi-sectoral framework.

This chapter continues the analysis of multi-sectoral models, with a focus on the determination of the domestic price level under a fixed exchange rate.[1] With monetary policy devoted to ensuring that the exchange rate remains fixed at the stated level, the central bank loses control of the money supply and is unable to influence the aggregate price level. Changes in the domestic price level are caused by changes in the foreign price level and by real factors that cause changes in the relative price of the non-traded good and the terms of trade.

The analysis begins with the two-sector model, with the traded and non-traded sectors. A three-sector model is also analyzed, where there is one non-traded sector and two traded sectors representing the manufacturing and resource sectors. While this specification is appropriate for countries with large resource sectors, the same analysis holds for any small economy with well-defined export and import sectors.

2. THE TWO-SECTOR MODEL

The domestic economy produces a traded good and a non-traded good (the foreign economy has the same structure). Goods markets are competitive, and the law of one price holds for the traded good:

$$P^T = s\, P^{T*},$$

where s is the exchange rate, and p^T and p^{T*} denote the domestic and foreign prices of the traded good. As the exchange rate is fixed, the domestic traded-good price does not change unless the foreign price changes.

There is full employment of the labor force. Workers are assumed to be identical, so that the wage rates in the two sectors must be the same. In conjunction with the conditions for profit maximization, the equality of wage rates implies that

$$w^T = P^T f_L^T = P^N f_L^N = w^N,$$

where w is the wage rate, f_L denotes the marginal product of labor, and the superscripts T and N denote the sectors. In this two-sector model, the marginal products of labor are exogenous.[2]

The price level (the consumer price index), denoted as P, is specified as

$$P = 0.4\, P^T + 0.6\, P^N.$$

Under a fixed exchange rate, the central bank cannot hold the price level fixed as monetary policy must be directed toward keeping the exchange rate fixed.

This model is a long-run model with flexible wages and prices. In effect, the analysis is in terms of long-run, or steady-state, changes in the variables.

3. EXOGENOUS CHANGES IN PRODUCTIVITY

Increase in the Marginal Product of Labor in the Traded Sector

Suppose there is an exogenous increase in the marginal product of labor in the traded sector (an exogenous increase in f_L^T). The other exogenous variables are held fixed, including the marginal product of labor in the non-traded sector. With the increase in f_L^T, price times marginal product is greater than the wage rate in the traded sector:

$$P^T f_L^T > w^T = P^N f_L^N = w^N.$$

As firms in the domestic economy react to this condition, several changes occur. Note that because the exchange rate and the foreign traded-good price are fixed, the law of one price implies that the domestic traded-good price cannot change. But as the value of marginal product is greater than the initial wage rate, firms in the traded sector have an incentive to increase the number of workers and increase the wage rate to attract new workers. In the non-traded sector, firms respond by matching the higher wage rate in the traded sector. And since firms in the non-traded sector have not experienced a change in productivity, these firms increase their price to cover the increase in average cost associated with the increase in the wage rate.

With these endogenous changes, wages in the two sectors are equal and the value of the marginal product of labor equals the wage rate in each sector. In response to an exogenous 10 per cent

Figure 11.1: Exogenous increase in f_L^T

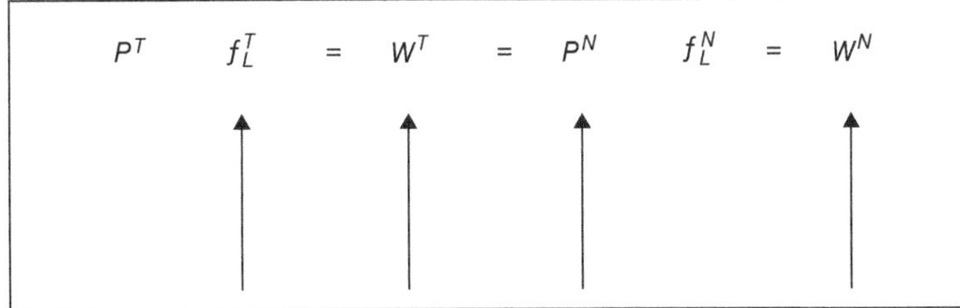

increase in f_L^T, there is no change in p^T, increases in w^T and w^N of 10 per cent, and an increase in p^N of 10 per cent. Figure 11.1 provides a summary. Given that the non-traded good has a weight of 0.6 in the price level, the 10 per cent increase in the price of the non-traded good results in a 6 per cent increase in the price level. Under a fixed exchange rate, the central bank is unable to prevent the price level from rising.[3]

While it may be surprising that a productivity increase causes an *increase* in the price level, this is what happens. While the price of the traded good does not change, the productivity change increases both the wage rate and the price of the non-traded good.[4] But the inflation is not of the variety where the prices of all goods rise by the same percentage amount. In this two-sector model with a fixed exchange rate, the rise in the price level is associated with a rise in the relative price of the non-traded good.

Increase in the Marginal Product of Labor in the Non-traded Sector

Suppose there is an exogenous increase in f_L^N. Immediately after the exogenous increase, price times marginal product is greater than the wage rate in the non-traded good sector. The exogenous increase in productivity implies that firms in the non-traded sector can produce the good more cheaply and, through competition, the price of the non-traded good falls.

By how much will the price of the non-traded good fall? One must determine the effects, if any, on the traded-good price and the wage rate. With a fixed exchange rate and a fixed foreign traded-good price, the law of one price implies that the domestic traded-good price does not change. Likewise, with p^T and f_L^T unchanged, the equilibrium wage rate in the traded sector is unchanged. And because the wages in the two sectors are linked, the wage rate in the non-traded sector does not change. Therefore, the exogenous increase in the marginal product of labor in the non-traded sector causes a proportionate fall in the price of the non-traded good. If the marginal product increases by 10 per cent, the price of the non-traded good falls by 10 per cent.

This productivity change therefore causes a decrease in the consumer price index. The 6 per cent fall in the price level, caused by the 10 per cent fall in the price of the non-traded good, is a natural adjustment that occurs in response to a change in the underlying structure of the economy. And the relative price change is again associated with a change in the price level in a fixed exchange rate regime. In summary, an exogenous 10 per cent increase in f_L^N results in a decrease in P^N of 10 per cent, no change in w^N or w^T, no change in P^T, and a decrease in P of 6 per cent (see Figure 11.2).

Figure 11.2: Exogenous increase in f_L^N

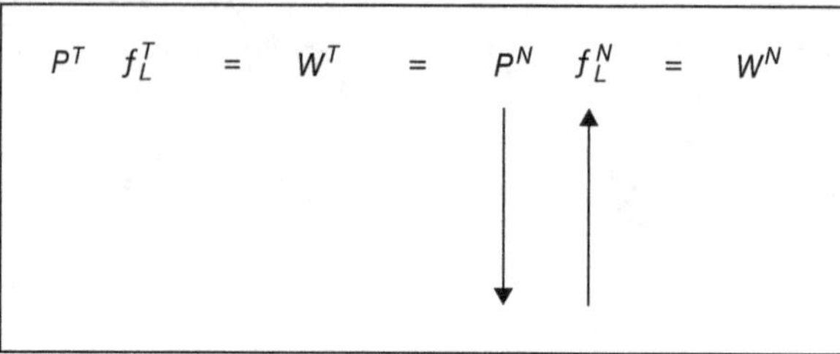

Productivity Changes and the Real Exchange Rate

The real exchange rate, q, is defined as $\dfrac{s\,P^*}{P}$. With an exogenous increase in the marginal product of labor in the traded sector, the price level rises and q falls: there is a real appreciation of the domestic currency. With an exogenous increase in the marginal product of labor in the non-traded sector, the price level falls and q rises: there is a real depreciation of the domestic currency. These real shocks cause changes in the real exchange rate.

4. MONETARY CHANGES

Changes in Domestic Credit

Under a fixed exchange rate, the exogenous policy instrument of the central bank is domestic credit. Foreign exchange reserves are endogenous, with reserves changing to keep the exchange rate fixed. In a small economy, an increase in domestic credit causes a proportional decrease in foreign exchange reserves, with no net effect on the money supply. Changes in domestic credit therefore have no effect on goods prices or the price level. The central bank is unable to exert any influence on the consumer price index.

Changes in the Price of the Foreign Traded Good

Suppose there is an exogenous increase in the price of the foreign traded good (caused by an increase in the money supply in the large foreign economy).[5] Immediately after the change, the domestic traded good is cheaper:

$$P^T < s\,P^{T*}.$$

Consumers, both domestic and foreign, would want to buy the domestic traded good. With a fixed exchange rate, the domestic price of the traded good must increase.

With the increase in the price of the traded good, firms in the traded sector increase the wage rate in an attempt to increase the number of workers (at the initial wage rate, an increase in labor increases profit). But firms in the non-traded sector also increase wages, and the price of the non-traded good increases to cover the increase in costs. The exogenous increase in the price of the foreign traded good therefore causes both domestic goods prices to rise, and the consumer price index rises proportionately.

Imported Inflation

When the foreign price level is rising year after year, caused by a continual increase in the foreign money supply, the domestic price level also rises year after year. Each increase in the price of the foreign traded good causes increases in the domestic prices of both goods, traded and non-traded. With these changes happening every year, the foreign inflation causes inflation in the domestic economy. This result is called imported inflation. Under a fixed exchange rate, with other exogenous factors fixed, an x per cent inflation rate in the foreign economy causes an x per cent inflation rate in the domestic economy.

A Note on the PPP Theory

The PPP theory tends to work well if the prices of all goods move together, rising or falling by the same amount in percentage terms. Under a fixed exchange rate, the PPP theory implies that the domestic price level is determined exclusively by the foreign price level:

$$P = s\,P^*.$$

But when there is differential productivity growth, the domestic price level changes without any change in the foreign price level. When the productivity growth rates in the traded and non-traded sectors are not the same, the domestic price level and the real exchange rate move permanently away from the values predicted by the PPP theory.

5. PRICE LEVEL MOVEMENTS IN CANADA, JAPAN, AND THE UNITED STATES UNDER BRETTON WOODS

Under the Bretton Woods system, each country fixed the value of their currency to the US dollar. While Canada had a flexible exchange rate for part of this period, the Canadian dollar was fixed to the US dollar between May 1962 and May 1970 (as well as between 1946 and 1950). Most other countries had rigidly fixed exchange rates, with no or very few changes in the level of the exchange rate. The Japanese yen, for example, was fixed at a rate of 360 yen to 1 US dollar for the entire period. This section examines aggregate price level movements in Canada and Japan (relative to the United States) during the latter part of the Bretton Woods era.[6]

Canada and the United States, 1962–1970

Between May 1962 and May 1970, the value of the Canadian dollar was fixed to the US dollar at a rate of 92.5 cents US to 1 Canadian dollar. With similar productivity growth in the two countries, the Canadian inflation rate was determined predominantly by the US inflation rate.

Figure 11.3: Canadian and US inflation rates

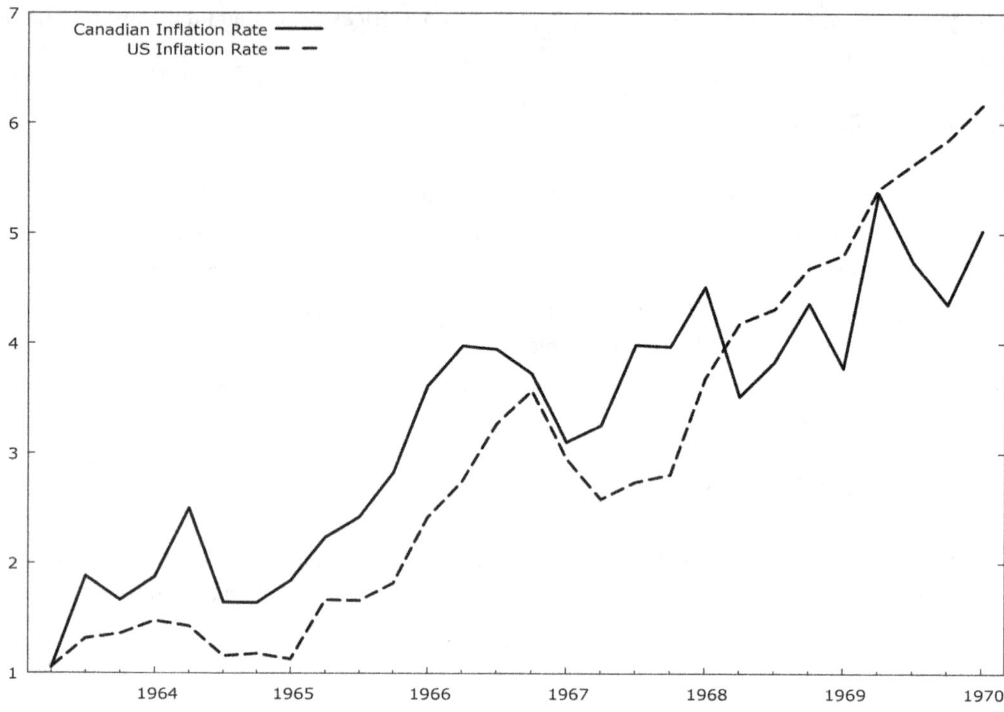

Data sources: International Monetary Fund and Statistics Canada

Figure 11.3 shows US and Canadian annual inflation rates, based on quarterly data, with each price level measured as a consumer price index (CPI).[7] In the first few years of the fixed exchange rate regime, US and Canadian inflation rates were between 1 per cent and 2 per cent. In 1965, the US inflation rate began an upward trend and the Canadian inflation rate was pulled up to these higher levels. Figure 11.4 shows the corresponding movements in Canadian and US price levels. The PPP theory worked fairly well in this case, as the real exchange rate changed by only 2 per cent over the eight-year period.

Japan and the United States, 1960–1971

While Canadian and US inflation rates were similar under Bretton Woods, this was not the case with respect to Japanese and American inflation rates. The main difference between these cases relates to the phenomenal growth in productivity in Japan in the 1960s.[8]

Figure 11.5 shows movements in traded and non-traded productivity indexes in Japan (each index is set equal to 100 in 1960).[9] The traded sector includes manufacturing, the largest sector in the Japanese economy, as well as the agriculture and mining sectors. Productivity increased substantially more in the traded sector. In terms of growth rates, the average annual growth rate of productivity was 8.5 per cent in the traded sector and 5.1 per cent in the non-traded sector.

Figure 11.4: Canadian and US price levels

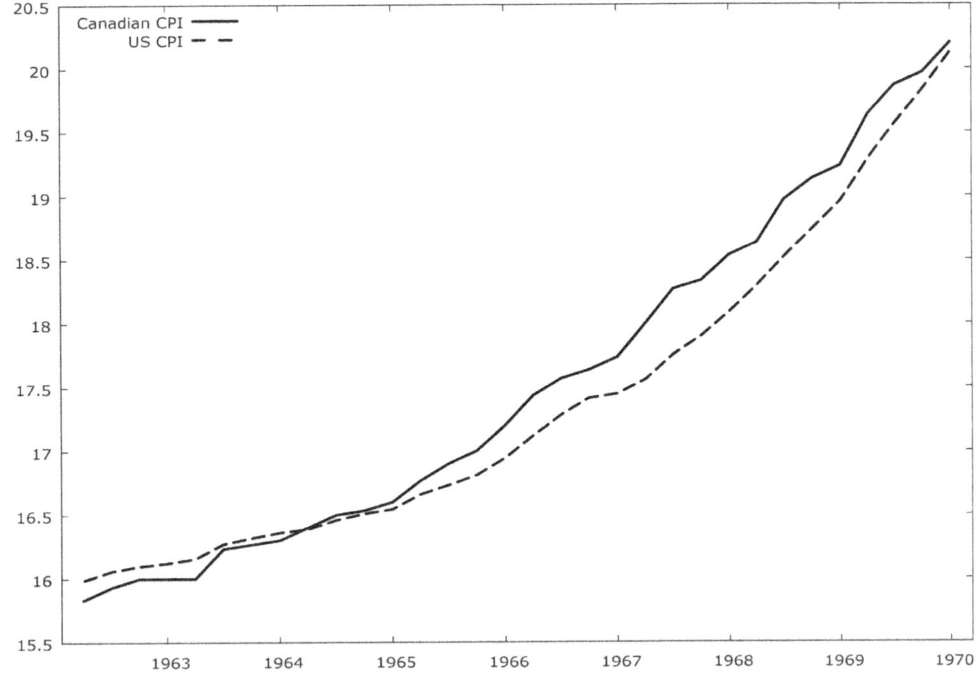

Data sources: International Monetary Fund and Statistics Canada

Figure 11.5: Sectoral productivity in Japan

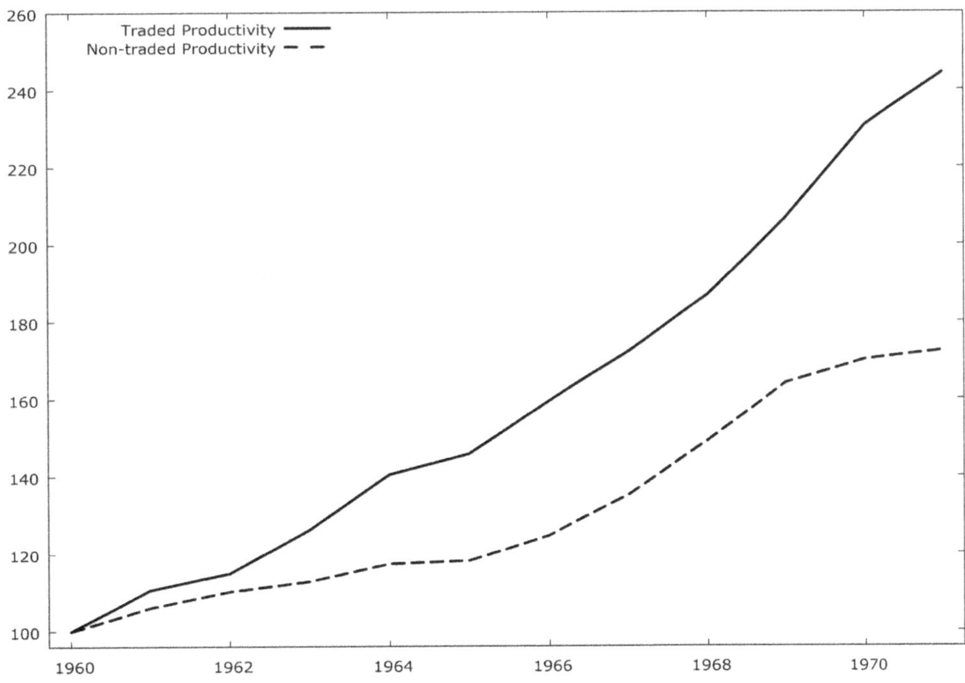

Data source: Groningen Growth and Development Centre, with the author's calculations

Figure 11.6: US and Japanese inflation rates

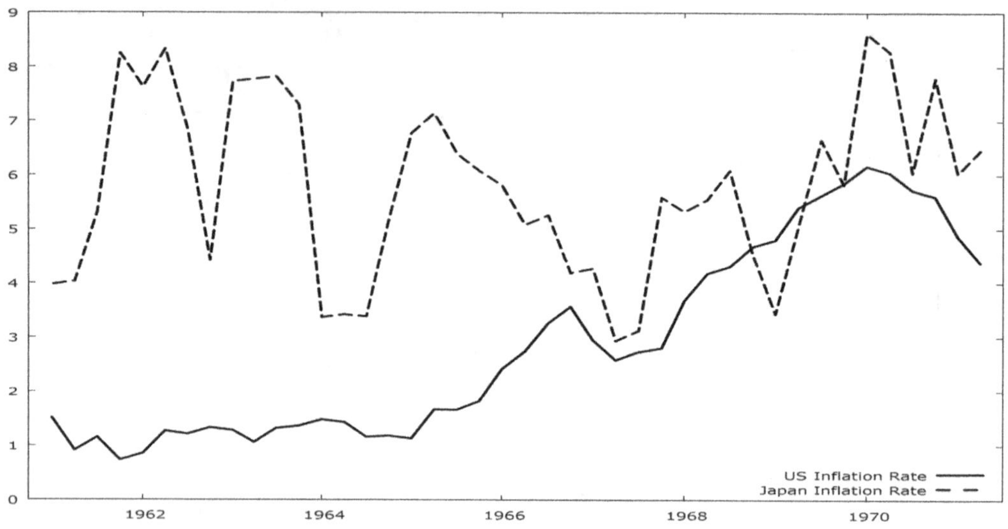

Data sources: International Monetary Fund

In the first half of the 1960s, as predicted by the two-sector model, the relatively high productivity growth rate in the traded sector caused a high inflation rate in Japan. For this period, the Japanese inflation rate ranged between 3 per cent and 8 per cent, whereas the average US inflation rate was 1.3 per cent (see Figure 11.6). In the latter 1960s, the growth rate of traded-sector productivity was still high, but it was often matched by high growth in the non-traded sector. This more balanced growth resulted in the Japanese inflation rate being closer to the (now higher) US inflation rate. Figure 11.7 depicts movements in price levels. The rise in the price level in Japan, relative to the price level in the United States, resulted in a real appreciation of the yen of about 35 per cent.

6. THE THREE-SECTOR MODEL

Suppose that each economy has three sectors. The non-traded sector is denoted as N and the traded sectors are denoted as R for the resource good and as M for the manufactured good. The law of one price holds for both traded goods:

$$P^R = s\, P^{R*},$$

$$P^M = s\, P^{M*}.$$

In the three-sector model, the marginal product of labor in each sector is *diminishing* and each sector has an upward sloping long-run supply curve. There is full employment, and workers are mobile between sectors. In this model, workers will move in response to certain exogenous changes.

Figure 11.7: Price levels in the United States and Japan

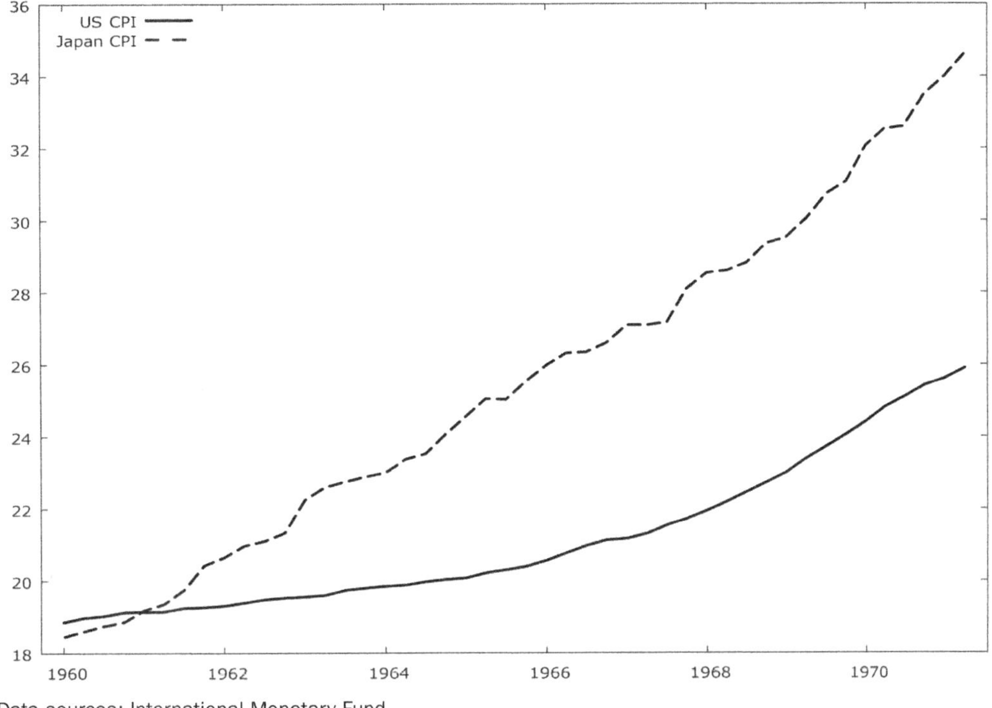

Data sources: International Monetary Fund

The consumer price index, or the price level, is specified as

$$P = 0.2\ P^R + 0.2\ P^M + 0.6\ P^N,$$

where each weight reflects the typical fraction of expenditure on that good.

Increase in the Foreign Resource Price

Suppose there is an exogenous 10 per cent increase in P^{R*}, a change that could be due to an exogenous increase in foreign demand for the resource good. Immediately after the change, the law of one price does not hold for the resource good:

$$P^R < s\ P^{R*}.$$

The resource good in the domestic economy is now cheaper. As consumers try to purchase the resource good from domestic firms, the domestic price increases. Under a fixed exchange rate, P^R must increase by 10 per cent to restore equilibrium. And given that the foreign price of the manufactured good is unchanged, the domestic price of the manufactured good does not change.

Assuming that the domestic economy exports the resource good and imports the manufactured good, the exogenous increase in the foreign price of the resource good causes an increase in the terms of trade of the domestic economy (denoted as TOT):

$$\text{TOT} = \frac{P^R}{P^M} = \frac{sP^{R*}}{sP^{M*}} = \frac{P^{R*}}{P^{M*}}.$$

The domestic economy is now exporting the resource good at a higher price and importing the manufactured good at a *relatively* lower price. This increase in the terms of trade is akin to an increase in real income, in that it allows domestic residents to purchase more goods than before the exogenous change. In effect, the domestic economy's opportunity set has expanded.

The price of the non-traded good in the domestic economy is determined by the interaction of supply and demand in that market. With the increase in the terms of trade, domestic residents are richer and increase spending on all goods (all goods are assumed to be normal goods). The demand curve for the non-traded good shifts to the right. With an upward-sloping supply curve, both price and production increase (in the non-traded sector, domestic production equals domestic consumption).[10]

With increases in both P^R and P^N, the resource and non-traded sectors will want to expand employment (price times marginal product is greater than the initial wage rate in these sectors).[11] When the expanding sectors increase wage rates, the manufacturing sector cannot initially match the wage increases (manufacturing firms cannot increase their price, and it is only profitable to pay higher wages if productivity rises). Labor is mobile between sectors, with workers leaving the manufacturing sector and finding employment in one of the expanding sectors. The changes in the quantity of labor induce changes in the marginal product of labor in each sector. In the resource and non-traded sectors, the marginal product of labor falls as they expand employment. And as labor leaves manufacturing, there is an endogenous increase in the marginal product of labor. With this higher level of productivity, firms in the manufacturing sector are then able to offer an increase in the wage rate for the remaining workers.

In the new equilibrium (see Figure 11.8), the wage rate equals the value of the marginal product of labor in each of the three sectors. As the levels of employment change, there are induced changes in the marginal products. In conjunction with the price changes, the profit-maximizing actions of firms ensure that the equalities in this equation hold.[12] In total, the following endogenous changes occur in response to an exogenous 10 per cent increase in P^{R*}: an increase in P^R of 10 per cent; as the number of workers in the resource sector increases, a decrease in f_L^R of (say) 2 per cent; an increase in the wage rate of 8 per cent; no change in P^M; as the number of workers falls in the manufacturing sector, an increase in f_L^M of 8 per cent; an increase in P^N of (say) 9 per cent; and as labor in the non-traded sector increases, a decrease in f_L^N of 1 per cent.

Under a fixed exchange rate, the domestic consumer price index changes when foreign traded-good prices change. In this case, the domestic price of the resource good increases by 10 per cent and the domestic price of the non-traded good rises by 9 per cent. Given the weights in the price index, the consumer price index rises by 7.4 per cent. In a fixed exchange rate regime, the central bank is unable to prevent this upward movement in the domestic price level.

Figure 11.8: Increase in the foreign resource price

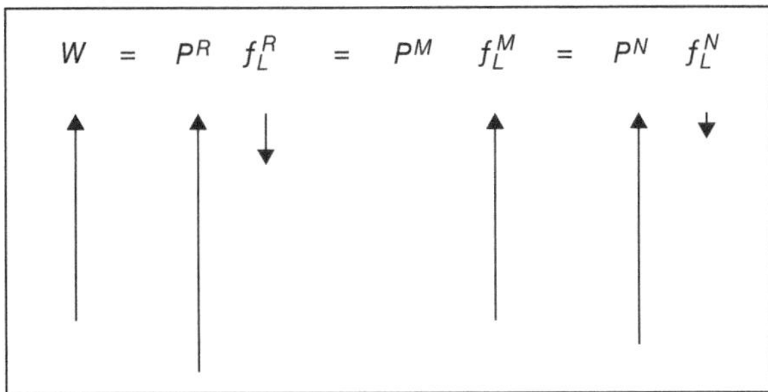

7. REAL SHOCKS AND PRICE LEVEL MOVEMENTS UNDER A FIXED EXCHANGE RATE

From 2002 to 2007, world resource prices rose sharply. The commodity price index, a weighted average of the US dollar prices of resource products important to the Canadian economy, increased by more than 140 per cent over this six-year period (see Chapter 10). While Canada had a flexible exchange rate over this period, it is interesting to examine what may have happened had Canada been operating under a fixed exchange rate regime (with the Canadian dollar fixed to the US dollar). Under a fixed exchange rate, the three-sector model predicts that the real shocks that caused increases in world resource prices would be transmitted to the domestic economy and cause increases in the domestic price level.

One can do a simple calculation based on the specification of the three-sector model. For example, if world resource prices rise by 10 per cent per year, the three-sector model suggests that the Canadian inflation rate would be approximately 7.4 per cent higher than the US inflation rate. If the US inflation rate was 2 per cent, the Canadian inflation rate would be 9.4 per cent. And with variability in the annual change in world resource prices, the annual inflation rate could be variable.

A Counterfactual Experiment

A simulation can be done using the actual movements in the real exchange rate and the US price level.[13] Given a set of simplifying assumptions, one can simulate the path for the Canadian price level assuming that the exchange rate was fixed. If one is willing to assume that "monetary neutrality" holds under any exchange rate regime, movements in real variables such as the real exchange rate and real GDP in the counterfactual experiment would be the same as the actual movements in these variables.

Suppose that, at the start of 2000, the Bank of Canada began fixing the Canadian dollar at 1.42857 Canadian dollars for 1 US dollar (70 cents US for each Canadian dollar). Using the movements in the US price level and the real exchange rate, along with the maintained assumptions, one can generate the path that the Canadian price level would have taken over the period between 2000 and 2007. The predicted price level, for every period t, is calculated as follows (with quarterly data):[14]

Figure 11.9: Predicted price level

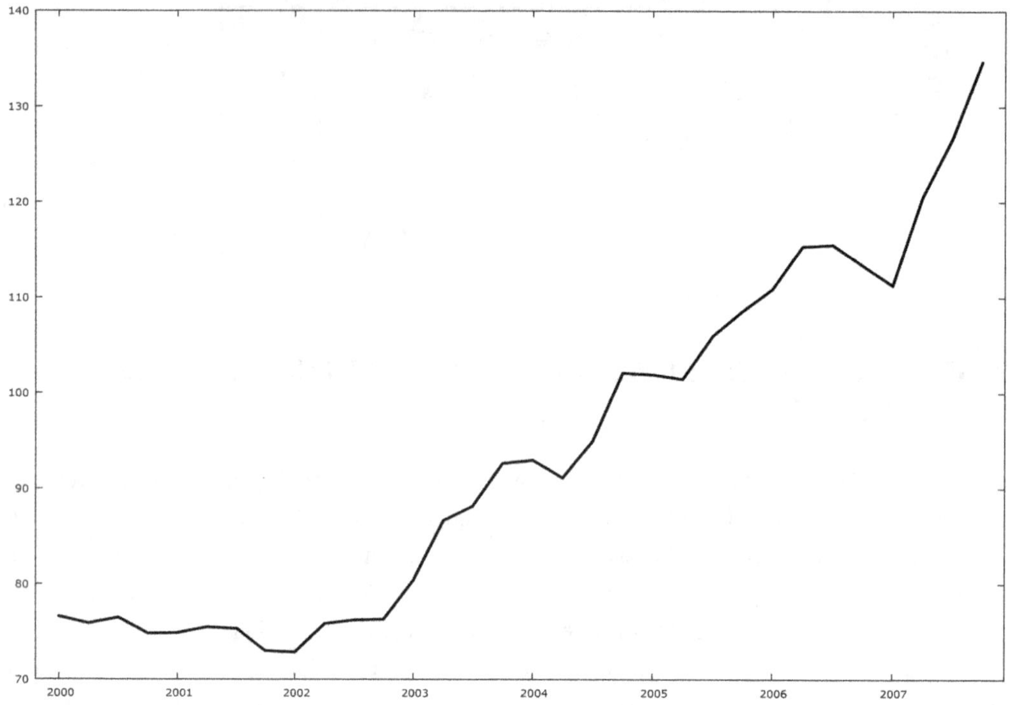

Data sources: International Monetary Fund and Statistics Canada (with the model's predictions)

$$predicted\ P_t\ =\ \frac{1.42857\ P_t^*}{q_t}.$$

Given the simplicity of the setup, one should regard the simulation and results as strictly an interesting pedagogical experiment.

The simulation result is shown in Figure 11.9. Between 2000 and 2002, the predicted Canadian price level has a slight downward trend. But beginning in 2003, the price level begins to trend upward such that the price level is 70 per cent higher by the end of 2007. The average annual inflation rate over the period is 7.3 per cent. Figure 11.10 depicts the predicted Canadian inflation rate, along with the actual US inflation rate. The predicted Canadian inflation rate is significantly higher under the fixed exchange rate regime. And the variability is higher, with the predicted inflation rate ranging from −3 per cent to 21 per cent.[15]

An applied exercise in Data Analytics examines the predicted movements in the Canadian price level, assuming that the Canadian–US dollar exchange rate was fixed at par beginning in 2008. These results will be of interest, given that this period includes both the recession in 2008 and 2009 and the downward movement in world commodity prices between 2014 and 2016.

Figure 11.10: Predicted inflation rate

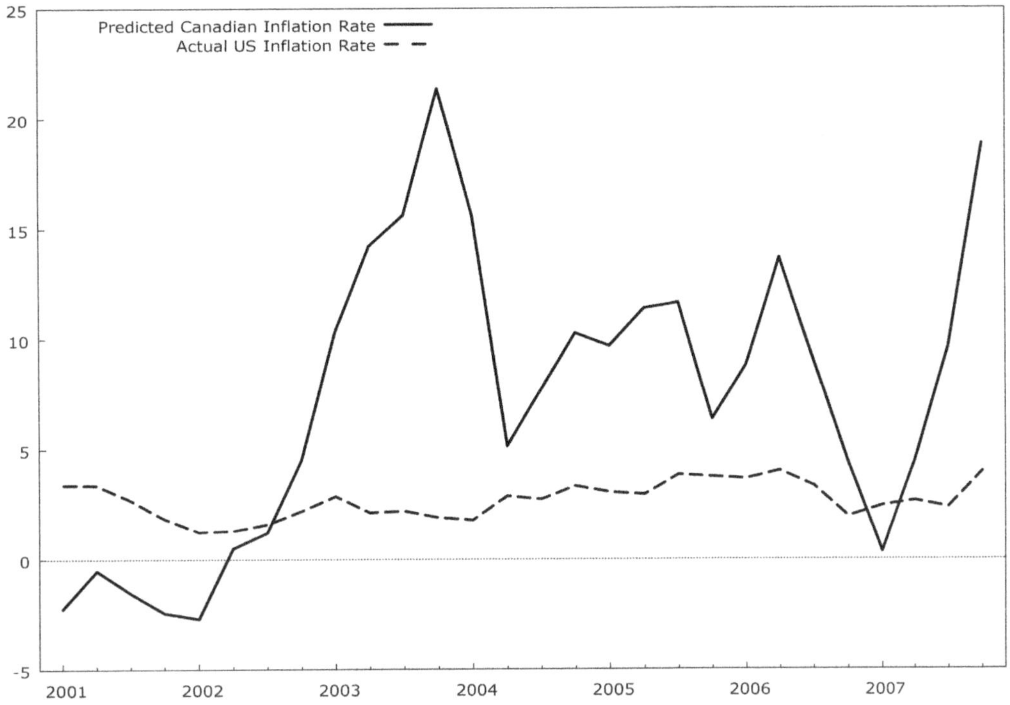

Data sources: International Monetary Fund and Statistics Canada (with the model's predictions)

8. CONCLUSION

Under a fixed exchange rate, the central bank in a small economy is unable to influence the domestic price level. If a country such as Canada returned to a fixed exchange rate regime, with the Canadian dollar fixed to the US dollar, the Bank of Canada would no longer be able to implement the policy of keeping the annual Canadian inflation rate between 1 per cent and 3 per cent.

With a fixed exchange rate, the domestic price level is affected by the foreign price level and by real factors that cause changes in the domestic relative price of the non-traded good and the terms of trade.[16] A low inflation rate in the large foreign economy does not guarantee a low and stable inflation rate in the domestic economy, as the real shocks impacting the economy can cause the domestic inflation rate to deviate from the foreign inflation rate. If the economy experienced real shocks, such as domestic productivity shocks or shifts in world demand for traded goods, these shocks would impact the domestic price level. Depending on the particular real shocks impacting the economy, the domestic inflation rate could be significantly above, or significantly below, the inflation rate in the foreign economy.

PRACTICE QUESTIONS

1. Fill in the blanks
   (a) In the two-sector model with a fixed exchange rate, the price of the domestic traded good only changes if the price of the ______ changes.
   (b) In the two-sector model with a fixed exchange rate, an exogenous increase in the marginal product of labor in the traded sector causes the price of the traded good to ______ and the price of the non-traded good to ______.
   (c) In the two-sector model with a fixed exchange rate, an exogenous increase in the marginal product of labor in the non-traded sector causes the wage rate to ______ and the price of the non-traded good to ______.
   (d) In the two-sector model, the marginal product of labor in the non-traded sector is ______, meaning that it is fixed and does not change unless it changes ______.
   (e) Based on the definition of imported inflation, imported inflation occurs under a ______.

2. Fill in the blanks
   (a) In the early 1960s, Japan had a high inflation rate because productivity growth in the ______ sector was high. At the time, the yen was fixed to the ______.
   (b) In the two-sector model with a fixed exchange rate, a decrease in the domestic price level can be caused by an exogenous increase in ______ and an exogenous decrease in the foreign ______.
   (c) The last time that Canada experienced "imported inflation" was in the year ______.
   (d) In the three-sector model with a fixed exchange rate, an exogenous increase in the world price of the resource good causes the price of the non-traded good to ______ and the marginal product of labor in the non-traded sector to ______.
   (e) Consider a three-sector model with a fixed exchange rate. In response to an exogenous increase in the foreign price of the resource good, production of the resource good ______ and the marginal product of labor in the resource sector ______.

3. Assume the exchange rate is fixed. Using the two-sector model, explain how an exogenous increase in the marginal product of labor in the traded sector affects prices, wages, and the price level in the long run.

4. Assume the exchange rate is fixed. Using the two-sector model, explain how an exogenous increase in the price of the foreign traded good affects prices and wages.

5. In the two-sector model with a fixed exchange rate, is it possible for an exogenous increase in productivity to cause an increase in the price level? Explain.

6. Consider the three-sector model with a fixed exchange rate. Write down the equation for the terms of trade and indicate what this equation measures (suppose the economy is similar to Canada). Explain what determines the terms of trade in a small economy (use the terms of trade equation with the law of one price conditions).

7. In the early 1960s, the inflation rate in Japan was much higher than in the United States. What was the main factor that caused the high Japanese inflation rate? Explain using the two-sector model.

DATA ANALYTICS

1. Conduct a simulation experiment, like that in Section 7, where the path of the Canadian price level is simulated under conditions of a fixed exchange rate. Adopt the same assumptions (such as monetary neutrality), but assume that the Bank of Canada begins fixing the Canadian–US dollar exchange rate at par at the start of 2008 (and continues to hold it fixed at par). Using the movements in the US price level P* and the real exchange rate q, calculate the predicted Canadian price level, for every period t, as follows:

$$predicted\ P_t = \frac{1.00\ P_t^*}{q_t}.$$

Collect monthly data on the Canadian consumer price index and the exchange rate from CANSIM, and collect monthly data on the US consumer price index from the FRED database or the International Monetary Fund's IFS database. Create plots of the predicted Canadian price level and the predicted Canadian inflation rate over the period since 2008. Comment.

APPENDIX: THE TWO-SECTOR MODEL WITH DIMINISHING MARGINAL PRODUCTS

Assume that, in each sector, the marginal product of labor is diminishing, so that each demand for labor curve is downward sloping. In equilibrium, each sector's value of marginal product equals the wage rate, both sectors are paying the same wage rate, and there is full employment. The following condition holds:

$$P^T f_L^T = w^T = P^N f_L^N = w^N.$$

This equilibrium condition is depicted in Figure 11.11 (the diagram can be used for any exchange rate regime). The wage rate (denoted w) is measured on the vertical axis, and the

Figure 11.11: Labor market equilibrium

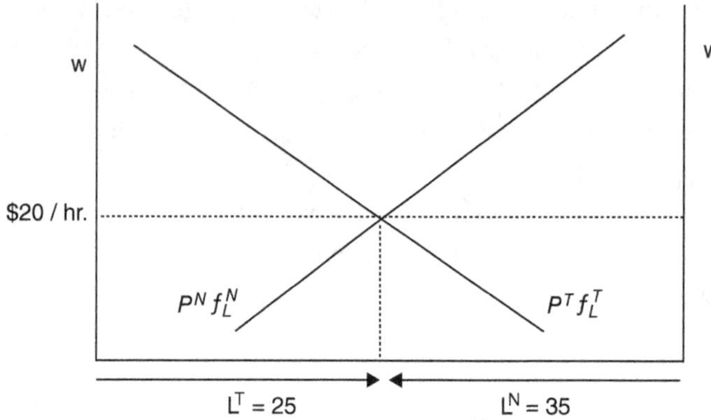

horizontal axis measures the total quantity of labor (the total number of workers in the domestic economy). The total number of workers is fixed at 60. The demand for labor in the traded sector, determined by $P^T f_L^T$, is downward sloping because the marginal product of labor falls as L^T increases (along this curve, the price of the traded good is fixed). The demand for labor in the traded sector is measured from left to right in the diagram. At a wage rate of \$20 per hour, traded-goods firms demand 25 workers. The demand for labor in the non-traded sector is measured from right to left on the horizontal axis. The demand curve for labor in the non-traded sector also incorporates a diminishing marginal product (along this curve, the price of the non-traded good is fixed). At a wage rate of \$20 per hour, firms in the non-traded sector demand 35 workers. The equilibrium wage rate is determined where the two curves cross in the diagram. At the equilibrium wage rate of \$20 per hour, the aggregate supply of workers equals the aggregate demand for workers.

As an exercise, suppose there is an exogenous 10 per cent increase in f_L^T, an exogenous change that shifts the labor demand curve for the traded sector. Suppose that, in addition, there is a 10 per cent increase in the price of the non-traded good that shifts the labor demand curve of the non-traded sector. Denote the new equilibrium at a point where the wage rate has increased by 10 per cent but there is no change in the number of workers employed in each sector.

NOTES

1   The analysis applies to both countries on a fixed exchange rate and countries within a currency union.
2   An appendix outlines the standard two-sector diagram when there is a diminishing marginal product in each sector.
3   An increase in f_L^T causes both real income and the price level to rise. With a fixed exchange rate, the associated increase in the demand for money causes an increase in the supply of money.
4   David Ricardo (1817), in the chapter "On Foreign Trade," wrote that "… the prices of home commodities… are, independently of other causes, higher in those countries where manufactures flourish."
5   A devaluation of the domestic currency (an exogenous increase in s) has the same effects.

6 Bordo (1993) notes that the analysis of Bretton Woods is often split into two periods, 1946-1959 and 1959-1971 (only in the latter phase were all currencies fully convertible). Bordo et al. (2010) provide an interesting study of Canada's period with a flexible exchange rate from 1950 to 1962.

7 The Canadian price level is CANSIM series V41690973. The consumer price indices for the US and Japan are taken from the International Monetary Fund's IFS database.

8 McKinnon (2006) discusses both Japan under Bretton Woods and China during the 1996 to 2005 period when the renminbi was rigidly fixed to the US dollar.

9 The annual data are taken from the GGDC 10 Sector Database. See Timmer et al. (2015). Three sectors are regarded as traded and seven sectors as non-traded (see the appendix in Chapter 10).

10 The effects of relative price changes on demand are examined in Chapters 12 and 14.

11 And given the assumptions, the only way to increase production is to increase the number of workers.

12 The extent of endogenous change in each marginal product depends on the slope of the marginal product curve and the magnitude of the change in the number of workers. It is assumed that these numbers are consistent with the equilibrium conditions.

13 Bordo and Eichengreen (2007) and Bordo et al. (2010) use general equilibrium models to conduct counterfactual experiments to examine, respectively, the world price level between 1928 and 1971 and the Canadian economy between 1950 and 1962.

14 The data for the Canadian-US dollar exchange rate and the Canadian price level are taken from CANSIM (series V37426 and V41690973, respectively), and the US price level data are taken from the IMF's IFS database.

15 Policy analysts may wonder if fixing the exchange rate allows for better private sector decisions and a more efficient economy. Of course, this argument for a fixed exchange rate is not valid if the public is not confident that the exchange rate will remain fixed at its current level. In addition, real shocks can generate price movements that are more difficult to predict under a fixed exchange rate, thereby causing difficulties in making optimal decisions in the uncertain environment. As international economists have long understood, when policymakers fix the exchange rate and close off one avenue through which excess pressure can be eliminated, that pressure can feed through the economy and impact prices and other variables.

16 For empirical analyses on the determination of the relative price of the non-traded good, the real exchange rate, and other variables in Canada during the classical gold standard, see Viner (1924) and Dick and Floyd (1992). For econometric analyses that examine both sectoral productivity growth and changes in the terms of trade, see Imai (2010) on Japanese inflation under Bretton Woods and Berka and Devereux (2013) on European real exchange rates.

CHAPTER 12

The Terms of Trade and the Exchange Rate

1. INTRODUCTION

An important relative price in an open economy is the terms of trade: the price of exports relative to the price of imports. For a small economy, this relative price is determined on world markets. But fluctuations in world prices can have a profound impact on the income, consumption, and welfare of domestic residents. Moreover, in conjunction with the monetary policy framework adopted by the central bank, fluctuations in world prices impact both the nominal and real exchange rates of the small economy.

This chapter uses a one-period Ricardian model of trade, extended to incorporate money into the model. The model, called the "terms of trade–exchange rate model," is a two-sector model with an export good and an import good. It is assumed that the domestic economy is small and the exchange rate is flexible. The analysis addresses the following questions. What factors cause long-term movements in the terms of trade in a small open economy? How do changes in the terms of trade affect real variables such as consumer spending, exports, and imports? What is the long-term relationship between the terms of trade, the real exchange rate, and the nominal exchange rate? The model is capable of explaining the close relationship between the terms of trade and the exchange rate, as well as the strong positive co-movement between nominal and real exchange rates evident in many economies.

While fluctuations in the real exchange rate are related to both fluctuations in the terms of trade and divergent movements in non-traded goods prices between countries, this chapter abstracts from non-traded goods to focus attention on export and import goods and the terms of trade.

2. THE BASIC SETUP

The model is a long-run model, with a single period, so there is no asset accumulation.[1] There are two goods, X and Y, and the world markets for these goods are competitive. It is assumed, for simplicity, that the domestic economy only produces good X (the domestic economy exports X and imports Y).[2] Production of good X is exogenous, as are the foreign prices of goods X and Y. Foreign price movements play an integral role in the determination of the exchange rate and the terms of trade in the small domestic economy.

Consumers use money to purchase goods. In this one-period model, the demand for money depends on the price level and consumption. The central bank is assumed to follow a zero-inflation policy, adjusting the nominal money supply (if necessary) to keep the domestic price level fixed. This simplification allows the analysis to focus on real factors in the determination of real and nominal exchange rates.

3. KEY EQUATIONS IN THE MODEL

The Equal Expenditure Condition

To maximize utility, the consumer chooses consumption of goods X and Y (denoted as c^X and c^Y) such that the ratio of marginal utilities equals the relative price. It is assumed that the utility functions are logarithmic, so that the marginal utility of consumption equals the inverse of consumption:

$$\frac{u'(c^X)}{u'c^Y} = \frac{P^X}{P^Y} \rightarrow \frac{\frac{1}{c^X}}{\frac{1}{c^Y}} = \frac{P^X}{P^Y} \rightarrow P^X c^X = P^Y c^Y,$$

where P^X and P^Y denote the domestic prices of goods X and Y. The last equality is the equal expenditure condition, implying that the consumer allocates expenditure to equalize expenditure on the two goods. This condition incorporates a relative price effect, whereby an increase in the relative price of good X induces a decrease in the consumption of good X relative to the consumption of good Y (for a given level of income).

Balanced Trade

The domestic economy has a comparative advantage in the production of good X and specializes completely in the production of this good. In a one-period model, there is no asset trade, and trade in goods must be balanced. In nominal terms, the value of exports equals the value of imports:

$$P^X \left[Q^X - c^X \right] = P^Y c^Y,$$

where exports equal $\left[Q^X - c^X \right]$ and imports equal c^Y because there is no domestic production of good Y (the model abstracts from investment and government spending).

The Law of One Price and the Terms of Trade

Good X produced in the domestic economy is identical to the good X produced in the foreign economy. Competition ensures that the law of one price holds (with zero tariffs and transport costs):

$$P^X = sP^{X*},$$

where s denotes the nominal exchange rate (an increase in s is a depreciation of the domestic currency). The law of one price also holds for good Y, and the equilibrium nominal exchange rate must be consistent with both law of one price conditions.[3]

The price of exports relative to the price of imports is called the terms of trade. The domestic economy exports X and imports Y, so the relative price ratio $\dfrac{P_X}{P_Y}$ is the terms of trade. When $\dfrac{P_X}{P_Y}$ increases, there is a terms-of-trade improvement. The domestic economy then sells its export good at a relatively higher price and imports the foreign good at a relatively lower price. A decrease in the equilibrium $\dfrac{P_X}{P_Y}$ is a terms-of-trade deterioration.

Given the law of one price conditions, prices in the large foreign economy determine the terms of trade (denoted as TOT):

$$TOT = \frac{P^X}{P^Y} = \frac{sP^{X*}}{sP^{Y*}} = \frac{P^{X*}}{P^{Y*}}.$$

Foreign changes in demand and supply cause changes in the foreign relative price ratio, and therefore cause changes in the terms of trade. In the small domestic economy, any exogenous changes that affect domestic demand or supply leave the terms of trade unchanged. Likewise, changes in the nominal exchange rate have no effect on the terms of trade.[4]

The Consumer Price Index and Money Market Equilibrium

The domestic price level (the consumer price index), denoted as P, is measured as the geometric mean of the prices P^X and P^Y:

$$P = P^{X\,0.5} P^{Y\,0.5}.$$

The statistical agency that calculates the price index has determined that consumers spend one-half of their total expenditure on each good. Each good has a weight equal to 0.5.

In this one-period model, the nominal demand for money depends on the price level and aggregate consumption (denoted as c). Setting money demand equal to money supply (denoted as M^s) yields the equilibrium condition:[5]

$$M^s = P\,c = P\,c^{X\,0.5}c^{Y\,0.5},$$

where aggregate consumption is measured as the geometric mean of the consumption of X and Y. This equation is consistent with the quantity theory of money, with the consumption velocity of money equal to 1. Under a flexible exchange rate, this equation determines the domestic price level. As the central bank follows a fixed price level policy, this equation forms the basis on which the central bank determines the required change in the nominal money supply to maintain the policy target.

The Real Exchange Rate

The real exchange rate, denoted as q, is a measure of the relative price of foreign goods to domestic goods, and is calculated as follows (where P* is the foreign price level):

$$q = \frac{s\,P^*}{P}.$$

An increase in q is a real depreciation of the domestic currency. If there are similar inflation rates in the two countries, real and nominal exchange rates move together.

Endogenous and Exogenous Variables

In general, the seven equations determine the seven endogenous variables (c^X, c^Y, P^X, P^Y, P, s, and q) and the exogenous variables are M^s, P^{X*}, P^{Y*}, and Q^X (domestic production of Y is zero). But the central bank alters the money supply to keep the price level fixed, so P is exogenous and M^s is endogenous. This assumption is analytically convenient because any change in the price of X is necessarily offset by an opposite change in the price of Y.

4. ON THE REAL EXCHANGE RATE

This chapter uses a definition of the real exchange rate based on consumer price indices, with different weights in the two indices. To understand the rationale for this approach, it is useful to consider some alternative measures of the real exchange rate.

Consumption-Based Price Indices with Equal Weights

Suppose consumers in each country spend equal nominal amounts on each good. Although production patterns in the two countries are different, the weights in the consumption-based price indices are identical. The real exchange rate is

$$q = \frac{s\,P^{X*0.5}\,P^{Y*0.5}}{P^{X0.5}\,P^{Y0.5}} = \frac{s^{0.5}\,P^{X*0.5}\,s^{0.5}P^{Y*0.5}}{P^{X0.5}\,P^{Y0.5}}.$$

Using the law of one price conditions, this definition of the real exchange rate equals 1. Thus, if one abstracts from non-traded goods and assumes that the weights in the price indices are the same, movements in the real exchange rate cannot be explained.

Production-Based Price Indices

Another measure of the real exchange rate is based on price indices called GDP deflators, where the weights in the index are based on domestic production shares (rather than consumption expenditure shares). The domestic economy is assumed to specialize in the production of good X, so the price of X gets a weight of one. If the foreign GDP deflator has equal weights, the real exchange rate is

$$q = \frac{s\,P^{X*0.5}\,P^{Y*0.5}}{P^{X}} = \frac{s^{0.5}\,P^{X*0.5}\,s^{0.5}P^{Y*0.5}}{P^{X\,0.5}\,P^{X\,0.5}} = \left[\frac{P^{Y}}{P^{X}}\right]^{0.5},$$

where both law of one price conditions have been used. An increase in q, a real depreciation of the domestic currency, is associated with a decrease in the relative price of good X, a terms-of-trade deterioration. With this measure, changes in the world relative price cause changes in the real exchange rate.

Consumption-Based Price Indices with Unequal Weights

Suppose the domestic consumer price index has equal weights, but the weights in the foreign consumer price index are higher on good Y. For example, suppose the two price indices are specified as

$$P = P^{X\,0.5}\,P^{Y\,0.5},$$

$$P^{*} = P^{X*0.1}\,P^{Y*0.9}.$$

These weights imply that foreign consumers have a larger share of expenditure on Y. In addition, note that the weight on the price of good X (the domestic economy's export good) in the domestic price index is higher than the weight on the price of X in the foreign index (and the weight on good Y, the foreign export good, in the foreign price index is higher than the weight on the price of Y in the domestic index).[6]

Given these assumed weights, and using the law of one price conditions, the real exchange rate equals

$$q = \frac{s\,P^{X*0.1}\,P^{Y*0.9}}{P^{X\,0.5}\,P^{Y\,0.5}} = \left[\frac{P^{Y}}{P^{X}}\right]^{0.4}.$$

The real exchange rate is a function of the relative price, and the relationship is akin to that in the production-based measure of the real exchange rate.

The Real Exchange Rate

In the analysis, the real exchange rate is measured as

$$q = \left[\frac{P^{Y}}{P^{X}}\right]^{0.4}.$$

A terms-of-trade deterioration is associated with a real depreciation of the domestic currency, and a terms-of-trade improvement is associated with a real appreciation of the domestic currency. It is important to emphasize that the real exchange rate does not depend on the nominal exchange rate. Nonetheless, real and nominal exchange rates will move together in response to certain exogenous shocks.

5. EXOGENOUS CHANGES IN THE FOREIGN RELATIVE PRICE

Suppose that, initially, all domestic and foreign prices equal 100. Both consumer price indices are equal to 100, and both the nominal and real exchange rate equal 1. Suppose that, due to shifts in demand or supply in the large foreign economy, P^{X*} increases by 9 per cent (from 100 to 109), and P^{Y*} decreases by 1 per cent (from 100 to 99). In total, the foreign relative price of good X has increased by approximately 10 per cent (the foreign consumer price index is almost unchanged, falling from 100 to 99.957).[7]

The increase in the foreign relative price of good X, through the law of one price conditions, causes an increase in the domestic relative price of good X:

$$\frac{P^X}{P^Y} = \frac{P^{X*}}{P^{Y*}} = \frac{109}{99} = 1.1010.$$

For a given initial exchange rate, the changes in foreign prices would cause the domestic price of X to increase 9 per cent and the domestic price of Y to fall 1 per cent. But with the fixed price level policy, this result cannot hold in the new long-run equilibrium (the price level would equal 103.88, almost 4 per cent higher than the initial price level). But the relative price of X must increase, so P^X has to rise, P^Y has to fall, and the nominal exchange rate must change.

The increase in demand for domestic currency on the foreign exchange market causes the domestic currency to appreciate. The nominal exchange rate, s, has to fall so that it is consistent with all of the following conditions: the law of one price conditions for goods X and Y, the domestic relative price of good X, or the terms of trade, equal to 1.1010, and the consumer price index equal to 100. Figure 12.1 depicts the appreciation of the domestic currency required to satisfy these conditions. When the exchange rate falls from 1.0 to 0.96265, there is a new long-run equilibrium.

In general terms, the domestic currency needs to appreciate by about 4 per cent. Then the 9 per cent increase in the foreign price of good X is offset by the 4 per cent appreciation and the domestic price of good X increases by about 5 per cent. For good Y, the 4 per cent appreciation of the domestic currency and the 1 per cent fall in the foreign price mean that the equilibrium domestic price of good Y falls by about 5 per cent. The increase in the price of good X is offset by the fall in the price of good Y and the consumer price index remains unchanged.

In the new equilibrium, the domestic relative price of X equals 104.929/95.302, which equals 1.1010. The increase in the foreign relative price of good X causes a terms-of-trade improvement in the domestic economy.[8] While the adjustment process that occurs in response to the exogenous shock may be complicated,[9] with the central bank making ongoing decisions regarding the appropriate response in terms of changes in the money supply, the theory outlines the long-run equilibrium conditions.[10] There is an improvement in the terms of trade, the domestic currency appreciates, and the central bank keeps the consumer price level fixed.

Figure 12.1: Law of one price conditions

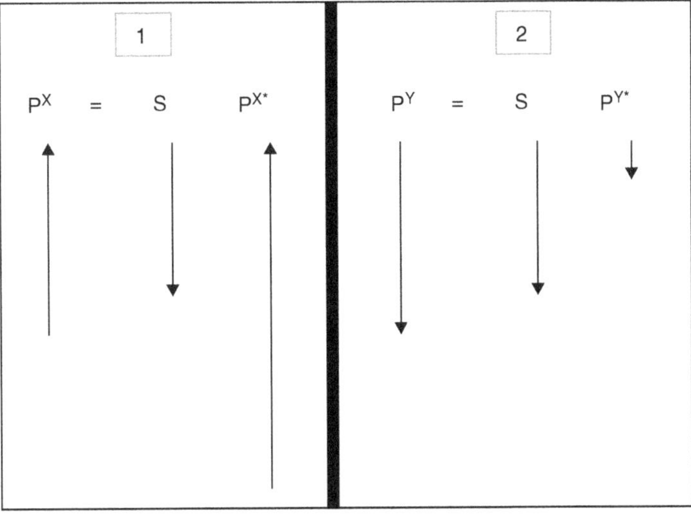

Positive Co-Movement between Nominal and Real Exchange Rates

The domestic currency appreciates from 1.0 to 0.96265, an appreciation of approximately 3.74 per cent. The real exchange rate also moves lower, meaning there is a real appreciation of the domestic currency. The real exchange rate was equal to 1 before, and now equals[11]

$$q = \frac{sP^*}{P} = \frac{0.96265 \, P_X^{*\,0.1} \, P_Y^{*\,0.9}}{100} = \frac{0.96265\,(99.957)}{100} = 0.96224,$$

a real appreciation of 3.78 per cent from the initial value of 1.[12] There is both a real and a nominal appreciation of the domestic currency.

The Terms of Trade, Nominal GDP, and Consumption

When there is a terms-of-trade improvement, there are two effects on the consumption of each good. There is a real income effect and a relative price effect. The increase in the terms of trade implies that the domestic economy is richer because it now exports good X at a relatively higher price. There is a real income effect because there is a terms-of-trade gain.[13] And there is a relative price effect on the demands for the two goods, with the increase in the relative price of good X, in itself, inducing consumers to shift consumption from good X to good Y. The model allows one to calculate the exact movements in consumption.

Suppose the production of X, denoted as Q^X, equals 10. In this Ricardian model of trade, the domestic economy is specializing in the production of X. When the relative price of X increases, the domestic production of X does not increase. It cannot increase because the domestic economy is already producing as much of good X as possible, given the full employment of workers and the assumed constant level of productivity in the sector. But the increase in the terms of trade does make the domestic economy richer, because X is now exported at a relatively higher price and Y is imported at a relatively lower price. In terms of a production possibility frontier and indifference curve diagram in international trade theory, the world relative price line rotates outward and expands the consumption possibilities set of the domestic economy.

Before the exogenous change, nominal GDP was equal to 1000 dollars and consumers spent 500 dollars on each good:

$$P^X Q^X = P^X c^X + P^Y c^Y,$$

$$100\,(10) = 100\,(5) + 100\,(5).$$

After the exogenous increase in the foreign relative price of good X, nominal GDP increases to 1049.29, with each of the 10 units of good X now selling for 104.929 dollars. The consumer equalizes expenditure on the two goods, spending 524.645 dollars on each good. At the new equilibrium prices, the consumer purchases 5 units of good X and 5.505 units of good Y:

$$P^X Q^X = P^X c^X + P^Y c^Y,$$

$$104.929\,(10) = 104.929\,(5) + 95.302\,(5.505).$$

There is equal expenditure on each good, as depicted in Figure 12.2. But as the relative price of good Y has decreased, utility-maximizing behavior implies that consumers purchase relatively more units of good Y. Consumer substitute toward the good that has fallen in relative price. In terms of good X, the real income effect of the terms of trade gain increases desired consumption, but the higher price of good X results in a decrease in the quantity demanded of good X. These two effects offset each other exactly and the consumption of good X is unchanged. For good Y, both effects work toward higher levels of consumption. The terms of trade gain results in an increase in demand for good Y, and the lower price induces a further increase in desired consumption of good Y.

As the consumption of X is unchanged and the consumption of Y is higher, consumers experience a higher level of utility.

Balanced Trade, Exports, and Imports

Initially, both P^X and P^Y were equal to 100, so the relative price of X was 1. Balanced trade implies the following condition:

$$P^X \left[Q^X - c^X \right] = P^Y c^Y,$$

$$Q^X - c^X = c^Y.$$

In the initial condition, consumption was equal to 5 units of each good. After the exogenous change that improved the terms of trade, the relative price of X equals 1.1010 and balanced trade implies (with Q^X equal to 10)

Figure 12.2: Equal expenditure condition

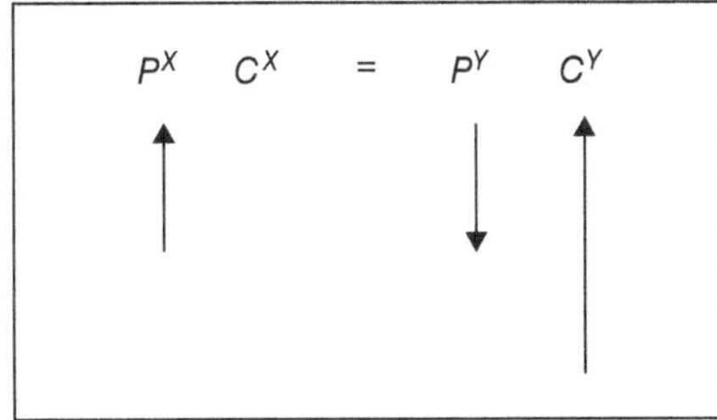

$$1.1010\left[10 - c^X\right] = c^Y.$$

With the equilibrium prices, the equal expenditure condition implies (as noted) that the equilibrium levels of consumption are as follows:

$$c^X = 5;\ c^Y = 5.505.$$

The domestic economy still exports 5 units of good X (consuming the other 5 units) but now receives 5.505 units of good Y in exchange.

Consumption, Zero Inflation, and the Money Supply

The money market equilibrium condition is specified as follows:

$$M^s = Pc.$$

In the new long-run equilibrium, the increase in consumption increases the nominal demand for money. To prevent a fall in the consumer price index, the central bank must accommodate the increase in money demand by increasing the nominal money supply. In a growing economy, a central bank following a zero-inflation policy must ensure that the growth in the nominal money supply matches the growth in consumption (in this model, the consumption elasticity of real money demand equals unity).

6. EXOGENOUS CHANGES IN DOMESTIC PRODUCTION

Suppose there is an exogenous increase in the domestic production of good X, with Q^X increasing from 10 to 11 (due to, for example, an innovation or an increase in the skills of workers). How does this exogenous increase in output affect prices, the exchange rate, income, consumption, and exports and imports?

The Terms of Trade, Prices, and the Exchange Rate

In this small economy, the increase in production has no effect on the terms of trade. The domestic relative price of good X equals the foreign relative price of good X, and foreign prices are exogenous and unchanged. Moreover, with the zero-inflation policy of the central bank, the increase in domestic output has no effect on domestic prices or the exchange rate.

The domestic price of good X, through the law of one price, is linked to the foreign (or world) price, and the domestic economy is too small to have any effect on world demand and world supply for good X (it does increase world production of good X, but the impact is so small that the effect on world price is negligible). Note that if P^X fell, P^Y would also have to fall to keep the terms of trade unchanged. But P^X and P^Y cannot both fall as the zero-inflation policy would be violated. And it is not possible for P^X to fall and P^Y to increase, as these price changes would violate the condition that the equilibrium domestic relative price of good X equals the fixed foreign relative price of good X (as well as violating at least one of the law of one price conditions). Therefore, there can be no effect on domestic prices or the exchange rate.

Growth and the Real Exchange Rate

The real exchange rate is determined by the relative price of good X, so the real exchange rate does not change in response to the exogenous increase in domestic production. Indeed, given the assumptions, the domestic price level, the nominal exchange rate, and the real exchange rate are all unchanged. This result is interesting, in that there is long-term growth but no change in real exchange rate. The lack of a simple relationship between growth and changes in the real exchange rate is not an uncommon result, also holding in the two-sector model with a traded and non-traded good.[14]

Nominal GDP, Consumption, and Money

When production of good X increases from 10 to 11, with P^X unchanged at 100, nominal GDP increases from 1000 to 1100. The equal expenditure condition implies that c^X and c^Y increase from 5.0 units to 5.5 units, with the 10 per cent increase in real income causing a 10 per cent increase in consumption of each good.

The increase in consumption increases nominal money demand. To ensure that the consumer price index remains fixed, the central bank must accommodate the increase in money demand by increasing the nominal money supply.[15]

Exports and Imports

Before the exogenous change, trade was balanced with exports and imports equal to 5 units of each good. With production of good X increasing from 10 to 11, and the associated increases in consumption of each good, balanced traded implies that

$$P^X \left[Q^X - c^X \right] = P^Y c^Y,$$

$$100 \left[11 - 5.5 \right] = 100 \left(5.5 \right).$$

Both exports and imports increase from 5 to 5.5 units. The growth in the domestic economy causes growth in the volume of trade, without any effect on prices or the exchange rate.

7. EXOGENOUS CHANGES IN THE FOREIGN PRICE LEVEL

Suppose the foreign central bank increases the nominal money supply and there is an increase in the foreign price level (with the foreign prices of goods X and Y both increasing from 100 to 110). With the increases in the foreign prices, the domestic prices are lower than the exchange rate-adjusted foreign prices:

$$P^X < s\ P^{X*},$$

$$P^Y < s\ P^{Y*}.$$

Given the zero-inflation policy in the domestic economy, the domestic prices of goods X and Y cannot increase. But the associated increase in demand for domestic currency will cause the domestic currency to appreciate. From the initial level of 1.0, the domestic currency appreciates to a level of 0.90909 in the new equilibrium and both law of one price conditions again hold as equalities.

While the domestic currency appreciates, the domestic prices of goods X and Y are unchanged (the relative price remains at 1). The purely monetary change in the foreign economy has no effect on the terms of trade. Likewise, the other real variables in the domestic economy, including the real exchange rate, consumption, exports, and imports, are all unchanged.

8. THE TERMS OF TRADE AND EXCHANGE RATES

Figure 12.3 shows movements in Canada's terms of trade and the Canadian–US dollar exchange rate from 1997 to 2015 (the data are monthly).[16] The exchange rate is measured as the inverse of s, so that an increase in the line represents an appreciation of the Canadian dollar. The terms of trade variable is measured as the export price index divided by the import price index.

Improvements in the terms of trade tend to be associated with increases in the value of the Canadian dollar and terms-of-trade deteriorations tend to be associated with decreases in the value of the Canadian dollar. There is a positive correlation between the two variables, with a correlation coefficient equal to 0.91. While the consumer price indices in Canada and the United States both trended upward at a low rate during this period, the terms of trade changes were quite pronounced. And as predicted by the analysis, these swings in the terms of trade tended to be positively correlated with movements in the value of the Canadian dollar (an exercise in Data Analytics examines the terms of trade and the exchange rate in the period since 2015).

Figure 12.4 depicts movements in the Canadian–US dollar nominal and real exchange rates (measured as 1/s and 1/q) between 1980 and 2016 (using quarterly data, with the same variables as outlined in Chapter 10).[17] The strong positive correlation between nominal and real exchange rates suggests that these longer term movements may have been caused predominantly by real shocks.[18] In terms of the model in this chapter, fluctuations in the real exchange rate are caused by exogenous changes on world markets that affect Canada's terms of trade. With similar Canadian

Figure 12.3: Terms of trade and the exchange rate

Data source: Statistics Canada

Figure 12.4: Real and nominal exchange rates

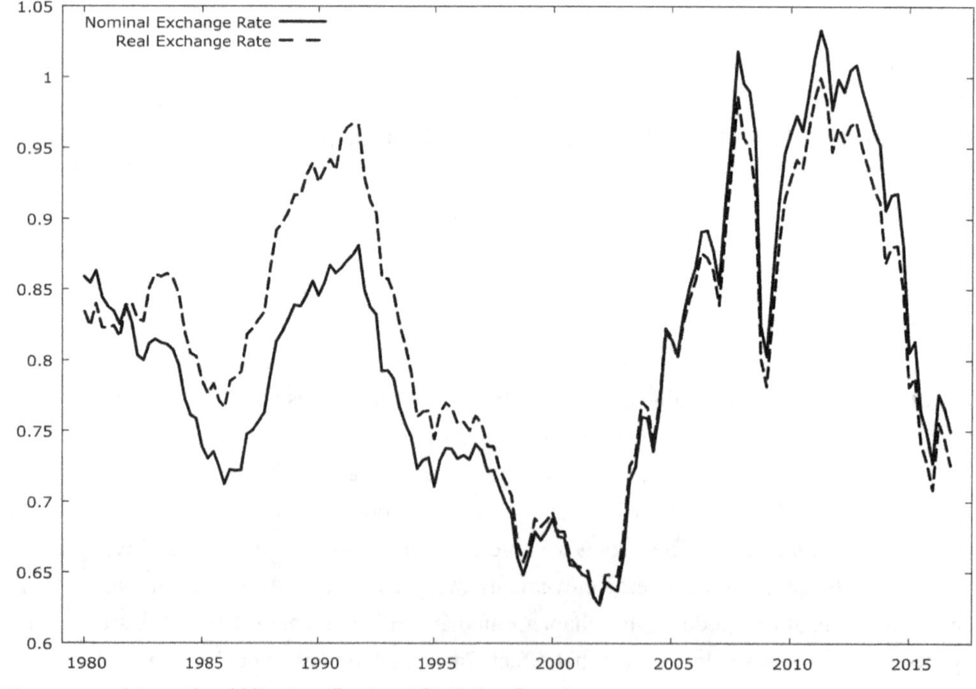

Data sources: International Monetary Fund and Statistics Canada

and American monetary policy, this conclusion implies that fluctuations in the nominal exchange rate were also caused predominantly by real shocks such as terms of trade shocks.[19]

9. THE COMMODITY PRICE INDEX AND THE CANADIAN DOLLAR

Canada exports large quantities of resource products from four broad categories: forestry products, agricultural products, metals and minerals, and energy products.[20] Because of the importance of these products to the Canadian economy, a commodity price index is calculated. This index is a weighted-average of the US dollar prices of these resource products, with the weight for each price reflecting the importance of that product in terms of Canada's total resource exports.

The terms of trade variable in Figure 12.3 is calculated as the price of exports divided by the price of imports, with both variables measured in Canadian dollars. The commodity price index is based on the US dollar prices of Canada's resource exports. There appears to be a close correlation between movements in the Canadian–US dollar exchange rate and the commodity price index. In particular, the Canadian dollar tends to depreciate when the commodity price index has decreased and tends to appreciate when the commodity price index has increased.

It is interesting to examine the evidence, focusing first on the 1980s and then on the 1990–2017 period (these data are monthly).[21]

The 1980s

Figure 12.5 shows movements in the commodity price index and the Canadian–US dollar exchange rate over the 1980s, where there is a strong positive correlation between the two variables. In the period 1980 to 1986, the Canadian dollar tended to be depreciating, falling from 86 cents US in 1980 down to around 70 cents in 1986. During this period, the commodity price index tended to be falling. Between 1986 and 1990, there was a strong upward movement in the value of the Canadian dollar, and this appreciation in the Canadian dollar was matched closely by the rise in the commodity price index.

This evidence is interesting because, in the late 1980s, the Canadian interest rate had moved significantly higher and the rise in the Canadian dollar was often attributed to the interest rate increases. While the tight Canadian monetary policy likely played a role in the appreciation, the evidence in Figure 12.5 suggests that the real factors underlying the rise in the commodity price index could have also played a prominent role. Indeed, John Crow, governor of the Bank of Canada between 1987 and 1994, had noted that the appreciation of the Canadian dollar was associated with the terms of trade improvement caused by the rise in world commodity prices.[22] The evidence in Figure 12.5 provides support for his assertion.

From 1990 to 2017

Figure 12.6 shows movements in the commodity price index and the Canadian–US dollar exchange rate between 1990 and 2017. While the correlation between the variables is low in the 1990s, the very close co-movement after 2002 dominates one's perception of the figure. Indeed,

Figure 12.5: The 1980s

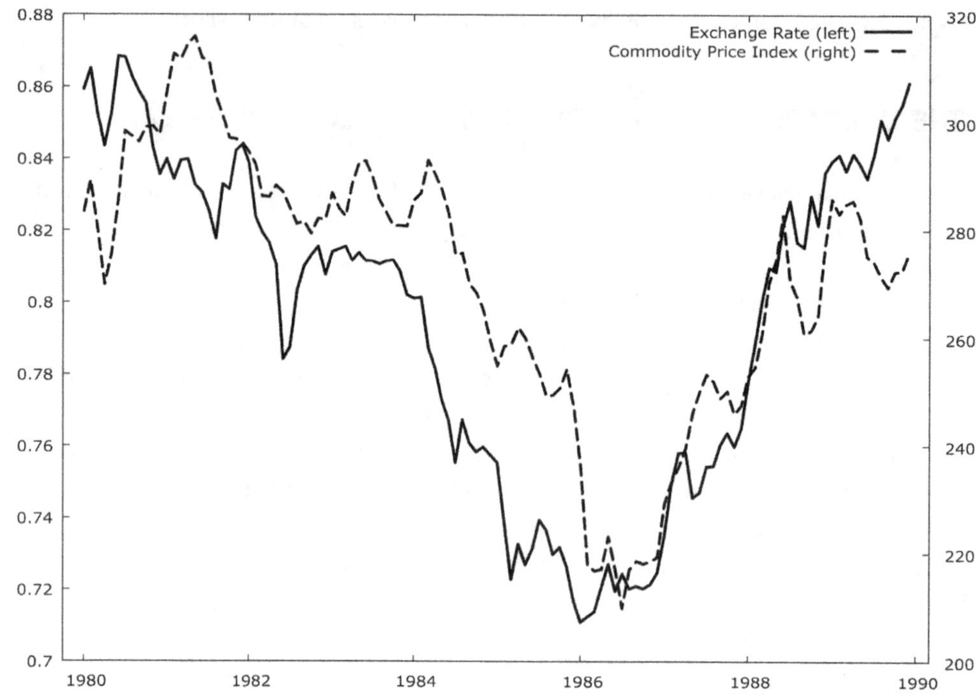

Data source: Statistics Canada

Figure 12.6: From 1990 to 2017

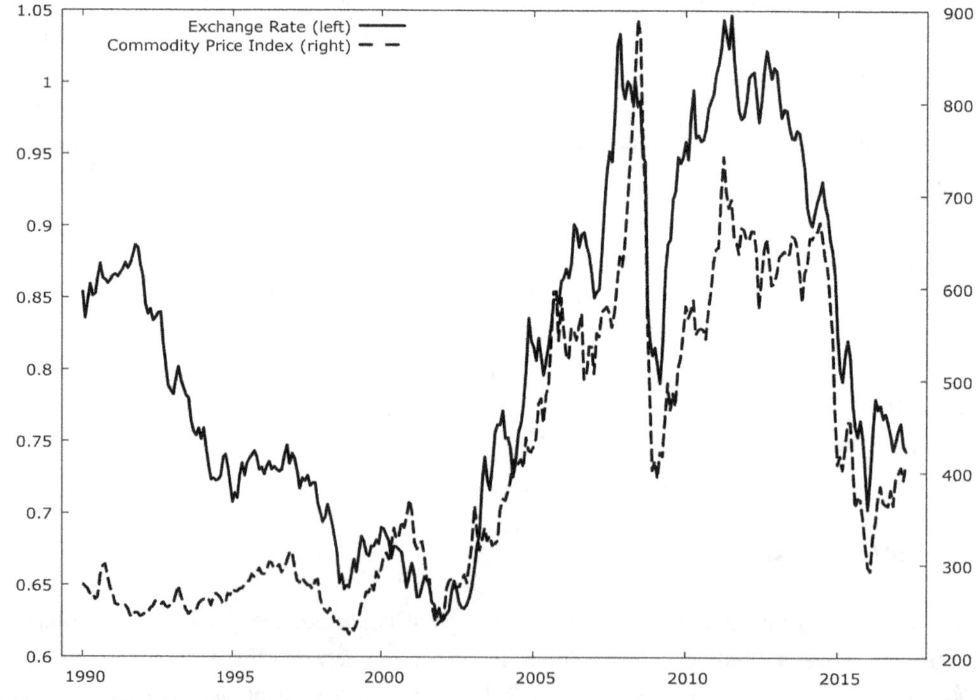

Data source: Statistics Canada

the movement in the value of the Canadian dollar between 2002 and 2008 is unprecedented in Canadian economic history, with the Canadian dollar rising from about 62 cents US to a level above par. And this appreciation is matched closely by the large rise in the commodity price index, which rises from the mid-200s to nearly 900 over these 6–7 years.

With the onset of the 2008–2009 financial crisis and worldwide recession, both variables collapsed together, with the Canadian dollar depreciating to a level below 80 cents. And in the immediate period thereafter, both variables moved sharply upward. By 2010, the Canadian dollar returned to a level around par and the commodity price index increased substantially in percentage terms.[23] In 2014 and 2015, both variables again move substantially lower in tandem. By 2017, the commodity price index had moved to a level around 400, and the value of the Canadian dollar had dipped to 75 cents US.

10. CONCLUSION

An important relative price in an open economy is the terms of trade, the price of the export good relative to the price of the import good. For a small economy, fluctuations in the terms of trade are caused by fluctuations in the foreign (or world) relative price of these goods and are therefore caused by fluctuations in the world demand and supply conditions.[24] Moreover, when both the domestic and foreign central banks follow low inflation rate policies, these real shocks are the main cause of fluctuations in the nominal exchange rate.

In the case of Canada and the US, the central banks have followed similar inflation policies during the flexible exchange rate regime. The Bank of Canada has tended to conduct monetary policy in a way that generated a Canadian inflation rate similar to the US inflation rate. In this environment, a large fraction of the long-term movements in the Canadian–US dollar exchange rate may well have been caused by real factors, including the factors that cause long-term changes in Canada's terms of trade.[25]

PRACTICE QUESTIONS

1. Fill in the blanks
   (a) The price of exports divided by the price of imports is called the _____.
   (b) The equal expenditure condition is derived from the utility-maximizing condition that the ratio of marginal utilities equals the _____.
   (c) Suppose the domestic economy exports good X and imports good Y. An exogenous increase in the foreign relative price of good X causes the terms of trade in the domestic economy to _____. If the central bank is following a zero-inflation policy, the nominal price of good Y is _____ in the new equilibrium.
   (d) In the terms of trade–exchange rate model, an exogenous increase in the production of good X (the export good) causes exports to _____ and imports to _____ (assume that foreign prices are fixed). In this one-period model, trade must be balanced.

    (e) The commodity price index is a weighted average of the US dollar prices of products from four sectors of the Canadian economy: forestry, _______, _______, and energy.

2. Consider the terms of trade–exchange rate model, where the two goods are an export good (denoted as X) and an import good (denoted as Y). Provide the definition of the terms of trade. What determines the terms of trade in this small economy? Explain (use equations).

3. Consider the terms of trade–exchange rate model with goods X and Y (X is the export good). The central bank holds the domestic price level fixed (the prices of goods X and Y have equal weights). Suppose there is an exogenous change in foreign prices: the foreign price of good X rises by 9 per cent and the foreign price of good Y falls by 1 per cent.

    (a) Explain how the exogenous change in foreign prices affects the terms of trade in the domestic economy.

    (b) Explain how the exogenous change in foreign prices affects consumption of good Y.

    (c) Why does this model assume that trade is balanced? Explain.

4. Use the terms of trade–exchange rate model, with two goods X and Y (the domestic economy produces and exports good X). Assume the central bank has a zero-inflation policy. How does an exogenous increase in the domestic production of good X affect prices, the terms of trade, and the exchange rate? Explain. Assume that foreign prices are unchanged.

5. Consider the terms of trade–exchange rate model and suppose the domestic economy exports good X. Suppose that foreign prices change and the domestic economy experiences an increase in the terms of trade. Using the equal expenditure condition, explain why consumption of good X remains the same.

DATA ANALYTICS

1. (a) Collect monthly data on import and export price indices for Canada from 2007 to 2012 (CANSIM Table 228-0063, now labeled Table 12100087, series V54059123 and V54060791). Create a plot of the terms of trade, defined as the export price index divided by the import price index.

    (b) Collect monthly data on the Canadian–US dollar exchange rate from 2007 to 2012 (series V37426). Measure the exchange rate as Canadian dollars per US dollar. Plot the terms of trade and the exchange rate on the same plot (measured on different axes). Do these series move together? What happened to these variables during the Great Recession? Comment.

2. Using the same data sources, collect data and construct a plot of the exchange rate and the terms of trade over the period since the start of 2015. Comment.

NOTES

1 All changes in exogenous variables can be regarded as permanent changes.
2 There are zero-cost brokers in the domestic economy who import good Y and resell it at the domestic price P^Y. In competitive equilibrium, these brokers earn zero profit.
3 The law of one price for good Y is subsumed in the equation below that determines the terms of trade. The equilibrium nominal exchange rate can be determined with either law of one price condition, but one must ensure that the equilibrium exchange rate is consistent with both equations.
4 Robert Mundell (2001), a Canadian-born economist who won the Nobel Prize in 1999, provides an interesting comment related to the Marshall–Lerner condition (named after economists Alfred Marshall and Abba Lerner), emphasizing that one should not confuse the terms of trade with the exchange rate.
5 The utility-maximizing consumer, in this one-period model, equates the marginal utility of real money with the marginal utility of "consumption." This relationship generates the demand for money function.
6 Obstfeld and Rogoff (2005) adopt the same approach in their simulation analysis.
7 If P^{X*} increases to 109.467 (rather than 109.0) and P^{Y*} falls to 99, the foreign price level remains at 100.
8 In terms of the numbers, the prices must satisfy $P^X = 1.1010\,P^Y$. On substitution into the price index,

$$P = 100 = P^{X\,0.5}\,P^{Y\,0.5} = \left[1.1010\,P^Y\right]^{0.5} P^{Y\,0.5} = \left[1.1010\right]^{0.5} P^Y.$$ The equilibrium prices are

$$P^Y = \frac{100}{\sqrt{1.1010}} = \frac{100}{1.04929} = 95.302 \; and \; P^X = 1.1010\,P^Y = 1.1010\,(95.302) = 104.929.$$

The law of one price conditions hold: $P^X = s\,P^{X*} = 0.96265\,(109) = 104.929$, and

$$P^Y = s\,P^{Y*} = 0.96265\,(99) = 95.302.$$

9 In an intertemporal model, a permanent increase in the terms of trade would increase the future value of the domestic currency and, through interest rate parity, result in an appreciation in the current period.
10 In practice, the central bank may respond to any initial upward pressure on the price level by reducing the money supply. But, as noted in the text, the central bank eventually has to expand the money supply to accommodate the increase in money demand related to the increase in consumption (to prevent a fall in P).
11 The real exchange rate can also be calculated as $q = \left[\dfrac{P^Y}{P^X}\right]^{0.4} = \left[\dfrac{95.302}{104.929}\right]^{0.4} = 0.96224$.
12 The nominal appreciation is smaller, due to the 0.04 per cent fall in the foreign price level which, in itself, would induce a 0.04 per cent nominal depreciation of the domestic currency.
13 Cao and Kozicki (2017) provide empirical evidence on how changes in the terms of trade have affected real income in Canada.
14 Growth in the traded good sector results in a real appreciation of the domestic currency whereas growth in the non-traded sector results in a real depreciation. See the discussion in Chapter 10.
15 If the central bank is not following the zero inflation policy, and holds the money supply fixed, an increase in production increases consumption and nominal money demand and thereby reduces the price level. With the fall in the individual goods prices, the domestic currency appreciates until the law of one price conditions hold.
16 The import and export price indices are available in CANSIM Table 228-0063, now labeled Table 12100087, with series numbers V54059123 and V54060791. The exchange rate is series V37426.
17 The data for the Canadian-US dollar exchange rate and the Canadian price level are taken from CANSIM (series V37426 and V41690973, respectively), and the US price level data are taken from the IMF's IFS database.
18 If the movement in the real exchange rate appears to be a permanent change, this suggests that it was not likely to be caused by monetary shocks in conjunction with temporary price stickiness.

19 The real exchange rate is also affected by movements in the prices of non-traded goods in the two countries, which are affected by the real shocks such as shocks to sectoral productivity growth.

20 These resource commodities are Canada's claim to fame in international trade, accounting for a significant fraction of Canada's exports. One could say that, in terms of Canada's exports, the acronym FAME refers to forestry, agriculture, metals and minerals, and energy.

21 The commodity price index, measured in US dollars, is a Fisher-ideal commodity price index, denoted CANSIM V52673496 in Table 176-0075, now labeled Table 10100132. Chen and Rogoff (2003) conduct empirical analyses of the relationship between world commodity prices and the real exchange rates of the resource-abundant economies of Australia, Canada, and New Zealand.

22 See the discussion in Crow (1993b). For an analysis of interest rate and exchange rate determination during this period, see Floyd (1995).

23 The commodity price index did not return to the level set before the financial crisis.

24 This chapter abstracted from government policy changes such as changes in tariff rates. In an interesting quantitative analysis, Betts et al. (2017) use a three-sector model (agriculture, industry, and services) to examine the effects of South Korean trade policy over the period 1963 to 2000. For an empirical study on terms of trade fluctuations and the business cycle, see Schmitt-Grohe and Uribe (2018).

25 For interesting empirical studies of the relationship between the Canadian-US dollar real exchange rate, the terms of trade (or commodity prices), and other factors, see (for example) Amano and Van Norden (1995), Chen and Rogoff (2003), Floyd (2010), and Choudhri and Schembri (2014).

PART V

Topics in International Macroeconomics

CHAPTER 13

The IS–LM–IRP Model of the Business Cycle

1. INTRODUCTION

What factors cause the business cycle? In some periods, the economy is booming with large increases in production; at other times, the economy grows more slowly. And in some periods, aggregate production falls and the economy is in a recession. What factors cause the short-term fluctuations in production that are evident in real-world economies?

The theory of the business cycle in this chapter is based on the IS–LM–IRP model. This model is a variation of the Mundell–Fleming model, a widely used framework for analyzing the business cycle in undergraduate macroeconomics.[1] Like the Mundell–Fleming model, the IS–LM–IRP model incorporates international trade in both goods and assets and is a demand-side model of the business cycle.[2] In this framework, fluctuations in aggregate expenditure (aggregate demand) cause short-term fluctuations in production. The fluctuations in aggregate demand, in turn, are caused by changes in monetary and fiscal policy, changes in expectations, and changes in foreign variables such as foreign real GDP (gross domestic product) and the foreign interest rate.

The exchange rate is flexible, and the analysis focuses on the short run with a fixed price level. The discussion includes analysis that addresses the following questions. What is the short-run relationship between movements in the exchange rate, the interest rate, and aggregate production? How do changes in foreign variables affect the domestic economy in the short run? How do changes in the expectations of firms and consumers impact the key macroeconomic variables in the short run? What are the short-run macroeconomic effects of monetary and fiscal policy? This chapter provides the background to address these issues from the perspective of the IS–LM–IRP framework and briefly discusses a few related empirical matters.

An appendix examines an alternative specification of the IS–LM–IRP model under a flexible exchange rate, and another appendix examines the model under a fixed exchange rate.

2. PRELIMINARIES

The IS–LM–IRP model is a small economy model, meaning that foreign variables are taken as given.[3] The three equilibrium conditions in the model are represented by three curves: the IS curve represents goods market equilibrium; the LM curve represents money market equilibrium; and the IRP curve represents interest rate parity, an equilibrium relationship that links the expected returns on domestic and foreign bonds. These equilibrium conditions form the basis of aggregate demand for the domestic good.

The Short Run

The short run is a period of time such as a quarter or a year. In this model, the domestic price level is assumed to be fixed in the short run. In effect, the short-run aggregate supply curve is horizontal and does not shift. Short-run fluctuations in real GDP are caused by factors that cause shifts in aggregate demand.

The Exchange Rate

The exchange rate, denoted as s, is the domestic currency price of foreign currency (an increase in s is a depreciation of the domestic currency). The exchange rate is a factor in determining the expected return on foreign bonds and therefore affects the IRP curve. And the exchange rate affects exports and imports and therefore affects the IS curve.

The Domestic Good and the Foreign Good

It is assumed that there is one domestic good and one foreign good, and these goods are similar but not identical. The prices of the two goods, adjusted for the exchange rate, will not be the same. The relative price between domestic and foreign goods is called the real exchange rate, denoted as q, and is defined as follows (where P and P* denote, respectively, the domestic and foreign price levels):

$$q = \frac{s\,P^{*}}{P}.$$

The numerator, sP*, measures the price of the foreign good for domestic residents. For example, if P* equals $10 US and the nominal exchange rate s equals 1.20 (1 US dollar costs $1.20 Canadian), the price of the US good is $12 Canadian. If the Canadian price level is $4 Canadian, the real exchange rate equals 3 Canadian goods per 1 US good.

The domestic price level is fixed in the short run, and the foreign price level is exogenous. Changes in the nominal exchange rate result in changes in the real exchange rate.

Net Exports and the Real Exchange Rate

The balance of trade in nominal terms (denoted as B_T) is the value of exports less the value of imports (both measured in domestic currency):

$$B_T = PEX - sP^* IM^f,$$

where EX denotes exports of the domestic good and IM^f denotes imports of the foreign good (measured in units of the foreign good). The balance of trade in real terms, measured in terms of the domestic good, is obtained by dividing through by the domestic price level. The real balance of trade, or net exports (denoted NX), is

$$\frac{B_T}{P} = NX = EX - q\, IM^f.$$

The term qIM^f equals imports of the foreign good measured in units of the domestic good, and is denoted as IM. Net exports are exports less imports (both measured in units of the domestic good):

$$NX = EX - IM.$$

As discussed below, a real depreciation of the domestic currency (holding other factors fixed) causes net exports to increase (and vice versa).

3. THE IS CURVE: BACKGROUND

The IS curve represents goods market equilibrium, with variable production. This condition is based on the following identity (production equals sales plus inventory changes):

$$y = c + I + g + NX.$$

The variable y denotes aggregate production of the domestic good (real GDP) and the right-hand side represents aggregate demand (AD). In equilibrium, production equals aggregate demand. The components of AD are consumer spending (c), investment spending (I), government spending (g), and net exports (NX). While this equation is an identity, it forms the basis of the condition representing equilibrium in the goods market. The theory behind the IS curve sets out the determinants of each component of aggregate demand.

Domestic production is sold to consumers, firms, the government, and foreigners. Consumer spending includes purchases of goods and services by domestic consumers. Investment spending includes purchases of machines and equipment by domestic firms, as well as inventory changes. Government spending counts the purchases of goods and services by governments, and exports are purchases by foreigners of goods produced in the domestic economy.

Why are imports subtracted at the end of the identity? Imports are purchases of goods produced in other countries. Because the identity represents the production, sales, and change in inventory of the *domestic good*, imports should not enter this identity. In fact, imports do not enter this identity. Consumer spending by domestic consumers, denoted as c, includes all spending by domestic consumers, regardless of whether these goods are produced in the domestic economy or the rest of the world. The variable c is (measured in units of the domestic good)

$$c = c^d + qc^f,$$

where c^d denotes consumer spending by domestic residents on the domestic good and c^f denotes consumer spending by domestic residents on the foreign good. The variables c, I, and g all count imports, and then imports are subtracted at the end of the equation.

The identity can be written in two ways:

$$y = c + I + g + EX - IM,$$

$$y = c^d + I^d + g^d + EX,$$

where

$$IM = q[c^f + I^f + g^f].$$

Macroeconomists tend to use the first identity.

Consumption, Investment Spending, and Government Spending

Consumer spending depends on after-tax real income (denoted as y-T, where y is real income and T denotes taxes), expected future real income (EFI), expected future taxes (EFT), the nominal interest rate (denoted i), and the expected inflation rate (denoted as π^e).[4] Increases in y-T, increases in EFI, and decreases in EFT increase consumer spending because they increase lifetime after-tax real income. Decreases in i or increases in π^e decrease the expected real interest rate and therefore induce consumers to increase spending in the current period.

Investment spending is the purchase of new machines and equipment by firms.[5] Investment spending depends on the expected real interest rate and expected future profit (denoted as EFP). With a lower nominal interest rate (holding other factors fixed), more investment projects are profitable and investment spending increases. An increase in expected inflation induces firms to increase purchases this period, as this period's price level has decreased relative to the expected future price level. With an improvement in the expected future business environment, expected future profit increases and firms increase investment spending this period.

Government spending is exogenous.

Net Exports

Exchange rate movements affect net exports. A nominal depreciation of the domestic currency, holding the domestic and foreign price levels fixed, causes a real depreciation, meaning that the domestic good has become relatively cheaper. Foreign residents increase their purchases of the domestic good, and domestic residents reduce their purchases of the foreign good (shifting expenditure toward the domestic good). The real depreciation therefore increases net exports. Likewise, increases in the foreign price level make the domestic good relatively cheaper (for a given exchange rate and domestic price level) and increase net exports.[6]

Net exports are also affected by changes in real income and the real interest rate. An increase in domestic real income (an increase in y) causes domestic residents to increase their spending on all goods, including the foreign good (imports increase and net exports fall). Similarly, an increase in foreign real income (an increase in y*) causes foreign residents to increase their spending on all goods, including the domestic good, so that domestic exports and net exports increase. Decreases in the nominal interest rate and increases in the expected inflation rate increase consumer and investment spending. Given that a portion of this spending is on imported goods, there is a decrease in net exports.

Exogenous and Endogenous Variables

Exogenous variables are held fixed, but they can change exogenously. The exogenous variables from the IS curve are the fiscal policy variables g and T, the expectations variables EFI, EFT, EFP, and π^e, and the foreign variables y* and P*. The endogenous variables are the interest rate, production, and the exchange rate (as well as the variables that depend on these variables).

4. GOODS MARKET EQUILIBRIUM AND THE IS CURVE

The IS curve represents goods market equilibrium. At all points on the IS curve, production (real GDP) equals the sum of consumer spending, investment spending, government spending, and net exports. Along any given IS curve, the variables i and y change, inducing changes in the variables that depend on i and y (the exogenous variables, the exchange rate, and the domestic price level are held fixed along any given IS curve). The IS curve is downward sloping, as shown in Figure 13.1 (this figure shows all three curves, the IS, LM, and IRP curves). When the interest rate falls, consumer and investment spending both increase and induce an increase in real GDP.[7] The associated increase in real income generates increases in consumption (and smaller increases in imports) in response to a multiplier process. As the interest rate falls, these changes all occur and the induced increase in aggregate expenditure implies a higher level of real GDP.

The IS curve shifts to the right with each of the following changes: an exogenous increase in g or decrease in T;[8] an exogenous increase in EFP, EFI, or π^e; an exogenous decrease in EFT; an exogenous increase in y* or P*; and an endogenous increase in s (a depreciation of the domestic currency).

Consider an increase in g, and suppose the additional government spending is on the domestic good (hold the interest rate fixed). An increase in g, in itself, increases c+I+g+NX (or $c^d+I^d+g^d+EX$), implying that y is higher. The increase in y also generates an increase in c (and a smaller increase in IM), reflecting the increased consumer spending associated with the increase in real income. This induced effect on c causes a further increase in y. In total, both g^d and c^d increase. Holding other factors fixed, the increase in g implies a higher level of y (at any level of the interest rate), so that the IS curve shifts to the right.

To take another example, a depreciation of the domestic currency shifts the IS curve to the right. The depreciation makes the domestic good relatively cheaper, causing exports to increase and

Figure 13.1: IS–LM–IRP diagram

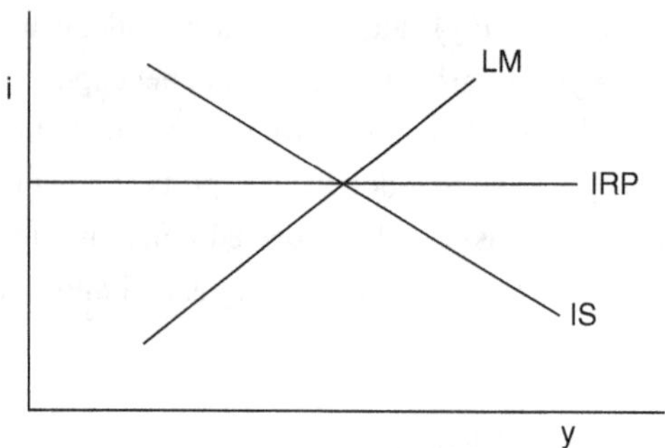

imports to fall. This increase in net exports induces an increase in real income, generating further increases in consumer spending and imports. In total, both net exports and consumer spending are higher, implying a higher level of y (at a given level of the interest rate).

5. MONEY MARKET EQUILIBRIUM AND THE LM CURVE

The LM curve represents money market equilibrium, where the money supply (denoted as M^s) equals desired money demand (denoted as M^d). Money consists of currency and transactions deposits at private banks (money does not earn interest). The quantity of money in existence, the money supply, is determined by the central bank. The demand for money depends on the price level, real income, and the interest rate:[9]

$$M^d = P\,L(i, y).$$

Increases in the price level and real income are associated with a higher level of transactions and cause domestic residents to want to hold more money. An increase in the interest rate on bonds increases the opportunity cost of holding money and therefore reduces the quantity of money demanded.

At any point on the LM curve, the supply of money equals the demand for money, or the amount of money in existence equals the amount of money the public *wants* to hold:

$$M^s = P\,L(i, y).$$

Along any given LM curve, M^s and P are fixed. The LM curve is upward sloping because an increase in real income must be associated with an increase in the interest rate (holding other factors fixed). An increase in real income causes money demand to rise so that, to maintain equilibrium, the interest rate must rise to reduce the demand for money back to the initial level (equal to the fixed money supply).

With a fixed price level, the only factor that shifts the LM curve is a change in the money supply. An exogenous increase in the money supply shifts the LM curve down to the right because, at a given level of output, the interest rate must fall to generate a higher demand for money and maintain money market equilibrium.

6. INTEREST RATE PARITY AND THE IRP CURVE

The IRP condition holds when the expected returns on domestic and foreign bonds are equal:

$$i = i^* + \frac{s^e - s}{s},$$

where the foreign interest rate is denoted as i*, the exchange rate *this period* is s, and the expected future exchange rate is s^e. In equilibrium, the domestic interest rate equals the foreign interest rate plus the expected rate of appreciation of the foreign currency (relative to the domestic currency). Domestic bonds and foreign bonds are then regarded as equally good investments.

The IRP curve is a horizontal line at the level of the expected return on the foreign bond, $i^* + \frac{s^e - s}{s}$. If the foreign interest rate equals 4 per cent and the expected rate of appreciation of the foreign currency equals 1 per cent, the expected return on foreign bonds equals 5 per cent for domestic investors, and the IRP curve is horizontal at 5 per cent. Interest rate parity holds at all points on the IRP curve.

The foreign interest rate and the expected future exchange rate are exogenous. Three changes shift the IRP curve up: an increase in the foreign interest rate, an increase in the expected future exchange rate (increasing $\left[\frac{s^e - s}{s}\right]$ for a given s), and an appreciation of the domestic currency this period (with the fall in s increasing $\left[\frac{s^e - s}{s}\right]$ for a given s^e).

7. METHOD OF ANALYSIS AND EXOGENOUS VARIABLES

The following method is used to determine the effects of exogenous changes. The initial equilibrium is denoted as point A, where all three curves intersect. At that interest rate and that level of production, the goods and money markets are in equilibrium and interest rate parity holds. When an exogenous change occurs, point B is denoted at the intersection of the IS and LM curves. If B lies below the IRP curve, actions in the foreign exchange market cause the domestic currency to depreciate (and vice versa). The change in the exchange rate then shifts both the IS and IRP curves, resulting in a new short-run equilibrium, denoted as point C.

The exogenous variables can be categorized as follows: the fiscal policy variables g and T; the expectations variables EFI, EFT, EFP, π^e, and s^e; the monetary policy variable M^s; and the foreign variables y*, P*, and i*.

A Note on the Expected Future Exchange Rate

The expected future exchange rate is taken to be an exogenous variable. In general, one always needs to be aware of the assumptions regarding the expected future exchange rate and the other expectations variables.[10] These variables are all taken to be exogenous.

Figure 13.2: Increase in the money supply

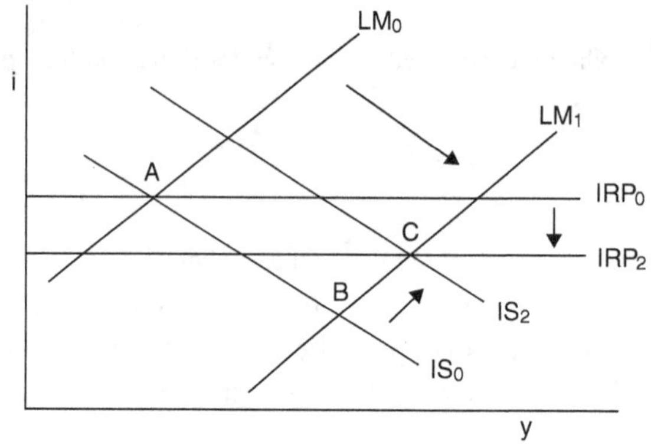

8. MONETARY POLICY

How does an exogenous increase in the money supply affect the interest rate, the exchange rate, and production in the short run? The increase in the money supply shifts the LM curve to the right from LM$_0$ to LM$_1$ in Figure 13.2, putting downward pressure on the domestic interest rate. The IS and LM curves cross at B, a point below the IRP$_0$ curve. With the domestic interest rate less than the expected return on foreign bonds, the domestic currency depreciates (as domestic residents try to acquire foreign currency to be able to buy foreign bonds). The depreciation shifts both the IS and IRP curves. The depreciation makes the domestic good relatively cheaper and therefore increases net exports and shifts the IS curve to the right from IS$_0$ to IS$_2$; and the increase in s, for a given s^e, decreases $\left[\dfrac{s^e - s}{s}\right]$ and shifts the IRP curve down from IRP$_0$ to IRP$_2$. The short-run equilibrium is established at point C. The new equilibrium has a lower domestic interest rate, a higher level of output, and a depreciated domestic currency.[11]

The increase in the money supply affects the economy by decreasing the interest rate and inducing a depreciation of the domestic currency. The decrease in the interest rate generates increases in consumer spending and investment spending, and the depreciation results in an increase in net exports. These increases in aggregate demand increase production. This increase in production activates a multiplier process: the increase in production increases real income and induces further increases in consumption and imports. The new short-run equilibrium, established at point C, incorporates all these changes. With a flexible exchange rate and a fixed price level, monetary policy has a significant short-run effect on production.

With a fixed price level, the short-run aggregate supply curve is horizontal and not shifting (the capital stock and total factor productivity are fixed). This assumption implies that any shift in aggregate demand generates a change in production. With the increase in the money supply, the induced changes in the interest rate, exchange rate, and real income generate increases in both domestic spending and exports. Domestic firms experience increases in sales and respond by increasing production. This increase in production is associated with an increase in employment (representing some combination of more workers and increases in hours worked for existing workers).

Figure 13.3: Rightward shift in the IS curve

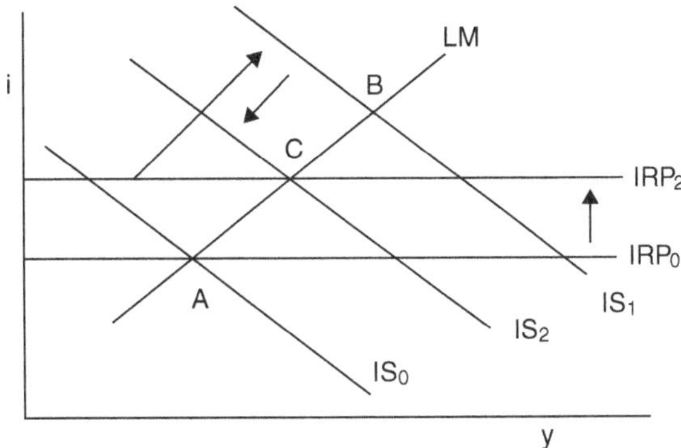

9. CHANGES IN FOREIGN REAL GDP

Suppose there is an exogenous increase in foreign real GDP (assume the foreign interest rate and foreign price level are unchanged). This increase in foreign real income increases spending by foreign residents, including their spending on the domestic good. Domestic exports increase, and the IS curve shifts to the right from IS_0 to IS_1 in Figure 13.3. At point B, the domestic interest rate lies above the IRP curve. The domestic currency therefore appreciates, and the decrease in s affects both the IS and IRP curves. The appreciation of the domestic currency makes the domestic good relatively more expensive, thereby reducing net exports and shifting the IS curve leftward from IS_1 to IS_2. And the decrease in s, for a given s^e, increases $\left[\dfrac{s^e - s}{s}\right]$, shifting the IRP curve up from IRP_0 to IRP_2. The new short-run equilibrium is established at point C, with a higher domestic interest rate, a higher level of output, and an appreciated domestic currency.

The increase in foreign real GDP increases exports, and the appreciation of the domestic currency reduces exports. But exports must rise because it is the initial effect that causes the other effects. The appreciation of the domestic currency increases imports, as does the rise in real income (the higher interest rate reduces consumer and investment spending, and part of these reductions may be on imported goods). But in total, net exports are definitely higher.

The induced changes in the interest rate and real income also cause changes in investment spending and consumer spending. The rise in the interest rate results in a decrease in investment spending (expected future profit and expected inflation are exogenous and held fixed). While the increase in real income acts to increase consumer spending, the rise in the interest rate acts to reduce consumer spending. In theory, consumer spending can rise or fall.[12]

Canadian and American Business Cycles

The IS–LM–IRP model predicts that a boom in the United States causes a boom in Canada. Likewise, a US recession causes a recession in Canada. While this prediction depends on the assumption that other exogenous variables are fixed (or change to accentuate the boom or exacerbate the recession), the short-term movements in real GDP are similar in the two countries.

Figure 13.4: Canadian and US growth rates

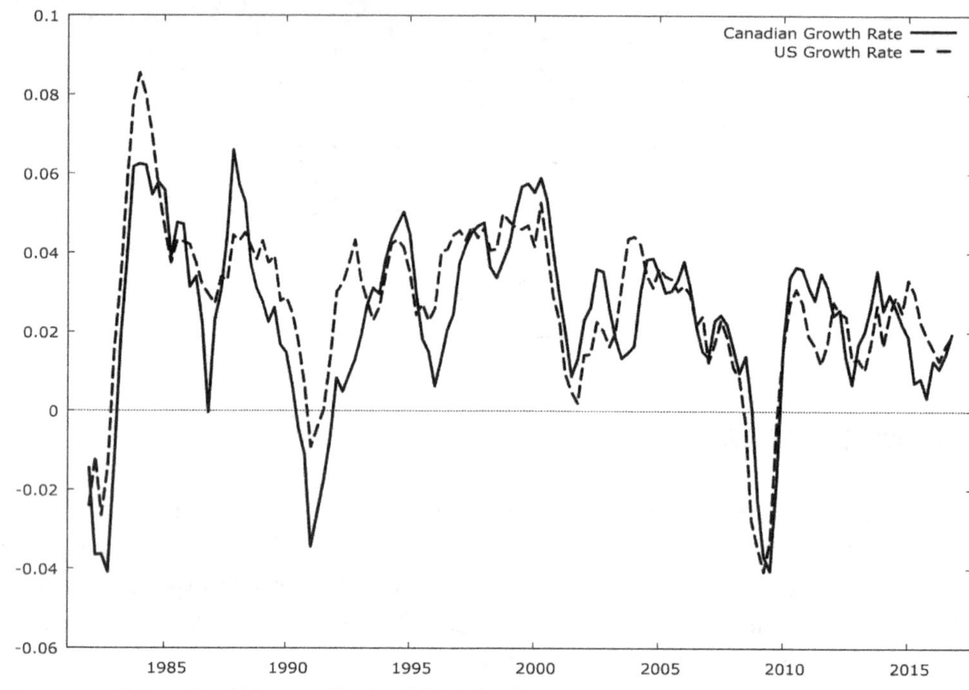

Data sources: International Monetary Fund and Statistics Canada

Since 1980, there were Canadian recessions in 1981–1982, 1990–1991, 2008–2009, and 2020. In each period, the US economy was also in recession. The close link between the growth rates of real GDP is shown in Figure 13.4, which covers the period from 1982 to 2016. The high correlation between Canadian and American growth rates is striking.[13] It should be emphasized, however, that the positive correlation may arise for reasons apart from the link between US real GDP and Canadian exports. The relationship could be due to a multitude of factors, ranging from the similarity in short-term monetary policies in the two countries to the similarity in supply-side factors such as changes in total factor productivity.[14]

An applied exercise in Data Analytics examines the level and growth rate of real GDP in Canada since 2016, and thus includes the recession in 2020.

10. FISCAL POLICY AND OTHER EXOGENOUS FACTORS

Fiscal policy consists of government spending and income tax policy. Suppose the government increases spending on the domestic good (hold other exogenous factors, including taxes, fixed). The increase in government spending shifts the IS curve to the right from IS_0 to IS_1 (the diagram for this exogenous change is the same as in Figure 13.3). The domestic interest rate lies above the IRP line at point B, indicating that the domestic currency will appreciate. This appreciation shifts the IS curve back from IS_1 to IS_2 and shifts the IRP curve up from IRP_0 to IRP_2. The new short-run equilibrium is at point C, with a higher interest rate and a higher level of real GDP.

With any exogenous change that shifts the IS curve rightward, there are four effects. There is the initial effect, the exogenous change. In this case, the exogenous variable g increases. There are the effects associated with the multiplier process, with the increase in real income inducing increases in consumer spending and imports. There are the interest-rate effects, such that the increase in the interest rate decreases both consumer spending and investment spending. And there is the exchange-rate effect, whereby the appreciation reduces net exports.

With a flexible exchange rate, fiscal policy tends to be relatively ineffective.[15] The increase in government spending causes the domestic interest rate to rise and the domestic currency to appreciate, and these effects counteract the direct effect of the fiscal expansion. While government spending increases, the effect on consumption may be small and both investment spending and net exports fall. Real GDP necessarily increases given the assumptions, but fiscal policy may have a small effect on real GDP.[16]

Figure 13.3 can be used to analyze any exogenous change that shifts the IS curve to the right (provided there is no shift in the LM curve and no shift in the IRP curve other than that associated with the change in the current-period exchange rate). For example, a decrease in taxes, an increase in expected future profit, an increase in the foreign price level, an increase in expected future real income, a decrease in expected future taxes, and an increase in the expected inflation rate all generate an IS–LM–IRP diagram like Figure 13.3.

11. EXPECTATIONS

Changes in expectations regarding the future state of the economy affect the current state of the economy. Suppose that, all of a sudden, managers at firms become more pessimistic about the future state of the economy, such that there is a decrease in expected future profit. How does this change affect real GDP in the short run? Because there is now a pessimistic view about the future, firms will not be buying as many machines this period as in the previous period. Investment spending falls and the IS curve shifts leftward from IS_0 to IS_1 in Figure 13.5. At point B, the domestic interest rate lies below the IRP curve. The domestic currency therefore depreciates, shifting the IS curve rightward to IS_2 and the IRP curve downward to IRP_2. The new short-run equilibrium occurs at point C. As real GDP has decreased, the economy is in a recession.

The decrease in expected future profit causes investment spending to fall. While the interest rate is lower in the new equilibrium, the decrease in the interest rate only moderates the extent of the reduction in investment spending. In total, investment spending is lower. It is the fall in investment spending that causes the other effects (such as the lower interest rate) to occur in the first place.[17]

This recession is caused by the exogenous change in expectations (there are many factors that could change expectations, both factors within industries and factors affecting the entire economy). Because the managers of firms believe that their requirements for machines in the near future will be less than previously expected, firms reduce purchases of machines this period, and the process begins whereby the economy moves to a lower level of aggregate production.

Figure 13.5: Leftward shift in the IS curve

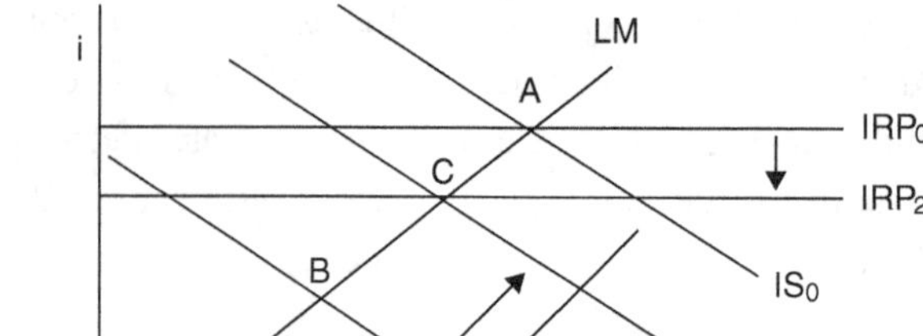

In practice, decreases in expected future profit may occur in response to a recession caused by other factors. That is, the economy contracts, and once firms recognize this fact, they revise their expectations. The decrease in expected future profit then results in a decrease in investment spending that exacerbates the recession. Similarly, the onset of a recession often results in workers revising their expectations, such that expected future real income is reduced (as some workers expect to be laid off in the near future). As consumers reduce spending in the current period, the lower spending translates into lower aggregate production.

12. CHANGES IN THE FOREIGN INTEREST RATE

An exogenous increase in the foreign interest rate (holding foreign real GDP and the foreign price level fixed) shifts the IRP curve up from IRP$_0$ to IRP$_1$ in Figure 13.6 (an exogenous increase in the expected future exchange rate has the same effects). The IS and LM curves cross at point B (the same as A), with the domestic interest rate below the new IRP curve. With the resulting depreciation of the domestic currency, net exports increase and the IS curve shifts rightward to IS$_2$. And the increase in s, for a given s^e, reduces the expected return on foreign bonds and shifts the IRP curve down from IRP$_1$ to IRP$_2$. The new short-run equilibrium occurs at point C, with a higher level of production and a higher domestic interest rate.

Even though the domestic interest rate has increased, acting to decrease investment spending and reduce consumer spending, aggregate demand and real GDP are higher. The main impetus to the increase in aggregate demand is the depreciation of the domestic currency, and the associated increase in net exports. In addition, the increase in real income increases consumer spending.[18]

13. THE GREAT RECESSION IN 2008–2009

Many countries went into recession in 2008–2009, an event now called the Great Recession. The recession in a small economy like Canada can be interpreted from the perspective of the IS–LM–IRP model, with the short-run fall in production caused by factors that decreased aggregate spending.

Figure 13.6: Increase in the foreign interest rate

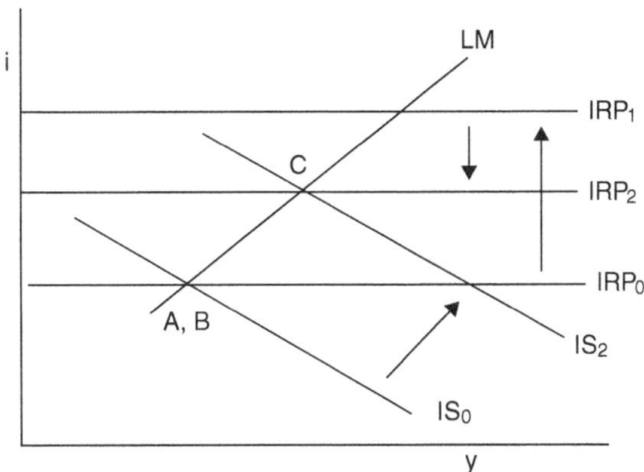

In this recession, like most recessions, the IS, LM, and IRP curves are *all* shifting. This recession may have been caused by factors that shifted the IS curve to the left.[19] The decrease in US real GDP (the US recession) decreased Canadian exports, and the decreases in expected future profit and expected future real income resulted in decreases in investment and consumer spending. These factors all caused the IS curve to shift leftward.[20] While the depreciation of the Canadian dollar (relative to the US dollar) and an increase in government spending were moderating influences, the negative effects on domestic spending were larger. Thus, the IS curve shifted to the left, resulting in a lower level of aggregate demand. While there was a large increase in the nominal money supply (shifting the LM curve to the right), as well as a decrease in the US interest rate (shifting the IRP curve down), the level of aggregate demand fell.[21] In terms of the IS–LM–IRP model, the decrease in aggregate spending caused aggregate production to fall and the Canadian economy was in a recession.

14. CONCLUSION

In the IS–LM–IRP model, short-term fluctuations in real GDP are caused by changes in aggregate demand. Changes in foreign variables, changes in expectations, and monetary and fiscal policy induce changes in aggregate expenditure and generate short-term fluctuations in production.

That fluctuations in aggregate demand are a predominant cause of the business cycle is a common view (in some models, the price level is flexible in the short run, but the nominal wage rate is fixed). But many macroeconomists and policymakers believe that both demand-side and supply-side factors are important for short-term fluctuations in production.[22]

PRACTICE QUESTIONS

1. Fill in the blanks
   (a) An increase in the interest rate causes investment spending to ______, and an increase in expected future profit causes investment spending to ______.

    (b) Two factors that can cause a short-run increase in exports are ______ of the domestic currency and ______ in foreign real income.

    (c) As one moves down along a given IS curve (the domestic interest rate falls), investment spending ______ and government spending ______.

    (d) Along any given LM curve, the money supply is ______. Along any given IRP curve, the foreign interest rate is ______.

    (e) Holding other factors fixed, a depreciation of the domestic currency in this period (an increase in s) ______ the expected return on foreign bonds for domestic investors and results in ______ shift in the IRP curve.

2. Fill in the blanks

Use the IS–LM–IRP model with a flexible exchange rate to determine the short-run effects of each exogenous change.

    (a) When there is an exogenous increase in the money supply, investment spending ______ and exports ______ in the short run.

    (b) When there is an exogenous increase in the money supply, the induced change in the exchange rate causes the ______ curve to shift rightward because ______ increase.

    (c) An exogenous increase in government spending causes ______ in the interest rate and ______ in investment spending.

    (d) An exogenous decrease in foreign real GDP (holding the foreign interest rate and the foreign price level fixed) causes exports to ______ and investment spending to ______.

    (e) An exogenous decrease in expected future profit causes investment spending to ______ and real GDP to ______.

3. (a) Using a diagram, explain why the LM curve is upward sloping.

    (b) Does a decrease in the domestic interest rate cause the IS curve to shift? Explain.

    (c) Suppose the interest rate falls, but expected future profit also falls. What happens to investment spending? Explain.

4. The exchange rate is flexible. Suppose there is a decrease in government spending. Draw the IS–LM–IRP diagram, showing points A, B, and C. Explain how exports and imports are affected by the endogenous changes in the interest rate, real income, and the exchange rate.

5. Consider the IS–LM–IRP model with a flexible exchange rate. Suppose there is an exogenous increase in the money supply. Draw the IS–LM–IRP diagram, and indicate why the various curves shift. List the short-run effects on consumer spending and exports. Explain.

6. Suppose there is an exogenous increase in foreign real GDP (hold the foreign interest rate and price level fixed). Draw the IS–LM–IRP diagram. Comment on whether exports rise or fall.

DATA ANALYTICS

1. Access CANSIM Table 36100104 and collect quarterly data on exports, investment spending, and real GDP over the period since 2000. Plot the ratio of exports to real GDP and comment. Plot investment spending and highlight periods when there was a reduction in investment spending. In addition, calculate the "cyclical" components of (the logarithms of) exports, investment spending and real GDP using a Hodrick–Prescott filter. Plot the variables and discuss.
2. Using data from question 1, create time-series plots of the level and growth rate of Canadian real GDP since 2016. Comment on aspects of the plots, including the size of the 2020 recession.
3. Collect Canadian data on the M1+ money supply (CANSIM series V37151), the price level (V41690973), and real GDP (V62305752) over the period 1988 to 1993 (where necessary, convert the monthly data to quarterly data). Calculate and plot the quarterly percentage change in the real money supply and real GDP. Comment.

APPENDIX A: AN ALTERNATIVE SPECIFICATION OF THE MODEL

In this specification, the IRP curve is represented as the equality of domestic and foreign interest rates. This formulation assumes that changes in the current-period exchange rate are matched by equivalent changes in the expected future exchange rate.[23] The IRP curve only shifts when there is a change in the foreign interest rate (the other aspects of the model are the same).

Monetary Policy

An increase in the money supply shifts the LM curve rightward from LM_0 to LM_1 in Figure 13.7. The domestic interest rate lies below the IRP curve at the intersection of the IS and LM curves at B, indicating a depreciation of the domestic currency. The depreciation makes the domestic good relatively cheaper, increasing net exports and shifting the IS curve from IS_0 to IS_2. The new short-run equilibrium is established at point C, with an increase in production and no change in the domestic interest rate.

The expansionary monetary policy has no short-run effect on the interest rate, but it increases aggregate demand. Monetary policy works, in this specification, by affecting the exchange rate and thereby influencing net exports. The associated increase in production also generates an increase in real income that increases consumer spending. While investment spending is unchanged, net exports and consumer spending increase. With a fixed price level, monetary policy is an effective tool in affecting real GDP (and employment) in the short run.

Figure 13.7: Increase in the money supply

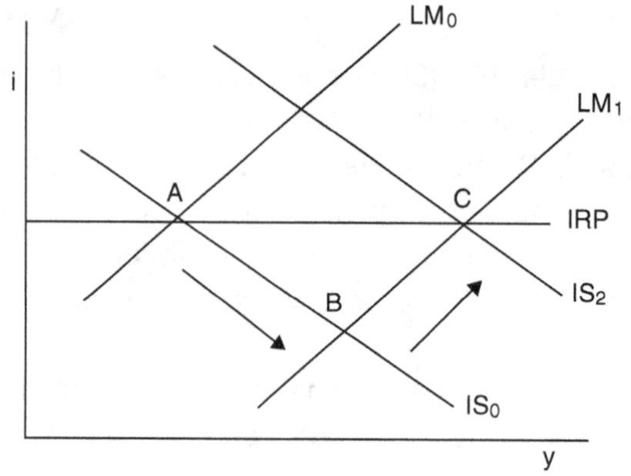

Fiscal Policy and Other Factors that Shift the IS Curve

An exogenous increase in government spending shifts the IS curve rightward from IS$_0$ to IS$_1$ in Figure 13.8. With the domestic interest rate above the IRP curve at point B, the domestic currency appreciates. The appreciation decreases net exports and shifts the IS curve back to the left. Given that the LM and IRP curves are unchanged, the IS curve shifts back completely to IS$_0$. The increase in government spending has no short-run effect on real GDP.

While the increase in government spending, in itself, increases aggregate demand, the associated reduction in net exports offsets the increase in government spending. The government spending multiplier, defined as $\dfrac{\Delta y}{\Delta g}$, equals 0. Consumer and investment spending are unchanged, and the increase in government spending is offset fully by the decrease in net exports.[24]

This result holds for any exogenous factor that shifts the IS curve. Consider, for example, an exogenous increase in expected future profit that increases investment spending. The exogenous change shifts the IS curve rightward, but the resulting appreciation of the domestic currency decreases net exports and shifts the IS back. With no shifts in the LM and IRP curves, the new short-run equilibrium is at the same level of real GDP.[25]

Change in the Foreign Interest Rate

An increase in the foreign interest rate shifts the IRP curve up in Figure 13.9 (hold foreign real income and the foreign price level fixed). With the domestic interest rate now lower than the foreign rate, the depreciation of the domestic currency increases net exports and shifts the IS curve rightward from IS$_0$ to IS$_2$. The domestic economy experiences an increase in real GDP, and the associated increase in real income increases both consumer spending and imports. While the higher interest rate acts to decrease investment spending and moderate the increase in consumer spending, real GDP is higher. The new short-run equilibrium is at point C.

Figure 13.8: Rightward shift in the IS curve

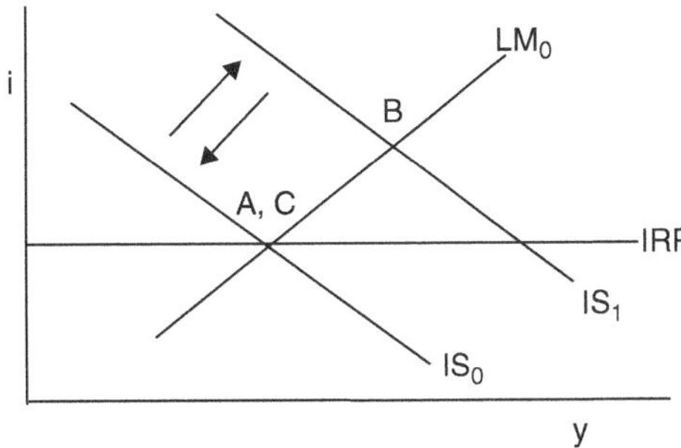

Figure 13.9: Increase in the foreign interest rate

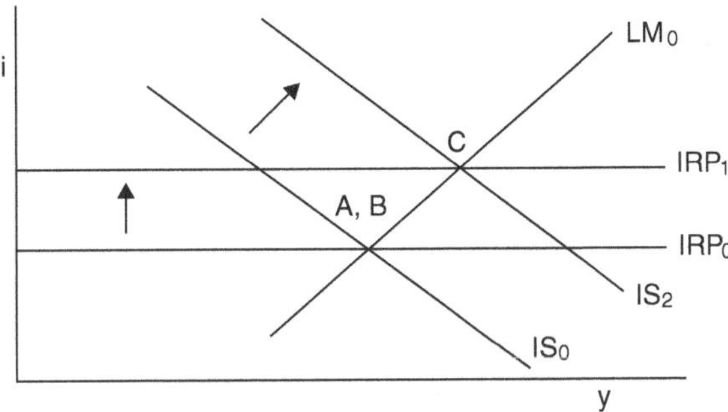

APPENDIX B: THE IS–LM–IRP MODEL UNDER A FIXED EXCHANGE RATE

Under a fixed exchange rate (let s equal 1), the central bank uses foreign exchange reserves to keep the exchange rate fixed. The money supply equals domestic credit, D, plus foreign exchange reserves, R:[26]

$$M^S = D + R.$$

While the central bank has control of D, the variable R is endogenous. For example, if the central bank buys foreign currency and sells domestic currency, foreign exchange reserves and the domestic money supply increase and the LM curve shifts to the right.

When the public expects the exchange rate to remain fixed at the current level, so that s equals s^e, the interest rate parity condition implies that the domestic interest rate equals the foreign interest rate. This assumption is adopted until near the end of this appendix.

In the diagram, the equilibrium point under a fixed exchange rate regime is determined at the intersection of the IS and IRP curves. The initial equilibrium is denoted as point A and the new equilibrium is denoted C. The LM curve adjusts endogenously. As domestic residents eliminate any excess money demand or supply that arises, there is a change in foreign exchange reserves and the money supply that shifts the LM curve to the new equilibrium point.

Figure 13.10: Rightward shift in the IS curve

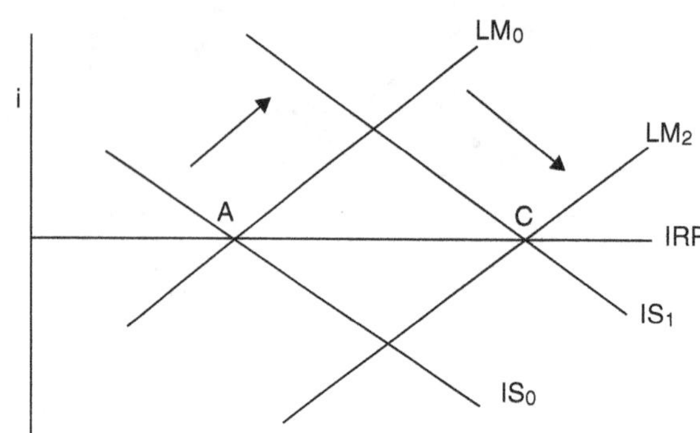

Exogenous Shift in the IS Curve

Suppose there is an increase in government spending, an increase in foreign real income, or some other exogenous change that shifts the IS curve rightward from IS_0 to IS_1 in Figure 13.10. With the exchange rate fixed and the domestic interest linked to the foreign interest rate, the exogenous change causes output to increase. And with the associated increase in real income, domestic residents increase spending on consumer goods, both domestic and foreign. With the higher level of real income, the demand for money increases. As domestic residents sell foreign bonds and then sell foreign currency for domestic currency, the central bank is forced to supply the desired increase in domestic money. These transactions increase reserves and the money supply, shifting the LM curve rightward from LM_0 to LM_2. The new short-run equilibrium is at point C.

Fiscal policy is effective under a fixed exchange rate.[27] An increase in government spending on the domestic good results in an increase in consumer spending on the domestic good, so the government spending multiplier is necessarily greater than 1 (in terms of the equation $y = c^d + I^d + g^d + EX$, the variables g^d and c^d increase and I^d and EX are unchanged). Likewise, a decrease in taxes causes consumer spending to increase and generates an increase in real GDP.

When the IS curve shifts to the left (for example, due to an exogenous decrease in foreign real income), the money supply decreases and shifts the LM curve leftward. In the new equilibrium, production is lower and the domestic economy is in a recession. Under a fixed exchange rate, recessions in the foreign economy cause recessions in the domestic economy.[28]

Exogenous Change in Domestic Credit

An increase in domestic credit shifts the LM curve rightward to LM_1 in Figure 13.11, creating an excess money supply. Domestic residents sell domestic currency on the foreign exchange market, acquiring foreign currency to purchase foreign bonds. The central bank must supply this foreign currency, generating a decrease in the money supply. This process continues, decreasing reserves and the money supply, until the LM curve shifts back to LM_0. The increase in domestic credit is offset by an equivalent decrease in reserves, and the money supply is unchanged. The new equilibrium at C is at the same point as the original equilibrium at A.

Figure 13.11: Increase in domestic credit

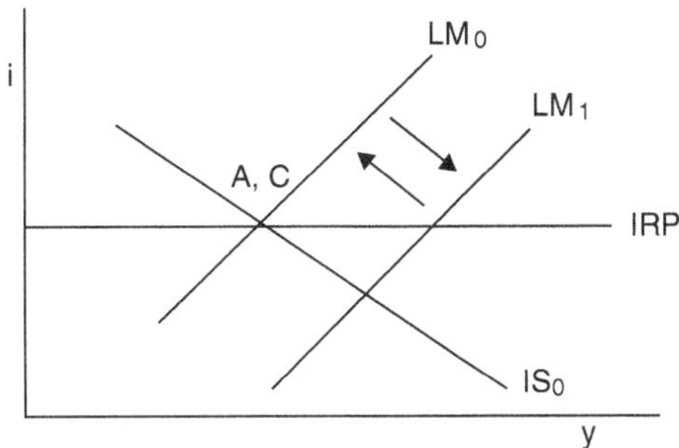

The increase in domestic credit has no effect on the domestic interest rate or real GDP.[29] This ineffectiveness of monetary policy implies that the central bank is unable to implement a stabilization policy under a fixed exchange rate.[30]

Exogenous Change in the Foreign Interest Rate

With an increase in the foreign interest rate, the IRP curve shifts upward from IRP$_0$ to IRP$_1$ in Figure 13.12. Domestic bonds are unattractive, and the attempted selling of domestic bonds increases the interest rate. This process continues until the domestic interest rate has increased to match the higher foreign interest rate. The higher interest rate results in decreases in both consumer and investment spending, and these expenditure decreases result in a fall in real GDP. Through the multiplier process, the fall in real income results in further decreases in consumer spending, imports, and output. In total, aggregate expenditure and aggregate production are lower, with the new short-run equilibrium at point C. With the higher interest rate and lower real income, the demand for money is lower. Domestic residents therefore sell domestic currency, acquiring foreign currency to purchase foreign bonds. These transactions result in decreases in foreign exchange reserves and the money supply, shifting the LM curve leftward to intersect the IS and IRP curves at point C.

A Currency Crisis

Suppose that the public comes to expect the domestic currency to be devalued in the near future (the exchange rate remains fixed in the current period, but there is an expectation that the domestic currency will be devalued within the next while). The exogenous increase in s^e increases the expected return on foreign bonds, shifting the IRP curve upward (the diagram is the same as Figure 13.12). The unattractiveness of domestic bonds results in the attempted selling of domestic bonds until the interest rate increases sufficiently to equal the higher expected return on foreign bonds (the foreign interest rate plus the expected rate of devaluation). In the short run, the higher interest rate reduces consumer and investment spending which, along with the decrease in consumer spending associated with the multiplier process, results in a lower level of real GDP.[31] The resulting decrease in money demand generates a decrease in foreign exchange reserves, shifting the LM

Figure 13.12: Increase in the foreign interest rate

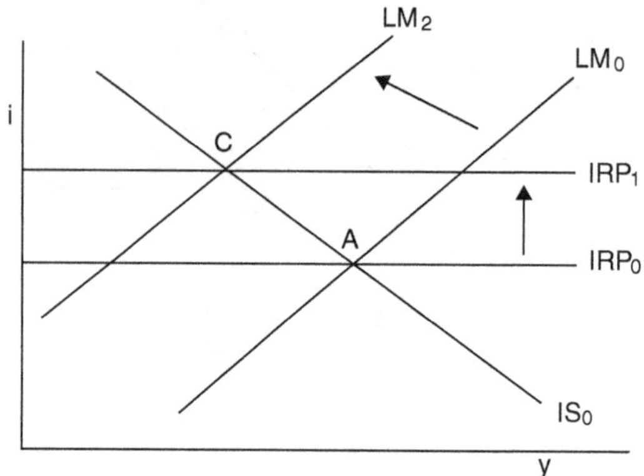

curve leftward to C. The exogenous change in expectations therefore causes aggregate production to fall, either exacerbating an existing recession or causing a new recession.

NOTES

1 Fleming (1962) and Mundell (1963) developed macroeconomic models that linked domestic and foreign interest rates. Dornbusch (1976), in an important extension, incorporated expectations into a model like the Mundell–Fleming model.
2 Chapter 6 outlines a dynamic model that provides an alternative model of business cycles, a "real business cycle" theory in which short-term fluctuations in production are caused by supply-side factors such as exogenous changes in total factor productivity.
3 For diagrammatical analyses of short-term fluctuations in output in a model with two large economies, see Floyd (1985, 2010).
4 The variable y represents both production and real income. All factors of production are owned by domestic residents. GDP equals gross national product (GNP). Taxes are measured in real terms.
5 Changes in inventory are assumed to equal 0.
6 A real depreciation unambiguously increases net exports. This approach is standard in the literature; see, for example, the discussion in Dornbusch (1980, 58–63).
7 Imports also increase when the interest rate falls, but consumption and investment spending increase more because they include both the domestic and foreign components of spending.
8 For simplicity, T is exogenous. If T equals τ y, where τ is the income tax rate, a decrease in τ decreases T for a given level of y and increases consumption (with expected future real income and expected future taxes held fixed).
9 An exogenous variable could be added to the money demand function, allowing for changes in money demand due to factors such as financial innovation or movements in expected future interest rates.
10 In an alternative specification, adopted in Mundell's (1963) seminal paper and in an appendix, the IRP curve is represented as the equality of domestic and foreign interest rates. This formulation assumes that any change in the current-period exchange rate is matched by an equivalent change in the expected future exchange rate.
11 An exogenous decrease in the demand for money (at each level of the interest rate) has the same effects as an exogenous increase in the money supply.

12 The income effect is small when the change in output is temporary, but consumption typically moves in the same direction as real GDP.

13 Canada's real GDP is measured by CANSIM series V62305752, and the data on US real GDP are taken from the International Monetary Fund's IFS database. The data are quarterly, with the Canadian growth rate measured as $\left[\dfrac{y_t - y_{t-4}}{y_{t-4}} \right]$, and the US growth rate measured similarly. On an interesting aside, Canadian real GDP fell in both 2015:1 and 2015:2 (before increasing in 2015:3); based on another definition of recession, that of at least two consecutive quarters of negative growth, there was a small recession in the first half of 2015.

14 Floyd (2010, 327–40) provides an interesting interpretation of the empirical evidence on the international transmission of business cycles in industrialized nations.

15 Floyd (1979, 1980) examines short-run movements in production and employment in a model that encompasses both traded and non-traded goods. Some core propositions within the Mundell–Fleming framework are altered in the multi-sectoral framework, particularly with respect to the effects of fiscal policy.

16 In an alternative specification of the IS-LM-IRP model outlined in an appendix, an increase in government spending has no short-run effect on real GDP under a flexible exchange rate.

17 The fall in real income reduces money demand. The public tries to buy bonds, resulting in a higher bond price and a lower interest rate. It is not the central bank that reduces the interest rate (the nominal money supply is fixed).

18 Consumption increases if the positive real-income effect outweighs the negative interest-rate effect.

19 In the recessions in 1981-1982 and 1990-1991, Canadian monetary policy played a role in that movements in the nominal money supply were associated with decreases in the real money supply (shifting the LM curve leftwards). In these recessions, the Bank of Canada was striving to reduce the inflation rate.

20 In some IS-LM-IRP models, changes in stock prices affect wealth and consumption and shift the IS curve.

21 A fact well known to macroeconomists, highlighted again during the Great Recession, is that interest rates on corporate bonds (relevant to firms' investment spending) do not always move proportionally with interest rates on government bonds. See, for example, the discussion in Hall (2009).

22 Chapter 6 discusses a real business cycle model that focuses on supply-side factors; for an application to Canada, see Mendoza (1991). Multi-sectoral models that allow for terms of trade fluctuations have also been used in business cycle research (see, for example, Mendoza 1995).

23 Mundell (1963) used this formulation in his seminal paper.

24 For an advanced discussion of the government spending multiplier in a large economy like the United States, see (for example) Hall (2009).

25 An exogenous decrease in foreign real GDP (holding the foreign interest rate and price level fixed) has no short-run effect of real GDP in the domestic economy. The initial change reduces net exports and shifts the IS curve leftward, but the depreciation of the domestic currency increases net exports and shifts the IS curve back to its initial position. The flexible exchange rate acts as an "automatic stabilizer," insulating the domestic economy from output fluctuations in the large foreign economy.

26 The equation abstracts from the banking system, and sets the money multiplier equal to 1.

27 This result was highlighted by Mundell (1963).

28 In the Great Depression in the early 1930s, Canada was operating under the gold standard system (a fixed exchange rate system). For empirical analyses of Canada in the Great Depression, see, for example, Betts et al. (1996) and Amaral and McGee (2002).

29 With an exogenous decrease in the demand for money (at each level of the interest rate), the diagram is the same as Figure 13.11. A fixed exchange rate regime works well as an "automatic stabilizer" in

response to exogenous shifts in money demand, in that there is no change in real GDP. But for shocks that shift the IS curve, where a flexible exchange rate regime acts as a perfect automatic stabilizer, the fixed exchange rate regime does not stabilize the economy. One factor in the choice between fixed and flexible exchange rates is the extent to which the exchange rate regime acts as an automatic stabilizer in response to unpredictable shocks that impact the economy.

30 The government and the central bank may, in certain cases, consider a devaluation of the domestic currency. A devaluation increases net exports and shifts the IS curve to the right, generating a short-run increase in production (the diagram is the same as Figure 13.10).

31 The expected inflation rate is assumed to be fixed (if it increased, the IS curve would shift rightward).

A Dynamic Model with a Non-traded Good

1. INTRODUCTION

While economies have a large traded-good sector, consisting of the manufacturing, agriculture, and resource sectors, there are a large number of industries that provide services almost exclusively for the domestic market. These service sectors, along with the construction sector, comprise the non-traded sector in the economy. In industrialized economies, the magnitude of the non-traded sector is typically larger than the traded sector. To understand the range of factors that can impact prices and the exchange rate in the economy, it is essential to embed a non-traded sector into the standard open-economy macroeconomic model.

This chapter outlines a dynamic model with both a traded good and a non-traded good. As highlighted in earlier chapters, dynamic models allow one to conduct a rigorous analysis of trade and current account imbalances. Multi-sectoral models allow for an in-depth analysis of the fundamental determinants of real and nominal exchange rates. The dynamic model with a non-traded good brings these two critical elements together in a coherent framework for analysis.

While the price of the traded good is tightly linked to the international price of the same good, through the law of one price condition, the price of the non-traded good is determined by demand and supply conditions in the domestic market. But in a general equilibrium setting, as in the aggregate economy, impacts in one sector have effects in other sectors. Exogenous changes affecting the demand for the traded good can impact the price of the non-traded good, and exogenous changes originating in the non-traded sector can affect the traded-good price and the exchange rate.[1] A multi-sectoral analysis allows one to examine the general equilibrium interactions, the determinants of real and nominal exchange rates, and the relationship between the exchange rate and the trade balance.

It should be noted that two factors that may be important in exchange rate determination are ignored in the analysis. First, while real exchange rate fluctuations are related to both terms-of-trade fluctuations and divergent movements in non-traded goods prices between countries, this chapter assumes that the export and import goods are identical and therefore abstracts from changes in the terms of trade (Chapter 12 examines the relationship between the exchange rate and the terms of trade). Second, the model is essentially a real model of the real exchange rate and abstracts from monetary factors. While movements in the real exchange rate can be caused by monetary shocks when prices are sticky, the impact of monetary shocks on the real exchange rate dissipates over the longer term. The current-period analysis can be taken to apply to a horizon where goods prices are flexible.

2. THE BASIC SETUP

A representative agent maximizes lifetime utility subject to an intertemporal budget constraint (the terms consumers, domestic residents, and agent are used interchangeably).[2] There are two periods: the current period, denoted as t, and the future period, denoted t+1. There is perfect foresight of future variables. There are two goods: a non-traded good, denoted as N and a traded good, denoted as T. The domestic traded good is identical to the foreign traded good, so that with competition and zero tariffs and transport costs, the law of one price condition holds (in each period):

$$P_{t+j}^{T} = s_{t+j}\ P_{t+j}^{T*}\ for\ j = 0, 1,$$

where P^T is the domestic price of the traded good, P^{T*} is the foreign price of the traded good (all foreign variables are denoted with a *), and s is the exchange rate measured as the foreign currency price of domestic currency. An increase in s is a depreciation of the domestic currency. Sectoral output is exogenous.[3] For simplicity, the model abstracts from investment spending, government spending, and taxes. The domestic economy is assumed to be a small economy, so that all foreign variables are exogenous.

This chapter develops a real model, assuming that monetary neutrality holds. The exchange rate is flexible, and the central bank is following a zero-inflation policy. The price level (the consumer price index), denoted as P, is measured as

$$P = 0.5\ P^N + 0.5\ P^T,$$

where the equal weights are based on an assumption that consumers tend to spend an equivalent amount on each good. The exogenous foreign price level P* is also measured with equal weights. With zero inflation in the domestic economy, any increase in the equilibrium domestic price of the non-traded good must be matched by an equivalent decrease in the price of the traded good (and vice versa). And the real exchange rate, denoted as q,

$$q = \frac{s\ P^*}{P},$$

will move together with the nominal exchange rate when the domestic and foreign inflation rates both equal zero.

Lifetime Utility and Household Budget Constraints

Utility depends on consumption (denoted c) of traded and non-traded goods, with lifetime utility, denoted as V, represented as

$$V = u\left(c_t^T\right) + u\left(c_t^N\right) + \frac{u\left(c_{t+1}^T\right) + u\left(c_{t+1}^N\right)}{1+\gamma},$$

where the fixed parameter γ denotes the marginal rate of time preference.

The current-period budget constraint, with taxes equal to zero, is[4]

$$P_t^T y_t^T + P_t^N y_t^N = P_t^T c_t^T + P_t^N c_t^N + s_t J_t.$$

The left-hand side represents nominal income, with current-period production denoted as y_t^T and y_t^N. The right-hand side equals, in nominal terms, consumer spending plus the net acquisition of foreign assets in the current period (the model abstracts from domestic assets).[5] The variable J measures the agent's holding of net foreign assets (the agent starts the current period with zero net foreign assets). When J_t is positive, the agent has acquired foreign bonds in the current period; when J_t is negative, the agent has acquired a foreign loan in the current period. Note that the variable c_t^T measures aggregate traded-good consumption, which can be purchased from domestic firms at P_t^T or imported at $s_t P_t^{T*}$. With the law of one price condition, these prices are the same. And traded-good firms in the domestic economy can sell the good domestically or export the good to the foreign economy. The constraint can be written in real terms by dividing through by the price of the traded good:

$$y_t^T + z_t y_t^N = c_t^T + z_t c_t^N + \frac{J_t}{P_t^{T*}},$$

where the variable z denotes the relative price of the non-traded good, $\frac{P^N}{P^T}$, and the law of one price condition has been used.

The period t+1 constraint, in nominal terms, is

$$P_{t+1}^T y_{t+1}^T + P_{t+1}^N y_{t+1}^N + \left(1+i_t^*\right) s_{t+1} J_t = P_{t+1}^T c_{t+1}^T + P_{t+1}^N c_{t+1}^N.$$

The agent obtains nominal income from the production of the traded and non-traded goods. In addition, there may be foreign interest earnings or foreign loan payments from the period t foreign bond holdings or foreign loans. For simplicity, the same foreign nominal interest rate i_t^* applies to both foreign bonds and foreign loans. Dividing by P_{t+1}^T yields

$$y_{t+1}^T + z_{t+1} y_{t+1}^N + \frac{\left(1+i_t^*\right) J_t}{P_{t+1}^{T*}} = c_{t+1}^T + z_{t+1} c_{t+1}^N,$$

where the law of one price condition has again been used.

The intertemporal constraint merges the current and future budget constraints. Substituting one equation into the other and rearranging yields

$$y_t^T + z_t\, y_t^N + \frac{y_{t+1}^T + z_{t+1}\, y_{t+1}^N}{\left(1 + r_t^{*T}\right)} = c_t^T + z_t\, c_t^N + \frac{c_{t+1}^T + z_{t+1}\, c_{t+1}^N}{\left(1 + r_t^{*T}\right)},$$

where the foreign real interest rate, r_t^{*T} is measured as[6]

$$1 + r_t^{*T} = \frac{\left(1 + i_t^*\right) P_t^{T*}}{P_{t+1}^{T*}}.$$

While there are different measures of real return, this real interest rate is measured in terms of the traded good. The intertemporal constraint implies that, over the lifetime, the present value of aggregate lifetime consumption equals the present value of aggregate lifetime real income.

Equilibrium Conditions and the Trade Balance

The current-period equilibrium condition in the market for the non-traded good is[7]

$$y_t^N = c_t^N.$$

Current-period production (supply) of the non-traded good must equal current-period consumption (demand) of the non-traded good (and likewise in the future period). The relative price of the non-traded good adjusts to maintain the equality of supply and demand.

Net exports (the trade balance) in period t, denoted as NX_t, equal production of the traded good less total spending on the traded good by domestic consumers (with all variables measured in terms of the traded good):

$$NX_t = y_t^T - c_t^T.$$

As consumers begin the current period with zero foreign assets and zero foreign debt, the current account balance is equal to net exports in the current period.[8] If the domestic economy produces more units of the traded good than are purchased by domestic consumers, the remaining traded goods are exported and generate a current-period surplus on both the current account and the trade account.

When the current-period equilibrium condition for the non-traded sector is merged with the equation for the current-period household budget constraint, one obtains the current-period constraint on the economy:

$$y_t^T - c_t^T = \frac{J_t}{P_t^{T*}}.$$

Of course, the left-hand side equals net exports. When domestic production of the traded good exceeds domestic consumption, the surplus of the traded good is exported and leads to an accumulation of the foreign bond by domestic residents (J_t is positive).[9] The balance of trade surplus equals private saving, with the magnitude of the surplus equal to the net accumulation of foreign bonds (in real terms). And if net exports are negative, private saving and J_t are negative, meaning that domestic residents have received a foreign loan.

Merging the intertemporal constraint with the non-traded goods equilibrium conditions for both periods,

$$y_t^N = c_t^N,$$

$$y_{t+1}^N = c_{t+1}^N,$$

yields the following equation:

$$c_{t+1}^T = y_{t+1}^T + \left(1 + r_t^{*T}\right)\left[y_t^T - c_t^T\right], \; or$$

$$c_t^T + \frac{c_{t+1}^T}{\left(1 + r_t^{*T}\right)} = y_t^T + \frac{y_{t+1}^T}{\left(1 + r_t^{*T}\right)}.$$

The present value of lifetime traded-good consumption equals the present value of the lifetime traded-good production. This constraint implies that a balance of trade surplus in the current period ($y_t^T > c_t^T$) must be matched, given the assumption of zero net foreign assets at the start of period t, with a balance of trade deficit in the future period ($c_{t+1}^T > y_{t+1}^T$). The more general case, where initial net foreign assets do not equal zero, is discussed in an appendix in Chapter 5 and in Chapter 15.

3. CONSUMPTION RELATIONSHIPS AND EQUILIBRIUM CONDITIONS

The representative agent maximizes lifetime utility subject to the intertemporal constraint. From the maximization process, there are three equations that represent the agent's behavior, one *intertemporal* condition and two *intra-temporal* (within-period) conditions.

The Euler Equation for Traded-Good Consumption

The consumer chooses consumption of the traded good such that the Euler equation holds:

$$u'\left(c_t^T\right) = \frac{\left(1 + r_t^{*T}\right)}{1 + \gamma} \, u'\left(c_{t+1}^T\right).$$

As discussed extensively in the one-good models in Chapters 4–9, the Euler equation is a marginal cost- (discounted) marginal benefit condition. The same underlying logic holds in this two-sector model. If the agent decreases current traded-good consumption by 1 unit, the agent experiences a decrease in current-period utility and the marginal cost is $u'\left(c_t^T\right)$. With the funds available from the decrease in traded-good consumption, the agent purchases foreign bonds in the current period t and the foreign bond pays off $(1+r_t^{*T})$ in real terms in the future period t+1. When those foreign bonds are cashed in and the funds are spent, there is a discounted gain in future utility from the additional future traded-good consumption. This is the (discounted) marginal benefit. The agent always ensures that the Euler equation for the traded good holds. And if r_t^{*T} equals γ, the agent smooths consumption of the traded good over time.

Note that while consumers can smooth traded-good consumption, consumers may not be able to smooth non-traded consumption. Non-traded consumption in any period is constrained by the magnitude of non-traded production in that period, and current and future production may not be equal.

Intra-Temporal Consumption Allocation

In the current period, the agent chooses consumption of the two goods: traded and non-traded. Consumers allocate their expenditure to maximize lifetime utility. As in the microeconomic theory of demand, consumers allocate within-period consumption based on the condition that the ratio of marginal utilities equals the relative price:

$$\frac{u'\left(c_t^N\right)}{u'\left(c_t^T\right)} = \frac{P_t^N}{P_t^T}.$$

Equivalently, the agent allocates consumption such that the marginal utility per dollar of expenditure on each good is equalized. The ratio of marginal utilities is called the marginal rate of substitution (MRS). This condition implies that a decrease in the relative price of the non-traded good results in a reallocation of consumer demand toward the relatively cheaper non-traded good. With any change in the relative price, there is a reallocation and thus induced changes in the marginal utilities, such that the intra-temporal condition holds as an equality.[10]

This intra-temporal condition is the curve denoted as MRS in Figure 14.1. As c_t^N increases, the marginal utility of non-traded consumption falls. Marginal utility is diminishing, which generates the downward-sloping MRS curve. With c_t^T held fixed along any given marginal rate of substitution curve, any increase in c_t^N results in a decrease in the marginal utility of the non-traded good and a decrease in the MRS. And when c_t^T changes, the curve shifts.[11] An increase in c_t^T, for example, decreases $u'\left(c_t^T\right)$ and results in a higher marginal rate of substitution at each level of c_t^N. The current-period MRS curve shifts up with an increase in current-period consumption of the traded good.

Equilibrium in the Current-Period Market for the Non-Traded Good

Current-period equilibrium in the market for the non-traded good is depicted in Figure 14.1. Production of the non-traded good is exogenous, shown as the vertical line denoted as y_t^N. The downward sloping curve represents the MRS. The relative price of the non-traded good adjusts to keep demand equal to supply in the domestic market for the non-traded good. At the equilibrium relative price, consumers are willing to buy the quantity of the non-traded good produced in the current period.

Figure 14.1: Market for the non-traded good

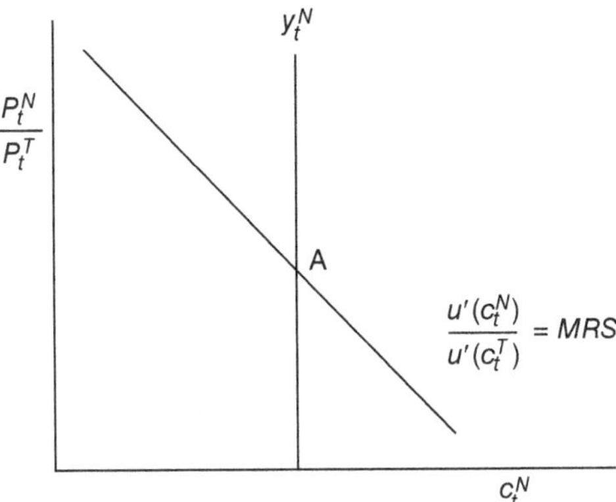

To maximize lifetime utility, consumers ensure that current-period spending is allocated between the two goods such that the intra-temporal condition holds. This implies that consumption of the non-traded good is always at a point on the MRS curve, where the ratio of marginal utilities equals the relative price ratio. When using numerical examples, it is convenient to assume that there are logarithmic utility functions. In this case, each marginal utility equals the inverse of consumption, and the intra-temporal condition simplifies to the "equal expenditure condition":

$$\frac{P_t^N}{P_t^T} = \frac{u'\left(c_t^N\right)}{u'\left(c_t^T\right)} = \frac{\dfrac{1}{c_t^N}}{\dfrac{1}{c_t^T}} \rightarrow P_t^N c_t^N = P_t^T c_t^T.$$

The last equation is the equal expenditure condition. Given the current-period prices of the two goods, consumers equalize the magnitude of spending on each good. For example, if total spending in the current period is \$100, then \$50 is spent on the non-traded good and \$50 is spent on the traded good. Given the assumptions, this equal expenditure on each good is the condition that results in the maximization of lifetime utility. And using the equal expenditure condition, it is straightforward to explain how changes in the current-period relative price or in lifetime real income affect current-period spending on the two goods. For example, if the current-period relative price of the non-traded good increases, the ratio of non-traded consumption to traded-good consumption must decrease in the current period. Of course, this result is consistent with the ratio of marginal utilities being equal to the relative price.

Two Interesting Results

With exogenous increases in traded or non-traded production, lifetime real income increases and the initial effect is an increase in demand for all four goods: c_t^T, c_t^N, c_{t+1}^T, and c_{t+1}^N. All goods are normal goods. But consumption also depends on the prices of the traded and non-traded goods. In this model, there are two interesting results.

(1) When traded-good production increases, consumption of the traded good increases, but consumption of the non-traded good does not change.

(2) When non-traded production increases, consumption of the non-traded good increases, but consumption of the traded good does not change.

Consider result (1). With any increase in traded-good production, the associated increase in lifetime real income increases the demand for both traded and non-traded goods. But with a fixed supply of the non-traded good, the excess demand for the non-traded good results in an increase in the relative price of the non-traded good. As the price of the non-traded good rises and the price of the traded good falls, consumers reallocate expenditure by increasing spending on the traded good and decreasing spending on the non-traded good. In the new equilibrium, traded-good consumption is higher and non-traded consumption is unchanged. While the increase in lifetime real income increases desired non-traded consumption, this change is offset exactly by the increase in the relative price of the non-traded good.

Recall the condition derived from the intertemporal constraint and the non-traded good equilibrium conditions:

$$c_t^T + \frac{c_{t+1}^T}{\left(1+r_t^{*T}\right)} = y_t^T + \frac{y_{t+1}^T}{\left(1+r_t^{*T}\right)}.$$

This condition and the Euler equation for traded-good consumption together imply that, when the foreign real interest rate and the marginal rate of time preference both equal zero so that consumption smoothing holds, traded-good consumption is determined as follows:

$$c_t^T = \frac{y_t^T + y_{t+1}^T}{2}.$$

In equilibrium, current-period traded-good consumption is determined strictly by current and future traded-good production.

With result (2), an increase in non-traded production increases lifetime real income and increases desired spending on both traded and non-traded goods. But with any given increase in supply of the non-traded good, consumers will not initially want to purchase all of the extra non-traded production because they want to increase spending on the traded good as well. There is therefore an excess supply of the non-traded good, resulting in a decrease in the relative price of the non-traded good. As consumers reallocate expenditure in response to the relative price change, they increase desired spending on the non-traded good and decrease it on the traded good. In the new equilibrium, traded-good consumption is unchanged and the increase in non-traded consumption is equal to the increase in non-traded production.

These results are indeed interesting, and help to simplify the analysis of exogenous changes. But one must understand that the results are based on the underlying transactions and attempted transactions outlined in the paragraphs above.

4. EXOGENOUS CHANGES IN SECTORAL OUTPUT

Any exogenous change in sectoral output induces changes in lifetime real income, consumption, the relative price of the non-traded good, and the exchange rate, and may induce changes in net exports. It is assumed that the foreign real interest rate and the marginal rate of time preference both equal zero, so that there is consumption smoothing of the traded good. The trade balance is initially assumed to equal zero. And the central bank is following a fixed price level policy, so that the prices of traded and non-traded goods must always move in opposite directions. With the fixed domestic price level, and an exogenously fixed foreign price level, real and nominal exchange rates will move together in response to exogenous changes in sectoral output.

Temporary Increase in Traded-Good Production

Suppose there is an exogenous increase in current-period production of the traded good y_t^T, but future traded-good production y_{t+1}^T is unchanged (and other exogenous variables, such as current and future production of the non-traded good, are unchanged). This exogenous change is called a temporary increase in traded-good production (or output). Lifetime real income increases, resulting in an increase in demand for both traded and non-traded goods. And given that the exogenous increase in production is temporary, consumers increase private saving to be able to smooth traded-good consumption.

The induced increase in current-period consumption of the traded good shifts the MRS curve to the right from MRS_0 to MRS_1 in Figure 14.2, implying an increase in demand for the non-traded good. With production of the non-traded good unchanged, there is an excess demand for the non-traded good at point B. The current-period relative price of the non-traded good increases such that the new equilibrium is at point C. With the central bank following a fixed price level policy, there is an increase in the current-period price of the non-traded good and a decrease in the current-period price of the traded good.

In terms of consumption, there are two effects. The increase in lifetime real income causes increases in demand for both goods, traded and non-traded. And as the relative price of the non-traded good increases, there is a reallocation of consumer spending that results in a decrease in non-traded consumption and an increase in traded consumption. There is both an income effect, due to the increase in lifetime real income, and a relative price effect. The increase in lifetime real income increases the demand for the non-traded good, but the rise in the relative price of the non-traded good results in an exactly offsetting decrease in the quantity demanded of the non-traded good. In total, traded consumption increases and non-traded consumption is unchanged.

Using the equal expenditure condition shown in Figure 14.3, along with the fixed price level policy of the central bank, one can calculate the percentage changes in the relevant variables. If the exogenous temporary increase in traded-good production results in a 10 per cent increase in current-period traded good consumption, then the current-period price of the non-traded good increases by 5 per cent and the current-period price of the traded good decreases by 5 per cent. These movements are summarized by the lengths and directions of the arrows in Figure 14.3.

Figure 14.2: Upward shift in the MRS curve

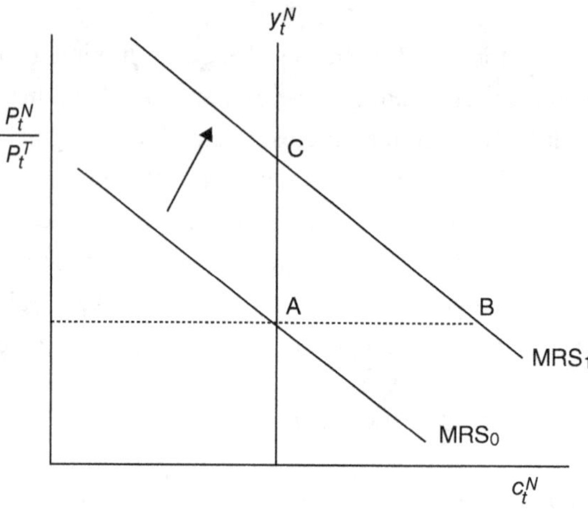

Figure 14.3: Equal expenditure condition

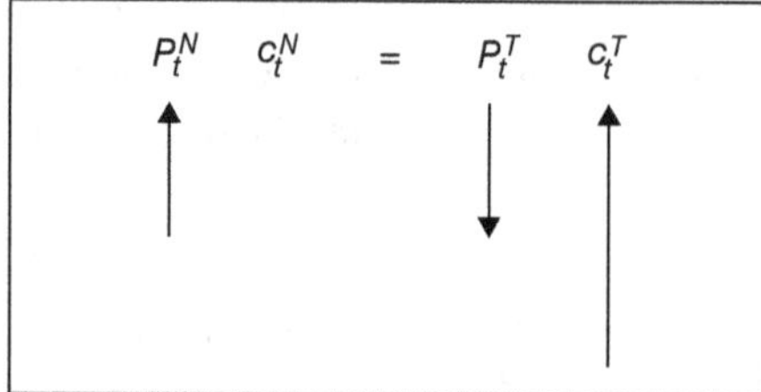

Given that the exogenous change in traded production is temporary, consumers increase both current-period traded-good consumption and current-period saving, with the latter representing purchases of foreign bonds. Consumers want to increase foreign bond holdings to be able to increase future traded-good consumption and therefore smooth traded-good consumption. In terms of net exports,

$$NX_t = y_t^T - c_t^T = \frac{J_t}{P_t^{*T}},$$

the increase in current-period production of the traded good exceeds the increase in current-period consumption of the traded good. Both net exports and the real magnitude of the foreign bond purchases increase. With the trade balance initially equal to zero, there is now a trade balance surplus. The temporary increase in traded-good output increases current-period net exports.

With the central bank acting to hold the price level fixed, the current-period traded-good price decreases. In terms of the law of one price condition for the traded good (along with a fixed foreign price of the traded good),

$$P_t^T = s_t \, P_t^{*T},$$

the decrease in the domestic traded-good price results in an appreciation of the domestic currency (a decrease in s_t). The lower domestic traded-good price, for a given exchange rate, indicates the domestic traded good is cheaper, and this inequality results in an increase in demand for the domestic currency to purchase the cheaper domestic traded good (with no demand for the foreign currency, as the foreign traded good is overpriced). There is an appreciation of the domestic currency until the law of one price for the traded good holds as an equality. The change in the exchange rate results in domestic and foreign producers remaining competitive in international goods markets.

It is interesting to note that, in this case of a temporary increase in traded-good output, there is both a current-period increase in the trade balance and a current-period appreciation of the domestic currency.

Permanent Increase in Traded-Good Production

With a permanent increase, both current and future production of the traded good increase by the same amount. Lifetime real income increases, and consumers do not need to increase current-period saving to smooth traded-good consumption. The MRS curve shifts to the right, the current-period price of the non-traded good increases, and the current-period price of the traded good decreases (with the consumer price index unchanged). The appearance of the diagram is the same as Figure 14.2, though the larger increase in current-period traded-good consumption results in a larger rightward shift of the MRS curve. In the new equilibrium, the increase in lifetime real income and the increase in the current-period relative price of the non-traded good together have effects that result in an increase in current-period consumption of the traded good and no change in the current-period consumption of the non-traded good.

The lower traded-good price implies that the current-period exchange rate variable s_t decreases, meaning that the domestic currency appreciates. The increase in current-period traded-good production is matched by an equivalent increase in current-period traded-good consumption, and net exports are unchanged. The domestic currency appreciates, and the trade balance is unaffected.

Increase in "Expected" Future Production of the Traded Good

Any exogenous increases in future output increase lifetime real income and cause changes in the desired levels of current-period variables. Suppose there is an exogenous increase in future production of the traded good, with current-period traded-good production unchanged and both current and future non-traded production held fixed. Consumers expect, or with perfect foresight know, that this increase in traded-good production will occur in period t+1, and therefore revise upward their level of lifetime real income. Consumers initially increase their demands for all goods and take actions to ensure that they smooth consumption of the traded good.

With an increase in current-period traded-good consumption, the MRS curve shifts to the right. The diagram is again the same as Figure 14.2. There is an excess demand for the current-period non-traded good at point B, resulting in an increase in the price of the non-traded good and a decrease in the price of the traded good (as the central bank ensures that the consumer price index remains unchanged). The price changes induce consumers to reallocate within-period spending toward the relatively cheaper traded good. In the new equilibrium, current-period consumption of the traded good is higher and current-period consumption of the non-traded good is unchanged. In terms of the equal expenditure condition, the movements are as shown in Figure 14.3.

With no change in current-period production and real income, consumers need to obtain a foreign loan to increase current-period spending on the traded good. And indeed, with current traded-good production unchanged, all additional purchases of the traded good must be imported. If future production of the traded good is "expected" to increase by 20 units, the foreign loan is equivalent to 10 units of the traded good and current-period consumption of the traded good increases by those 10 units. In the new equilibrium in the current period, there is a balance of trade deficit. And of course, as with all exogenous increases in traded-good production, the lifetime utility of consumers increases.[12]

In terms of the law of one price condition, the lower equilibrium domestic traded-good price, with a fixed foreign traded-good price, implies that the domestic currency appreciates in the current period. The exchange rate variable s_t decreases. In the case of an exogenous future increase in traded-good production, the induced changes in the current period are that the trade balance worsens and the domestic currency appreciates.

Note that, in period t+1, consumers experience the increase in real income associated with the increase in traded-good production of 20 units. Consumers pay back the foreign loan of 10 units and increase consumption of the traded good by 10 units. Consumers smooth consumption of the traded good.

Permanent Increase in Production of the Non-Traded Good

Suppose there is a permanent increase in non-traded production, meaning that both current and future non-traded production increase by the same amount (with traded-good production held fixed). With a permanent increase, one can focus the discussion on the current period. In Figure 14.4, the vertical line representing current-period production of the non-traded good shifts to the right. If y_t^N increases by 20 units, consumers will initially want to spend the associated increase in real income on both goods. But if non-traded supply increases by 20 units and the demand for the non-traded good increases by 10 units, there is excess supply of the non-traded good. The relative price of the non-traded good falls, and this relative price change induces consumers to reallocate this period's spending toward the non-traded good. In the new equilibrium, consumption of the non-traded good increases by 20 units, so that supply equals demand at point C, and consumption of the traded good is unchanged (note that because c_t^T is unchanged, the MRS curve does not shift).

In terms of net exports in the current period,

$$NX_t = y_t^T - c_t^T,$$

current-period production of the traded good is fixed, and current-period consumption of the traded good is unchanged. There is no effect on net exports. But as the current-period price of the non-traded good decreases and the current-period price of the traded good increases, the law of one

Figure 14.4: Increase in non-traded production

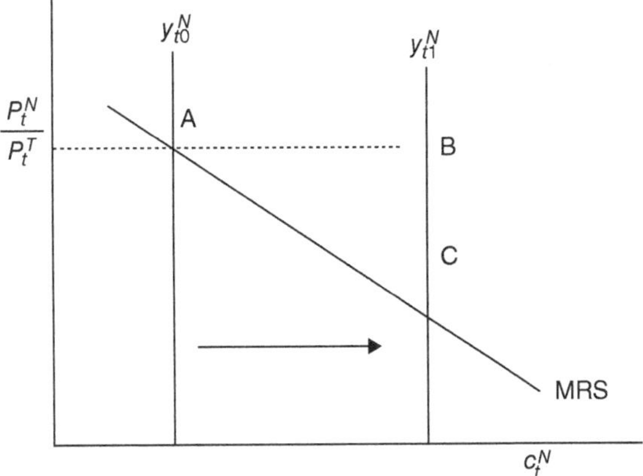

price condition for the traded good indicates that the current-period exchange rate, denoted as s_t, increases. The permanent increase in non-traded production causes a depreciation of the domestic currency in the current period. With the increase in production and the increase in the present value of lifetime real income, the lifetime utility of consumers increases.

Sectoral Output Changes, the Exchange Rate, and Net Exports

In this dynamic model, there is no simple relationship between current-period movements in the exchange rate and net exports. While a temporary increase in traded-good output, a future increase in traded-good output, and a permanent increase in traded-good output all generate an appreciation of the domestic currency in the current period, these changes induce current-period net exports, respectively, to increase, decrease, or remain unchanged. And a permanent increase in non-traded production induces a depreciation of the domestic currency, but there is no effect on net exports. In a dynamic model, where consumers choose saving and consumption to maximize lifetime utility, there is no simple relationship between movements in the exchange rate and movements in net exports.

5. OTHER EXOGENOUS CHANGES

Monetary Policy

In the analysis, central bank policy ensured that the price level (the consumer price index) remained fixed. Suppose, instead, that monetary policy involves exogenous money supply changes. An increase in the money supply creates a situation where consumers have excess cash balances. As consumers attempt to spend the excess cash balances with a fixed supply of goods, there are increases in the prices of traded and non-traded goods and a depreciation of the domestic currency. But the money supply change has no effect on the relative price of the non-traded good, the real exchange rate, or net exports.[13]

Foreign Traded-Good Prices

Suppose there is a permanent decrease in the foreign traded-good price (hold domestic sectoral output and the foreign real interest rate fixed). With no effect on lifetime real income, and no change in the foreign real interest rate, consumption, the domestic relative price ratio, and net exports are unaffected. The lower foreign traded-good price implies that the domestic traded good, at the initial exchange rate, is overpriced. As residents demand foreign currency to purchase the foreign traded good, the domestic currency depreciates until the law of one price for the traded good holds as an equality. With an unchanged domestic relative price ratio, and the central bank following the fixed price level policy, there is no effect on the domestic price of the traded good. A decrease in the current-period foreign price of the traded good results in a current-period depreciation of the domestic currency, with no change in the current-period domestic price of the traded good.

Relative Demand Shifts

With a more general utility function, the intra-temporal condition is altered (an appendix provides details):

$$\frac{u'\left(c_t^N\right)}{u'\left(c_t^T\right)} = \frac{\alpha\, c_t^T}{c_t^N} \rightarrow P_t^N c_t^N = \alpha\, P_t^T c_t^T,$$

where α is a parameter in the utility function (in the previous analysis, α was equal to 1). If α equals 1.5, for example, the utility-maximizing allocation of current-period expenditure (in nominal terms) is 60 per cent on the non-traded good and 40 per cent on the traded good. This specification permits exogenous changes in tastes that generate relative demand shifts.

Suppose an exogenous change in tastes results in α increasing from 1.5 to 2. The diagram for the current-period relative price is the same as Figure 14.2, and the equilibrium movements in the variables are depicted in Figure 14.5. Given current-period expenditure and prices, the exogenous change implies that consumers want to spend less on the traded good and more on the non-traded good. The MRS curve shifts up to the right, and the equilibrium relative price of the non-traded good increases. With fixed production, consumption of the non-traded good does not change. And given the assumptions, traded-good consumption does not change. While the change in tastes generates a desire to alter spending patterns, the increase in the relative price of the non-traded good results in a situation where consumers are content to undertake the same real purchases as before the change. In effect, there are two offsetting effects on demand. And with the decrease in the equilibrium domestic traded-good price, the domestic currency appreciates. In equilibrium, the exogenous change in tastes affects prices and the exchange rate but has no effect on consumption or net exports.

Figure 14.5: Shift in relative demand

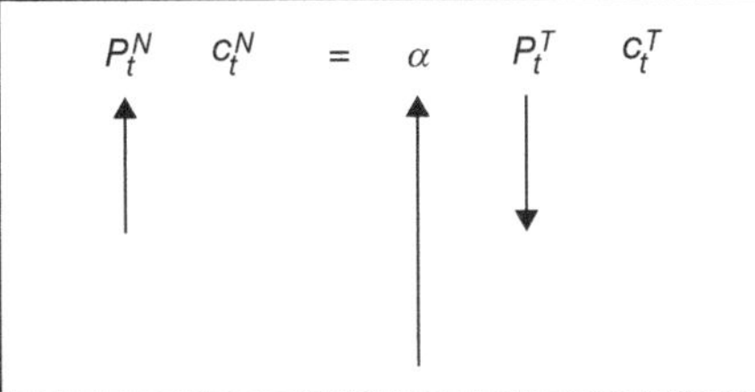

6. SECTORAL PRODUCTION IN CANADA

The statistical agencies in the United States, Canada, and Mexico have developed the North American Industry Classification System (NAICS). This framework decomposes the economy into twenty sectors. For the Canadian economy, one approach is to assign fourteen sectors within the NAICS to the non-traded sector and six sectors to the traded sector (an appendix to Chapter 10 discusses measurement issues related to sectoral decomposition). The non-traded sector consists of service sectors and the construction sector, whereas the traded sector consists of the manufacturing sector, the resource sector, and a few other sectors.

Figure 14.6 depicts traded and non-traded production between 1997 and 2017, with quarterly data measured at annual rates in billions of chained (2007) dollars.[14] Production in the non-traded sector ranges from 60 per cent to 65 per cent of the aggregate economy. In addition, the traded sector tends to be more volatile, with larger percentage changes in production (additional evidence on volatility is provided in Chapter 10, as well in the following section of this chapter). The dynamic model with a non-traded good predicts that these fluctuations in traded-good production cause movements in the exchange rate and net exports. An applied exercise in Data Analytics examines the validity of these relationships. Of course, factors such as changes in government spending and changes in the foreign real interest rate may also be factors in the determination of net exports and the exchange rate.[15]

7. A NOTE ON MULTI-SECTORAL OPEN ECONOMY MACROECONOMICS

It may be beneficial to decompose the economy into more than two sectors. Of course, the standard three-sector model is a widely used framework that yielded significant insights (see Chapter 10 and the academic literature cited therein). Other forms of disaggregation may also be useful.[16] In a five-sector framework, for example, one could include two sectors of non-traded goods, representing the service and construction sectors, and three sectors representing manufacturing, resources, and a composite sector that encompasses other sectors. This section provides further information on sectoral production in Canada within this five-sector framework.

The additional disaggregation yields information that a two-sector framework does not provide. In particular, the difference in the relative volatility of services and construction is evident in Figure 14.7. While the annual growth rate of production in the service sector is relatively smooth,

Figure 14.6: Traded and non-traded production

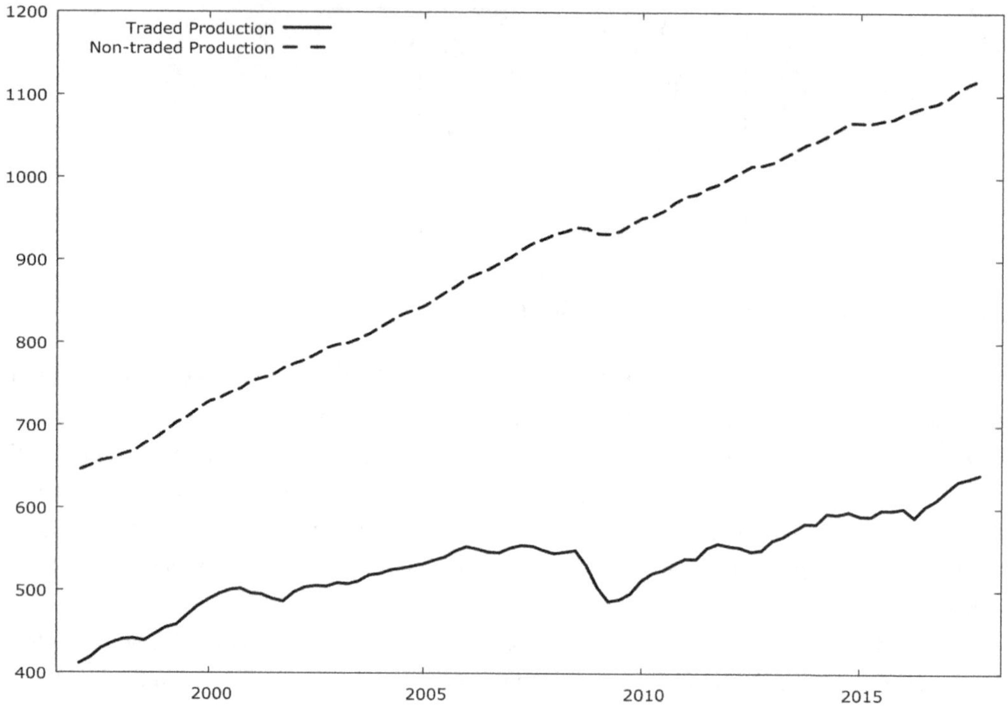

Data source: Statistics Canada, with the author's calculations

the growth rate in the construction sector has considerable volatility. The correlation coefficient between growth rates is 0.33, and the standard deviation of the growth rate in construction is about four times larger. The negative growth rate of production in the construction sector in the 2008–2009 recession is not surprising. But it is interesting that the construction sector contracted significantly in 2015, a time when the aggregate economy was not in a major downturn.

Figure 14.8 depicts annual growth rates in the resource and manufacturing sectors. These growth rates have tended to move together, with a correlation coefficient of 0.61. Both sectors are volatile, with standard deviations of growth rates about five times larger than in the service sector.[17] And each sector experienced periods of negative growth at times other than the Great Recession. For example, the resource sector experienced downturns in 2012 and 2015–2016 and the growth rate in manufacturing was often negative between 2002 and 2008 (an applied exercise in Data Analytics investigates measures of cyclical sectoral production).

Dynamic models with multiple sectors have been applied beneficially to various topics in international macroeconomics, including analyses of trade imbalances, the quantity of international trade (including the collapse in trade during the Great Recession), investment spending, the terms of trade, structural change, and the business cycle.[18] The models often incorporate sectoral capital and labor, with endogenous sectoral production. Some international, multi-sectoral models are within the tradition of the real business cycle (RBC) approach,[19] while others fall within the dynamic stochastic general equilibrium (DSGE) framework that encompasses RBC models

Figure 14.7: Growth rates: Services, construction

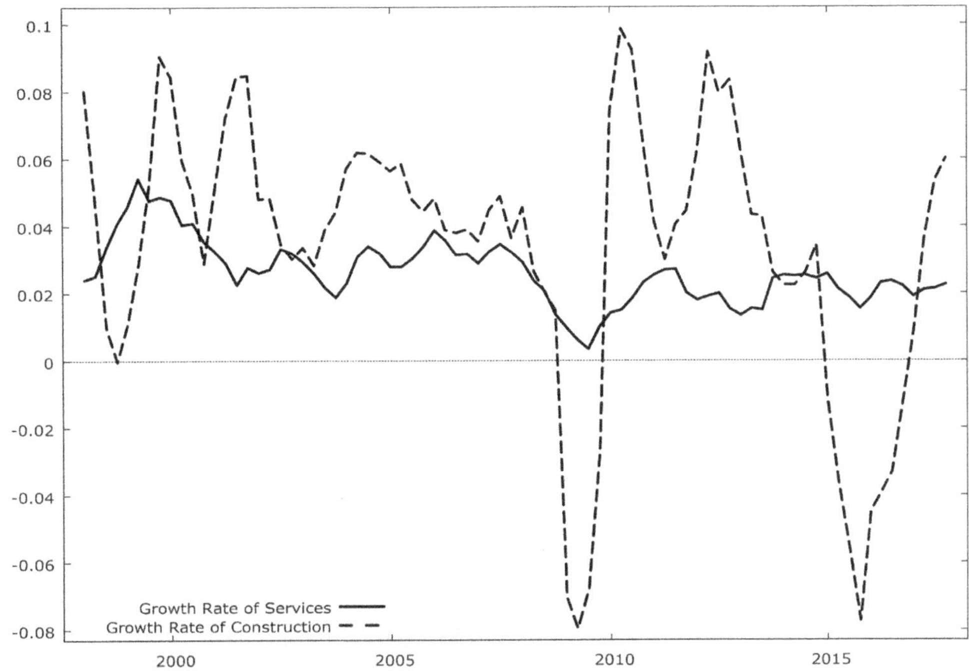

Data source: Statistics Canada

Figure 14.8: Growth rates: Resource, manufacturing

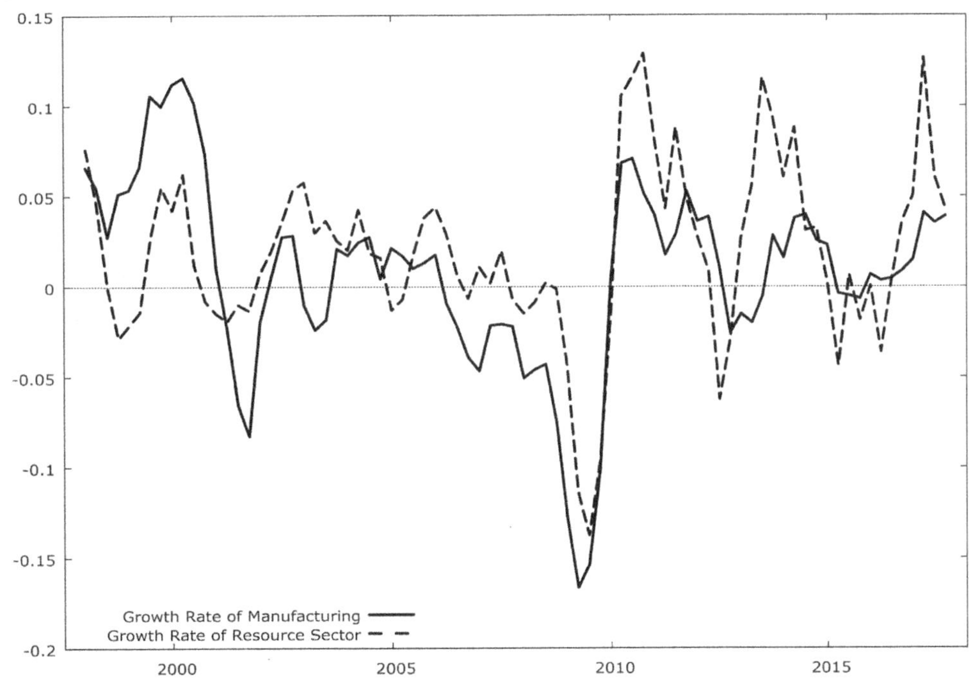

Data source: Statistics Canada

and various dynamic models with sticky prices or wages.[20] While empirical research based on dynamic, multi-sectoral models must confront difficult measurement issues related to sectoral decomposition and other matters,[21] further high-quality research in this framework is capable of providing significant improvement in understanding the economy.

8. CONCLUSION

This chapter examined a dynamic model with a non-traded good to analyze the determinants of the exchange rate, consumption, the relative price of the non-traded good, and net exports.[22] This two-sector model provided significant insights, including that related to the relationship between the exchange rate and net exports. Indeed, dynamic, multi-sectoral models are now an integral component in the toolkit of international macroeconomists.

PRACTICE QUESTIONS

1. Fill in the blanks. Use the dynamic model with a non-traded good. Assume that the exchange rate is flexible, and the central bank is acting to hold the price level fixed.

   (a) A temporary increase in production of the traded good causes consumption of the traded good to increase, and results in _____ in the current-period price of the non-traded good and _____ of the domestic currency (relative to the foreign currency).

   (b) A permanent increase in production of the non-traded good causes _____ of the domestic currency in the current period.

   (c) A temporary increase in output of the traded good causes _____ in net exports and _____ of the domestic currency (relative to the foreign currency) in the current period.

   (d) A future increase in output of the traded good causes the price of the non-traded good to _____ and the domestic currency to _____ in the current period.

   (e) A future increase in output of the traded good leaves current-period consumption of the non-traded good unchanged. The increase in lifetime income increases desired spending on the non-traded good, but this effect is offset by the decrease in desired spending caused by the _____ in the current-period _____.

2. Using the dynamic model with a non-traded good (with a flexible exchange rate and a fixed price level), explain how a temporary increase in traded-good production affects the price of the non-traded good, the exchange rate, and net exports in the current period. Use equations and the diagram representing equilibrium in the market for the non-traded good.

3. Use the dynamic model with a non-traded good. Assume the exchange rate is flexible and the central bank is acting to hold the price level fixed. Using the diagram and equations, explain how a permanent increase in output of the non-traded good affects the price of the non-traded good, the exchange rate, consumption (of each good), and net exports.

4. (a) An increase in production of the non-traded good causes the domestic currency to depreciate in the current period. Outline the mechanisms through which this change in the non-traded sector affects the exchange rate.

   (b) Provide an example of an exogenous change that causes both an increase in net exports and an appreciation of the domestic currency. Explain.

   (c) Explain how a permanent increase in output of the traded good affects the relative price of the non-traded good, consumption of the non-traded good, and the exchange rate in the current period. Use the diagram and equations. Assume that the central bank is holding the price level fixed.

   (d) With a permanent increase in output of the traded good, the current-period price of the non-traded good rises and the current-period price of the traded good falls. Using the equal expenditure condition, explain how consumption of the non-traded good is affected in the current period.

DATA ANALYTICS

1. (a) Collect monthly data on "goods" and "services" production since January 2014, available in CANSIM Table 36100434. Convert the data to quarterly data and create time-series plots of the levels and growth rates of these series. Comment.

   (b) Suppose traded-good output is measured by the production of goods. Assume that the permanent component of traded-good output increases steadily by 0.50 per cent per quarter. Calculate temporary traded-good output as the difference between traded-good output and permanent traded-good output. Plot temporary traded-good output and comment on the movements over time.

   (c) Collect quarterly data on exports and imports since 2014, available in CANSIM Table 36100104. Create a time-series plot of net exports. To what extent can the movements in net exports be explained by temporary changes in traded-good production? Comment.

2. Access CANSIM Table 36100434. Collect production data for the construction, manufacturing, and resource sectors (the resource sector combines the "agriculture, forestry, fishing and hunting" and "mining, quarrying, and oil and gas extraction" sectors). Convert the monthly data to quarterly and take logarithms of all variables. Using an HP filter (discussed in Chapter 6), calculate cyclical components of production. Construct various plots, with any two cyclical variables on a given plot. Comment on the two most interesting plots.

APPENDIX A: THE REAL EXCHANGE RATE

For this appendix, the price level (the consumer price index), denoted as P, is measured as a geometric mean with equal weights:

$$P = P^{T\,0.5}\, P^{N\,0.5}.$$

The exogenous foreign consumer price index P* is measured similarly. The real exchange rate, denoted q, is a complex measure of the relative price of foreign to domestic goods:

$$q = \frac{sP^*}{P} = \frac{sP^{T*0.5}\,P^{N*0.5}}{P^{T\,0.5}\,P^{N\,0.5}}.$$

Using the law of one price for the traded good, this equation simplifies to

$$q = \left[\frac{sP^{*N}}{P^N}\right]^{0.5} = \left[\frac{P^T}{P^N}\,\frac{P^{N*}}{P^{T*}}\right]^{0.5}.$$

With all foreign prices assumed to equal 1, the inverse of the real exchange rate equals

$$\frac{1}{q} = \left[\frac{P^N}{P^T}\right]^{0.5}.$$

A real appreciation of the domestic currency (an increase in 1/q) is associated with an increase in the relative price of the non-traded good. Under a flexible exchange rate with a zero-inflation policy, the real appreciation means that there is an increase in P^N, a decrease in P^T, and a nominal appreciation of the domestic currency.

APPENDIX B: NOMINAL AND REAL INTEREST PARITY

The nominal interest rate parity condition is

$$\left(1+i_t\right) = \frac{\left(1+i_t^*\right) s_{t+1}}{s_t}.$$

Domestic bonds and foreign bonds are equally good investments, both earning the same percentage return in nominal terms. Real interest rates measure returns in terms of goods and can be measured in terms of different bundles of goods.

Real Interest Rates in Terms of Traded Goods

Domestic and foreign residents consume the same traded good. Define the domestic and foreign real interest rates, measured in terms of the traded good, denoted as r_t^T and r_t^{*T}, as

$$\left(1+r_t^T\right) = \frac{\left(1+i_t\right)P_t^T}{P_{t+1}^T},$$

$$\left(1+r_t^{*T}\right) = \frac{\left(1+i_t^*\right)P_t^{T*}}{P_{t+1}^{T*}}.$$

The nominal IRP condition, together with the law of one price conditions, implies that

$$r_t^T = r_t^{*T}.$$

The equilibrium domestic real interest rate, measured in terms of the traded good, equals the foreign real interest rate measured in terms of the traded good.

Real Interest Rates in Terms of Composite Goods

Domestic and foreign residents consume both the traded good and their own non-traded good, with the consumer price indices defined with equal weights. With real interest rates based on these aggregate price levels,

$$1+ r_t = \frac{\left(1+i_t\right)P_t}{P_{t+1}},$$

$$1+ r_t^* = \frac{\left(1+i_t^*\right)P_t^*}{P_{t+1}^*},$$

the following condition holds:

$$1+ r_t = \frac{\left(1+r_t^*\right)q_{t+1}}{q_t}.$$

This condition is the real interest rate parity condition, with the approximate version written as[23]

$$r_t = r_t^* + \frac{q_{t+1} - q_t}{q_t}.$$

The equilibrium domestic real interest rate equals the foreign real interest rate plus the percentage rate of real depreciation of the domestic currency. In general, the domestic real interest rate (based on this measure) need not equal the foreign real interest rate. But these real rates are equal if changes in the current-period real exchange rate are matched by equivalent changes in the future real exchange rate.[24]

APPENDIX C: A NOTE ON THE MODEL

Manipulation of the equations yields results useful in determining the effects of exogenous changes. The reduced-form equation for c_t^T and the current-period equilibrium condition for the non-traded good imply that the current-period relative price of the non-traded good (denoted as z_t) is

$$z_t = \frac{\dfrac{y_t^T + y_{t+1}^T}{2}}{y_t^N}.$$

The future relative price is

$$z_{t+1} = \frac{\dfrac{y_t^T + y_{t+1}^T}{2}}{y_{t+1}^N},$$

so that

$$\frac{z_t}{z_{t+1}} = \frac{y_{t+1}^N}{y_t^N},$$

assuming that, initially, y_t^N equals y_{t+1}^N. While it is always necessary to provide the economic explanation, these equations are useful in that they allow for a verification of the ultimate effect on endogenous variables.

APPENDIX D: ON RELAXING THE EQUAL EXPENDITURE CONDITION

Suppose the current-period utility functions are (with the exogenous parameter $\alpha > 0$)

$$u\left(c_t^T\right) = \ln c_t^T,$$

$$u\left(c_t^N\right) = \alpha \ln c_t^N.$$

The intra-temporal condition is

$$\frac{u'\left(c_t^N\right)}{u'\left(c_t^T\right)} = \frac{\alpha\, c_t^T}{c_t^N} = \frac{P_t^N}{P_t^T} \;\rightarrow\; P_t^N c_t^N = \alpha\, P_t^T c_t^T.$$

Using the definition of total expenditure in the current period, with the intra-temporal condition, the share of current-period expenditure on the traded good is

$$\frac{P_t^T\, c_t^T}{P_t^N\, c_t^N + P_t^T\, c_t^T} = \frac{1}{1+\alpha}.$$

If α equals 1.5, for example, 40 percent of current-period expenditure is spent on the traded good.

APPENDIX E: GOVERNMENT SPENDING AND TAXES

For convenience, this chapter abstracted from government spending and taxes. To incorporate fiscal policy, one needs to add current and future government spending to the lifetime utility function (and, for simplicity, assume that separability holds). In addition, one needs to include the government budget constraints and revise the various period and intertemporal constraints. The current-period government budget constraint, in nominal terms, is

$$P_t^T g_t^T + P_t^N g_t^N = T_t,$$

where it is assumed that government spending is financed by lump-sum taxes. The government budget is balanced in both periods. In real terms, the current and future constraints are

$$g_t^T + z_t\, g_t^N = \frac{T_t}{P_t^T},$$

$$g_{t+1}^T + z_{t+1}\, g_{t+1}^N = \frac{T_{t+1}}{P_{t+1}^T}.$$

Of course, government spending on the traded good is included in the equation for net exports:

$$NX_t = y_t^T - c_t^T - g_t^T.$$

In this more general model with government spending and taxes, the following results hold. Any balanced-budget decrease in government spending on the traded good has the same effects on net exports and the exchange rate as the corresponding increase in traded-good production. For example, a temporary decrease in government spending on the traded good (matched by a temporary tax cut) increases current-period consumption of the traded good and shifts the MRS curve to the right. The diagram is the same as Figure 14.2, except that the vertical line, now called the net supply of the non-traded good, represents current-period non-traded production less current-period government spending on the non-traded good. The price of the non-traded good rises, and the price of the traded good and the exchange rate fall (the domestic currency appreciates). There is an increase in net exports, as traded-good consumption rises by less than the fall in government purchases of the traded good. The surplus production is exported, and consumers accumulate foreign bonds to allow for the desired increase in future consumption of the traded good. Net exports increase even though the domestic currency appreciates.

Likewise, an exogenous permanent decrease in government spending on the non-traded good has the same effects as the permanent increase in production of the non-traded good. The diagram for a permanent decrease in government spending on the non-traded good is the same as Figure

14.4, except that the vertical line now represents current-period net supply of the non-traded good.[25] Because a large share of government expenditure in industrialized economies is on non-traded goods and services, movements in this component of government spending could be an important determinant of the exchange rate.[26] And the model predicts that these exchange-rate movements occur without any effect on net exports.

NOTES

1 The model in this chapter, unlike the two-sector model in Chapter 10, incorporates both income and relative price effects on demand.
2 The seminal literature on a dynamic model with a non-traded good includes Dornbusch (1983), Stockman (1983), and Greenwood (1984).
3 For simplicity, it is assumed that domestic output is owned entirely by domestic residents, and domestic residents do not have any ownership rights to foreign output.
4 Abstracting from money does not distort the results given that monetary neutrality holds.
5 An appendix discusses the link between domestic and foreign real interest rates in an environment with both domestic and foreign bonds.
6 With multiple goods, there are different measures of the real interest rate (see an appendix). In models with identical traded goods, it is common to focus on the real interest rate measured in terms of the traded good.
7 Both traded and non-traded goods are perishable goods, like services or non-durable goods. They are not durable goods like cars, where consumers receive benefits, or utility, in multiple periods, and consumers can sell them in future periods.
8 The more general case is discussed in Chapters 5, 6, and 14.
9 If exports exceed imports, with all trade conducted in foreign currency, domestic residents accumulate foreign currency and then exchange it for foreign bonds.
10 In the future period, the agent will allocate consumption such that the future marginal rate of substitution equals the future relative price.
11 A change in c_t^T is the only factor, other than an exogenous change in tastes, that shifts this curve. With separability, a change in future consumption, traded or non-traded, has no effect on the current-period marginal rate of substitution and therefore does not shift this curve. An exogenous change in tastes is examined later on in the chapter.
12 Trade and current account deficits are not "bad." It is traditional in international macroeconomics to use the phrases "the trade balance improves" or "the trade balance worsens," but the terms increases and decreases are more appropriate. While the trade and current account balances have moved into deficit with this exogenous change, these deficits allow consumers to smooth traded-good consumption over time. The lifetime utility of consumers increases. For an advanced discussion of current account imbalances and welfare in a more general dynamic model with a non-traded good, see Blanchard (2007).
13 An appendix discusses the effects of various fiscal policy changes.
14 The NAICS data are taken from CANSIM Table 379-0031, now labeled Table 36100434. The resource sector combines the "agriculture, forestry, fishing and hunting" and "mining, quarrying, and oil and gas extraction" sectors.
15 The article by Pasula (2017), published in the *Australasian Journal of Economics Education*, discusses elements related to teaching the lecture material in this chapter in an undergraduate course. In addition, evidence is provided on the relationship between changes in the Canadian-US dollar exchange rate and changes in Canadian net exports.

16 In an interesting study examining relative price movements, Duarte and Restuccia (2019) disaggregate services into traditional and nontraditional services.

17 The composite sector encompasses retail trade, wholesale trade, and transportation and warehousing, sectors regarded as traded in some studies (and the calculations above) and non-traded in others. See the discussion in Chapter 10.

18 Interesting applications of dynamic, multi-sectoral open economy analyses are provided by, among many others, Engel and Wang (2011), Gorodnichenko et al. (2012), Eaton et al. (2016), and Kehoe et al. (2018). Herrendorf et al. (2014) survey the literature on long-term economic growth and structural change.

19 The RBC approach leads one naturally to think in terms of a multi-sectoral framework. For example, the factor that initiates a downturn may be a sector-specific weakening of the construction sector or a collapse in world commodity prices that decreases resource production. The seminal papers in the RBC literature are Kydland and Prescott (1982) and Long and Plosser (1983), with the latter based on a multi-sectoral model. In terms of open-economy multi-sectoral models, the formative empirical literature includes studies by Mendoza (1995) and Stockman and Tesar (1995).

20 To provide but one example, Gorodnichenko et al. (2012) incorporate wage stickiness.

21 There may be measurement issues associated with intermediate goods and value added (see, for example, Johnson 2014) and the component of investment spending called intellectual property products (see, for example, McGrattan and Prescott 2014). In the 2012 revision to national accounts, Statistics Canada began to include the category "intellectual property products" as a separate entry in investment spending.

22 Pasula (2025) uses the dynamic model with a non-traded good to examine reserve flows under a fixed exchange rate, with the demand for money modeled as in the intertemporal model of money (see Chapter 7). In addition, an empirical application of the model examines reserve flows in Japan from 1957 to 1971.

23 In a model with uncertainty, this condition would include a risk premium, representing default risk or consumption-related risk (as in the consumption capital asset pricing model). See Chapters 2 and 15.

24 In an important theoretical contribution, Rogoff (1992) demonstrates that temporary shocks to traded-good output have permanent effects on the real exchange rate.

25 The tax cut associated with a decrease in government spending on the non-traded good has no effect on traded-good consumption. In equilibrium, the increase in after-tax real income generated by the tax cut is spent entirely on the non-traded good (otherwise there is excess supply, and the relative price of the non-traded good falls until the result holds). On a related issue, note that the model in this chapter has relevance to the twin deficits literature (discussed in Chapter 5). To examine the impact of a tax cut (that increases the budget deficit to some extent) on the trade deficit, one must account not only for (current and future) aggregate government spending but for the composition of that spending on traded and non-traded goods.

26 For a study that investigates the relationship between government spending and the real exchange rate, see Galstyan and Lane (2009).

CHAPTER 15

A Two-Country Dynamic Model of Real Interest Rates and Current Account Balances

1. INTRODUCTION

What determines the real interest rate in an economy? In the dynamic model in Chapter 6, the real interest rate in the small domestic economy is determined exclusively by the real interest rate in the large foreign economy. In this framework, exogenous changes in the small economy affect the current account balance but not the real interest rate. When an exogenous change generates a current account surplus, for example, the magnitude of the acquisition of foreign bonds by domestic residents is too small to impact the foreign real interest rate. But if the domestic economy is a large economy, these same exogenous changes impact both the current account and the real interest rate. With large economies, there is a joint determination of real interest rates and current account balances.

This chapter uses a two-country version of the dynamic model in Chapter 6, with both economies assumed to be "large," and examines the determination of real interest rates, current account balances, and other macroeconomic variables. The model, widely used in open-economy macroeconomics, is within the traditions of neoclassical growth theory, real business cycle theory, and the intertemporal approach to the current account.[1] In each economy, consumers maximize lifetime utility, firms maximize lifetime profit, and prices are flexible. Production is an endogenous variable, with changes in production caused by exogenous changes in total factor productivity and other exogenous changes that induce changes in the capital stock (the quantity of labor is fixed). And the model embeds the simplifications from Chapter 6, the two-period setup with perfect foresight of future variables, identical domestic and foreign goods, and monetary neutrality.[2] In this framework, changes in real interest rates and current account balances are caused by changes in exogenous variables such as total factor productivity, government spending, taxes, and the marginal rate of time preference.[3]

Extending the basic structure of Chapter 6 to two large economies is a straightforward exercise, though the extra level of interaction in a two-country framework adds complications. But there are significant benefits to learning the material, as the analysis provides the background for an understanding of important aspects of the workings of the global economy. The main questions addressed are as follows. With unrestricted international asset trade, what is the relationship between domestic and foreign real interest rates and between real rates and the marginal products of capital? How do current and future exogenous changes in total factor productivity, government spending, taxes, and tastes affect real interest rates, current account balances, and other macroeconomic variables? In addition, the chapter provides a concise discussion of the implications of the framework for some current issues in the global economy, such as global imbalances, low world real interest rates, and the allocation of capital between developed and developing economies.

2. BASIC SETUP

It is taken for granted that the reader understands the model in Chapter 6, including the assumptions, identities, and economic relationships (Euler equation for consumption, total factor productivity, marginal product of capital, and so on). While there is repetition where necessary, the discussion is concise. The focus is on aspects that arise from having two large countries and on outlining and utilizing a diagram that allows for an examination of the effects of exogenous shocks. The analysis regards the two countries as "the world."

Real Interest Rate Parity Condition

With perfect foresight and identical foreign and domestic goods, the nominal interest rate parity condition implies that domestic and foreign bonds earn the same equilibrium real return (all international borrowing and lending is done at this same equilibrium real interest rate). Thus, the real interest rate parity condition holds (Chapter 7 provides the derivation):[4]

$$r_t = r_t^*,$$

where r_t is the domestic real interest rate and r_t^* is the foreign real interest rate (the notation * denotes foreign variables). Given the equality of rates, one may refer to the world real interest rate r_t^w. And domestic and foreign firms, acting to maximize lifetime profit, ensure that their net marginal products of capital equal the world real interest rate:[5]

$$r_t^w = f'\left(K_{t+1}\right) - \delta = f'\left(K_{t+1}^*\right) - \delta^*,$$

where δ and δ^* denote the constant rates of depreciation (there are no taxes on interest earnings or returns to capital). With the equality of the equilibrium returns on different investments, the world real interest rate is said to be determined on international capital markets.

It should be noted that, in more general models with uncertainty and multiple goods, domestic and foreign real rates are linked in a more complicated real interest rate parity condition (an appendix examines this case).

Net Exports in the Domestic and Foreign Economies

In this two-country world, where the exports of one country are necessarily the imports of the other, net exports in the domestic economy equal the negative of net exports in the foreign economy. A trade surplus in one country is matched by a trade deficit in the other. If each country begins the current period with zero net assets denominated in the currency of the other country, current-period net exports equal the current account.[6] These conditions yield the identities:[7]

$$NX_t = CA_t = -NX_t^* = -CA_t^*.$$

World National Saving and World Investment Spending

The world real interest rate is determined by world saving and world investment spending. National saving, denoted as S^{nat} and defined as private saving plus government saving, equals output (denoted as y) less the sum of consumer spending (c) and government spending (g). Domestic and foreign goods are identical, with the market being the world market. Letting world supply equal world demand yields the goods-market equilibrium condition (where I denotes investment spending):[8]

$$y_t + y_t^* = c_t + I_t + g_t + NX_t + c_t^* + I_t^* + g_t^* + NX_t^*.$$

Using the restriction on net exports and the definition of national saving, this equilibrium condition can be rewritten:

$$\left[y_t - c_t - g_t\right] = I_t - [y_t^* - c_t^* - g_t^*] + I_t^*,$$

$$S_t^w = S_t^{nat} + S_t^{nat*} = I_t + I_t^* = I_t^w,$$

where S^w is world saving and I^w is world investment spending. All else fixed, an increase in the world real interest rate induces an increase in saving and a decrease in investment spending in each country and the world economy. This equilibrium condition incorporates the mechanism that the world real interest rate adjusts to keep world saving equal to world investment. All else fixed, exogenous changes that increase world saving reduce the world real interest rate, and exogenous changes that increase world investment increase the world real rate.

World saving and world investment spending are depicted on the left-hand side of the diagram in Figure 15.1. In equilibrium, world saving equals world investment spending. At the initial equilibrium (point A), the world real interest rate equals 2 per cent and world saving and world investment (on the horizontal axis) equal 40 units (all variables measured in terms of goods).

In numerical examples, it is assumed the two economies are of equal size and have the same underlying economic relationships (for example, the same responsiveness to interest rate changes). For each economy, the initial values for output, consumption, investment spending, government spending, and net exports are 100, 60, 20, 20, and 0. National saving and investment spending both equal 20 in each economy and world saving and investment equal 40.

Figure 15.1: World saving and world investment, and national saving and investment in the domestic economy

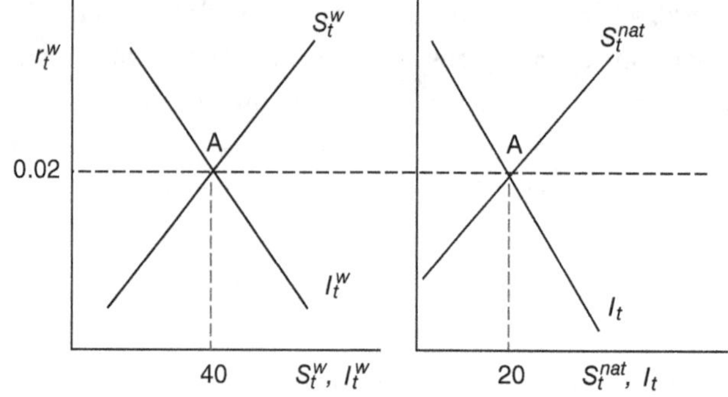

The right-hand side depicts national saving and investment spending in the domestic economy, with the real interest rate on the vertical axis and national saving and investment spending on the horizontal axis (the analogous diagram for the foreign economy is not shown). This part of the diagram is used to determine current-period net exports (current account), where

$$NX_t = CA_t = \left[y_t - c_t - g_t \right] - I_t = S_t^{nat} - I_t.$$

Net exports equal production less the sum of consumption, government spending, and investment spending, and net exports also equal the difference between national saving and investment spending (national saving and investment spending both equal 20 in the initial equilibrium at A, and net exports equal 0).

With exogenous changes, there are shifts in the curves that can generate changes in the world real interest rate and the trade and current account balances. The initial world real interest rate is assumed to equal the marginal rate of time preference (in each country). Total factor productivity, government spending, and the marginal rate of time preference are exogenous (government budgets are balanced, until noted otherwise).

3. CHANGES IN TOTAL FACTOR PRODUCTIVITY

Increases in total factor productivity are caused by, among other factors, increases in skills, innovations, and other factors such as decreases in regulation.[9] Of course, in a dynamic framework, changes in (expected) future variables can impact current-period variables, such as consumer spending, investment spending, the current account, and the real interest rate. The extent to which an exogenous change happens in the current period or in the future is a critical factor in determining the effects. For any given change, other exogenous factors in both economies are held fixed.

Temporary Increase in Domestic Total Factor Productivity

The initial equilibrium is at point A in Figure 15.2, with the world real interest rate equal to 2 per cent and the current account balanced. An exogenous temporary increase in domestic total factor productivity generates an increase in current-period production and real income. Private saving

Figure 15.2: Temporary increase in domestic total factor productivity

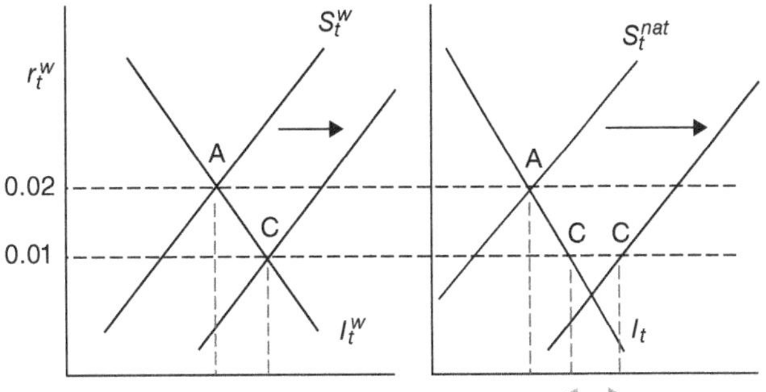

increases at the initial real interest rate, as consumers want to smooth consumption (consumers want to purchase assets this period to increase future consumption). As the domestic economy is large, there is an increase in world saving at the initial real interest rate, and the world saving curve shifts to the right (the national saving curve for the domestic economy also shifts rightward). There is no incentive, initially, to alter investment spending in the current period (the future marginal product of capital is not affected by a temporary change, and the real interest rate has not yet changed).[10] The increase in desired world saving, reflecting the desired increase in asset purchases, results in downward pressure on the world real interest rate and the equilibrium real rate falls from 2 per cent to 1 per cent. The induced reduction in real interest rates throughout the world economy moderates the increase in saving in the domestic economy and reduces saving in the foreign economy, while generating increases in investment spending in both countries. The temporary increase in domestic total factor productivity thus causes a reduction in the world real interest rate (in each economy, the reduction in the equilibrium real rate is associated with an increase in the future capital stock and a decrease in the future marginal product of capital).[11] In the new equilibrium at point C, world saving and investment are higher.

In the domestic economy, the temporary increase in real income results in an improvement in net exports and the current account. Consider the identity that the current account equals national saving less investment. With the temporary increase in real income, the increase in desired saving implies a rightward shift in the national saving curve. As the real interest rate falls, desired saving is reduced to some extent, but national saving is higher.[12] The reduction in the real rate induces an increase in investment spending, as domestic firms increase their current-period purchases of capital. At the new equilibrium real interest rate of 1 per cent, national saving exceeds investment spending. The current account moves from being balanced to a surplus, with the magnitude of the surplus equal to the distance between C and C (indicated by the ↔ symbol). In terms of the identity,

$$CA_t = y_t - c_t - I_t - g_t,$$

the increase in domestic production is larger than the associated increases in consumer and investment spending. The current account surplus in the domestic economy is matched by a deficit in the foreign economy (current-period production is unchanged in the foreign economy, and consumer and investment spending increase in response to the decrease in the real rate).

Figure 15.3: Temporary increase in foreign total factor productivity

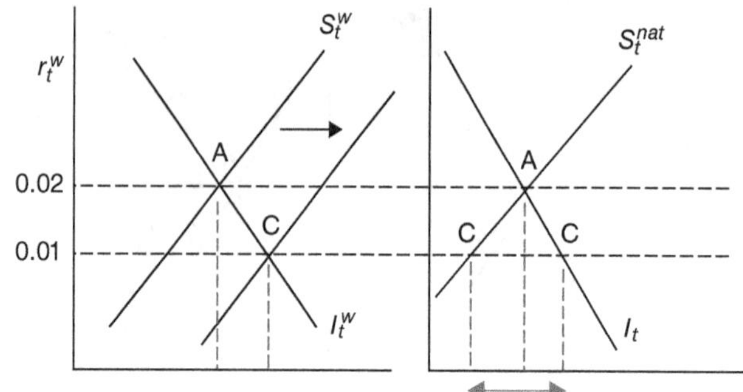

In the new equilibrium, consumers (domestic and foreign) are not smoothing consumption. With the real interest rate less than the marginal rate of time preference, the Euler equation implies that consumers find it optimal to have consumption falling over time.

Temporary Increase in Foreign Total Factor Productivity

This exogenous change increases national saving in the foreign economy, but has no initial effect on investment spending (only a future change in total factor productivity affects the future marginal product of capital). Desired saving increases because foreign consumers want to spread the increase in real income over both periods. The world saving curve shifts to the right in Figure 15.3. With the fall in world real interest rate to the new equilibrium point at C, there is a moderation in the increase in foreign saving, a decrease in domestic saving, and increases in investment spending in both economies.[13] In the new equilibrium, the world real interest rate is lower, and world saving and investment are higher.

In terms of the domestic economy, the saving and investment curves have not shifted (the domestic exogenous variables are fixed). The factor that impacts the domestic economy is the reduction in the world real interest rate, which generates an endogenous decrease in saving and an endogenous increase in investment spending. In the right-hand side of Figure 15.3, the new equilibrium points are denoted as C. In the move from A to C, the reduction in the real rate implies, initially, that the domestic future marginal product of capital exceeds the real rate. Domestic firms increase current-period investment spending until these real returns are equalized. The induced reduction in national saving means that current consumption increases. The domestic economy has a current account deficit, with the magnitude of the deficit equal to the distance between C and C (indicated by the ↔ symbol).

Is a current account deficit bad? There are no distortions in this model, meaning that there are no externalities and no market failures. The choices of consumers and firms are the optimal choices. Though the current account deficit implies that domestic residents have accumulated foreign debt, they are capable of repaying these debts, and it is in their interest to accumulate these debts. By borrowing, domestic residents achieve the highest possible level of lifetime utility. If the government restricted trade, requiring a balanced current account, the lifetime utility of domestic consumers would be lower.

Figure 15.4: Temporary increases in total factor productivity in both economies

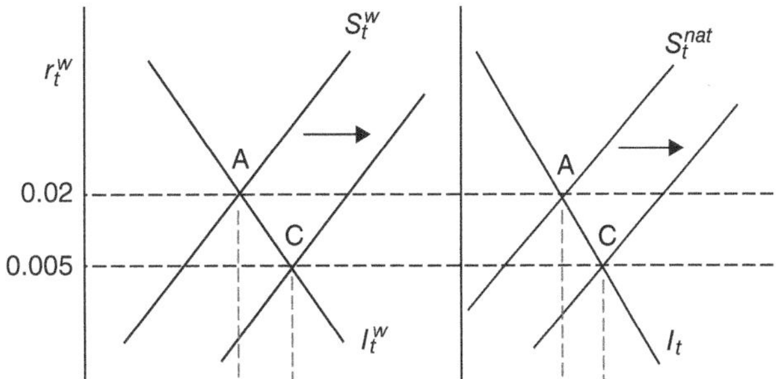

Temporary Increases in Total Factor Productivity in Both Economies

Suppose there is a temporary increase in total factor productivity (of the same magnitude) in both the domestic and foreign economies. The increases in desired current-period saving in the two economies shift the world saving curve to the right in Figure 15.4. As residents in both economies attempt to accumulate assets, to be able to spread the temporary increase in their real income over the two periods, there is downward pressure on the world real interest rate. In the new equilibrium at point C, the world real interest rate is lower, and world saving and investment are higher.

In the right-hand side diagram for the domestic economy, the national saving curve shifts to the right. With this exogenous change, the world real interest rate falls to a level where national saving and investment spending are equal in the domestic economy (and in the foreign economy). With desired saving increasing in both economies, there is a larger reduction in the world real interest rate and therefore a larger increase in investment spending. In the new equilibrium, net exports and the current account are unchanged. Current-period production increases, but the increases in domestic spending (the sum of consumer and investment spending) are of the same magnitude. Domestic residents do not accumulate any foreign assets, but the induced increase in current-period investment spending results in an increase in the future capital stock and a corresponding increase in future production. Domestic saving is associated with an equivalent increase in domestic investment spending.

Increases in Current and Future Domestic Total Factor Productivity: Example 1

There are often cases where both current and future total factor productivity increase (an increase in the current-period skills of workers, for example, typically means that future skills will be higher as well). This subsection and the next one examine this type of exogenous change.

How do exogenous increases in current and future total factor productivity affect the curves? An increase in current-period total factor productivity has no direct effect on investment spending (because it has no effect on the future marginal product of capital).[14] But when future total factor productivity increases, current-period investment spending increases. The increase in future total factor productivity increases the future marginal product of capital, and it is profitable for firms to purchase capital in the current period to allow for an increase in the future capital stock.[15] This

Figure 15.5: Increases in domestic current and future total factor productivity: Example 1

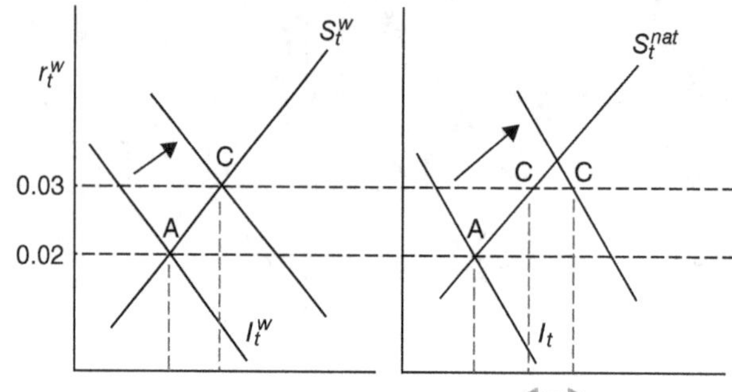

exogenous change therefore causes both the domestic investment spending curve and the world investment spending curve to shift to the right. In terms of current-period national saving, exogenous increases in current and future total factor productivity have opposite effects. While an increase in current total factor productivity increases current-period desired saving at the initial real interest rate, an increase in future total factor productivity decreases it. In Example 1, it is assumed that the magnitudes of the exogenous increases in current and future total factor productivity are such that, in total, desired current-period national saving is unchanged at the initial world real interest rate.

Given this assumption, the exogenous change shifts the world investment curve to the right in Figure 15.5 but leaves the world saving curve unchanged. In the world capital market, domestic firms seek funds to finance their current-period investment spending. But at the initial world real interest rate, neither domestic nor foreign residents are willing to supply any additional funds. Therefore, this excess demand for funds results in an increase in the world real interest rate. In the new equilibrium, the higher real interest rate in fact generates the necessary increase in world saving to match the increase in world investment spending. The equilibrium world real interest rate rises from 0.02 to 0.03, and world saving and investment increase.

In the diagram for the domestic economy, the investment spending curve shifts to the right but the national saving curve is unchanged.[16] With the rise in the equilibrium world rate, there is both a moderation of the increase in desired investment spending and an increase in desired national saving. In the new equilibrium, investment spending exceeds national saving, and the domestic economy has a current account deficit. While current-period production increases, the associated increases in investment spending and consumer spending are larger. The larger magnitude for domestic spending, relative to domestic production, implies that these goods must be imported.

It is worth highlighting that current-period investment spending increases in the domestic economy even though the real interest rate has increased (as noted in Chapter 6, this situation is not uncommon). The increase in future total factor productivity increases the future marginal product of capital, and it is profitable for domestic firms to acquire additional capital even though there is a higher real interest rate on loans to finance the investment spending.

Figure 15.6: Increases in domestic current and future total factor productivity: Example 2

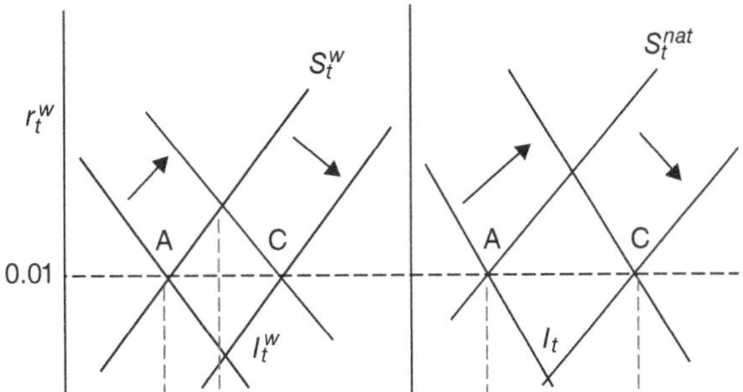

Increases in Current and Future Domestic Total Factor Productivity: Example 2

Consider another example with exogenous increases in both current and future domestic total factor productivity. The future increase, by shifting the future marginal product of capital upward, increases current-period investment spending and results in rightward shifts of both the domestic investment and world investment curves. In this example, it is assumed that the current increase in total factor productivity is significantly larger than the future increase, such that desired current-period domestic national saving increases and generates rightward shifts in the world saving and domestic saving curves. Indeed, the magnitudes are assumed to be such that the curves shift exactly as shown in Figure 15.6, so that the equilibrium world real interest rate remains unchanged at point C. In this case, while domestic firms demand funds to finance the increase in investment spending, there is also a willingness from domestic consumers to increase current-period saving. In total, domestic national saving and investment spending increase by the same amount, and there is no pressure on the world real interest rate to change.

In terms of domestic production and spending, the increase in current-period production is purchased entirely by domestic consumers and domestic firms undertaking investment spending (purchasing additional machines). The increase in current production and real income is of the magnitude that consumers can increase current consumption as well as increase saving by an amount just sufficient to finance the investment spending undertaken by domestic firms (national saving equals investment spending). There is no need to borrow from foreigners, and net exports remain at zero (and given that foreign production is unchanged, foreign net exports must equal zero because, with an unchanged world interest rate, foreign spending is unchanged).

4. FISCAL POLICY AND OTHER FACTORS

Balanced-Budget Temporary Decrease in Domestic Government Spending

Consider a balanced-budget change in fiscal policy, where the domestic government decreases both current-period taxes and spending (future taxes and government spending are unchanged). With this temporary tax cut, and the associated increase in lifetime after-tax real income, domestic consumers want to increase both current-period consumption and saving (to increase future consumption and smooth consumption). The decrease in current-period government spending, with production unchanged and a less than proportionate increase in consumer spending, increases national saving. Both the domestic national saving curve and the world saving curve shift to the right, with the diagram identical to Figure 15.2. Domestic residents want, at the initial world real interest rate of 2 per cent, to increase saving to be able to spread the available funds from the tax cut over both periods. There is no incentive, initially, to alter investment spending in the current period (the future marginal product of capital is not affected by the exogenous change, and the real interest rate has not yet changed). The increase in desired world saving reduces the equilibrium world real interest rate to 1 per cent, depicted as C in the figure. The induced reduction in real interest rates throughout the world economy moderates the increase in domestic saving, reduces foreign saving, and generates increases in investment spending in both countries. The temporary decrease in government spending thus causes a reduction in the world real interest rate and, in the process, generates purchases of capital that result in a decrease in the future marginal product of capital in both economies.

The temporary decrease in government spending results in an improvement in net exports and the current account balance. At the new equilibrium world real interest rate, national saving exceeds investment spending (as depicted in Figure 15.2). In terms of the identity,

$$CA_t = y_t - c_t - I_t - g_t,$$

current-period production is unchanged and the decrease in government spending is larger than the sum of the increases in consumer and investment spending. There is a current account surplus, and domestic residents accumulate foreign assets. Of course, the surplus in the domestic economy is matched by a foreign current account deficit. The foreign current account balance is negative, because production is unchanged and consumer and investment spending increase in response to the decrease in the world real interest rate.

In the new equilibrium, consumers (domestic and foreign) are not smoothing consumption. With the real interest rate less than the marginal rate of time preference, the Euler equation implies that consumers find it optimal to have consumption falling over time.

The effects of a temporary decrease in government spending in the domestic economy on the world real interest rate and current account balances are the same as the effects of a temporary increase in domestic total factor productivity (as in Figure 15.2). Likewise, a temporary balanced-budget decrease in government spending in the foreign economy has the same effects as in Figure 15.3 (the temporary increase in foreign total factor productivity).

On the Effects of Fiscal Policy in the Model

Current-period decreases in government spending have the same effects as current-period increases in total factor productivity. But the effects of decreases in future government spending are not the same as increases in future total factor productivity. Changes in future total factor productivity do, but future changes in government spending do not, shift the future marginal product of capital curve. This result follows from the specification of the model. While government spending yields utility to consumers, government spending does not enter the production function. In addition, with lump-sum taxes, the only effect of a tax change is through the impact on lifetime after-tax real income (whereas a model with a more detailed tax regime could generate various substitution effects on spending, employment, and production).[17]

Balanced-Budget Decrease in Future Taxes

Suppose current-period government spending and taxes are unchanged, but the domestic government announces a decrease in future taxes matched by a decrease in future government spending (a balanced-budget decrease in future taxes). The decrease in future tax increases lifetime after-tax real income, resulting in an increase in desired consumption in both periods. To increase current-period consumption with no change in current-period after-tax real income, domestic consumers must decrease current-period private saving. Domestic residents need to get a loan from foreigners (and foreigners will, based on the initial conditions, only be willing to do so at a higher real interest rate). The world saving curve shifts to the left in Figure 15.7, and as domestic residents demand funds on the international capital market, the world real interest rate increases. With a higher real rate, foreign saving increases, the decrease in domestic national saving moderates, and current-period investment spending decreases in both economies.[18] These adjustments work toward eliminating the original excess demand for funds on the international capital market. In the new equilibrium at point C, the world real interest rate is higher and world saving and investment are lower.

In the diagram for the domestic economy, national saving is less than investment spending in the new equilibrium. There is a current account deficit in the domestic economy, and domestic residents have received a loan from foreigners.[19] In the domestic economy, current-period consumption increases more than investment spending decreases (and production and government spending are unchanged). The current account balance moves to a deficit, with the magnitude equal to the distance between C and C (indicated by the ↔ symbol).

Current-Period Tax Decrease Matched by a Future Tax Increase

Suppose the domestic government reduces current taxes and increases future taxes, with government spending fixed in both periods. The current-period government budget is now in deficit, and the government finances the deficit by selling newly issued domestic government bonds. Suppose the government reduces current-period taxes by 10 units and announces that it will increase future taxes by 10.2 (all variables measured in terms of goods). With a real interest rate equal to 0.02, the government knows that future taxes have to increase by 10.2 to be able to repay the debt (principal and interest) and pay for government spending over the two periods.[20] When the new tax regime is introduced, domestic residents determine that the change in the tax package has no effect on their lifetime after-tax real income. While the current-period tax cut increases lifetime after-tax real income, the increase in the future tax decreases it by the same amount in present value terms. With unchanged lifetime after-tax real income and a given real interest rate, current-period

Figure 15.7: Decrease in future taxes and government spending

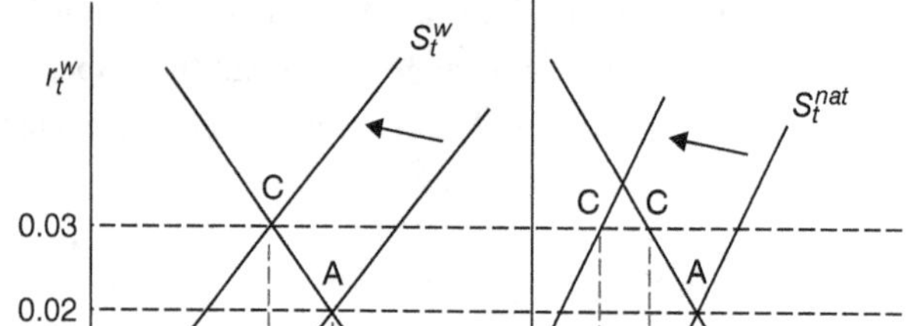

consumer spending does not change. Consumers use the funds from the current-period tax cut to purchase the newly issued domestic bonds. That is, desired private saving in the current-period increases by the amount of the tax cut, with consumers willingly purchasing the government bonds this period to be able to pay the increase in future taxes without having to reduce future consumption (the purchase of 10 units of government bonds in the current period, with a real return of 2 per cent, yields 10.2 units in the future period, the amount needed to pay the higher future taxes). By saving the entire current-period tax cut, consumers can smooth consumption. Given the equality of the real rate and the marginal rate of time preference, smoothing is the choice that maximizes lifetime utility. The change in the tax regime has no effect on consumption, a result known as the Ricardian equivalence theorem.[21]

Current-period national saving equals the sum of private saving (the first term in square brackets in the equation below) and government saving (the second term in square brackets, equal to the government budget surplus):[22]

$$S_t^{nat} = \left[y_t - c_t - T_t\right] + \left[T_t - g_t\right] = y_t - c_t - g_t.$$

While there is an increase in current-period private saving, there is an exogenous decrease in government saving with the current-period tax cut and the budget deficit. The changes in private and government saving offset each other, and national saving is unchanged. There is therefore no shift in the national saving curve or the world saving curve, and the specified change in taxes leaves the world real interest rate unchanged. While a new sale of government bonds is often regarded as putting upward pressure on the real interest rate (when there is no corresponding change in desired saving), in this case domestic consumers willingly purchase the newly issued bonds (at the existing real rate of 2 per cent) because they know that they must increase current-period saving to pay for the increase in future taxes (without having to cut future consumer spending).

With no change in lifetime after-tax real income and no effect on the real interest rate, the new tax regime has no effect on current-period consumer spending or investment spending. With current production unchanged and government spending fixed, the current account balance remains unchanged (the current-period tax cut generates a budget deficit, but there is not a current account deficit).[23] In this model, a tax cut matched by a future tax increase (of the same present value) has no effect on consumption, investment spending, the real interest rate, or the current account balance.[24]

Decrease in the Domestic Marginal Rate of Time Preference

Suppose tastes change in the domestic economy, such that there is an exogenous decrease in the marginal rate of time preference from 2 per cent to 0 per cent (the foreign marginal rate of time preference remains at 2 per cent). Domestic residents are now more patient in that they discount the future at a lower rate. In fact, domestic consumers do not discount the future at all, being indifferent between a current-period basket of 100 units of goods and the same basket of 100 units of goods in the future (whereas foreign residents, with a marginal rate of time preference of 2 per cent, unambiguously prefer the current-period basket).

With the exogenous change, the domestic national saving curve shifts to the right (the diagram is the same as Figure 15.2). At an initial world real interest rate of 2 per cent, domestic consumers want to increase current-period saving and decrease current-period consumer spending. This rightward shift of the national saving curve implies a rightward shift in the world saving curve, indicating that domestic residents want to accumulate assets (with the change in tastes, the 2 per cent real return on assets is attractive). As domestic residents acquire assets, the world real interest rate is reduced. As both economies adjust to the reduction in real interest rates, desired saving falls in the foreign economy and moderates in the domestic economy, and investment spending increases in both economies. In the new equilibrium at point C, the world real interest rate is lower, now equal to 1 per cent, and world saving and investment are higher.

The exogenous decrease in the marginal rate of time preference from 2 per cent to 0 per cent in the domestic economy reduces the equilibrium world real interest rate from 2 per cent to 1 per cent. The equilibrium world real interest rate now lies between the marginal rates of time preference in the two economies. The decrease in the marginal rate of time preference has no direct effect on the marginal products of capital (determined by future total factor productivity and the real interest rate). But the induced reduction in the equilibrium world real rate induces firms to acquire more capital, resulting in reductions in the marginal products of capital in both economies.

In terms of the current account balance in the domestic economy, the decrease in current-period consumption (associated with the current-period increase in desired saving) results in an improvement of the current account. Domestic residents accumulate foreign assets, allowing for an increase in future consumption. With the world real interest rate greater than the marginal rate of time preference in the domestic economy, domestic consumers have future consumption higher than current consumption. Foreign residents, on the other hand, increase current-period consumption and will have future consumption lower than current-period consumption. Each economy is maximizing their lifetime utility, and each economy faces the same equilibrium world real interest rate, but the two economies now have a different marginal rate of time preference. The more patient domestic consumers have rising consumption over time, whereas foreign consumers have falling consumption over time.

Decrease in the Foreign Marginal Rate of Time Preference

With an exogenous decrease in the foreign marginal rate of time preference, the equilibrium world real interest rate falls (the diagram is the same as Figure 15.3). In the current period, the foreign economy has a current account surplus and the domestic economy a deficit (the fall in the world real rate increases current-period spending in the domestic economy).

5. CURRENT ISSUES IN THE GLOBAL ECONOMY

This section outlines some current topics of interest from the perspective of the model. The discussion is limited to a concise summary of each issue, along with some insights from, and references to, the advanced literature in international macroeconomics.

Global Imbalances

While the term "global imbalances" is often used to mean current account (or trade) surpluses or deficits in general, it is sometimes taken to mean excessive deficits or surpluses (based on some criteria). Some economists regard the state of current account imbalances in the global economy as a situation that needs to be rectified by policy actions (some applied exercises in Data Analytics examine elements of the US current account balance). In an International Monetary Fund (2019) assessment, for example, some nations (for example, United States, United Kingdom, Argentina) had current account deficits deemed to be excessive, and others (Germany, Netherlands, Korea) had surpluses higher than warranted.[25] Whether, and what, policy action is needed is a matter of dispute.

In the model in this chapter, imbalances are not a problem.[26] A current account imbalance allows firms to maximize lifetime profit and consumers to maximize lifetime utility. The implied acquisition of foreign debt in the case of a current account deficit can be repaid in the future (given the conditions in the economy).[27] It is also important to note that, with positive net foreign assets at the start of the current period, the domestic economy could run current account deficits in both the current and future periods (see Chapter 5). Thus, in a many-period model, a string of periods with current account deficits need not suggest that imbalances are excessive.[28]

But in models with externalities, imperfections in credit or goods markets, non-competitive markets, or government-induced distortions, there may be a basis for policy actions that improve society's welfare (lifetime utility). For example, with innovations that create market power for innovating firms, there are benefits associated with the innovations but there may also be deadweight-weight losses associated with non-competitive pricing.[29] Government action may increase welfare.[30] The question of whether policies that reduce "excessive" current account imbalances improve welfare is embedded within this line of argument.[31]

Low World Real Interest Rates

Real interest rates in the world economy were low for the decade of the 2010s. Using a measure of the ex-post US real interest rate, calculated as the ten-year government bond rate less the forward annual inflation rate, Figure 15.8 depicts movements over the period 1970 to 2020. The US

Figure 15.8: The ex-post US real interest rate

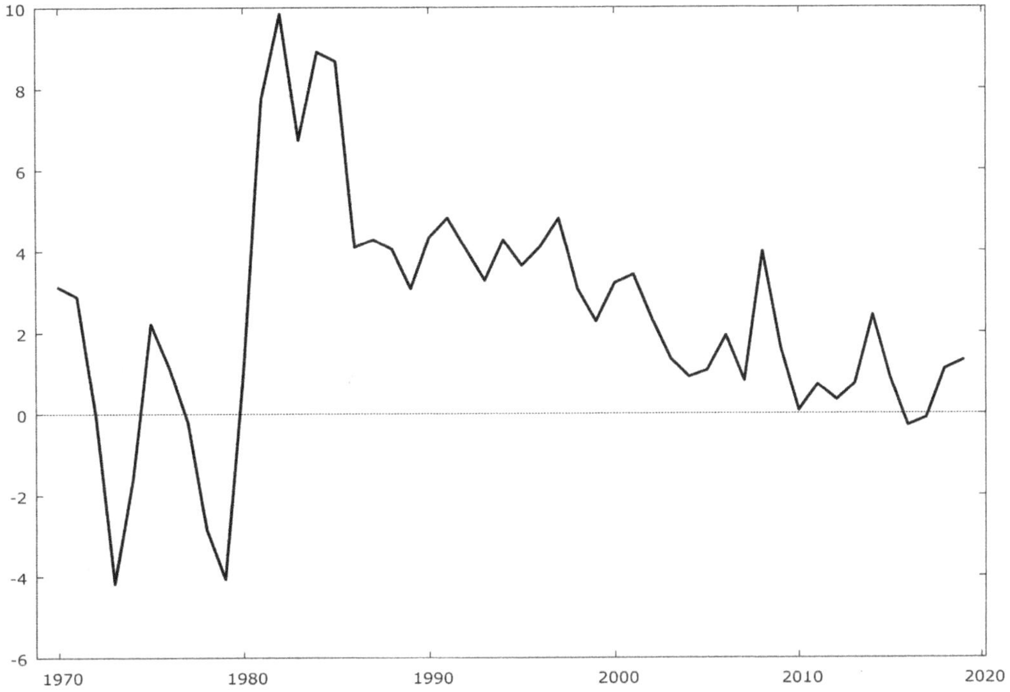

Data sources: Statistics Canada and US Bureau of Labor Statistics via FRED

real interest rate was low in the 1970s, rose sharply in the early 1980s, and then moved downward in each subsequent decade. The (approximate) decadal averages are 0 per cent for the 1970s, 6 per cent for the 1980s, 4 per cent for the 1990s, 2 per cent for the 2000s, and 1 per cent for the 2010s.[32]

In terms of the model, downward movements of the US real interest rate (a measure of the world real rate) are consistent with various exogenous changes. A lower growth rate of world output, caused by changes in current and future total factor productivity, results in a lower world real interest rate. For example, an exogenous decrease in future total factor productivity in either economy results in a reduction in world investment and an expansion in world saving (at the initial real rate), generating the downward movement in the world real rate. Reductions in the world real rate could also be associated with factors that primarily affect world saving at the initial world real rate. For example, an exogenous decrease in the marginal rate of time preference in the foreign economy increases world saving (at the initial real rate) and induces a reduction in the world rate. And certain fiscal policy changes, such as (expected) future tax increases, have the same effect. While some of these factors have been forwarded as possible causes of the downward movements in the real rate in recent decades, insights from more general saving-investment models have highlighted other factors (including demographic change, trends in the aggregate quantity of labor, and long-term movements in the relative price of capital).[33] Of course, empirical analyses are required to discriminate between alternative factors. An exercise in Data Analytics examines whether or not specific exogenous changes are consistent with movements in US real rates and current account balances over a specific period.

Figure 15.9: Equal net marginal products

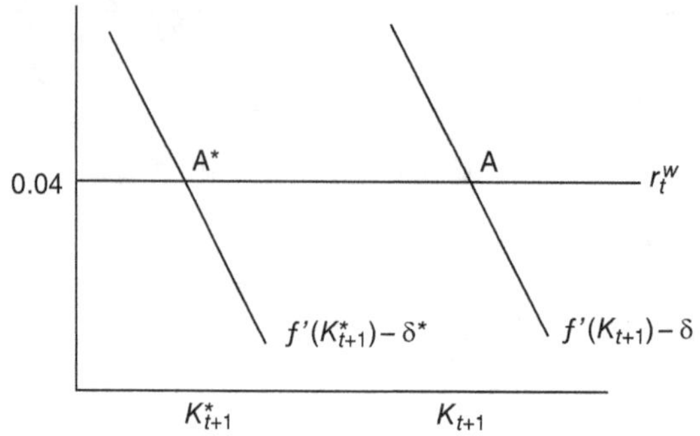

The Marginal Product of Capital in Developed and Developing Economies

The model predicts that domestic and foreign net marginal products of capital are equal. The model can be applied to two large economies such as the United States and Europe, where one may expect similar marginal products. But if the domestic and foreign economies represent "developed" and "developing" economies, the equality of marginal products may be an issue. And if the net marginal product of capital tends to be significantly higher in developing economies, some questions arise. Why doesn't more capital flow from developed to developing economies? And would more capital flows in this direction generate significant benefits to the global economy?

But the model, not having incorporated any intrinsic or policy barriers to the international flow of capital, is consistent with the equality of net marginal products between economies with significantly different quantities of capital. Consider Figure 15.9, which extends the diagram in Chapter 6 (assume, for simplicity, that each economy has the same number of workers).[34] The domestic (developed) economy has a higher capital stock than the foreign (developing) economy, but the equilibrium net marginal products of capital are the same. The marginal product curve for the developed economy is further to the right, because the developed economy has a higher level of total factor productivity. And the lower level of capital in the developing economy does not generate a higher marginal product, given a diminishing marginal product, because the lower total factor productivity in the developing economy offsets the effect of the diminishing marginal product. Net marginal products are equal in the developed and developing economies.

Whether net marginal products of capital are the same in developed and developing economies, and in the global economy in general, is an empirical question. While there is some empirical support for equal marginal products, the evidence points to the need to incorporate additional factors into the analysis (such as, among other factors, variations in the relative price of capital goods to consumption goods).[35]

6. CONCLUSION

The two-country dynamic model allows for an analysis of the joint determination of real interest rates and current account balances in large economies. The chapter analyzed the impact of various exogenous changes, in both the current period and in the future, on real rates and current accounts, as well as on other macroeconomic variables such as production, consumption, investment spending, and saving.

Of course, the model abstracts from issues that may be important. Extensions of the model that incorporate other factors, such as demographic change or movements in the relative price of capital, may be needed to tackle certain issues of prominence in the global economy. These more general models may require both multiple periods and multiple sectors (such as consumption-good and capital-good sectors). And if the focus of the research involves a shorter time horizon, monetary factors may need to be included. Of course, monetary factors are essential for analyses pertaining to alternative exchange rate regimes.[36] But the two-country dynamic model provides a useful benchmark in assessing the performance of these alternative specifications and in examining current issues in the global economy.

PRACTICE QUESTIONS

1. Fill in the blanks
   (a) An exogenous temporary increase in domestic total factor productivity _____ the world real interest rate. In the new equilibrium, world saving is _____.
   (b) An exogenous temporary decrease in domestic total factor productivity will, in the current period, increase the current account in _____ and decrease the current account balance in _____.
   (c) Suppose there is an exogenous temporary increase in foreign total factor productivity. In the new equilibrium, the domestic economy has _____ current-period national saving and _____ current-period investment spending.
   (d) An exogenous temporary increase in foreign total factor productivity impacts variables in the domestic economy: current-period consumption increases, in response to the induced decrease in _____, but current-period production remains the same because _____ do not change.
   (e) Consider the domestic economy. At the initial real interest rate, an exogenous increase in current total factor productivity _____ current-period saving and an exogenous increase in future total factor productivity _____ current-period saving.
2. Fill in the blanks
   (a) A balanced-budget temporary decrease in government spending in the domestic economy results in _____ in the world real interest rate and _____ in world investment spending.
   (b) Assume the government budget is always balanced. An exogenous increase in future taxes in the domestic economy results in _____ in current-period national saving at the initial real interest rate, and generates _____ in the equilibrium world real interest rate.

(c) An exogenous decrease in the marginal rate of time preference in the domestic economy results in _____ in the world real interest rate and _____ in investment spending in the domestic economy.

(d) An exogenous decrease in the marginal rate of time preference in the foreign economy results in _____ in the world real interest rate and _____ in the current account balance in the domestic economy.

(e) Compared to the mid-1980s, the US real interest rate in the mid-2010s was _____. In terms of the model, this implies that the net marginal product of capital in the United States in the mid-2010s was _____ than in the mid-1980s.

3. (a) Explain why the world saving curve is upward sloping.

(b) Using the equation for national saving, explain how a temporary increase in domestic total factor productivity affects national saving at the initial real interest rate.

(c) Outline the effects, at the initial world real interest rate, of an exogenous future increase in domestic total factor productivity on current-period national saving and current-period investment spending.

(d) Suppose domestic total factor productivity is unchanged, but exogenous changes in the foreign economy decrease the world real interest rate. What are the effects on investment spending and the marginal product of capital in the domestic economy? Explain.

(e) Suppose, in the domestic economy, a current-period tax decrease is matched by a future tax increase such that lifetime after-tax real income is unchanged (with current and future government spending fixed). Explain why current-period desired saving increases (at the initial real interest rate).

4. Using the saving-investment diagram, explain how an exogenous temporary increase in domestic total factor productivity affects the following current-period variables:

(a) the world real interest rate, world saving, and world investment spending; and

(b) national saving, investment spending, and current account balance in the domestic economy.

5. Suppose there are exogenous increases in both current and future domestic total factor productivity, such that domestic national saving is unchanged at the initial real interest rate. Using the saving-investment diagram, explain how the exogenous change affects the world real interest rate and current account balances.

6. Using the saving-investment diagram, explain how an exogenous decrease in the marginal rate of time preference in the foreign economy affects the world real interest rate, world saving, world investment spending, and current account balances.

7. Using a diagram that depicts the net marginal product of capital curves for the two economies, explain how it is possible for net marginal products to be

equal even though the economies have different levels of total factor productivity.

DATA ANALYTICS

1. Using FRED, the online database at the Federal Reserve Bank of St. Louis, collect quarterly data on US real GDP, the US current account balance, and the US federal government budget deficit since 1970. Divide the latter two variables by US real GDP and examine the co-movements of the two variables on a time-series plot.

2. Using the FRED database, collect data on the interest rate on 1-year US government bonds and the US consumer price index since 1970. Convert the monthly data to annual data and calculate the forward annual inflation rate and the ex-post real interest rate.

   (a) Create a plot of the US real rate and comment on the long-term movements.

   (b) In terms of the model, can the increase in the US real rate in the early 1980s be explained by (expected) future increases in total factor productivity? Elaborate. Comment on other information that may be needed to confirm the validity of this explanation.

   (c) Find a period when the US real rate fell. Comment on whether the fall is more consistent with an exogenous change that increases world saving or decreases world investment spending (at the initial real rate).

3. Using the data in question 1, locate a five-year period, relative to the previous five-year period, when the US real interest rate is lower and the US current account deficit is larger. Then consider the two-country model in terms of the US and the rest of the world. Determine the effects of each exogenous change: (a) a decrease in future US total factor productivity; (b) a decrease in future total factor productivity in the rest of the world; (c) a decrease in the marginal rate of time preference in the US; (d) a decrease in the marginal rate of time preference in the rest of the world; and (e) a balanced budget increase in future taxes in both the domestic and foreign economies. Comment on whether each exogenous change is, or is not, consistent with the movements in the US current account balance and real interest rate.[37]

APPENDIX: REAL INTEREST RATE PARITY CONDITION

The real interest rate parity condition specified in Section 2 relies on underlying assumptions of perfect foresight, identical domestic and foreign goods, zero portfolio transactions costs, and no taxes on asset returns (or the same tax rates on domestic and foreign returns). In a more general case, with uncertainty and domestic and foreign goods that are not identical, the real interest rate parity condition is

$$r_t^e + \varphi_t = r_t^{e*} + \frac{q_{t+1}^e - q_t}{q_t},$$

where the superscript e denotes expected, φ is the risk premium, and q is the real exchange rate (the relative price of foreign to domestic goods). In this framework, (expected) real interest rates need not be equal. If foreign bonds are riskier, the risk premium φ_t is positive and foreign and domestic expected real rates can differ. Likewise, if investors expect changes in the real exchange rate over time, domestic and foreign expected real interest rates can differ (further discussion is provided in Chapters 2 and 14).[38]

The simplification of real interest rate equality is useful in some theoretical analyses, and there are cases where it tends to hold in practice. But the more general condition may be a better representation of the link between domestic and foreign expected real interest rates, especially when the risk premium is volatile and real exchange rate movements are not permanent. Rejecting the equality of foreign and domestic real interest rates need not imply a rejection of the more general real interest rate parity condition.[39]

NOTES

1 The model is in the tradition of the closed-economy theory of the real interest rate of Irving Fisher (1930).

2 Monetary factors have no effect on the real interest rate (or the current account balance) in the model. This result relies on the assumptions of current-period price flexibility and perfect foresight of future variables. Under alternative conditions, central-bank actions under a flexible exchange rate may cause changes in the real rate (or, with uncertainty, the expected real interest rate). The model's applicability to a given time horizon depends on, among other things, the degree of price flexibility at that horizon.

3 The determinants of real interest rates and current account balances are the same under any exchange rate regime.

4 With unrestricted international asset trade between many economies, all the real interest rates are linked.

5 By relaxing an assumption in Chapter 6, domestic firms could be allowed to have partial ownership of the foreign capital stock, and vice versa (the capital would not leave the country, but the non-resident owners would have a claim on the output of that capital). But relaxing this assumption adds complications. For example, changes affecting the foreign marginal product of capital could affect domestic saving, complicating the diagrammatical analysis. The relaxation is therefore not adopted. But firms can import new capital for their own ownership and use.

6 With zero initial net foreign assets, the analysis can abstract from the wealth effects of interest rate changes.

7 In period t+1, the condition on net exports holds but current accounts need not equal net exports.

8 The relative price of consumption and investment goods equals unity.

9 On reductions in total factor productivity, see Chapter 6 and academic papers such as Hansen and Ohanian (2016).

10 With perfect foresight (or rational expectations in models with uncertainty), consumers and firms anticipate the effects described in the subsequent sentences. In that sense, once the exogenous change occurs, there is an incentive to take the actions subsequently explained in the text. The step-wise description serves to highlight each effect.

11 The increase in the future foreign capital stock increases future foreign real income, resulting in a relatively small indirect effect on foreign national saving and thus on world saving.

12 In this two-period model, consumers initially want to save less than one-half of the increase in current-period real income (initially, with the real interest rate equal to the marginal rate of time preference, consumers desire smoothed consumption). If current-period real income increases by 20 units, consumption can increase by (approximately) 10.1 units and the saving of 9.9 has a future pay-out of (approximately) 10.1 when the real rate is 0.02. This analysis is the initial effect. The fall in the real rate generates another effect, inducing a decrease in current-period saving and an increase in current-period consumption. In the new equilibrium, the real rate is below the marginal rate of time preference and, as implied by the Euler equation, current consumption exceeds future consumption. In the new equilibrium, current-period saving is higher but increases by less than 9.9 units (and the new real rate is 0.01).

13 The decrease in domestic national saving associated with the fall in the real interest rate is a movement along the domestic national saving curve (and the world saving curve). Note that the increase in investment spending implies an increase in the future capital stock and future real income, and thereby induces a small negative effect on current-period national saving. This indirect effect could be interpreted as a movement along, or as a relatively small leftward shift of, the current-period national saving curve (and the world saving curve). When the curves are derived as functions of the real interest rate and the exogenous variables, there is not a shift.

14 The current-period capital stock is given. Current-period purchases of capital can only be used for production in the future period. Firms look forward to determine if they should be purchasing capital for use in the future.

15 An increase in skills, for example, increases the marginal product of capital at the initial level of capital.

16 In the initial equilibrium, with the world real interest rate equal to the marginal rate of time preference, there is no need for domestic residents to save or borrow in the current period if the changes in current and future real income are such that consumption smoothing can arise without saving, either positive or negative.

17 See Chapters 5 and 6. Models with more general effects of fiscal policy are examined in (for example) Frenkel and Razin (1987) and Aschauer (1988). Ramey (2016) summarizes the empirical literature on the effects of fiscal policy.

18 With no shift in the marginal product of capital, the higher real interest rate implies a lower level of the future capital stock (in both economies). Domestic and foreign firms will not replace all of the depreciated capital. For example, whereas investment spending is normally 20 units to replace worn-out capital, firms replace only 18 units.

19 In the future period, domestic consumers use the tax cut to pay back the foreign loan and increase consumption.

20 If current and future taxes (and government spending) initially equal 20, current taxes are 10 and future taxes are 30.2 in the new regime.

21 The theorem and related corollaries are discussed in Chapter 5 and numerous other chapters. Frenkel and Razin (1987), among others, discuss both the theorem and the conditions under which it does not hold. For an interesting quantitative analysis on Ricardian equivalence, see Barczyk (2016).

22 The initial net government debt equals zero.

23 In this model, government budget deficits need not be associated with current account deficits. On the theory and empirics of "twin deficits," see Chapter 5.

24 In a more general model, a current-period sales tax cut, matched by a future sales tax increase (with unchanged lifetime after-tax real income), increases current-period consumer spending and affects other macroeconomic variables (Chapter 5 provides further discussion). On temporary tariff changes, see Aschauer (1987).

25 In the International Monetary Fund (2019) assessment, China's current account surplus, having narrowed in recent years, is no longer excessive.

26 Stockman (1988) provides an excellent discussion of many issues still relevant in today's global economy. For a concise discussion of the case that imbalances need not be a problem, see pages 535–6 and 540–1.

27 For an advanced discussion of issues related to non-payment of foreign debt, see Aguiar and Amador (2014).

28 Desroches and Francis (2010) and Rachel and Smith (2017) discuss long-term determinants such as demographics and financial development.

29 See the discussion of endogenous growth models in Grossman and Helpman (1994), who also highlight technology spill-over externalities.

30 Using a dynamic model with a non-traded good, Blanchard (2007) examines optimal policy for various distortions and notes that the optimal policy does not always reduce the trade imbalance. Corden (1994, 2007) also provides an excellent discussion of issues related to imbalances and welfare.

31 The current account measures net capital flows, but some analysts stress "gross" flows in the issue of global imbalances (Gourinchas and Rey 2014 discuss this matter and the related issue of "valuation effects"). Kehoe et al. (2018) use a multi-sectoral model of the US economy (and the rest of the world) to examine trade deficits, the real rate, employment, and other variables.

32 The interest rate on 10-year US government bonds is series V4429275 in CANSIM. The US consumer price index data, used to calculate the inflation rate, are series CPIAUCSL in FRED (Federal Reserve Economic Data). Using the interest rate on 91-day Treasury bills, the decadal averages are 1 per cent or 2 per cent lower (with negative real rates in both the 1970s and 2010s). The original data are converted to annual data using averaging.

33 See, for example, Bernanke (2005), Desroches and Francis (2010), and Rachel and Smith (2017).

34 Alternatively, each capital stock can be reinterpreted as the capital–labor ratio, with a fixed quantity of workers.

35 Excellent references for this broad literature include the seminal article by Lucas (1990), the empirical study by Caselli and Feyrer (2007), and the survey paper by Gourinchas and Rey (2014). An appendix in Chapter 6 discusses the case of a variable relative price of capital.

36 There is a tendency to focus on "the" interest rate (one nominal and one real), whereas there is an entire term structure of government bonds and a multitude of corporate bonds with different terms and risk characteristics. But macroeconomists are well aware of the need to conduct analyses with multiple rates (to provide one example, see Hall 2010).

37 An exogenous change that predicts a decrease in the real rate and a current account improvement may still be an important factor, in that another exogenous change may have decreased the real rate and deteriorated the current account. Empirical analyses are required to discriminate between factors.

38 The risk premium can capture both default risk (for example, during the "sovereign debt crisis" in the early 2010s) and more general risk characteristics (as in the consumption capital asset pricing framework).

39 For a discussion of empirical analyses, see (for example) Floyd (2010) and Engel (2014).

References

Abel, Andrew B. 1990. "Consumption and Investment." In *Handbook of Monetary Economics*, Volume 2, edited by B.M. Friedman and F.H. Hahn. New York: Elsevier.

Agarwal, Sumit., Nathan Marwell, and Leslie McGranahan. 2017. "Consumption Responses to Temporary Tax Incentives: Evidence from State Sales Tax Holidays." *American Economic Journal: Economic Policy* 9: 1–27.

Aguiar, Mark, and Manuel Amador. 2014. "Sovereign Debt." In *Handbook of International Economics*, Volume 4, edited by G. Gopinath, E. Helpman, and K. Rogoff. New York: North Holland.

Ahmed, Shaghil. 1986. "Temporary and Permanent Government Spending in an Open Economy: Some Evidence for the United Kingdom." *Journal of Monetary Economics* 17: 197–224. http://doi.org/10.1016/0304-3932(86)90028-0

Alexander, S. 1952. "Effects of a Devaluation on a Trade Balance." *International Monetary Fund Staff Papers* 2: 263–78. http://doi.org/10.2307/3866218

Altug, Sumru, and Warren Young. 2015. "Real Business Cycles after Three Decades: A Panel Discussion with Edward Prescott, Finn Kydland, Charles Plosser, John Long, Thomas Cooley, and Gary Hansen." *Macroeconomic Dynamics* 19: 425–45. http://doi.org/10.1017/S1365100513000424

Alvarez, Fernando, Andrew Atkeson, and Patrick J. Kehoe. 2009. "Time-Varying Risk, Interest Rates, and Exchange Rates in General Equilibrium." *The Review of Economic Studies* 76: 851–78. http://doi.org/10.1111/j.1467-937X.2009.00537.x

Alvarez, Fernando, and Francesco Lippi. 2014. "Persistent Liquidity Effects and Long-Run Money Demand." *American Economic Journal: Macroeconomics* 6: 71–107. https://doi.org/10.1257/mac.6.2.71

Amano, Robert A., and Simon van Norden. 1995. "Terms of Trade and Real Exchange Rates: The Canadian Evidence." *Journal of International Money and Finance* 14: 83–104. http://doi.org/10.1016/0261-5606(94)00016-T

Amaral, Pedro S., and James C. MacGee. 2002. "The Great Depression in Canada and the United States: A Neoclassical Perspective." *Review of Economic Dynamics* 5: 45–72. http://doi.org/10.1006/redy.2001.0141

Aschauer, David. 1987. "Some Macroeconomic Effects of Tariff Policy." *Economic Perspectives*. Federal Reserve Bank of Chicago.

Aschauer, David. 1988. "The Equilibrium Approach to Fiscal Policy." *Journal of Money, Credit and Banking* 20: 41–62. http://doi.org/10.2307/1992666

Asea, Patrick K., and W. Max Corden. 1994. "The Balassa-Samuelson Model: An Overview." *Review of International Economics* 2: 191–200. http://doi.org/10.1111/j.1467-9396.1994.tb00040.x

Attanasio, O. 1999. "Consumption." In *Handbook of Macroeconomics*, Volume 1, edited by J.B. Taylor and M. Woodford. New York: Elsevier.

Backus, David K., Espen Henriksen, and Kjetil. Storesletten. 2008. "Taxes and the Global Allocation of Capital." *Journal of Monetary Economics* 55: 48–61. http://doi.org/10.1016/j.jmoneco.2007.11.008

Backus, David K., Patrick J. Kehoe, and Finn E. Kydland. 1992. "International Real Business Cycles." *Journal of Political Economy* 100: 745–75. http://doi.org/10.1086/261838

Balassa, Bela. 1964. "The Purchasing Power Parity Doctrine: A Reappraisal." *Journal of Political Economy* 72: 584–96. http://doi.org/10.1086/258965

Baldwin, John R., and Beiling Yan. 2004. "The Law of One Price: A Canada/U.S. Exploration." *Review of Income and Wealth* 1: 1–10. http://doi.org/10.1111/j.0034-6586.2004.00108.x

Barczyk, Daniel. 2016. "Ricardian Equivalence Revisited: Deficits, Gifts, and Bequests." *Journal of Economic Dynamics and Control* 63: 1–24. http://doi.org/10.1016/j.jedc.2015.11.004

Barro, R. 1989. "The Neoclassical Approach to Fiscal Policy." In *Modern Business Cycle Theory*, edited by R. Barro. Cambridge. Harvard University Press.

Baxter, Marianne. 1995. "International Trade and Business Cycles." In *Handbook of International Economics*, Volume 3, edited by Gene Grossman and Kenneth Rogoff. New York: Elsevier. https://doi.org/10.1016/S1573-4404(05)80015-2

Beaudry, Paul, and Francisco Ruge-Murcia. 2017. "Canadian Inflation Targeting." *Canadian Journal of Economics* 50: 1556–72. http://doi.org/10.1111/caje.12307

Bergin, Paul. 2003. "Putting the 'New Open Economy Macroeconomics' to a Test." *Journal of International Economics* 60: 3–34. http://doi.org/10.1016/S0022-1996(02)00057-0

Berka, Martin, and Michael B. Devereux. 2013. "Trends in European Real Exchange Rates." *Economic Policy* 28: 193–242. http://doi.org/10.1111/1468-0327.12006

Betts, Caroline, Michael D. Bordo, and Angela Redish. 1996. "A Small Open Economy in Depression: Lessons from Canada in the 1930s." *Canadian Journal of Economics* 29: 1–36. http://doi.org/10.2307/136149

Betts, Caroline, Rahul Giri, and Rubina Verma. 2017. "Trade, Reform, and Structural Transformation in South Korea." *IMF Economic Review* 65: 745–91. http://doi.org/10.1057/s41308-017-0031-7

Betts, C., and T. Kehoe. 2017. "Real Exchange Rate Movements and the Relative Price of Non-Traded Goods." Unpublished manuscript.

Blanchard, Olivier. 2007. "Current Account Deficits in Rich Countries." *IMF Staff Papers* 54: 191–219. http://doi.org/10.1057/palgrave.imfsp.9450013

Blankenau, William, M. Ayhan Kose, and Kei-Mu Yi. 2001. "Can World Real Interest Rates Explain Business Cycles in a Small Open Economy?" *Journal of Economic Dynamics and Control* 25: 867–89. http://doi.org/10.1016/S0165-1889(00)00059-2

Boothe, Paul M., and Bradford G. Reid. 1989. "Asset Returns and Government Budgets in a Small Open Economy." *Journal of Monetary Economics* 23: 65–77. http://doi.org/10.1016/0304-3932(89)90062-7

Bordo, Michael. 1993. "The Bretton Woods International Monetary System: A Historical Overview." In *A Retrospective on the Bretton Woods System: Lessons for International Monetary Reform*, edited by M. Bordo and B. Eichengreen. Chicago: University of Chicago Press. http://doi.org/10.7208/chicago/9780226066905.001.0001

Bordo, M., A. Dib, and L. Schembri. 2010. "Canada's Pioneering Experience with a Flexible Exchange Rate in the 1950s: (Hard) Lessons Learned for Monetary Policy in a Small Open Economy." *International Journal of Central Banking* 6: 51–99.

Bordo, Michael, and Barry Eichengreen. 2007. "Implications of the Great Depression for the Development of the International Monetary System." In *The Defining Moment: The Great Depression and the*

American Economy in the Twentieth Century, edited by M. Bordo, C. Goldin, and E. White. Chicago: University of Chicago Press.

Bordo, Michael, Owen F. Humpage, and Anna J. Schwartz. 2015. "Foreign-Exchange-Market Operations in the Twenty-First Century." In *Strained Relations: U.S. Foreign-Exchange Operations and Monetary Policy in the Twentieth Century*, edited by M. Bordo, O. Humpage, and A. J. Schwartz. Chicago: University of Chicago Press. http://doi.org/10.7208/chicago/9780226051512.001.0001

Bordo, Michael, and Christopher M. Meissner. 2016. "Fiscal and Financial Crises." In *Handbook of Macroeconomics*, Volume 2, edited by J.B. Taylor and H. Uhlig. New York: North Holland. https://doi.org/10.1016/bs.hesmac.2016.04.001

Brock, William. 1974. "Money and Growth: The Case of Long Run Perfect Foresight." *International Economic Review* 15: 750–77. http://doi.org/10.2307/2525739

Brock, William. 1975. "A Simple Perfect Foresight Monetary Model." *Journal of Monetary Economics* 1: 133–50. http://doi.org/10.1016/0304-3932(70)90001-2

Burnside, Craig, Martin Eichenbaum, and Sergio Rebelo. 2016. "Currency Crisis Models." In *Banking Crises*, edited by G. Jones. London: Palgrave Macmillan. https://doi.org/10.1057/9781137553799_11

Burstein, Ariel, Martin Eichenbaum, and Sergio Rebelo. 2006. "The Importance of Nontradable Goods Prices in Cyclical Real Exchange Rate Fluctuations." *Japan and the World Economy* 18: 247–53. http://doi.org/10.1016/j.japwor.2006.02.003

Burstein, Ariel, and Gita Gopinath. 2014. "International Prices and Exchange Rates." In *Handbook of International Economics*, Volume 4, edited by G. Gopinath, E. Helpman, and K. Rogoff. New York: North Holland. https://doi.org/10.1016/B978-0-444-54314-1.00007-0

Cairncross, Alec, and Barry Eichengreen. 2003. *Sterling in Decline*. Oxford: Basil Blackwell. http://doi.org/10.1057/9780230596306

Canzoneri, Matthew, Robert Cumby, and Behzad Diba. 1999. "Relative Labor Productivity and the Real Exchange Rate in the Long Run: Evidence for a Panel of OECD Countries." *Journal of International Economics* 47: 245–66. http://doi.org/10.1016/S0022-1996(98)00021-X

Cao, Shutao, and Sharon Kozicki. 2017. "Real GDI, Productivity, and the Terms of Trade in Canada." *Review of Income and Wealth* 63 (Supplement 1): S134–48. https://doi.org/10.1111/roiw.12255

Caselli, Francesco, and James Feyrer. 2007. "The Marginal Product of Capital." *The Quarterly Journal of Economics*: 535–68. http://doi.org/10.1162/qjec.122.2.535

Champ, Bruce, Scott Freeman, and Joseph Haslag. 2011. *Modeling Monetary Economies*. New York: Cambridge University Press. http://doi.org/10.1017/CBO9780511977411

Chen, Yu-chin, and Kenneth Rogoff. 2003. "Commodity Currencies." *Journal of International Economics* 60: 133–60. http://doi.org/10.1016/S0022-1996(02)00072-7

Chinn, Menzie. 2000. "The Usual Suspects? Productivity and Demand Shocks and Asia-Pacific Real Exchange Rates." *Review of International Economics* 8: 20–43. http://doi.org/10.1111/1467-9396.00203

Choudhri, Ehsan, and Lawrence Schembri. 2014. "Productivity, Commodity Prices and the Real Exchange Rate: The Long-run Behaviour of the Canada-U.S. Exchange Rate." *International Review of Economics and Finance* 29: 537–51. http://doi.org/10.1016/j.iref.2013.08.003

Cochrane, John. 2001. *Asset Pricing*. Princeton: Princeton University Press.

Cochrane, John. 2011. "Discount Rates." *Journal of Finance* 66: 1047–108. http://doi.org/10.1111/j.1540-6261.2011.01671.x

Corden, W. Max. 1994. *Economic Policy, Exchange Rates, and the International System*. Oxford: Oxford University Press.

Corden, W. Max. 2007. "Those Current Account Imbalances: A Sceptical View." *The World Economy* 30: 363–82. http://doi.org/10.1111/j.1467-9701.2007.01000.x

Corden, W. Max, and J. Peter Neary. 1982. "Booming Sector and De-Industrialisation in a Small Open Economy." *Economic Journal* 92: 825–48. http://doi.org/10.2307/2232670

Costa Junior, Celso J., and Alejandro C. Garcia-Cintado. 2018. "Teaching DGSE Models to Undergraduates." *Economia* 19: 424–44. http://doi.org/10.1016/j.econ.2018.11.001

Crow, J. 1993a. "The Economy and Canadian Monetary Policy." *Bank of Canada Review.*

Crow, J. 1993b. "Monetary Policy under a Floating Rate Regime: The Canadian Experience." *Bank of Canada Review.*

Crucini, Mario J., and Anthony Landry. 2019. "Accounting for Real Exchange Rates using Micro-Data." *Journal of International Money and Finance* 91: 86–100. http://doi.org/10.1016/j.jimonfin.2018.11.002

Cumby, Robert. 1983. "Trade Credit, Exchange Control, and Monetary Independence: Evidence from the United Kingdom." *Journal of International Economics* 14: 53–67. http://doi.org/10.1016/0022-1996 (83)90019-3

Cumby, Robert, and M. Obstfeld. 1984. "International Interest Rate and Price Level Linkages under Flexible Exchange Rates: A Review of Recent Evidence." In *Exchange Rate Theory and Practice*, edited by J. Bilson and R. Marston. Chicago: University of Chicago Press.

De Gregorio, José, Alberto Giovannini, and Holger C. Wolf. 1994. "International Evidence on Tradables and Nontradables Inflation." *European Economic Review* 38: 1225–44. http://doi.org/10.1016/0014-292 1(94)90070-1

Desroches, Brigitte, and Michael Francis. 2010. "World Real Interest Rates: A Global Savings and Investment Perspective." *Applied Economics* 42: 2801–2816. http://doi.org/10.1080/00036840801964690

Devereux, Michael B., and Viktoria Hnatkovska. 2012. "The Extensive Margin, Sectoral Shares, and International Business Cycles." *Canadian Journal of Economics* 45: 509–34. http://doi.org/10.1111 /j.1540-5982.2012.01707.x

Devereux, Michael B., and Gregor Smith. 2021. "Testing the Present-Value Model of the Exchange Rate with Commodity Currencies." *Journal of Money Credit and Banking* 53: 589–96. http://doi.org/10.1111 /jmcb.12774

Dick, T., and J.E. Floyd. 1992. *Canada and the Gold Standard: Balance of Payments Adjustment under Fixed Exchange Rates, 1870–1913.* New York: Cambridge University Press.

Dornbusch, Rudiger. 1976. "Expectations and Exchange Rate Dynamics." *Journal of Political Economy* 84: 1161–76. http://doi.org/10.1086/260506

Dornbusch, Rudiger. 1980. *Open Economy Macroeconomics.* New York: Basic Books.

Dornbusch, Rudiger. 1983. "Real Interest Rates, Home Goods, and Optimal External Borrowing." *Journal of Political Economy* 91: 141–53. http://doi.org/10.1086/261132

Duarte, Margarida, and Diego Restuccia. 2010. "The Role of the Structural Transformation in Aggregate Productivity." *The Quarterly Journal of Economics* 125: 129–73. http://doi.org/10.1162/qjec .2010.125.1.129

Duarte, Margarida, and Diego Restuccia. 2019. "Relative Prices and Sectoral Productivity." *Journal of the European Economic Association* 18: 1400–33. http://doi.org/10.1093/jeea/jvz022

Duarte Margarida, and Alan C. Stockman. 2005. "Rational Speculation and Exchange Rates." *Journal of Monetary Economics* 52: 3–29. http://doi.org/10.1016/j.jmoneco.2004.08.004

Eaton, Jonathan, Samuel Kortum, Brent Neiman, and John Romalis. 2016. "Trade and the Global Recession." *American Economic Review* 106: 3401–38. http://doi.org/10.1257/aer.20101557

Edwards, Sebastian. 1999. "How Effective are Capital Controls?" *Journal of Economic Perspectives* 13: 65–84. http://doi.org/10.1257/jep.13.4.65

Edwards, Sebastian. 2003. "Exchange Rate Regimes, Capital Flows, and Crisis Prevention." In *Economic and Financial Crises in Emerging Market Economies*, edited by M. Feldstein. Chicago: University of Chicago Press. https://doi.org/10.7208/chicago/9780226241104.003.0002

Eichengreen, Barry. 2008. *Globalizing Capital: A History of the International Monetary System.* Princeton: Princeton University Press. http://doi.org/10.2307/j.ctt7pfmc

Eichengreen, Barry. 2015. "Secular Stagnation: The Long View." *American Economic Review* 105: 66–70. http://doi.org/10.1257/aer.p20151104

Eichengreen, Barry, and Andrew Rose. 2014. "Capital Controls in the 21st Century." *Journal of International Money and Finance* 48: 1–16. http://doi.org/10.1016/j.jimonfin.2014.08.001

Einzig, P. 1968. *Leads and Lags: The Main Cause of Devaluation.* London: Macmillan. http://doi.org/10.1007/978-1-349-00268-9

Eli, Shari, Joshua K. Hausman, and Paul W. Rhode. 2025. "The Model T." *The Journal of Economic History* 85: 110–51. http://doi.org/10.1017/S0022050725000014

Engel, Charles. 1996. "The Forward Discount Anomaly and the Risk Premium: A Survey of Recent Evidence." *Journal of Empirical Finance* 3: 123–92. http://doi.org/10.1016/0927-5398(95)00016-X

Engel, Charles. 2014. "Exchange Rates and Interest Parity." In *Handbook of International Economics*, Volume 4, edited by G. Gopinath, E. Helpman, and K. Rogoff. New York: North Holland. https://doi.org/10.1016/B978-0-444-54314-1.00008-2

Engel, Charles. 2016. "Exchange Rates, Interest Rates, and the Risk Premium." *American Economic Review* 106: 436–74. http://doi.org/10.1257/aer.20121365

Engel, Charles, Nelson C. Mark, Kenneth Rogoff, and Kenneth D. West. 2007. "Exchange Rate Models Are Not as Bad as You Think." *NBER Macroeconomics Annual* 22: 381–441. http://doi.org/10.1086/ma.22.25554969

Engel, Charles, and Jiang Wang. 2011. "International Trade in Durable Goods: Understanding Volatility, Cyclicality, and Elasticities." *Journal of International Economics* 83: 37–52. http://doi.org/10.1016/j.jinteco.2010.08.007

Epstein, Larry, and J. Allan Hynes. 1983. "The Rate of Time Preference and Dynamic Economic Analysis." *Journal of Political Economy* 91: 611–35. http://doi.org/10.1086/261168

Ferraro, Domenico, Kenneth Rogoff, and Barabara Rossi. 2015. "Can Oil Prices Forecast Exchange Rates? An Empirical Analysis of the Relationship between Commodity Prices and Exchange Rates." *Journal of International Money and Finance* 54: 116–41. http://doi.org/10.1016/j.jimonfin.2015.03.001

Fisher, Irving. 1930. *Theory of Interest.* New York: Macmillan.

Fleming, J.M. 1962. "Domestic Financial Policies under Fixed and under Floating Exchange Rates." *IMF Staff Papers* 9: 369–80. http://doi.org/10.2307/3866091

Flood, Robert, and Peter M. Garber. 2004. "Collapsing Exchange Rate Regimes: Some Linear Examples." *Journal of International Economics* 17: 1–13. http://doi.org/10.1016/0022-1996(84)90002-3

Flood, Robert, and Jeanne Olivier. 2005. "An Interest Rate Defense of a Fixed Exchange Rate?" *Journal of International Economics* 66: 471–84. http://doi.org/10.1016/j.jinteco.2004.09.001

Floyd, John E. 1979. "Government Expenditure Policies in the Small Open Economy." *Canadian Journal of Economics* 12: 377–93. http://doi.org/10.2307/134728

Floyd, John E. 1980. "Tax Policy in the Small Open Economy: A Monetary Approach to a Keynesian Problem." *The Scandinavian Journal of Economics* 82: 378–97. http://doi.org/10.2307/3439748

Floyd, John E. 1985. *World Monetary Equilibrium: International Monetary Theory in an Historical-Institutional Context.* Philadelphia: University of Pennsylvania Press.

Floyd, John E. 1995. "Are Canadian Interest Rates Too High?" *Canadian Public Policy* 21: 143–58. http://doi.org/10.2307/3551590

Floyd, John E. 2010. *Interest Rates, Exchange Rates and World Monetary Policy.* Berlin: Springer-Verlag. http://doi.org/10.1007/978-3-642-10280-6

Fox, John, Robert Andersen, and Joseph Dubonnet. 1999. "The Polls and the 1995 Quebec Referendum." *The Canadian Journal of Sociology* 24: 411–24. http://doi.org/10.2307/3341396

Frenkel, Jacob. 1976. "A Monetary Approach to the Exchange Rate: Doctrinal Aspects and Empirical Evidence." *The Scandinavian Journal of Economics* 78: 200–24. http://doi.org/10.2307/3439924

Frenkel, Jacob, and H.G. Johnson. 1976. *The Monetary Approach to the Balance of Payments.* London: Allen and Unwin.

Friedman, Milton. 1957. *A Theory of the Consumption Function.* Princeton: Princeton University Press. http://doi.org/10.1515/9780691188485

Friedman, Milton. 1959. "The Demand for Money: Some Theoretical and Empirical Results." *Journal of Political Economy* 67: 327–51. http://doi.org/10.1086/258194

Friedman, Milton. 1969. *The Optimum Quantity of Money and Other Essays*. Chicago: Aldine.

Friedman, Milton. 1997. "John Maynard Keynes." Federal Reserve Bank of Richmond *Economic Quarterly* 83: 2–23.

Friedman, Milton. 2008. "Quantity Theory of Money." In *The New Palgrave Dictionary of Economics*. London: Palgrave Macmillan.

Froot, Kenneth A., and Kenneth Rogoff. 1995. "Perspectives on PPP and Long-Run Real Exchange Rates." In *Handbook of International Economics*, Volume 3, edited by G. Grossman and Kenneth Rogoff. New York: Elsevier.

Galstyan, Vahagn, and Philip Lane. 2009. "The Composition of Government Spending and the Real Exchange Rate." *Journal of Money, Credit and Banking* 41: 1233–49. http://doi.org/10.1111/j.1538-4616.2009.00254.x

Glick, Reuven, and Kenneth Rogoff. 1995. "Global versus Country-Specific Productivity Shocks and the Current Account." *Journal of Monetary Economics* 35: 159–92. http://doi.org/10.1016/0304-3932(94)01181-9

Gorodnichenko, Yuriy, Enrique G. Mendoza, and Linda L. Tesar. 2012. "The Finnish Great Depression: From Russia with Love." *American Economic Review* 102: 1619–44. http://doi.org/10.1257/aer.102.4.1619

Gourinchas, Pierre-Olivier, and Hélène Rey. 2014. "External Adjustment, Global Imbalances, and Valuation Effects." In *Handbook of International Economics*, Volume 4, edited by G. Gopinath, E. Helpman, and K. Rogoff. New York: North Holland. https://doi.org/10.1016/B978-0-444-54314-1.00010-0

Greenwood, Jeremy. 1983. "Expectations, the Exchange Rate, and the Current Account." *Journal of Monetary Economics* 12: 543–69. http://doi.org/10.1016/0304-3932(83)90038-7

Greenwood, Jeremy. 1984. "Non-Traded Goods, the Trade Balance, and the Balance of Payments." *Canadian Journal of Economics* 17: 806–23. http://doi.org/10.2307/135075

Grossman, Gene M., and Elhanan Helpman. 1994. "Endogenous Innovation in the Theory of Growth." *Journal of Economic Perspectives* 8: 23–44. http://doi.org/10.1257/jep.8.1.23

Hall, Robert E. 1978. "Stochastic Implications of the Life Cycle-Permanent Income Hypothesis: Theory and Evidence." *Journal of Political Economy* 86: 971–87. http://doi.org/10.1086/260724

Hall, Robert E. 1989. "Consumption." In *Handbook of Modern Business Cycle Theory*, edited by R. Barro. Cambridge: Harvard University Press.

Hall, Robert E. 2009. "By How Much Does GDP Rise If the Government Buys More Output?" *Brookings Papers on Economic Activity* 2: 183–231. http://doi.org/10.1353/eca.0.0069

Hall, Robert E. 2010. "Why Does the Economy Fall to Pieces after a Financial Crisis?" *Journal of Economic Perspectives* 24: 3–20. http://doi.org/10.1257/jep.24.4.3

Hall, Robert E., and Thomas J. Sargent. 2018. "Short-Run and Long-Run Effects of Milton Friedman's Presidential Address." *Journal of Economic Perspectives* 32: 121–34. http://doi.org/10.1257/jep.32.1.121

Hansen, Gary D., and Lee E. Ohanian. 2016. "Neoclassical Models in Macroeconomics." In *Handbook of Macroeconomics*, Volume 2, edited by J.B. Taylor and H. Uhlig. Amsterdam: Elsevier. https://doi.org/10.3386/w22122

Hansen, Gary D., and Edward C. Prescott. 1993. "Did Technology Shocks Cause the 1990-1991 Recession?" *American Economic Review* 83: 280–6. https://doi.org/10.21034/wp.507

Harrod, R.F. 1939. *International Economics*. London: Nisbet and Company Ltd.

Helpman, Elhanan. 2004. *The Mystery of Economic Growth*. Cambridge: Harvard University Press.

Helpman, Elhanan, and Assaf Razin. 1982. "A Comparison of Exchange Rate Regimes in the Presence of Imperfect Capital Markets." *International Economic Review* 23: 365–88. http://doi.org/10.2307/2526445

Herrendorf, Berthold, Richard Rogerson, and Ákos Valentinyi. 2014. "Growth and Structural Transformation." In *Handbook of Economic Growth*, Volume 2, edited by J.B. Taylor and H. Uhlig. New York: Elsevier. https://doi.org/10.3386/w18996

Hodrick, Robert J., and Edward C. Prescott. 1997. "Postwar U.S. Business Cycles: An Empirical Investigation." *Journal of Money, Credit and Banking* 29: 1–16. http://doi.org/10.2307/2953682

Hoffmann, Mathias. 2013. "What Drives China's Current Account?" *Journal of International Money and Finance* 32: 856–83. http://doi.org/10.1016/j.jimonfin.2012.07.005

Hsieh, David A. 1982. The Determination of the Real Exchange Rate: The Productivity Approach." *Journal of International Economics* 12: 355–62. http://doi.org/10.1016/0022-1996(82)90045-9

Hynes, J. Allan. 1974. "On the Theory of Real Balance Effects." *Journal of Money, Credit and Banking* 6: 65–83. http://doi.org/10.2307/1991083

Imai, Hiroyuki. 2010. "Japan's Inflation under the Bretton Woods System: How Large was the Balassa–Samuelson Effect?" *Journal of Asian Economics* 21: 174–85. http://doi.org/10.1016/j.asieco.2009.10.003

International Monetary Fund. 2018. *Annual Report on Exchange Arrangements and Exchange Restrictions.*

International Monetary Fund. 2019. "External Sector Report: The Dynamics of External Adjustment." Washington, DC.

Iscan, Talan. 2015. "Windfall Resource Income, Productivity Growth, and Manufacturing Employment." *Open Economies Review* 26: 279–311. http://doi.org/10.1007/s11079-014-9330-z

Johnson, Harry G. 1972. "A Monetary Approach to Balance of Payments Theory." *Journal of Financial and Quantitative Analysis* 7: 1555–72. http://doi.org/10.2307/2329935

Johnson, Harry G. 1976. "Money, Balance of Payments Theory, and the International Monetary Problem." *The Bangladesh Development Studies* 4: 455–78.

Johnson, Robert C. 2014. "Five Facts about Value-Added Exports and Implications for Macroeconomics and Trade Research." *Journal of Economic Perspectives* 28: 119–42. http://doi.org/10.1257/jep.28.2.119

Jones, C.I. 2016. "The Facts of Economic Growth." In *Handbook of Macroeconomics*, Volume 2, edited by J.B. Taylor and H. Uhlig. New York: North Holland. https://doi.org/10.1016/bs.hesmac.2016.03.002

Kehoe, Timothy J., Kim J. Ruhl, and Joseph B. Steinberg. 2018. "Global Imbalances and Structural Change in the United States." *Journal of Political Economy* 126: 761–96. http://doi.org/10.1086/696279

Keynes, John M. 1923. *A Tract on Monetary Reform*. In *The Collected Writings of John Maynard Keynes*, edited by E. Johnson and D. Moggridge. London: Macmillan.

Keynes, John M. 1936. *The General Theory of Employment, Interest and Money*. In *The Collected Writings of John Maynard Keynes*, edited by E. Johnson and D. Moggridge. London: Macmillan.

Kollmann, Robert. 2001. "The Exchange Rate in a Dynamic-Optimizing Business Cycle Model with Nominal Rigidities: A Quantitative Investigation." *Journal of International Economics* 55: 243–62. http://doi.org/10.1016/S0022-1996(01)00087-3

Kouri, Pentti J. K., and Michael Porter. 1974. "International Capital Flows and Portfolio Equilibrium." *Journal of Political Economy* 82: 443–67.

Krugman, Paul. 1979. "A Model of Balance-of-Payments Crises." *Journal of Money Credit and Banking* 3: 311–25. http://doi.org/10.2307/1991793

Kydland, Finn E. 2006. "Quantitative Aggregate Economics." *American Economic Review* 96: 1373–83. http://doi.org/10.1257/aer.96.5.1373

Kydland, Finn E., and Edward C. Prescott. 1982. "Time to Build and Aggregate Fluctuations." *Econometrica* 50: 1345–70. http://doi.org/10.2307/1913386

Kydland, Finn E., and Edward C. Prescott. 1996. "The Computational Experiment: An Econometric Tool." *The Journal of Economic Perspectives* 10: 69–85. http://doi.org/10.1257/jep.10.1.69

Leiderman, Leonardo, and Assaf Razin. 1988. "Testing Ricardian Neutrality with an Intertemporal Stochastic Model." *Journal of Money, Credit and Banking* 20: 1–21. http://doi.org/10.2307/1992664

Leiderman, Leonardo, and Assaf Razin. 1991. "Determinants of External Imbalances: The Role of Taxes, Government Spending, and Productivity." *Journal of the Japanese and International Economies* 5: 421–50. http://doi.org/10.1016/0889-1583(91)90007-D

LeRoy, Stephen F. 1984a. "Nominal Prices and Interest Rates in General Equilibrium: Money Shocks." *Journal of Business* 57: 177–95. http://doi.org/10.1086/296258

LeRoy, Stephen F. 1984b. "Nominal Prices and Interest Rates in General Equilibrium: Endowment Shocks." *Journal of Business* 57: 197–213. http://doi.org/10.1086/296259

Leung, D., and S. Cao. 2009. "The Changing Pace of Labour Reallocation in Canada: Causes and Consequences." *Bank of Canada Review*.

Lewis, Karen K. 2011. "Global Asset Pricing." *Annual Review of Financial Economics* 3: 435–66. http://doi.org/10.1146/annurev-financial-102710-144841

Long, Jr., John B., and Charles Plosser. 1983. "Real Business Cycles." *Journal of Political Economy* 91: 39–69. http://doi.org/10.1086/261128

Lothian, James. 2016. "Uncovered Interest Parity: The Long and the Short of It." *Journal of Empirical Finance* 36: 1–7. http://doi.org/10.1016/j.jempfin.2015.12.001

Lucas, Robert E. 1976. "Econometric Policy Evaluation: A Critique." *Carnegie-Rochester Conference Series on Public Policy* 1: 19–46. http://doi.org/10.1016/S0167-2231(76)80003-6

Lucas, Robert E. 1990. "Why Doesn't Capital Flow from Rich to Poor Countries?" *American Economic Review* 80: 92–6.

Lucas, Robert E. 2000. "Inflation and Welfare." *Econometrica* 68: 247–74. http://doi.org/10.1111/1468-0262.00109

Lucas, Robert E. 2014. "Liquidity: Meaning, Measurement, Management." *Federal Reserve Bank of St. Louis Review* 96: 199–212.

Lustig, Hanno, and Adrien Verdelhan. 2007. "The Cross Section of Foreign Currency Risk Premia and Consumption Growth Risk." *American Economic Review* 97: 89–117. http://doi.org/10.1257/aer.97.1.89

Lustig, Hanno, and Adrien Verdelhan. 2011. "The Cross Section of Foreign Currency Risk Premia and Consumption Growth Risk: Reply." *American Economic Review* 101: 3477–500. http://doi.org/10.1257/aer.101.7.3477

Macdonald, R. 2007. "Not Dutch Disease, It's China Syndrome." *Canadian Economic Observer* 20: 1–11.

Marston, Richard C. 1987. "Real Exchange Rates and Productivity Growth in the United States and Japan." *NBER Working Paper* 1922. https://doi.org/10.3386/w1922

McCallum, Bennett T., and Marvin S. Goodfriend. 1989. "Demand for Money: Theoretical Studies." In *Money* (The New Palgrave Series), edited by J. Eatwell, M. Milgate, and P. Newman. New York: Norton. https://doi.org/10.1007/978-1-349-19804-7_13

McCandless, George. 2008. *The ABCs of RBCs: An Introduction to Dynamic Macroeconomic Models*. Cambridge: Harvard University Press. https://doi.org/10.4159/9780674033788

McGrattan, E., and Edward C. Prescott. 2014. "A Reassessment of Real Business Cycle Theory." *American Economic Review* 104: 177–82. http://doi.org/10.1257/aer.104.5.177

McKinnon, Ronald. 2006. "China's Exchange Rate Trap: Japan Redux?" *American Economic Review* 96: 427–31. http://doi.org/10.1257/000282806777212459

Melino, A. 2012. "Inflation Targeting: A Canadian Perspective." *International Journal of Central Banking* 8: 105-31.

Mendoza, Enrique. 1991. "Real Business Cycles in a Small Open Economy." *American Economic Review* 81: 797–810.

Mendoza, Enrique. 1995. "The Terms of Trade, the Real Exchange Rate, and Economic Fluctuations." *International Economic Review* 36: 101–37. http://doi.org/10.2307/2527429

Morales, J. 1988. "Inflation Stabilization in Brazil." In *Inflation Stabilization: The Experience of Israel, Argentina, Brazil, Bolivia, and Mexico*, edited by M. Bruno. Cambridge: MIT Press.

Mundell, Robert. 1963. "Capital Mobility and Stabilization Policy under Fixed and Flexible Exchange Rates." *Canadian Journal of Economics and Political Science* 29: 475–85. http://doi.org/10.2307/139336

Mundell, Robert. 2001. "On the History of the Mundell-Fleming Model." *IMF Staff Papers* 47: 215–27. https://doi.org/10.1016/0167-2231(79)90034-4

Mussa, Michael. 1979. "Empirical Regularities and the Behavior of Exchange Rates and the Theories of the Foreign Exchange Market." *Carnegie Rochester Conference Series on Public Policy* 11: 9–57. http://doi.org/10.1016/0167-2231(79)90034-4

Mussa, Michael. 2008. "IMF Surveillance over China's Exchange Rate Policy." In *Debating China's Exchange Rate Policy*, edited by M. Goldstein and N. Lardy. Washington: Peterson Institute for International Economics.

Neary, J.P., and D. Purvis. 1983. "Real Adjustment and Exchange Rate Dynamics." In *Exchange Rates and International Macroeconomics*, edited by J. Frenkel. Chicago: The University of Chicago Press.

Obstfeld, Maurice. 1981. "Capital Mobility and Devaluation in an Optimizing Model with Rational Expectations." *American Economic Review* 71: 217–21. https://doi.org/10.3386/w0557

Obstfeld, Maurice. 1986. "Speculative Attack and the External Constraint in a Maximizing Model of the Balance of Payments." *Canadian Journal of Economics* 19: 1–22. http://doi.org/10.2307/135168

Obstfeld, Maurice, and Kenneth Rogoff. 1995a. "The Mirage of Fixed Exchange Rates." *Journal of Economic Perspectives* 9: 73–96. http://doi.org/10.1257/jep.9.4.73

Obstfeld, Maurice, and Kenneth Rogoff. 1995b. "The Intertemporal Approach to the Current Account." In *Handbook of International Economics*, Volume 3, edited by G. Grossman and K. Rogoff. New York: Elsevier.

Obstfeld, Maurice, and Kenneth Rogoff. 1996. *Foundations of International Macroeconomics*. Cambridge: MIT Press.

Obstfeld, Maurice, and Kenneth Rogoff. 2000. "The Six Major Puzzles in International Macroeconomics: Is There a Common Cause?" *NBER Macroeconomics Annual* 15: 339–90. http://doi.org/10.1086/654423

Obstfeld, Maurice, and Kenneth Rogoff. 2005. "Global Current Account Imbalances and Exchange Rate Adjustments." *Brookings Papers on Economic Activity* 1: 67–146. http://doi.org/10.1353/eca.2005.0020

Obstfeld, Maurice, Jay C. Shambaugh, and Alan M. Taylor. 2005. "The Trilemma in History: Tradeoffs among Exchange Rates, Monetary Policies, and Capital Mobility." *Review of Economics and Statistics* 87: 423–38. http://doi.org/10.1162/0034653054638300

Oppenheimer, P. 1974. "Non-Traded Goods and the Balance of Payments: A Historical Note." *Journal of Economic Literature* 12: 882–8.

Ouyang, Alice Y., Ramkishen Rajan, and Thomas Willett. 2010. "China as a Reserve Sink: The Evidence from Offset and Sterilization Coefficients." *Journal of International Money and Finance* 29: 951–72. http://doi.org/10.1016/j.jimonfin.2009.12.006

Pasula, Kit. 1994. "Sterilization, Ricardian Equivalence, and Structural and Reduced-Form Estimates of the Offset Coefficient." *Journal of Macroeconomics* 16: 683–99. http://doi.org/10.1016/0164-0704(94)90007-8

Pasula, Kit. 1996. "Monetary Independence under Bretton Woods: Perspectives from a Stochastic, Maximizing Model." *Canadian Journal of Economics* 29: 643–64. http://doi.org/10.2307/136255

Pasula, Kit. 1997. "Monetary Non-Neutrality and the Intertemporal Approach to the Balance of Trade: The U.K. Trade Balance under Bretton Woods." *Review of International Economics* 5: 333–47. http://doi.org/10.1111/1467-9396.00061

Pasula, Kit. 2016. "The Risk Premium, Interest Rate Determination, and Monetary Independence under a Fixed, but Adjustable, Exchange Rate." *International Journal of Finance and Economics* 21: 313–31. http://doi.org/10.1002/ijfe.1548

Pasula, Kit. 2017. "Teaching the Exchange Rate and the Current Account Balance in a Dynamic Model with a Non-Traded Good." *Australasian Journal of Economics Education* 14: 31–51.

Pasula, Kit. 2020. "Reserve Flows and Monetary Autonomy under a Fixed Exchange Rate: The British Experience under Bretton Woods." *Applied Economics* 52: 1891–904. http://doi.org/10.1080/00036846.2019.1680793

Patinkin, D. 1965. *Money, Interest, and Prices: An Integration of Monetary and Value Theory*. New York: Harper and Row.

Persson, Torsten. 1984. "Real Transfers in Fixed Exchange Rate Systems and the International Adjustment Mechanism." *Journal of Monetary Economics* 13: 349–69. http://doi.org/10.1016/0304-3932(84)90037-0

Phelps, Edmund S. 1973. "Inflation in the Theory of Public Finance." *The Swedish Journal of Economics* 75: 67–82. http://doi.org/10.2307/3439275

Pigou, A. C. 1922. "The Foreign Exchanges." *The Quarterly Journal of Economics* 37: 52–74. http://doi.org/10.2307/1885909

Polak, Jacques J. 1998. "The IMF Monetary Model at 40." *Economic Modelling* 15: 395–410. http://doi.org/10.1016/S0264-9993(98)00019-4

Powell, J. 2005. *A History of the Canadian Dollar*. Ottawa: Bank of Canada.

Prescott, Edward C. 2006. "Nobel Lecture: The Transformation of Macroeconomic Policy and Research." *Journal of Political Economy* 114: 1–33. http://doi.org/10.1086/503205

Prescott, Edward C. 2016. "RBC Methodology and the Development of Aggregate Economic Theory." In *Handbook of Economic Growth*, Volume 2, edited by J.B. Taylor and H. Uhlig. New York: Elsevier.

Purvis, Douglas D. 1977. "The Exchange Rate Regime and Economic Policy in Theory and in Practice." *Canadian Public Policy* 3: 205–18. http://doi.org/10.2307/3549537

Rachel, L., and T.D. Smith. 2017. "Are Low Real Interest Rates Here to Stay?" *International Journal of Central Banking* 13: 1–42.

Ramey, V. 2016. "Macroeconomic Shocks and their Propagation." In *Handbook of Macroeconomics*, Volume 2, edited by J.B. Taylor and H. Uhlig. New York: North Holland. https://doi.org/10.1016/bs.hesmac.2016.03.003

Ricardo, David. 1817. On the Principles of Political Economy and Taxation, Volume 1. In *The Works and Correspondence of David Ricardo* (1951), edited by P. Sraffa, with collaboration of M.H. Dobb. Cambridge: Cambridge University Press.

Ricardo, David. 1951. Letters 1810 to 1815, Volume 6. In *The Works and Correspondence of David Ricardo*, edited by P. Sraffa, with collaboration of M.H. Dobb. Cambridge: Cambridge University Press.

Ricci, Luca Antonio, Gian Maria Milesi-Ferretti, and Jaewoo Lee. 2013. "Real Exchange Rates and Fundamentals: A Cross-Country Perspective." *Journal of Money, Credit and Banking* 45: 845–65. http://doi.org/10.1111/jmcb.12027

Rogoff, Kenneth. 1992. "Traded Goods Consumption Smoothing and the Random Walk Behavior of the Real Exchange Rate." *BOJ Monetary and Economic Studies* 10: 1–29.

Rogoff, Kenneth. 1996. "The Purchasing Power Parity Puzzle." *Journal of Economic Literature* 34: 647–68.

Rose, Andrew. 2011. "Exchange Rate Regimes in the Modern Era: Fixed, Floating, and Flaky." *Journal of Economic Literature* 49: 652–72. http://doi.org/10.1257/jel.49.3.652

Rose, Andrew. 2014. "Surprising Similarities: Recent Monetary Regimes of Small Economies." *Journal of International Money and Finance* 49: 5–27. http://doi.org/10.1016/j.jimonfin.2014.05.004

Sachs, Jeffrey D. 1987. "The Bolivian Hyperinflation and Stabilization." *American Economic Review* 77: 279–83.

Sachs, Jeffrey D., Richard N. Cooper, and Stanley Fischer. 1981. "The Current Account and Macroeconomic Adjustment in the 1970s." *Brookings Papers on Economic Activity* 1: 201–68. http://doi.org/10.2307/2534399

Sachs, Jeffrey D., and F. Larrain. 1993. *Macroeconomics in the Global Economy*. Englewood Cliffs: Prentice-Hall.

Samuelson, Paul. 1964. "Theoretical Notes on Trade Problems." *Review of Economics and Statistics* 46: 145–54. http://doi.org/10.2307/1928178

Schembri, L. 2008. "Canada's Experience with a Flexible Exchange Rate: Valuable Lessons Learned." *Bank of Canada Review*: 3–15.

Schmitt-Grohe, Stephanie, and Martín Uribe. 2018. "How Important are Terms-of-Trade Shocks?" *International Economic Review* 59: 85–111. http://doi.org/10.1111/iere.12263

Sidrauski, M. 1967. "Rational Choice and Patterns of Growth in a Monetary Economy." *American Economic Review* 57: 534–44.

Spence, Michael, and Sandile Hlatshwayo. 2012. "The Evolving Structure of the American Economy and the Employment Challenge." *Comparative Economic Studies* 54: 703–38. http://doi.org/10.1057/ces.2012.32

Stockman, Alan C. 1983. "Real Exchange Rates under Alternative Nominal Exchange-Rate Systems." *Journal of International Money and Finance* 2: 147–66. http://doi.org/10.1016/0261-5606(83)90012-8

Stockman, Alan C. 1988. "On the Roles of International Financial Markets and Their Relevance for Economic Policy." *Journal of Money, Credit and Banking* 20: 531–49. http://doi.org/10.2307/1992532

Stockman, Alan C. 1999. "Choosing an Exchange-Rate System." *Journal of Banking and Finance* 23: 1483–98. http://doi.org/10.1016/S0378-4266(99)00027-8

Stockman, Alan C., and L. Tesar. 1995. "Tastes and Technology in a Two-Country Model of the Business Cycle: Explaining International Co-Movements." *American Economic Review* 85: 168–85.

Taylor, Alan M., and Mark P. Taylor. 2004. "The Purchasing Power Parity Debate." *Journal of Economic Perspectives* 18: 135–58. http://doi.org/10.1257/0895330042632744

Thimme, Julian. 2017. "Intertemporal Substitution in Consumption: A Literature Review." *Journal of Economic Surveys* 31: 226–57. http://doi.org/10.1111/joes.12142

Timmer, M.P., G.J. de Vries, and K. de Vries. 2015. "Patterns of Structural Change in Developing Countries." In *Routledge Handbook of Industry and Development*, edited by J. Weiss and M. Tribe. London: Routledge.

Turnovsky, Stephen J. 2009. *Capital Accumulation and Economic Growth in a Small Open Economy*. Cambridge: Cambridge University Press. http://doi.org/10.1017/CBO9780511641978

Viner, J. 1924. *Canada's Balance of International Indebtedness, 1900–1913*. Cambridge: Harvard University Press.

Viner, J. 1937. *Studies in the Theory of International Trade*. New York: Harper and Brothers.

Volcker, Paul. 2007. "An Interview with Paul A. Volcker." In *Inside the Economist's Mind: Conversations with Eminent Economists*, edited by P. Samuelson and W. Barnett. Maiden: Blackwell.

Walsh, C. 2010. *Monetary Theory and Policy*. Cambridge: MIT Press.

Woodford, M. 2008. "Comment." *Brookings Papers on Economic Activity* 1: 420–39.

Yeager, L. 1976. *International Monetary Relations: Theory, History, and Policy*. New York: Harper and Row.

Index